Microsoft Project Essentials

Plan, Manage, and Deliver Projects with Confidence

Charles Waghmare

Apress®

Microsoft Project Essentials: Plan, Manage, and Deliver Projects with Confidence

Charles Waghmare
Mumbai, Maharashtra, India

ISBN-13 (pbk): 979-8-8688-1562-1   ISBN-13 (electronic): 979-8-8688-1563-8
https://doi.org/10.1007/979-8-8688-1563-8

Copyright © 2025 by Charles Waghmare

This work is subject to copyright. All rights are reserved by the Publisher, whether the whole or part of the material is concerned, specifically the rights of translation, reprinting, reuse of illustrations, recitation, broadcasting, reproduction on microfilms or in any other physical way, and transmission or information storage and retrieval, electronic adaptation, computer software, or by similar or dissimilar methodology now known or hereafter developed.

Trademarked names, logos, and images may appear in this book. Rather than use a trademark symbol with every occurrence of a trademarked name, logo, or image we use the names, logos, and images only in an editorial fashion and to the benefit of the trademark owner, with no intention of infringement of the trademark.

The use in this publication of trade names, trademarks, service marks, and similar terms, even if they are not identified as such, is not to be taken as an expression of opinion as to whether or not they are subject to proprietary rights.

While the advice and information in this book are believed to be true and accurate at the date of publication, neither the authors nor the editors nor the publisher can accept any legal responsibility for any errors or omissions that may be made. The publisher makes no warranty, express or implied, with respect to the material contained herein.

Managing Director, Apress Media LLC: Welmoed Spahr
Acquisitions Editor: Smriti Srivastava
Editorial Assistant: Jessica Vakili

Cover designed by eStudioCalamar

Cover image designed by Pixabay

Distributed to the book trade worldwide by Springer Science+Business Media New York, 1 New York Plaza, New York, NY 10004. Phone 1-800-SPRINGER, fax (201) 348-4505, e-mail orders-ny@springer-sbm.com, or visit www.springeronline.com. Apress Media, LLC is a Delaware LLC and the sole member (owner) is Springer Science + Business Media Finance Inc (SSBM Finance Inc). SSBM Finance Inc is a **Delaware** corporation.

For information on translations, please e-mail booktranslations@springernature.com; for reprint, paperback, or audio rights, please e-mail bookpermissions@springernature.com.

Apress titles may be purchased in bulk for academic, corporate, or promotional use. eBook versions and licenses are also available for most titles. For more information, reference our Print and eBook Bulk Sales web page at http://www.apress.com/bulk-sales.

Any source code or other supplementary material referenced by the author in this book is available to readers on GitHub. For more detailed information, please visit https://www.apress.com/gp/services/source-code.

If disposing of this product, please recycle the paper

> *"Blessed are those who find wisdom, those who gain understanding."*
>
> —**Proverbs 3:13**

I am deeply grateful to my Lord and Savior, Jesus Christ, for granting me the opportunity to write this book. All that I am and all that I have, I owe to Him. I praise Him for His countless blessings in my life.

This book is dedicated to my mother, late Mrs. Kamala David Waghmare. Your love and wisdom still guide me, shaping who I am today. Though you are gone, your memory lives on in my words and actions. To my father, Mr. David Genu Waghmare: You have always been my rock and source of strength. Your resilience, dedication, and unwavering support inspire me every day. Thank you for your love and guidance, which formed the foundation of my dreams.

This book reflects the values and lessons you both taught me. It acknowledges the support and sacrifices that have helped me navigate through life. I appreciate all that you have done for me.

I also dedicate this book to my beloved wife, Mrs. Priya Waghmare, in gratitude for her unwavering support, love, encouragement, and care.

With all my love,

Charles Waghmare

Table of Contents

About the Author xi

About the Technical Reviewer xiii

Acknowledgments xv

Introduction xvii

Chapter 1: Introduction to Microsoft Project: Understanding the Platform 1
    Introduction 3
    Importance of Microsoft Project 4
        Achieving Organizational Goals 6
        Optimizing Resource Utilization 7
        Enhancing Team Collaboration 7
        Ensuring Project Success 8
        Risk Management 8
        Quality Assurance 8
        Stakeholder Management 9
        Adaptability and Flexibility 9
        Continuous Improvement 9
        Conclusion 10
    Features of Microsoft Project 10
        Task Management 11
        Resource Management 12

TABLE OF CONTENTS

    Budget Management 14

    Collaboration and Communication 15

    Reporting and Analytics 16

    Automated Scheduling 23

    Integration and Customization 25

    Risk Management 25

    Time Tracking 26

    Portfolio Management 26

    Baseline and Variance Analysis 26

    Customizable Templates 27

Conclusion 27

Chapter 2: Getting Started with Microsoft Project 29

Introduction 29

Get Started with Microsoft Project 30

    Create and Save a Project 30

Defining Project Goals and Objectives in Microsoft Project 38

    Steps to Define Project Goals and Objectives 39

Communicate with Your Project Plan 42

    Save a Project Baseline 42

Update and View Project Schedule 49

    Communicate with the View the Project Schedule 58

Chapter 3: Managing Tasks with Microsoft Project 69

Introduction 69

Create and Modify Tasks 70

    Create Tasks 70

    Summary Tasks 73

Add Milestone 80
Put Tasks into Sequence 85
Add Task Duration to the Project 90
Create a Task Plan Using Microsoft Copilot 91
Gantt Charts in Microsoft Project 96
Benefits of Using Gantt Charts in Microsoft Project 100
Tips for Effective Use of Gantt Charts 100

Chapter 4: Resource Management Using Microsoft Project 103
Introduction 103
Create Resources 106
Assign Resources to Tasks 113
Resource Overallocation Problem 121
Resource Overallocation Impact on the Overall Project Cycle 122
Conclusion 125
Crucial to Resolve Resource Overallocation 125
Demonstration to Fix a Resource Overallocation Problem 127

Chapter 5: Fine-Tuning a Project Schedule 131
Introduction 131
Review of the Critical Path 133
Identify Schedule Issues with Task Inspector 141
Delay a Task or Assignment 147
Inactive Tasks in Microsoft Project 152
Identify Project Schedule Problems 158

TABLE OF CONTENTS

Chapter 6: Budget and Cost Management Using Microsoft Project 167

Introduction 167

Setting Up Your Project 168

Budget Planning 168

Cost Tracking 169

Cost Control 169

Reporting and Analysis 170

Best Practices 170

Handle Tricky Project Costs 171

Budget Work and Resource Cost 178

    Set Up Work Resources 178

    Enter the Maximum Capacity for Work Resources 183

    Enter Work Resource Pay Rates 187

Chapter 7: Seamless Integration of Microsoft Project with Microsoft 365 Family 195

Introduction 196

Collaboration and Communication Using Microsoft Project ... 197

    Collaboration Features in Microsoft Project 198

    Overview of Communication and Collaboration with Microsoft Project 199

Seamless Integration of Microsoft Project with Microsoft Teams 201

    Work on a Project in Teams 201

    Remove a Project Tab 205

    Delete a Project 206

Seamless Integration of Microsoft Project with Microsoft SharePoint Online 207

    Sync with a New SharePoint Site 207

    Sync with an Existing SharePoint Site 209

TABLE OF CONTENTS

Best Practices Around Microsoft Project...211
    Best Practices for Using Microsoft Project..212

Microsoft Project Keyboard Shortcuts 215
    Frequently Used Shortcuts 215
    Navigate Views and Windows..215
    Use the Main Window 217
    Use the Timeline View 217
    Outline a Project..218
    Select and Edit in a Dialog Box..218
    Select and Edit in a Sheet View..218
    Use a Network Diagram..219
    Use Office Art Objects..219

Conclusion 220

Chapter 8: Agile Project Management Using Microsoft Project 221

Introduction..221
An Introduction to Agile in Microsoft Project...222
Set Up an Agile Project...231
    Turn on Agile Feature for a Project...231
    Add Features to the Agile Backlog..235
    Create Sprint 243

Chapter 9: Microsoft Project Reports and Analytics 247

Introduction..247
Choosing the Fields in a Graphical Report...251
Focusing on Key Results in a Graphical Report 260

ix

TABLE OF CONTENTS

Chapter 10: Advanced Features of Microsoft Project and Future Trends in Project Management 273

Introduction 274

Advanced Features of Microsoft Project Available 274

Expert Tips for Efficient Analysis, Risk Management, and Quality Control 278

    Copy Data into Adjacent Rows 278

    Quickly Insert Multiple Tasks 281

    Enter Values Quickly with a Lookup Table 283

    Wrap Text in Table Cells 286

    Align Cell Data 290

    Copy Cell Formatting 294

    Change Currency Formatting 298

    Adjust Column and Row Size in Project 301

Index 309

About the Author

Charles Waghmare, presently a DBA (Doctor of Business Administration) scholar from the prestigious SP Jain School of Global Management, as well as an MBA from the same prestigious B-school, has more than 17 years of industry experience in the IT, engineering, and energy sectors. Charles is presently working with a global energy leader since 2019 as an Information and Records Management Specialist in the Microsoft 365 space. Before that, he worked for Capgemini for eight years in various roles, including Viva Engage Community Manager and an Overseer for a Drupal-based Enterprise Knowledge Management system.

He also developed a knowledge management platform for Capgemini's Digital Customer Experience (DCX) organization using SharePoint Online to manage client references and knowledge assets related to artificial intelligence and customer experience (CX). Further, he adopted Microsoft Azure Chatbots to automate communication channels with customers. Charles also worked for SIEMENS Information Systems Limited for five years. During his tenure there, he was a Community Manager of SAP-based communities, where he utilized TechnoWeb 2.0 – a Viva Engage-like platform – and on-premises SharePoint to manage SAP user-based communities. Also, Charles was the global rollout manager for a structured document management system built using SharePoint.

ABOUT THE AUTHOR

Charles has penned several books on Microsoft 365 technologies such as Viva Engage, SharePoint Online, Azure Chatbots, Microsoft Purview, and also on ChatGPT. Further, he loves reading motivational books in his spare time, his favorite being *The Monk Who Sold His Ferrari, The 5 AM Club, and The Wealth Money Can't Buy.*

About the Technical Reviewer

Kasam Shaikh is a prominent figure in India's artificial intelligence landscape, holding the distinction of being one of the country's first four Microsoft Most Valuable Professionals (MVPs) in AI. Currently serving as a Senior Architect, Kasam boasts an impressive track record as an author, having authored five best-selling books dedicated to Azure and AI technologies. Beyond his writing endeavors, Kasam is recognized as a Microsoft Certified Trainer (MCT) and influential tech YouTuber (@mekasamshaikh). He also leads the largest online Azure AI community, known as DearAzure | Azure INDIA, and is a globally renowned AI speaker. His commitment to knowledge sharing extends to contributions to Microsoft Learn, where he plays a pivotal role.

Within the realm of AI, Kasam is a respected Subject Matter Expert (SME) in Generative AI for the Cloud, complementing his role as a Senior Cloud Architect. He actively promotes the adoption of No Code and Azure OpenAI solutions and possesses a strong foundation in Hybrid and Cross-Cloud practices. Kasam Shaikh's versatility and expertise make him an invaluable asset in the rapidly evolving landscape of technology, contributing significantly to the advancement of Azure and AI.

In summary, Kasam Shaikh is a multifaceted professional who excels in both technical expertise and knowledge dissemination. His contributions span writing, training, community leadership, public

ABOUT THE TECHNICAL REVIEWER

speaking, and architecture, establishing him as a true luminary in Azure and AI. Kasam was recently recognized as Top AI Voice by LinkedIn, making him the sole exclusive Indian professional acknowledged by both Microsoft and LinkedIn for his contributions to artificial intelligence!

Acknowledgments

I wish to express my heartfelt gratitude to the following individuals who have profoundly impacted my life:

Late **Mr. Anil Malvankar**, former Deputy General Manager at SIEMENS, who graciously offered me my first job at SIEMENS. His mentorship and guidance were invaluable, and I remain deeply appreciative of his support until his passing in April 2024.

Late **Mr. Alwin Fernandis**, my beloved friend. Though he is no longer with us, his memory endures in my heart, and his influence continues to inspire me.

Introduction

Microsoft Project helps managers plan, execute, and monitor projects with detailed plans, schedules, Gantt charts, and Kanban boards. It enables resource assignment, workload management, and optimization. Integration with Teams and SharePoint enhances collaboration. Prebuilt reports and customizable dashboards provide project performance insights.

What Is in This Book

This book on Microsoft Project teaches readers essential skills for effective project management across any industry. It offers comprehensive step-by-step instructions for project setup and management, covering all aspects of Microsoft Project. Readers will learn resource assignments, workload management, cost estimation, budget tracking, and status updates. It also explains integration with Teams and SharePoint for enhanced collaboration.

Audience

This book on Microsoft Project attracts diverse readers, including project managers, team leaders, business analysts, students, IT professionals, consultants, entrepreneurs, construction professionals, healthcare administrators, nonprofit coordinators, and beginners. It offers practical insights, expert tips, and comprehensive coverage to enhance skills in project management, operational excellence, cost management, and project information management.

CHAPTER 1

Introduction to Microsoft Project: Understanding the Platform

Microsoft Project is a comprehensive project management software developed by Microsoft, designed to assist project managers in planning, executing, and controlling projects efficiently. It offers a robust suite of tools that enable users to manage tasks, resources, timelines, and budgets effectively. The software is widely used across various industries, including construction, IT, healthcare, and finance, to streamline project workflows and ensure successful project delivery. Project planning, resource and budget management, collaboration and communication, and analytics are some top tier features of Microsoft Project.

One of the standout features of Microsoft Project is its ability to create detailed project plans. Users can define project objectives, set milestones, and establish dependencies between tasks. The software provides a visual representation of the project timeline through Gantt charts, which help project managers track progress and identify potential bottlenecks. Additionally, Microsoft Project allows for the customization of project

CHAPTER 1 INTRODUCTION TO MICROSOFT PROJECT: UNDERSTANDING THE PLATFORM

templates, making it easier to adapt to different types of projects and organizational requirements. This flexibility ensures that project managers can tailor their plans to meet specific needs and goals.

Resource management is another critical aspect of Microsoft Project. The software enables users to allocate resources efficiently, ensuring that team members are assigned tasks based on their availability and skill sets. It also helps in tracking resource utilization and identifying overallocated resources, which can lead to project delays. By providing insights into resource allocation, Microsoft Project aids in optimizing workforce productivity and minimizing project risks. The ability to manage resources effectively is crucial for maintaining project schedules and ensuring that all tasks are completed on time.

Budget management is an integral part of project management, and Microsoft Project excels in this area. The software allows users to create detailed budget plans, track expenses, and monitor financial performance throughout the project life cycle. It provides tools for cost estimation, budget forecasting, and variance analysis, helping project managers stay within budget and avoid cost overruns. With real-time financial data, users can make informed decisions and take corrective actions when necessary. This financial oversight is essential for maintaining project viability and ensuring that resources are used efficiently.

Collaboration and communication are essential for successful project management, and Microsoft Project facilitates these aspects through its integration with other Microsoft tools, such as Teams and SharePoint. This integration enables seamless communication among team members, allowing for the sharing of project updates, documents, and feedback. The software also supports collaboration with external stakeholders, ensuring that everyone involved in the project is on the same page. Effective communication is vital for resolving issues promptly and keeping the project on track.

CHAPTER 1 INTRODUCTION TO MICROSOFT PROJECT: UNDERSTANDING THE PLATFORM

Microsoft Project also offers advanced reporting and analytics capabilities. Users can generate a variety of reports to gain insights into project performance, identify trends, and make data-driven decisions. These reports can be customized to meet specific requirements, providing project managers with the information they need to manage projects effectively. The ability to analyze project data helps in identifying areas for improvement and implementing best practices.

In conclusion, Microsoft Project is a versatile and robust project management tool that offers a wide range of features to support project planning, execution, and control. Its capabilities in task management, resource allocation, budget tracking, collaboration, and reporting make it an invaluable asset for project managers aiming to deliver projects on time and within budget. By leveraging Microsoft Project, organizations can enhance their project management processes, improve team productivity, and achieve their strategic goals. The software's flexibility and integration with other Microsoft tools ensure that it can adapt to various project types and organizational needs, making it a critical component of modern project management.

Introduction

Microsoft Project, or MS Project, provides a solution for managing projects of various sizes and complexities. It offers tools for planning, scheduling, and tracking project tasks, allowing project managers to create detailed project plans and monitor progress effectively. The software's resource management features enable users to allocate resources efficiently, track their utilization, and avoid overallocation, which helps in maintaining project timelines and optimizing productivity. Budget management includes tools for cost estimation, budget forecasting, and variance analysis, assisting project managers in keeping projects within budget and making informed financial decisions.

Collaboration is supported through integration with other Microsoft tools like Teams and SharePoint, enabling communication and document sharing among team members and stakeholders. This ensures that everyone involved in the project has access to the same information and can contribute effectively. Additionally, Microsoft Project's reporting and analytics capabilities offer insights into project performance, helping managers identify trends, make data-driven decisions, and implement best practices. By using these features, organizations can improve their project management processes, enhance team productivity, and achieve their strategic goals.

In this chapter, we will cover an introduction to project management, definition of project management, and significance of project management. Further, in pursuit of project management, we will explore Microsoft project management, specifically the MS Project desktop app, and explore some of its features in a detailed manner.

Note Microsoft Project and MS Project implies the same.

Importance of Microsoft Project

Define project management? Years ago, an inexperienced IT manager mishandled a critical project to upgrade the corporate phone system. He chose a new system without proper research or consulting users. The result was a system that disrupted communication and caused delays, leading to lost customers and business. This could have been avoided with proper project management, which is crucial for delivering solutions and solving business problems. Examples of projects include new product development, software deployment, community events, employee training, or relocating a business.

CHAPTER 1   INTRODUCTION TO MICROSOFT PROJECT: UNDERSTANDING THE PLATFORM

Project management involves using tools like Microsoft Project and skills such as communication, people management, negotiation, and budgeting. The Project Management Institute offers resources and credentials for learning more about project management methodologies. Projects have a start time, end date, cost commitments, and checkpoints, unlike ongoing operations. Applying project management methods and tools ensures your projects meet business needs successfully.

Effective scheduling can significantly contribute to organizational success. Consider the analogy of embarking on a journey by car without knowing your destination, travel companions, costs involved, or even the necessary maintenance for the vehicle. This scenario is akin to managing a project without a plan. Scheduling serves as a road map for achieving success. It provides direction and structure, ensuring that tasks are completed efficiently and effectively. While unforeseen changes may occur along the way, having a well-defined plan allows for adjustments while maintaining overall progress.

Unlike a simple to-do list, scheduling involves the sequencing of tasks, assignments, and cost management. Organizations utilize scheduling to oversee tasks, resources, and expenses at various levels of detail. The Project Online Desktop Client offers a robust database with multiple views and reports, facilitating communication of essential information to leaders, team members, and other stakeholders. This scheduling tool enables users to track progress and assess if project timelines are being met. Although the term "scheduling" is frequently used, we will refer to it as "planning" throughout this course. Your objective is to create a strategic plan for success. Utilize Microsoft Project Online or Desktop Client to meticulously plan your projects and adopt a structured approach to drive organizational success.

Project management is a critical discipline that plays a vital role in the successful execution of projects across various industries. It involves the application of knowledge, skills, tools, and techniques to project activities to meet project requirements. The importance of project management can be understood through its impact on achieving organizational goals, optimizing resource utilization, enhancing team collaboration, and ensuring project success. The foundation of project management is laid out in achieving organizational goals, optimizing resource utilization, enhancing team collaboration, ensuring project success, risk management, quality assurance, stakeholder management, adaptability and flexibility, and finally continuous improvement as shown in Figure 1-1. Let's go through the overview for each one of them in section.

Figure 1-1. *Foundation of project management*

Achieving Organizational Goals

One of the primary reasons project management is essential is its role in helping organizations achieve their strategic goals. Projects are often initiated to fulfill specific business objectives, such as launching a new product, improving processes, or expanding into new markets. Effective project management ensures that these projects are aligned with the organization's goals and are executed in a manner that maximizes their contribution to overall success. By setting clear objectives, defining scope, and establishing timelines, project managers can guide projects to completion while ensuring they deliver the intended value.

Optimizing Resource Utilization

Resource management is a critical aspect of project management. Projects require various resources, including human resources, materials, equipment, and finances. Effective project management ensures that these resources are allocated efficiently and used optimally. Project managers are responsible for identifying resource needs, assigning tasks based on team members' skills and availability, and monitoring resource utilization throughout the project life cycle. This helps prevent resource overallocation, reduces waste, and ensures that resources are available when needed. Optimizing resource utilization is crucial for maintaining project schedules and minimizing costs.

Enhancing Team Collaboration

Successful project management fosters collaboration and communication among team members. Projects often involve cross-functional teams working together to achieve common goals. Effective communication is essential for coordinating efforts, sharing information, and resolving issues promptly. Project managers facilitate collaboration by establishing clear communication channels, conducting regular meetings, and ensuring that team members are aware of their roles and responsibilities. Tools like project management software, collaboration platforms, and communication apps play a significant role in enhancing team collaboration. When team members work together seamlessly, projects are more likely to be completed on time and within budget.

Ensuring Project Success

Project management is crucial for ensuring project success. It involves planning, executing, and controlling project activities to meet defined objectives. Project managers use various methodologies, such as Agile, Waterfall, and Scrum, to manage projects effectively. These methodologies provide frameworks for organizing tasks, managing timelines, and adapting to changes. By following best practices in project management, project managers can mitigate risks, address challenges, and ensure that projects are delivered successfully. Key elements of project success include meeting deadlines, staying within budget, achieving quality standards, and satisfying stakeholders' expectations.

Risk Management

Risk management is an integral part of project management. Every project faces uncertainties and potential risks that can impact its success. Effective project management involves identifying, assessing, and mitigating risks to minimize their impact. Project managers develop risk management plans that outline strategies for addressing potential issues. They also monitor risks throughout the project life cycle and take proactive measures to prevent or mitigate them. By managing risks effectively, project managers can ensure that projects stay on track and achieve their objectives.

Quality Assurance

Quality assurance is another important aspect of project management. Projects must meet specific quality standards to deliver value to stakeholders. Project managers are responsible for defining quality criteria, establishing processes for quality control, and ensuring that project deliverables meet these standards. Quality assurance involves regular inspections, testing, and reviews to identify and address any issues. By maintaining high-quality standards, project managers can ensure that projects deliver the intended benefits and meet stakeholders' expectations.

Stakeholder Management

Stakeholder management is a critical component of project management. Projects often involve multiple stakeholders, including clients, team members, sponsors, and external partners. Effective stakeholder management involves identifying stakeholders, understanding their needs and expectations, and engaging them throughout the project life cycle. Project managers communicate regularly with stakeholders, provide updates on project progress, and address any concerns or issues. By managing stakeholder relationships effectively, project managers can ensure that stakeholders are satisfied with the project's outcomes and support its success.

Adaptability and Flexibility

Projects are dynamic and often subject to changes in scope, timelines, and resources. Effective project management involves being adaptable and flexible to accommodate these changes. Project managers use change management processes to evaluate and implement changes while minimizing their impact on the project. They also adjust plans and strategies to respond to new challenges and opportunities. Adaptability and flexibility are crucial for ensuring that projects remain viable and continue to meet their objectives despite changes.

Continuous Improvement

Continuous improvement is a key principle of project management. Project managers strive to enhance their processes, methodologies, and practices to achieve better results. This involves learning from past projects, analyzing performance data, and implementing best practices.

Continuous improvement helps organizations refine their project management capabilities, increase efficiency, and deliver higher-quality projects. By fostering a culture of continuous improvement, project managers can drive innovation and achieve long-term success.

Conclusion

In conclusion, project management is essential for the successful execution of projects and the achievement of organizational goals. It involves optimizing resource utilization, enhancing team collaboration, ensuring project success, managing risks, maintaining quality standards, and engaging stakeholders effectively. Project managers play a crucial role in guiding projects to completion, adapting to changes, and driving continuous improvement. By leveraging project management principles and practices, organizations can enhance their project management processes, improve team productivity, and achieve their strategic goals. The importance of project management cannot be overstated, as it is a critical discipline that contributes to the overall success and growth of organizations across various industries.

Features of Microsoft Project

Project Online Desktop Client provides new features to assist with managing your plan. The Project Online Desktop Client is obtained through a Microsoft 365 subscription, and updates are released regularly. For nonsubscription users, Project Professional 2021 is a similar alternative. The interface changes frequently to improve readability. Such changes also occur in other Microsoft programs like Word and Excel. You can verify the latest updates under File and then Account.

You can determine what version you have and read about the new features. Small enhancement features are often released around major Microsoft conferences such as Microsoft Ignite. These enhancements could be software fixes or feature improvements based on user feedback. If working on Agile or hybrid projects, the new task boards and sprint period management will be beneficial. The Sprints tab and Task Boards are new additions. There are also new reporting features, including options to report work status, task status, and sprint status via the Task Board Category. Note that even if a new feature is announced, it may not be available immediately as organizations often delay updates by three to six months to test with other internal programs and obtain IT department approval.

Sometimes, updates are rolled back if released too quickly, which is another reason for delayed global rollout of updates. More integration with Microsoft 365 is expected. Currently, there is the ability to import project plans into several other solutions. Project Online Desktop Client offers the latest features and stays updated through a Microsoft 365 subscription.

Microsoft Project is a comprehensive project management tool that offers a wide array of features designed to help project managers plan, execute, and control projects effectively. Here, we'll explore these features in detail, highlighting how they contribute to successful project management.

Task Management

One of the core features of Microsoft Project is its robust task management capabilities. Users can create detailed project plans by defining tasks, setting milestones, and establishing dependencies between tasks. This helps in organizing the project workflow and ensuring that all tasks are aligned with the project objectives. The software provides a visual representation of the project timeline through Gantt charts, which are instrumental in tracking progress and identifying potential bottlenecks.

CHAPTER 1 INTRODUCTION TO MICROSOFT PROJECT: UNDERSTANDING THE PLATFORM

These charts allow project managers to see the start and end dates of tasks, their duration, and how they interrelate, making it easier to manage complex projects. Shown in Figure 1-2 is a list of tasks created in the MS Project with their duration and start and finish dates.

	Task Mode	Task Name	Duration	Start	Finish
		Task 1	3 days	Fri 3/14/25	Tue 3/18/25
		Task 2	3 days	Wed 3/26/25	Fri 3/28/25
		Task 3	5 days	Fri 3/28/25	Thu 4/3/25
		Task 4	3 days	Wed 4/2/25	Fri 4/4/25
		Task 5	3 days	Mon 3/10/25	Wed 3/12/25
		Task 6	1 day	Wed 3/5/25	Wed 3/5/25
		Task 7	3 days	Wed 4/2/25	Fri 4/4/25

Figure 1-2. *List of tasks created in MS Project*

Resource Management

Efficient resource management is crucial for the success of any project, and Microsoft Project excels in this area. The software enables users to allocate resources effectively, ensuring that team members are assigned tasks based on their availability and skill sets. It helps in tracking resource utilization and identifying overallocated resources, which can lead to project delays. By providing insights into resource allocation, Microsoft Project aids in optimizing workforce productivity and minimizing project risks. This feature is particularly useful in large projects where multiple resources need to be managed simultaneously. To access resource management, click File ➤ Gannt Chart ➤ Resource Sheet as shown in Figure 1-3.

CHAPTER 1　INTRODUCTION TO MICROSOFT PROJECT: UNDERSTANDING THE PLATFORM

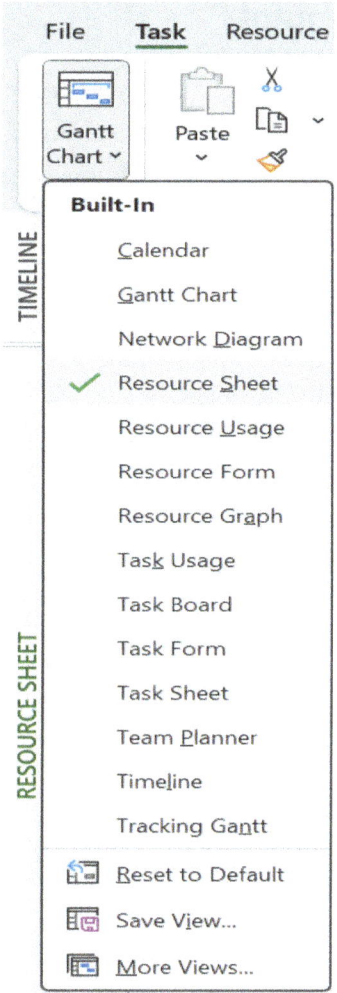

Figure 1-3. *Access resource sheet*

Figure 1-4 shows an example of the resource management sheet.

ⓘ	Resource Name	Type	Material	Initials	Group	Max	Std. Rate	Ovt. Rate	Cost/Use	Accrue	Base Calendar	C
1	Author	Material		A			$0.00		$0.00	Prorated		
2	Technical Reviewer	Work		T		100%	$0.00/hr	$0.00/hr	$0.00	Prorated	Standard	
3	Publisher	Cost		P						Prorated		
4	Designer	Work		D		100%	$0.00/hr	$0.00/hr	$0.00	Prorated	Standard	
5	Software Developere	Work		S		100%	$0.00/hr	$0.00/hr	$0.00	Prorated	Standard	

Figure 1-4. *An example of resource sheet*

13

CHAPTER 1   INTRODUCTION TO MICROSOFT PROJECT: UNDERSTANDING THE PLATFORM

Budget Management

Budget management is another critical aspect of project management, and Microsoft Project offers comprehensive tools for this purpose. Users can create detailed budget plans, track expenses, and monitor financial performance throughout the project life cycle. The software provides tools for cost estimation, budget forecasting, and variance analysis, helping project managers stay within budget and avoid cost overruns. With real-time financial data, users can make informed decisions and take corrective actions when necessary. This financial oversight is essential for maintaining project viability and ensuring that resources are used efficiently.

A resource can be made budgeted by accessing resource sheet, clicking on the task to be budgeted, and clicking on Budget as shown in Figure 1-5.

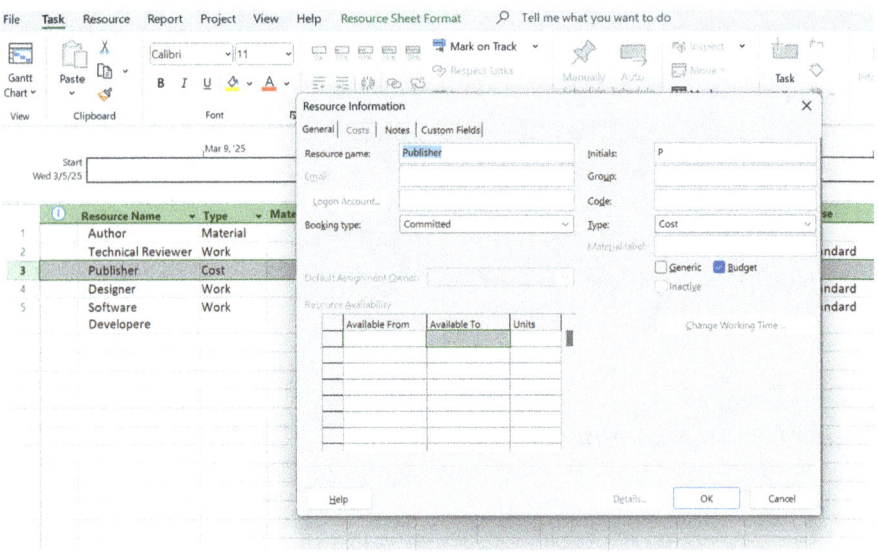

Figure 1-5. Resource to be made as budgeted

14

Collaboration and Communication

Effective collaboration and communication are essential for successful project management, and Microsoft Project facilitates these aspects through its integration with other Microsoft tools, such as Teams and SharePoint. This integration enables seamless communication among team members, allowing for the sharing of project updates, documents, and feedback. The software also supports collaboration with external stakeholders, ensuring that everyone involved in the project is on the same page. By fostering a collaborative environment, Microsoft Project helps in resolving issues promptly and keeping the project on track.

Microsoft Project enhances collaboration and communication through various advanced features, such as real-time collaboration on project plans, shared documents, and seamless integrations with other Microsoft 365 applications like Teams and SharePoint. These capabilities enable teams to work together efficiently. Here is a detailed overview:

Real-Time Collaboration

- **Simultaneous Editing:** Multiple users can concurrently edit the same project plan (MPP file), facilitating real-time collaboration and immediate feedback.

- **Cloud Storage:** Integration with OneDrive and SharePoint allows for cloud-based storage and access to project plans from any location.

- **Version Control:** Track changes and revert to previous versions of project plans, ensuring data integrity and collaborative workflows.

Communication and Sharing

- **Microsoft Teams Integration:** Integrate Microsoft Project with Teams to facilitate project-related discussions, file sharing, and task updates within a centralized platform.

CHAPTER 1   INTRODUCTION TO MICROSOFT PROJECT: UNDERSTANDING THE PLATFORM

- **SharePoint Integration:** Store and manage project documents, templates, and other assets in SharePoint, ensuring easy access and version control.

- **Email Notifications:** Configure project updates and task assignments to be sent via email, keeping team members informed and on track.

Reporting and Analytics

Microsoft Project offers advanced reporting and analytics capabilities that provide valuable insights into project performance. Users can generate a variety of reports to gain insights into project status, identify trends, and make data-driven decisions. These reports can be customized to meet specific requirements, providing project managers with the information they need to manage projects effectively. The ability to analyze project data helps in identifying areas for improvement and implementing best practices. This feature is particularly useful for stakeholders who need to stay informed about project progress and performance. As shown in Figure 1-6, different reports are available in MS Project.

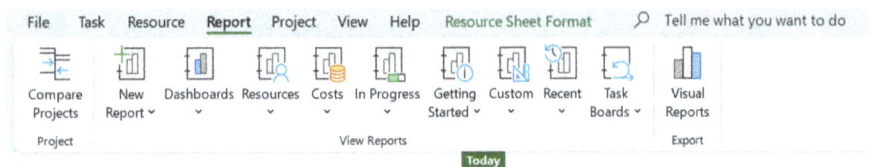

Figure 1-6. *Reports in MS Project*

Dashboards reports (Figure 1-6-1) show reports such as Burndown, Cost Overview, Project Overview, Upcoming Tasks, and Work Overview.

16

CHAPTER 1   INTRODUCTION TO MICROSOFT PROJECT: UNDERSTANDING THE PLATFORM

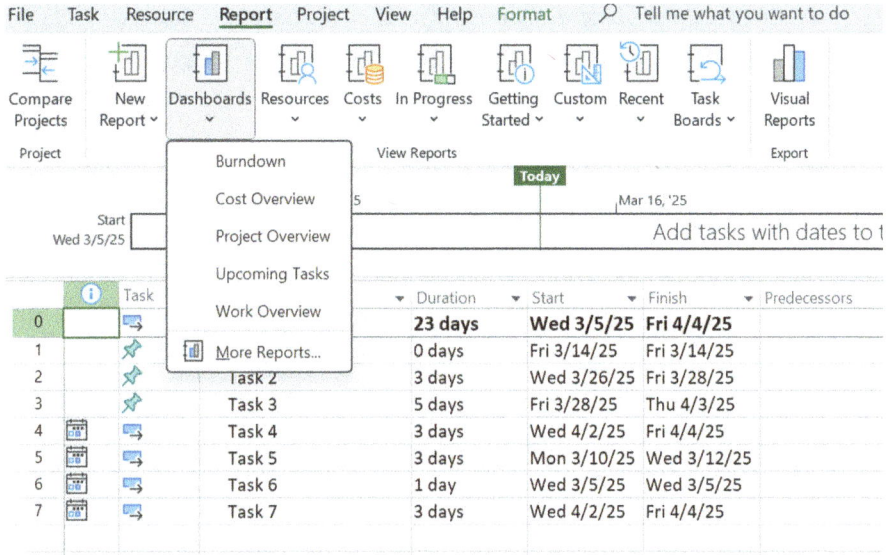

Figure 1-6-1. Dashboards reports

Below are the definitions for each report available in Dashboards:

- **Burndown**: Tracks completed tasks, remaining work, and progress. For details, see Create a burndown report.

- **Cost Overview**: This section details the current cost status of your project and its top-level tasks, including planned costs, remaining costs, actual costs, cumulative costs, baseline costs, and percentage of completion. This information helps in assessing whether the project will adhere to the budget.

- **Project Overview**: Completion percentage, upcoming milestones, and overdue tasks.

- **Upcoming Tasks**: Completed work this week, status of remaining tasks, and next week's new tasks.

17

CHAPTER 1   INTRODUCTION TO MICROSOFT PROJECT: UNDERSTANDING THE PLATFORM

- **Work Overview**: A project burndown chart and stats for top-level tasks, showing completion percentage and remaining work.

Resources reports, as shown in Figure 1-6-2, contain reports such as Overallocated Resources and Resource Overview.

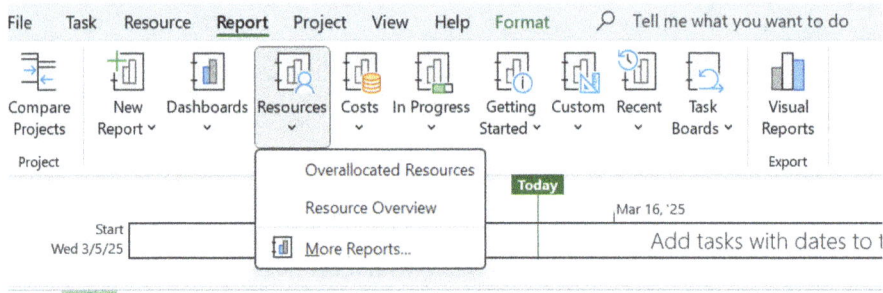

Figure 1-6-2. *Resources reports*

Below are the definitions of resources reports:

- **Overallocated Resources**: Displays actual and remaining work for all overallocated resources. Resolve these overallocations in the Team Planner View.

- **Resource Overview**: The work status of all personnel on your project, showing completed work and remaining tasks.

Costs reports, as shown in Figure 1-6-3, contain reports such as Cash Flow, Cost Overruns, Earned Value Report, Resource Cost Overview, and Task Cost Overview.

18

CHAPTER 1   INTRODUCTION TO MICROSOFT PROJECT: UNDERSTANDING THE PLATFORM

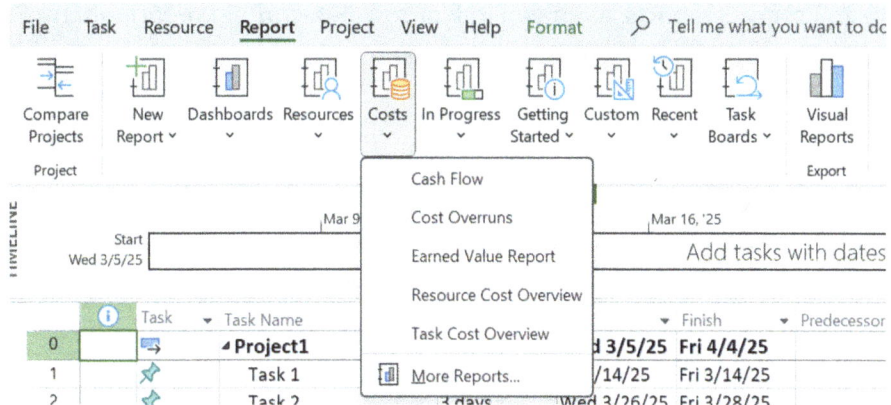

Figure 1-6-3. Costs reports

Below are the definitions of reports available under Costs reports:

- **Cash Flow**: Quarterly costs and cumulative costs for all top-level tasks. Use the Field List to display other costs or time periods.

- **Cost Overruns**: The cost variance for all top-level tasks and work resources indicates where actual costs surpass the baseline costs.

- **Earned Value Report**: This report tracks earned value, variance, and performance indices over time. It compares costs and schedules to a baseline to assess whether the project is proceeding as planned.

- **Resource Cost Overview**: Displays the costs of work resources, detailing in a table and showing cost distribution in a chart.

- **Task Cost Overview**: Displays top-level task costs with details in a table and distribution in a chart.

19

CHAPTER 1   INTRODUCTION TO MICROSOFT PROJECT: UNDERSTANDING THE PLATFORM

In Progress reports, as shown in Figure 1-6-4, contain reports such as Critical Tasks, Late Tasks, Milestone Report, and Slipping Tasks.

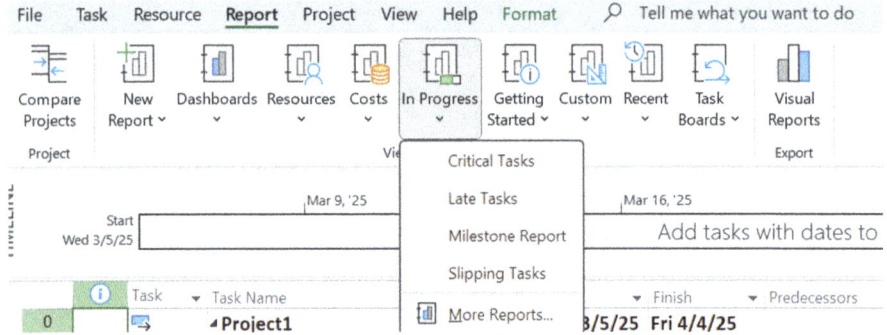

Figure 1-6-4. In Progress reports

Below are the definitions for each report under In Progress reports:

- **Critical Tasks**: Tightly scheduled tasks on your project's critical path, where any delay will cause the schedule to slip.

- **Late Tasks**: These are tasks that have commenced or concluded beyond their scheduled start and finish dates and are not progressing as intended.

- **Milestone Report**: Shows all project tasks with milestones, indicating their status as late, due, or completed.

- **Slipping Tasks**: Tasks in your project that are delayed beyond their baseline finish date.

Pick a report template to create your own reports as shown in Figure 1-6-5, which contains report formats such as Blank, Chart, Table, and Comparison.

CHAPTER 1   INTRODUCTION TO MICROSOFT PROJECT: UNDERSTANDING THE PLATFORM

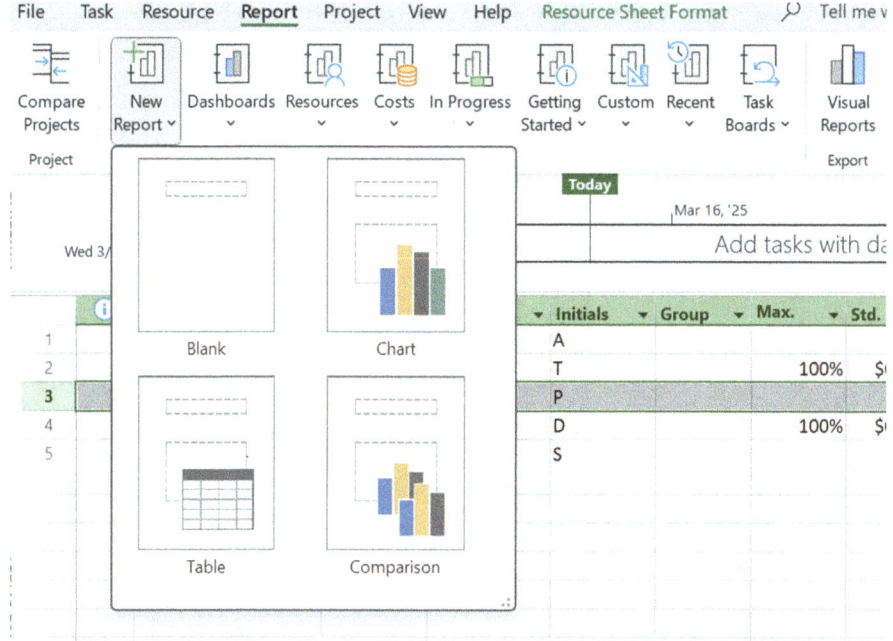

Figure 1-6-5. Access to new reports

Definitions of different report types are as follows:

- **Blank**: A blank canvas. Use the Report Tools Design tab to insert charts, tables, text, and images.

- **Chart**: This chart displays your project data, including actual work, remaining work, and default work. Utilize the Field List to select specific fields for comparison in the chart. Customize the chart using the buttons provided next to it.

- **Table**: Display project data including Name, Start, Finish, and % Complete fields. Use the Field List to select different fields and the Outline level box to choose the project outline levels. Customize the table using the Table Tools tabs.

21

CHAPTER 1   INTRODUCTION TO MICROSOFT PROJECT: UNDERSTANDING THE PLATFORM

- **Comparison**: Display two charts side by side with the same project data. Use the Field List to select fields for comparison in each chart.

Access to Visual Reports shows a list of reports shown in Figure 1-6-6 in both Microsoft Excel and Microsoft Visio formats.

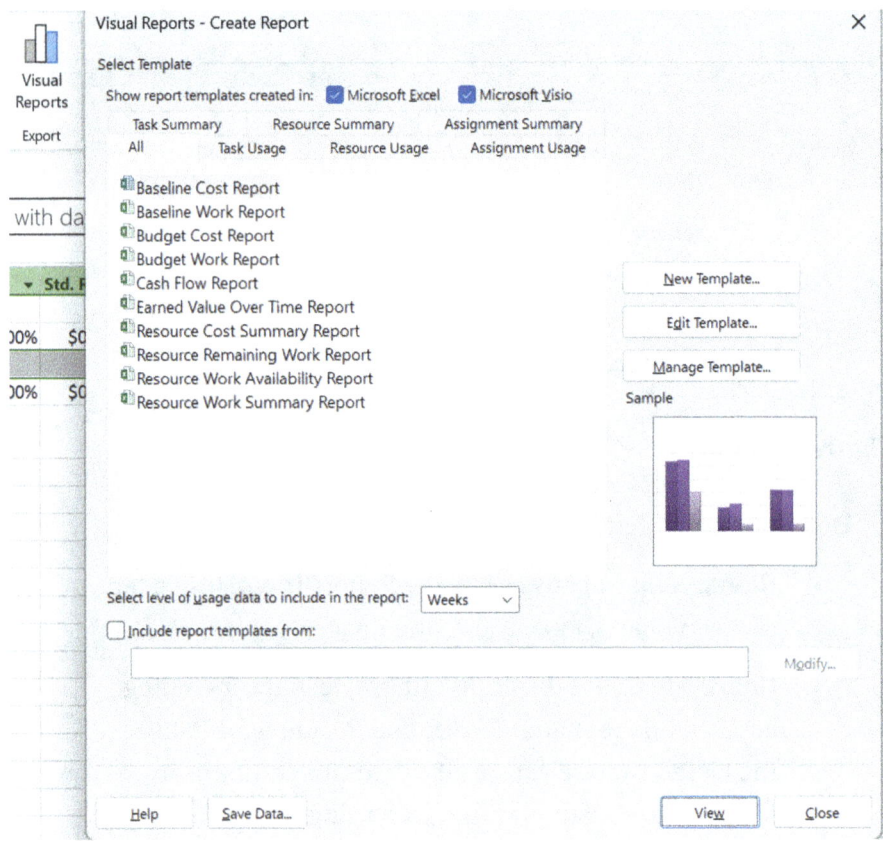

Figure 1-6-6. *Visual reports*

Below is the list of visual reports available for Microsoft Excel and Visio:

- Baseline Cost Report
- Baseline Work Report

CHAPTER 1   INTRODUCTION TO MICROSOFT PROJECT: UNDERSTANDING THE PLATFORM

- Budget Cost Report
- Budget Work Report
- Cash Flow Report
- Earned Value Over Time Report
- Resource Cost Summary Report
- Resource Remaining Work Report
- Resource Work Availability Report
- Resource Work Summary Report

Automated Scheduling

Automated scheduling is a powerful feature of Microsoft Project that helps in planning projects more accurately. The software provides dynamic scheduling based on the effort needed, project duration, and allotted team members. This helps in creating realistic project timelines and adjusting schedules as needed. Automated scheduling takes into account task dependencies, resource availability, and other constraints, ensuring that the project plan is feasible and achievable. This feature is particularly useful in complex projects where manual scheduling can be time-consuming and prone to errors. To configure automated scheduling, access task sheet ➤ click the individual task ➤ choose between Manually Scheduled and Auto Scheduled options for each task as shown in Figure 1-7.

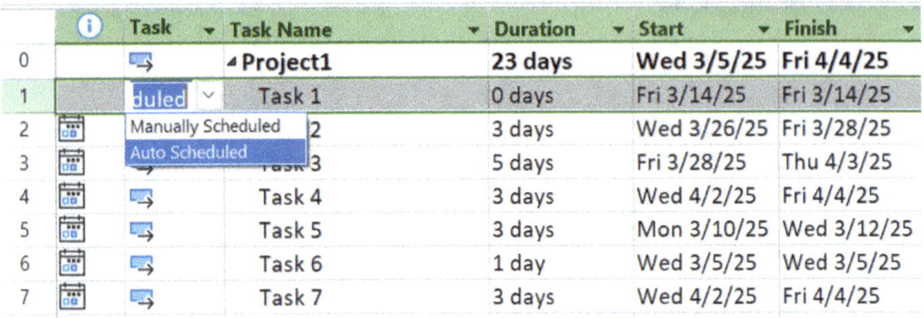

CHAPTER 1   INTRODUCTION TO MICROSOFT PROJECT: UNDERSTANDING THE PLATFORM

Figure 1-7. Configure manually scheduled or auto scheduled option for tasks

Manually scheduled and auto scheduled tasks are distinguished with icons shown in Figure 1-7-1 – manually scheduled with a pin and auto scheduled with a box and arrow.

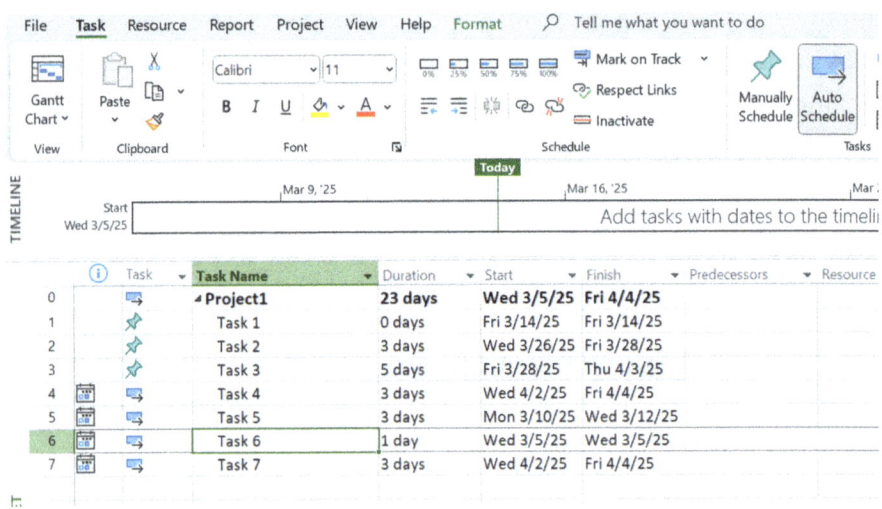

Figure 1-7-1. Distinguish manually scheduled and auto scheduled tasks

24

CHAPTER 1   INTRODUCTION TO MICROSOFT PROJECT: UNDERSTANDING THE PLATFORM

Integration and Customization

Microsoft Project integrates seamlessly with various Microsoft tools and platforms, such as Power BI for interactive dashboards and Azure for building secure, flexible experiences. This integration allows users to leverage the full suite of Microsoft products to enhance their project management processes. Additionally, Microsoft Project offers customization options that enable users to tailor the software to their specific needs. Users can create custom fields, views, and reports and automate workflows to streamline processes. This flexibility ensures that Microsoft Project can adapt to different project types and organizational requirements. Power BI integration with Microsoft Project is available under custom reports as shown in Figure 1-8.

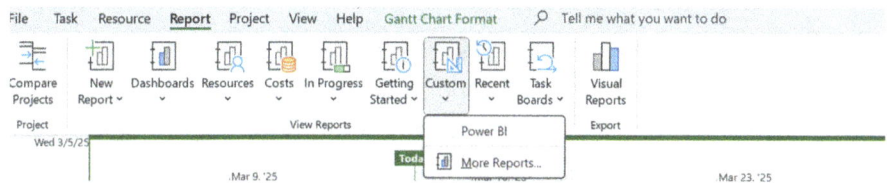

Figure 1-8.   Microsoft Project and Power BI integration

Risk Management

Risk management is an integral part of project management, and Microsoft Project provides tools to identify, assess, and mitigate risks. Users can create risk management plans that outline strategies for addressing potential issues. The software allows for the tracking of risks throughout the project life cycle and provides alerts when risks need to be addressed. By managing risks effectively, project managers can ensure that projects stay on track and achieve their objectives. This feature is particularly useful in projects with high levels of uncertainty or complexity.

25

Time Tracking

Time tracking is another important feature of Microsoft Project. The software allows users to track the time spent on tasks and compare it with the estimated time. This helps in monitoring project progress and identifying any deviations from the plan. Time tracking also provides insights into team productivity and helps in optimizing resource allocation. By keeping track of time, project managers can ensure that projects are completed on schedule and within budget.

Portfolio Management

For organizations managing multiple projects, Microsoft Project offers portfolio management capabilities. This feature allows users to manage a collection of projects as a portfolio, providing a high-level view of project performance and resource allocation. Portfolio management helps in prioritizing projects, aligning them with organizational goals, and optimizing resource utilization across projects. This feature is particularly useful for large organizations with complex project portfolios.

Baseline and Variance Analysis

Microsoft Project allows users to set baselines for their projects, which serve as reference points for measuring project performance. Baselines capture the original project plan, including tasks, timelines, and budgets. Variance analysis compares the current project status with the baseline to identify any deviations. This helps project managers understand the impact of changes and take corrective actions to keep the project on track. Baseline and variance analysis are essential for maintaining control over project performance and ensuring that projects meet their objectives.

Customizable Templates

Microsoft Project offers a variety of customizable templates that can be used to create project plans quickly and efficiently. These templates provide a starting point for different types of projects, such as IT projects, construction projects, and marketing campaigns. Users can customize these templates to meet their specific needs, saving time and ensuring consistency in project planning. Customizable templates are particularly useful for organizations that manage similar types of projects regularly.

Conclusion

In conclusion, Microsoft Project is a versatile and robust project management tool that offers a wide range of features to support project planning, execution, and control. Its capabilities in task management, resource allocation, budget tracking, collaboration, reporting, automated scheduling, integration, risk management, time tracking, portfolio management, baseline analysis, and customizable templates make it an invaluable asset for project managers. By leveraging these features, organizations can enhance their project management processes, improve team productivity, and achieve their strategic goals. Microsoft Project's flexibility and integration capabilities ensure that it can adapt to various project types and organizational needs, making it a critical component of modern project management.

With this, we have come to the end of this chapter. In this chapter, we have covered an introduction to project management, definition of project management, and significance of project management. Further, in pursuit of project management, we have explored Microsoft project management, specifically the MS Project desktop app, and explored some of its features in a detailed manner. In the next chapter, we will kick-start with setting up a project, defining project goals and objectives, and creating a project plan.

CHAPTER 2

Getting Started with Microsoft Project

In the previous chapter, we introduced project management, its definition, and significance. We also explored MS Project and some of its features. In this chapter, we will set up a project, define projects goals and objectives, and communicate with different stakeholders using Microsoft Project. With this, we will be able to establish our goals of creating and communicating a project plan using the Microsoft Project desktop app.

> **Note** Screenshots or features described in this chapter are used from the Microsoft Project desktop app.

Introduction

Microsoft Project is a powerful tool for managing tasks, resources, and deadlines. This chapter covers creating a basic project, setting up your work calendar, and modifying tasks. It also explains assigning resources and handling overallocation. Finally, learn to use built-in reports and visualizations to communicate your plan. This chapter aims to

CHAPTER 2   GETTING STARTED WITH MICROSOFT PROJECT

- Create and manage project files
- Organize tasks and milestones
- Define dependencies
- Assign resources to tasks
- Resolve resource overallocation
- Generate useful reports

Get Started with Microsoft Project

In this section, we will create and save a project, define the work calendar, and create a project with a calendar.

Create and Save a Project

To get your project schedule started, create a new project in Microsoft Project. Here's a straightforward way to do that with the following steps:

Step 1: On the home screen in the Microsoft Project desktop app, click the Microsoft Project icon shown in Figure 2-1.

Figure 2-1. *Microsoft Project desktop app icon*

CHAPTER 2   GETTING STARTED WITH MICROSOFT PROJECT

Step 2: Once you click the Microsoft Project icon, a Blank Project opens, which creates a new file automatically named "Project 1" as shown Figure 2-2.

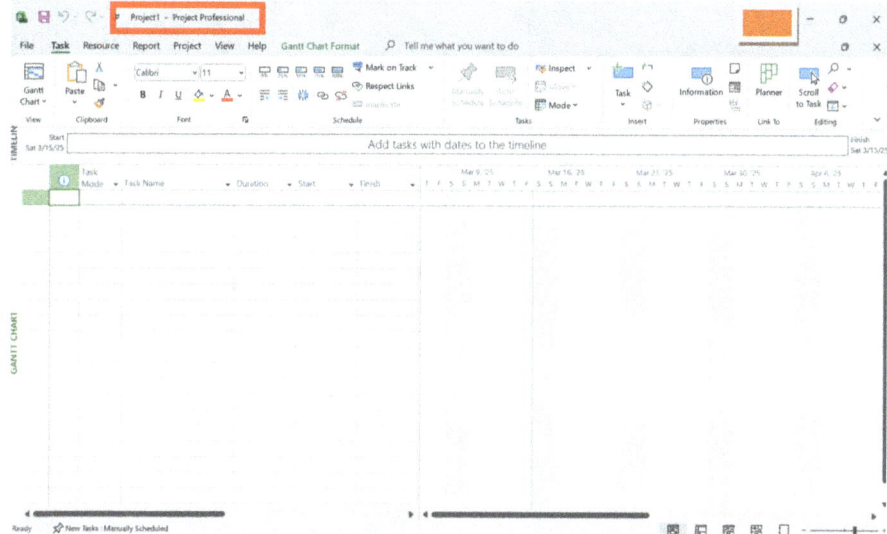

Figure 2-2. *Creation of "Project 1"*

Note   If a project is already open, you can use a keyboard shortcut Ctrl+N to create another new project. This one will be called "Project 2" as shown in Figure 2-3. Each new project created in a session is assigned a higher number as shown in Figure 2-4.

31

CHAPTER 2   GETTING STARTED WITH MICROSOFT PROJECT

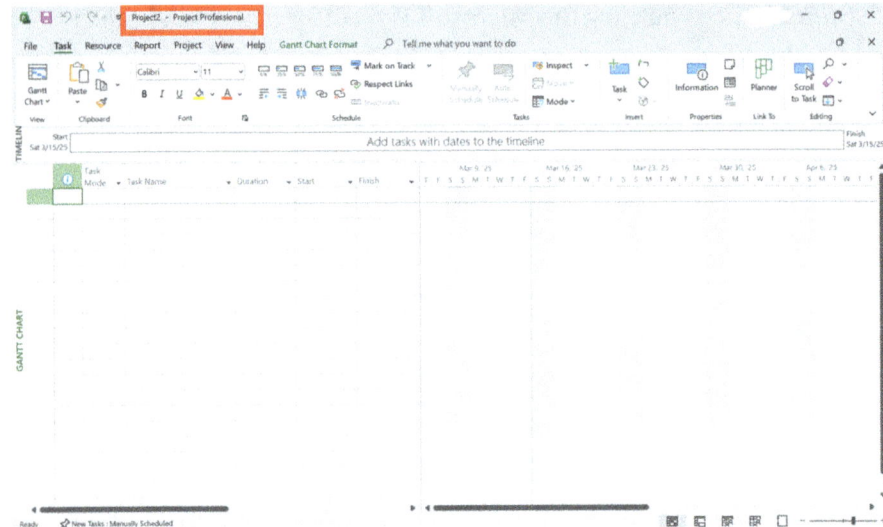

Figure 2-3. Creation of "Project 2"

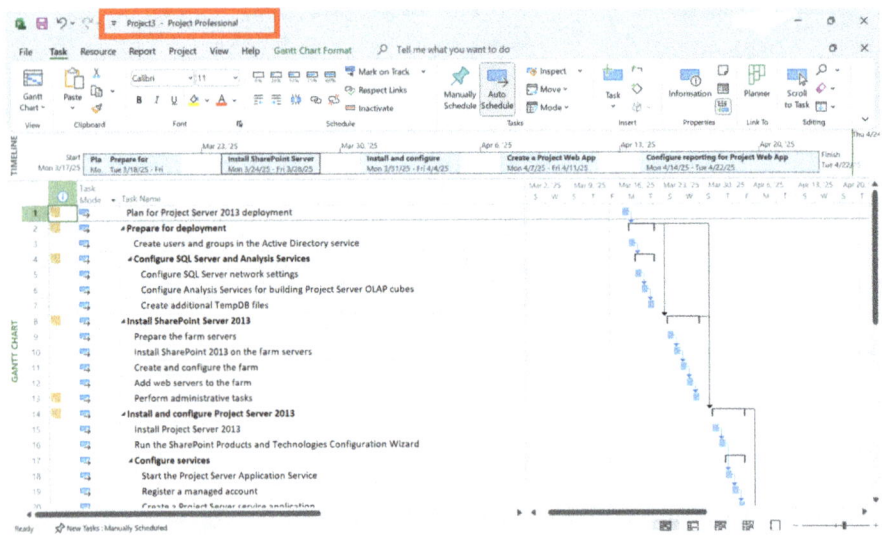

Figure 2-4. Creation of "Project 3"

CHAPTER 2   GETTING STARTED WITH MICROSOFT PROJECT

Step 3: To save any instance of the project, in the menu, click "File➤ Save As," and then, a screen appears as shown in Figure 2-5.

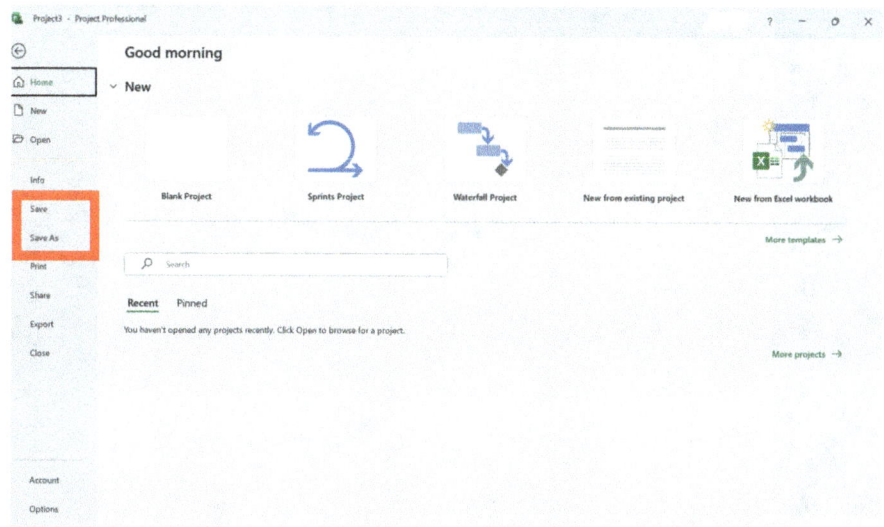

Figure 2-5. *To save any instance of the project*

Note   You can save the project either to your OneDrive or SharePoint as shown in Figure 2-6, and we will name this project "Install Project Server – Project" as shown in Figure 2-7.

33

CHAPTER 2   GETTING STARTED WITH MICROSOFT PROJECT

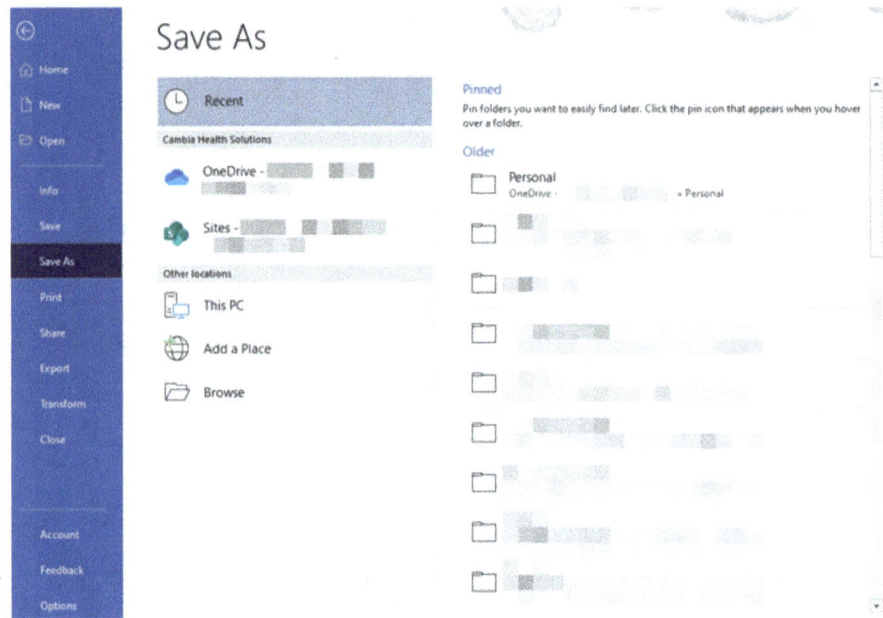

Figure 2-6. *Project file can be saved to OneDrive or SharePoint*

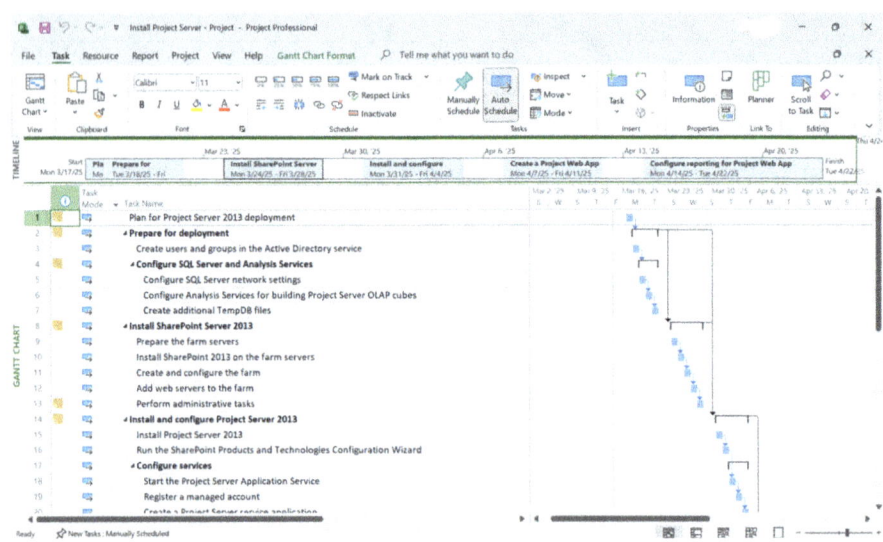

Figure 2-7. *Project saved with the name "Install Project Server – Project"*

Note In Microsoft Project, there are plenty of built-in Project templates available as shown in Figure 2-8 and Figure 2-8-1. When you create a new project, Microsoft Projects offers you an option whether to use a Blank template or a built-in template. The set of available templates for projects are as follows:

- Sprints project, budget
- Construction project, both commercial and residential
- Simple project
- Earned value project
- New business plan project
- Startup business plan project
- Annual report preparation project
- Marketing campaign project

CHAPTER 2 GETTING STARTED WITH MICROSOFT PROJECT

Figure 2-8. *Microsoft Project templates*

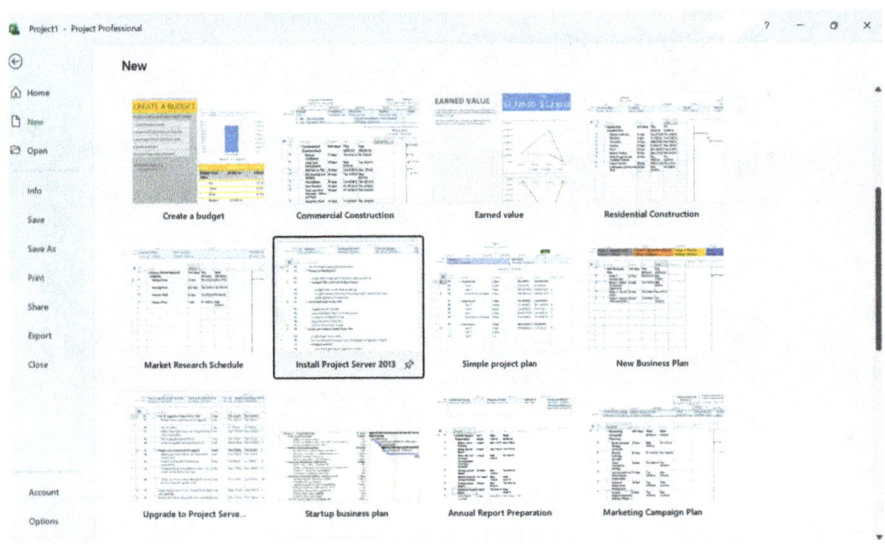

Figure 2-8-1. *Additional Microsoft Project templates*

Step 4: Now set the project start date, as follows:

- Go to the Project tab, and click Project Information as shown in Figure 2-9.

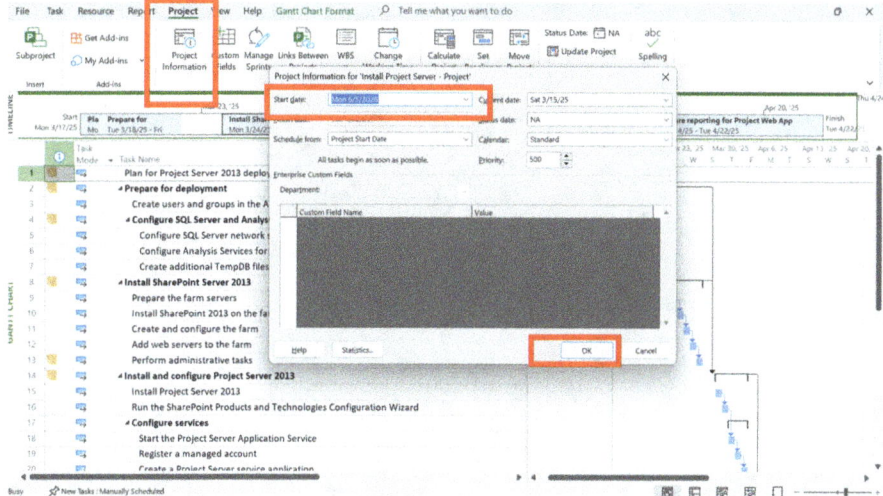

Figure 2-9. Access to Project Start Date

- The start date applies to tasks without a set start date or predecessors.
- Set the start date to June 5, 2028, as shown in Figure 2-9.
- Ensure the schedule from box is set to "Project Start Date, "so you can see when the project can finish. Click OK as shown in Figure 2-9.
- Finally, to save the file, go to the File tab and click Save.

Once the "Install Project Server – Project" is saved, all the dates get updated to the year of 2028 as shown in Figure 2-10.

37

CHAPTER 2   GETTING STARTED WITH MICROSOFT PROJECT

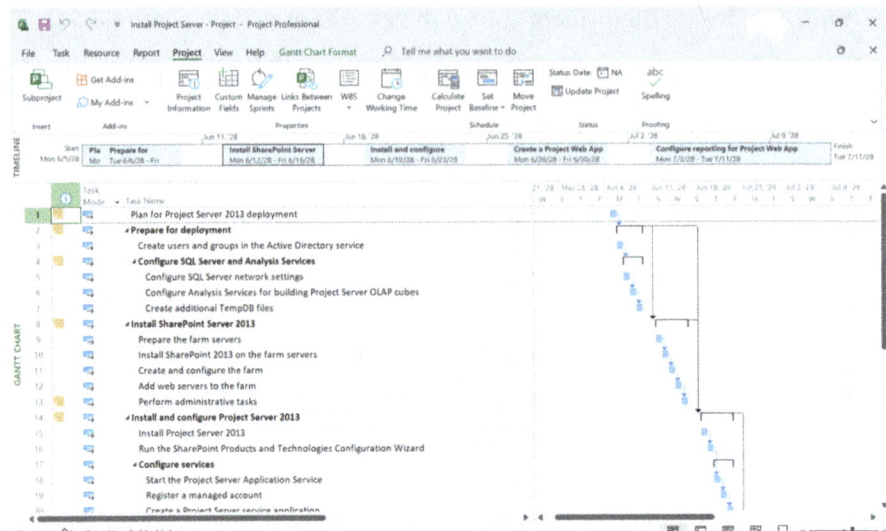

Figure 2-10. *Saved "Install Project Server – Project" with start date as June 5, 2028*

With this, we have come to the end of this section where we have experienced creating and saving a new Microsoft Project along with assigning a start date to the project. In the next section, we will explore the creation and modification of project tasks.

Defining Project Goals and Objectives in Microsoft Project

Defining project goals and objectives is a crucial step in project management, as it sets the foundation for planning, execution, and success. Project goals and objectives provide a clear direction and purpose for your project. Goals are broad, overarching targets that you aim to achieve, while objectives are specific, measurable steps that help you reach those goals. In Microsoft Project, you can define and track these elements to ensure your project stays on course.

Defining project goals and features is done using task management features of Microsoft Project, which we will be covering in depth in the next chapter; however, in this chapter, we will focus on understanding concepts that will provide enough exposure to gain practical experience in the next chapter.

Steps to Define Project Goals and Objectives

Defining projects and objectives is achieved by following the steps below:

- Understand the project scope
- Identify key stakeholders
- Define SMART project goals
- Define actionable project objectives
- Document goals and objectives in Microsoft Project
- Link goals and objectives to tasks
- Use Microsoft Project features to track progress
- Communicate goals and objectives
- Review and adjust goals and objectives

Understand the Project Scope: Before defining goals and objectives, it's essential to understand the project's scope. This includes the project's purpose, deliverables, constraints, and stakeholders. A clear scope helps in setting realistic and achievable goals.

Identify Key Stakeholders: Identify the key stakeholders involved in the project. These are individuals or groups who have an interest in the project's outcome. Engaging stakeholders early ensures their expectations are aligned with the project goals.

Define SMART Project Goals: Project goals should be broad, long-term achievements that the project aims to accomplish. They should align with the organization's strategic objectives. Use the SMART criteria to define goals:

- **Specific**: Clearly define what you want to achieve.
- **Measurable**: Ensure the goal can be measured to track progress.
- **Achievable**: Set realistic goals that can be accomplished with available resources.
- **Relevant**: Align the goal with broader business objectives.
- **Time-Bound**: Set a deadline for achieving the goal.

Define Actionable Project Objectives: Objectives are specific actions or steps taken to achieve the project goals. They should also follow the SMART criteria. For example, if a goal is to improve customer satisfaction, an objective might be to reduce response time to customer inquiries by 50% within six months.

Document Goals and Objectives in Microsoft Project:

- **Create a New Project**: Open Microsoft Project and create a new project.
- **Add Goals and Objectives**: Use the task list to add goals and objectives. You can create a task for each goal and subtasks for each objective.
- **Set Milestones**: Define milestones to mark significant points in the project. Milestones help in tracking progress toward goals and objectives.

Link Goals and Objectives to Tasks: Linking goals and objectives to specific tasks ensures that every task contributes to the project's overall purpose. This can be done by

- **Assigning Tasks**: Assign tasks to team members and link them to the relevant objectives.
- **Setting Dependencies**: Define dependencies between tasks to manage the sequence of activities.

Use Microsoft Project Features to Track Progress

- **Gantt Chart**: Use the Gantt chart to visualize the project timeline and track progress.
- **Task Information**: Enter detailed information for each task, including start and end dates, duration, and resources.
- **Progress Tracking**: Regularly update the status of tasks to reflect progress. This helps in identifying any deviations from the plan.

Communicate Goals and Objectives: Effective communication is key to ensuring that all team members and stakeholders understand the project goals and objectives. Use Microsoft Project's reporting features to generate reports and share them with stakeholders.

Review and Adjust Goals and Objectives: Projects are dynamic, and changes are inevitable. Regularly review the goals and objectives to ensure they remain relevant and achievable. Adjust them as necessary to accommodate any changes in the project scope or environment.

Benefits of Defining Goals and Objectives

- **Clarity and Focus**: Provides a clear direction and focus for the project
- **Alignment**: Ensures that the project aligns with organizational objectives

- **Motivation**: Motivates the team by providing clear targets to aim for
- **Performance Measurement**: Facilitates the measurement of project performance and success

Defining project goals and objectives in Microsoft Project is a critical step in ensuring project success. By following the steps outlined above, you can create a clear road map for your project, align your team's efforts, and track progress effectively. Regularly reviewing and adjusting your goals and objectives will help you stay on track and achieve your desired outcomes.

Communicate with Your Project Plan

In this section, we will explore on how we communicate with our project plan with different stakeholders involved in. We will be communicating using project baseline, project schedule, and project results with all stakeholders.

Save a Project Baseline

Once the project stakeholders approve your project plan, you need to save the approved schedule to compare actual progress with what you planned. In Project, a baseline holds a snapshot of your approved schedule. Let's follow below steps to accomplish this.

Step 1: To set a baseline, go to the Project tab, click Set Baseline in the Schedule section, and select Set Baseline from the drop-down menu as shown in Figure 2-11. This opens the Set Baseline dialog box. Ensure "Set Baseline" is selected, and "Baseline" appears in the box as shown in Figure 2-12.

CHAPTER 2 GETTING STARTED WITH MICROSOFT PROJECT

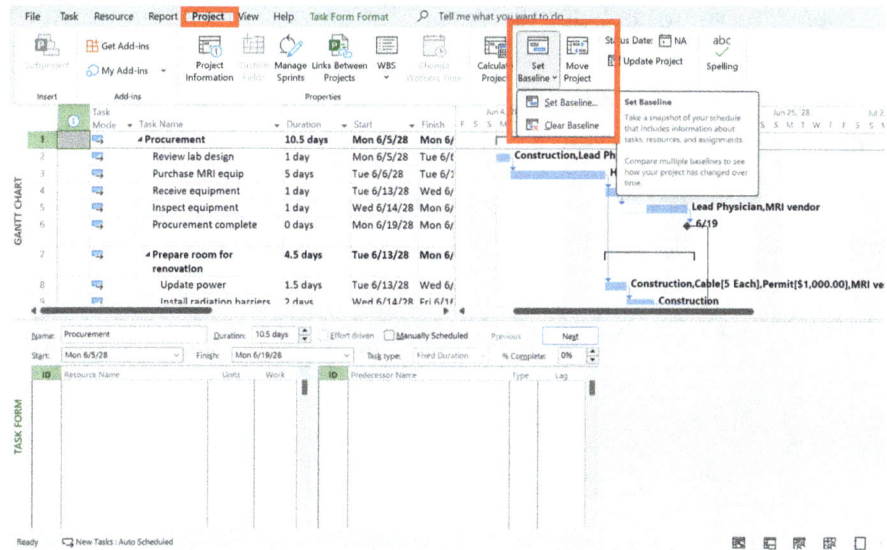

Figure 2-11. *Setting project baseline*

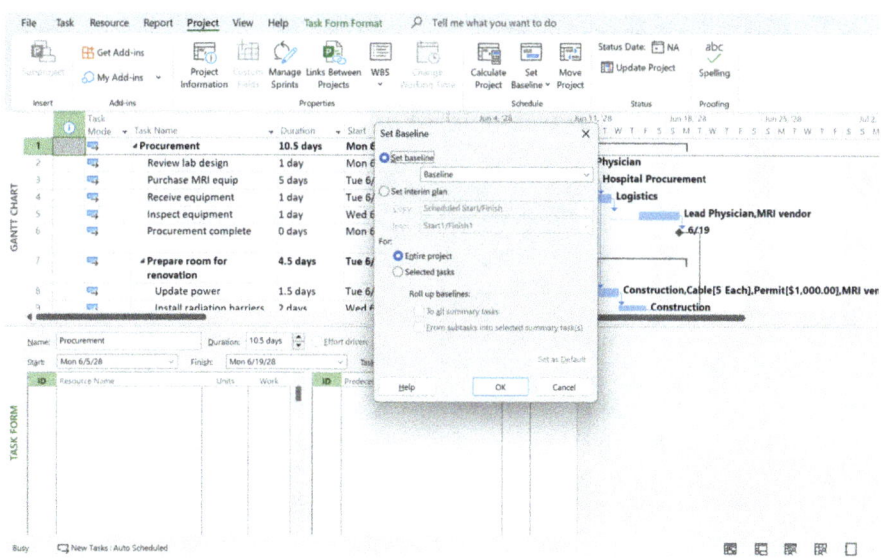

Figure 2-12. *Setting up baseline*

43

CHAPTER 2   GETTING STARTED WITH MICROSOFT PROJECT

Step 2: As shown in Figure 2-13, click the down arrow to choose from baseline options, but we will use "Baseline." Ensure the "For" option is set to "Entire project" to capture the entire schedule as shown in Figure 2-14. Click OK.

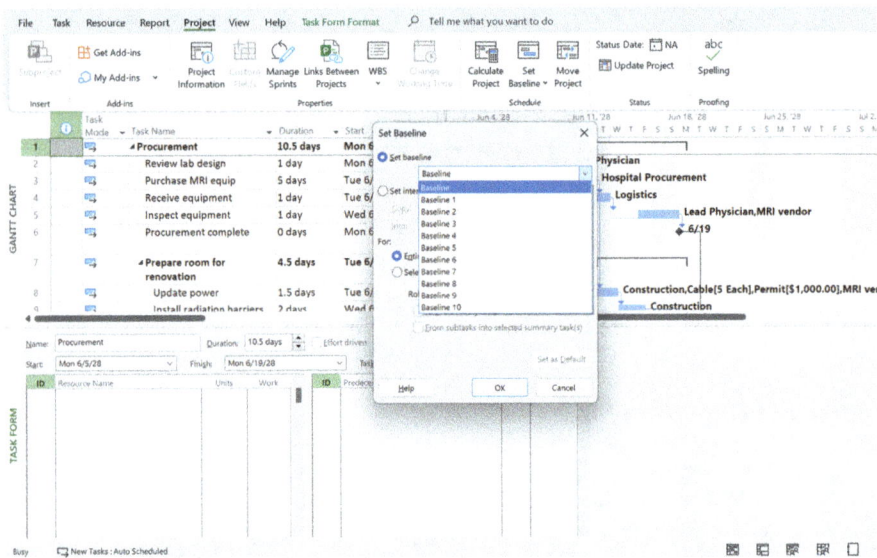

Figure 2-13. Choosing baseline from options

CHAPTER 2 GETTING STARTED WITH MICROSOFT PROJECT

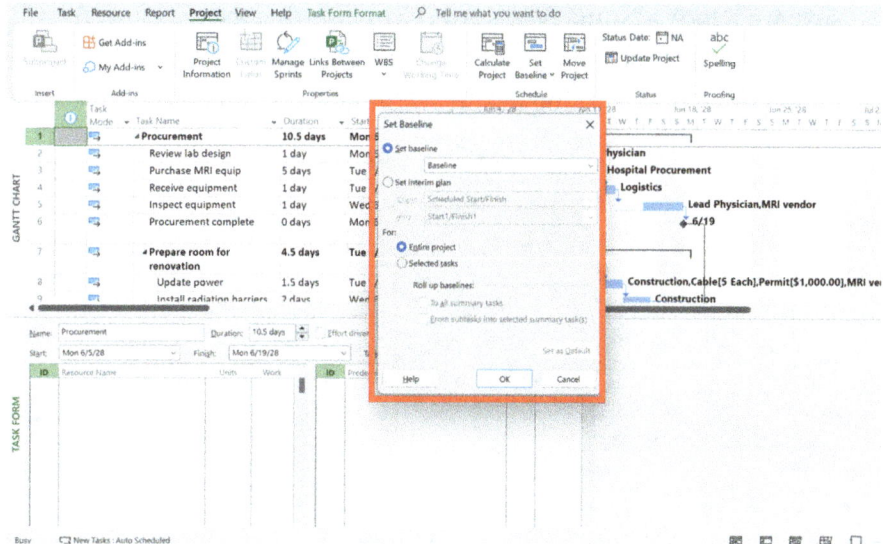

Figure 2-14. *Choosing "Baseline" as baseline and choosing Entire project option*

If you click Set baseline again, you'll see the date the baseline was saved, as shown in Figure 2-15. Click Cancel.

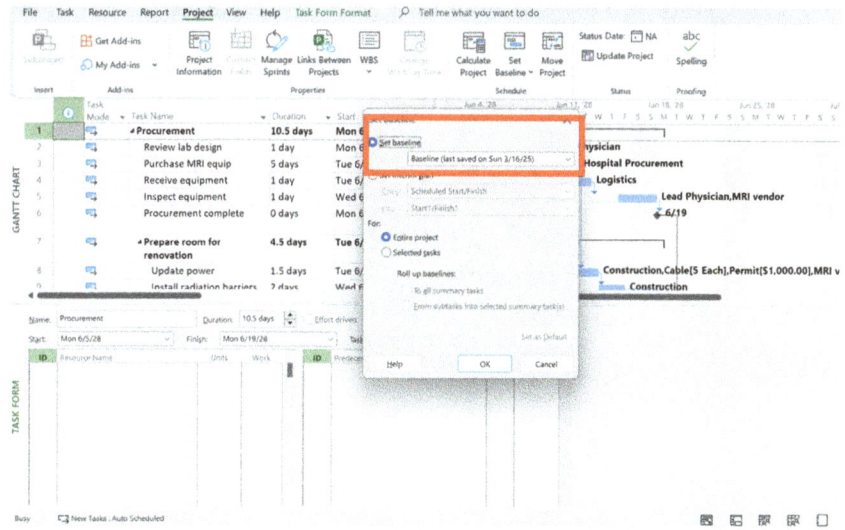

Figure 2-15. *Baseline date changed into baseline saved date*

45

CHAPTER 2 GETTING STARTED WITH MICROSOFT PROJECT

Next, we'll look at some fields saved when setting the baseline. As shown in Figure 2-16, change the table in the Gantt chart view by going to the View tab and then clicking the arrow under the Tables icon.

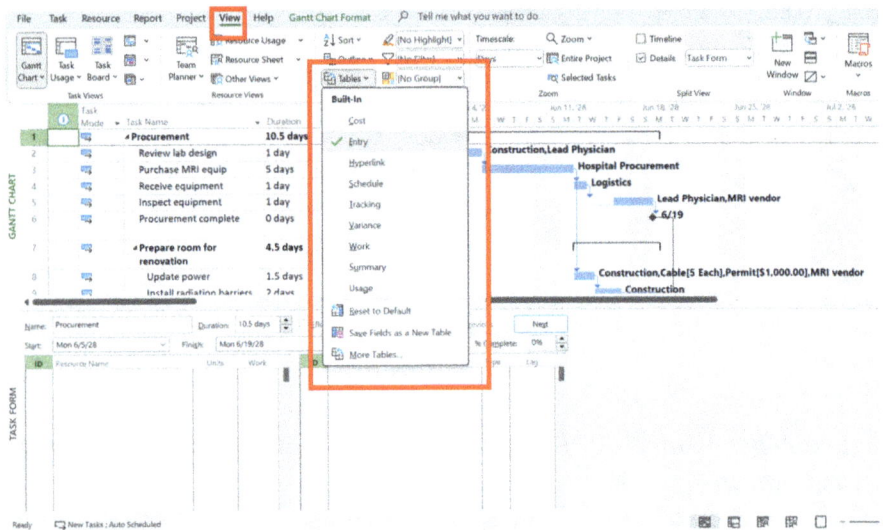

Figure 2-16.

Choose "More Tables" at the bottom, and select "Baseline" in the dialog box, as shown in Figure 2-17.

46

CHAPTER 2   GETTING STARTED WITH MICROSOFT PROJECT

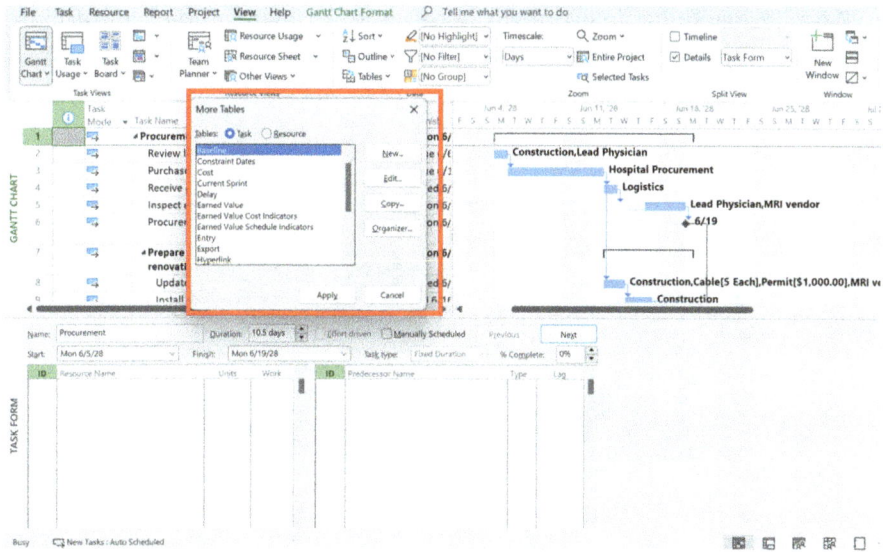

Figure 2-17. *Choose Baseline for the baseline view*

Once you click Apply as shown in Figure 2-17, the baseline saves fields for baseline duration, start, finish, work, and cost as shown in Figure 2-18.

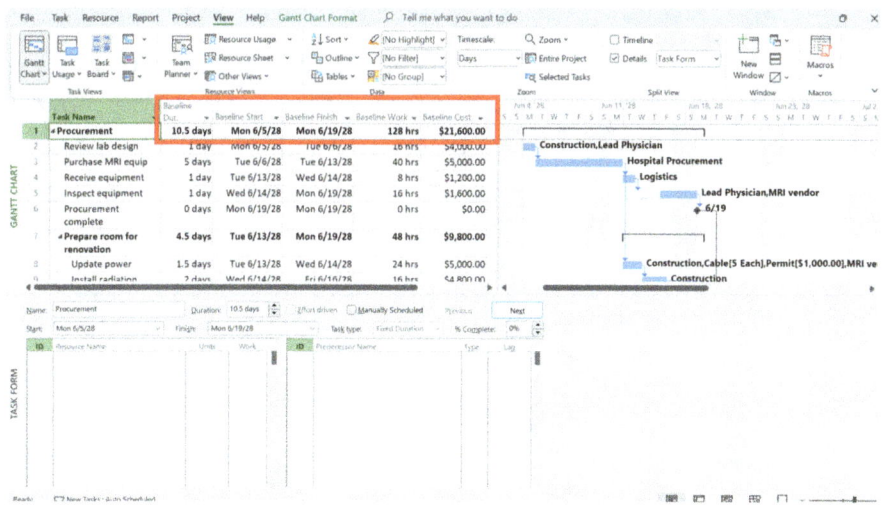

Figure 2-18. *Updated baseline fields*

47

CHAPTER 2   GETTING STARTED WITH MICROSOFT PROJECT

Another useful table is the Variance table. To switch tables, right-click the top-left corner of the table, and select "Variance" from the pop-up menu as shown in Figure 2-19.

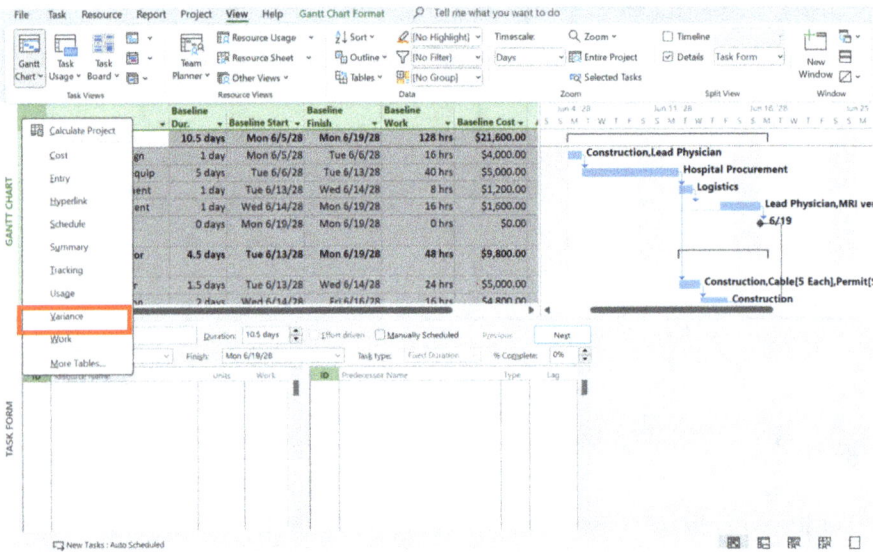

Figure 2-19. *Select Variance*

As highlighted in Figure 2-20, the Variance table shows scheduled start and finish dates compared to baseline dates, allowing you to track progress against the approved schedule. Differences will appear in the start and finish variance fields. Initially, variances are zero as the baseline matches the current schedule. That's how you save your approved schedule in a project baseline.

48

CHAPTER 2   GETTING STARTED WITH MICROSOFT PROJECT

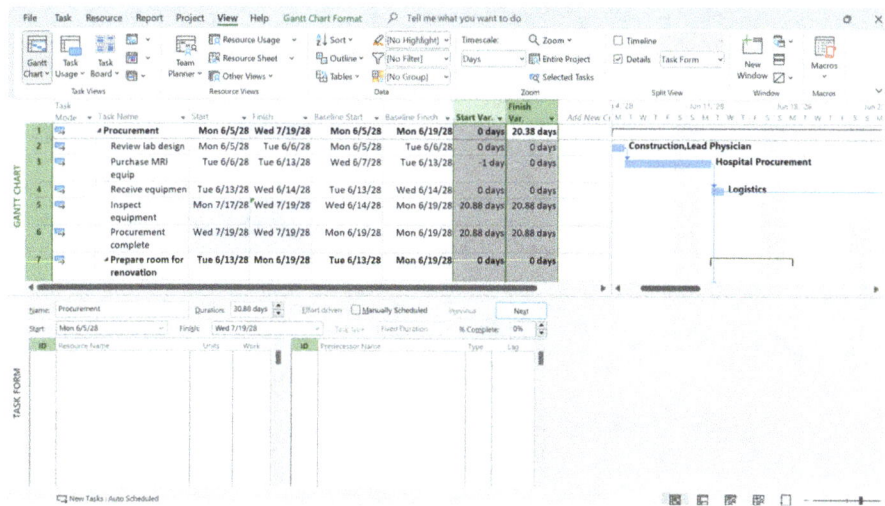

Figure 2-20. Variance of the project plan

So, with the help of baseline and variance, we are able communicate our project plans to all stakeholders involved in the project. In the next section, we will see how do we view and update our project schedule so that we can communicate this information to our stakeholders.

Update and View Project Schedule

When the team starts work on their assignments, it is time to start updating actual values in Project. To demonstrate a couple of simple ways to update progress, we will be updating tasks as described in the following steps.

Step 1: The first step is to change the table in the Gantt chart view to the tracking table because it has fields for actual and remaining values. To change the table as shown in Figure 2-21, go to the top-left corner of the table and right-click.

49

CHAPTER 2   GETTING STARTED WITH MICROSOFT PROJECT

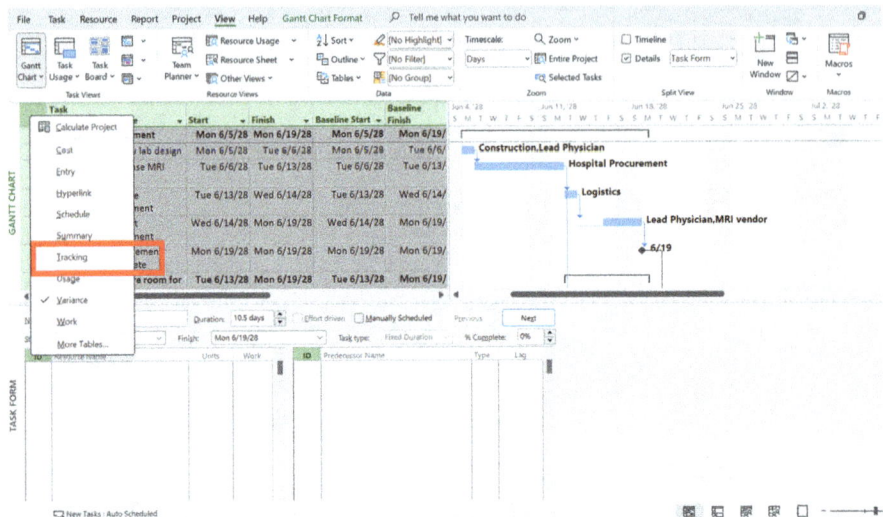

Figure 2-21. Access "Tracking" option

In the pop-up menu, select tracking. You will see fields like actual start, actual finish, percent complete, actual remaining duration, actual cost, and actual work as shown in Figure 2-22.

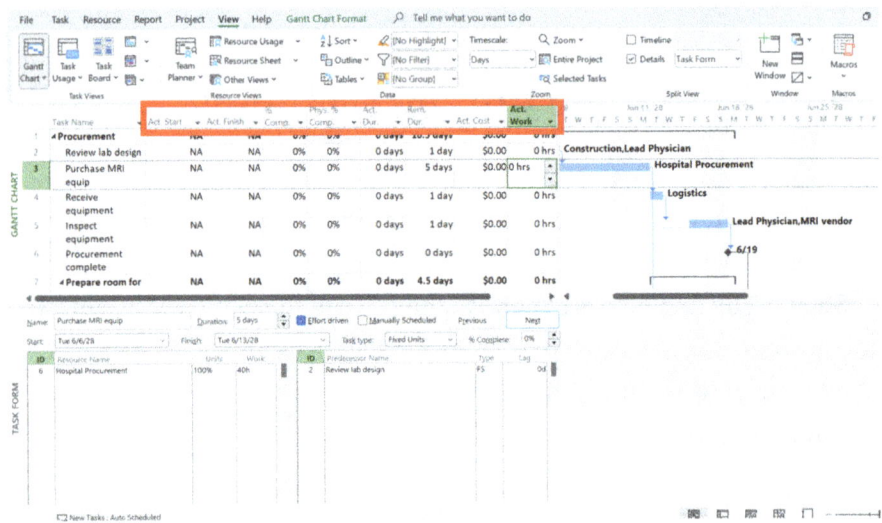

Figure 2-22. Addition of actual fields

CHAPTER 2   GETTING STARTED WITH MICROSOFT PROJECT

Step 2: Before adding any progress, set up the status date. Go to the Project tab and the Status section as shown in Figure 2-23.

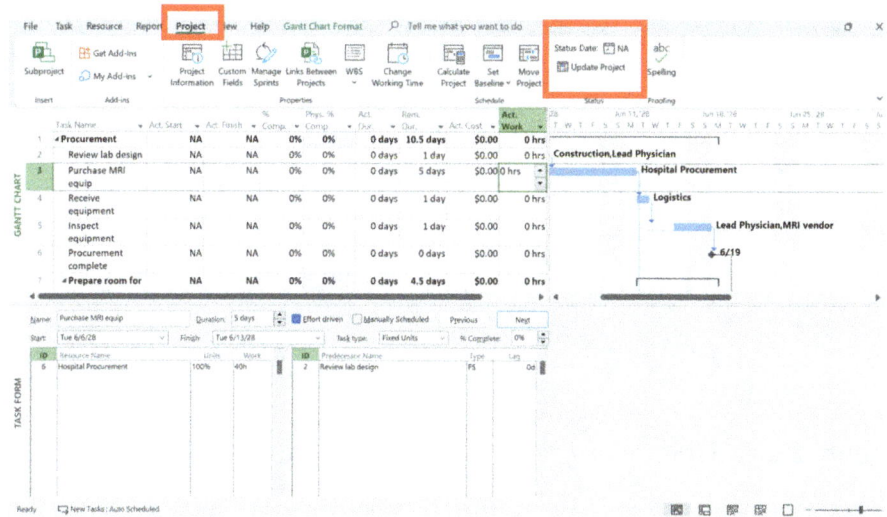

Figure 2-23. *Update project status date*

In Figure 2-23, where it says status date, click the calendar icon and enter the status date, for example, June 16, 2028, as shown in Figure 2-24. Once set, the date will appear in the ribbon as shown in Figure 2-24.

51

CHAPTER 2   GETTING STARTED WITH MICROSOFT PROJECT

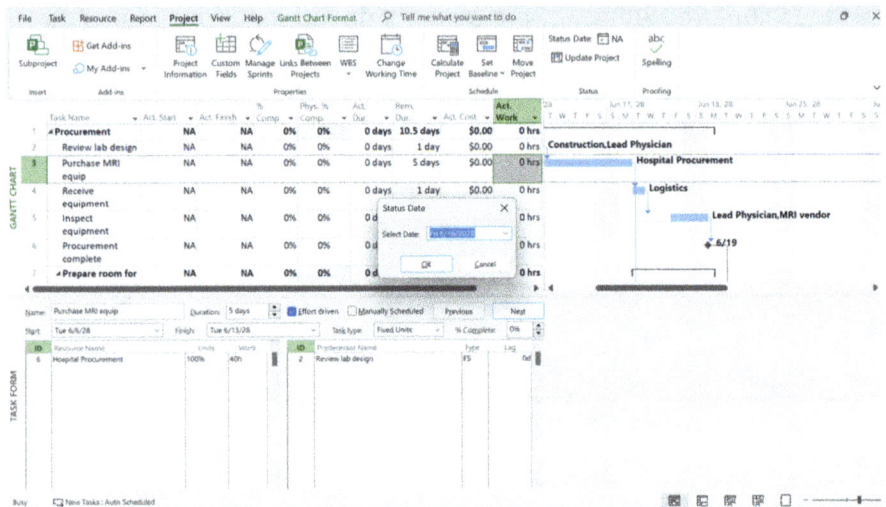

Figure 2-24. *Update project status date to June 16, 2028*

Step 3: Now, we can add some progress. Starting with task two, Review lab design, let's say this task completed as scheduled. Go to the Task tab, and in the Schedule section, click the down arrow next to Mark on Track, and then select Mark on Track as shown in Figure 2-25.

52

CHAPTER 2   GETTING STARTED WITH MICROSOFT PROJECT

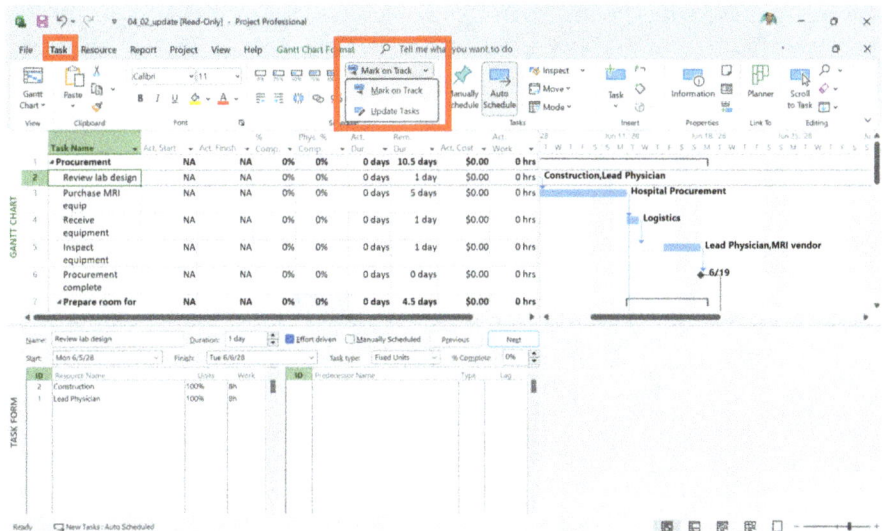

Figure 2-25. *Mark on Track tasks for task "Review lab design"*

This uses the original scheduled start date and sets it as the actual start and duration. Since the task was scheduled to complete before the status date, it shows as 100% complete as shown in Figure 2-26.

CHAPTER 2   GETTING STARTED WITH MICROSOFT PROJECT

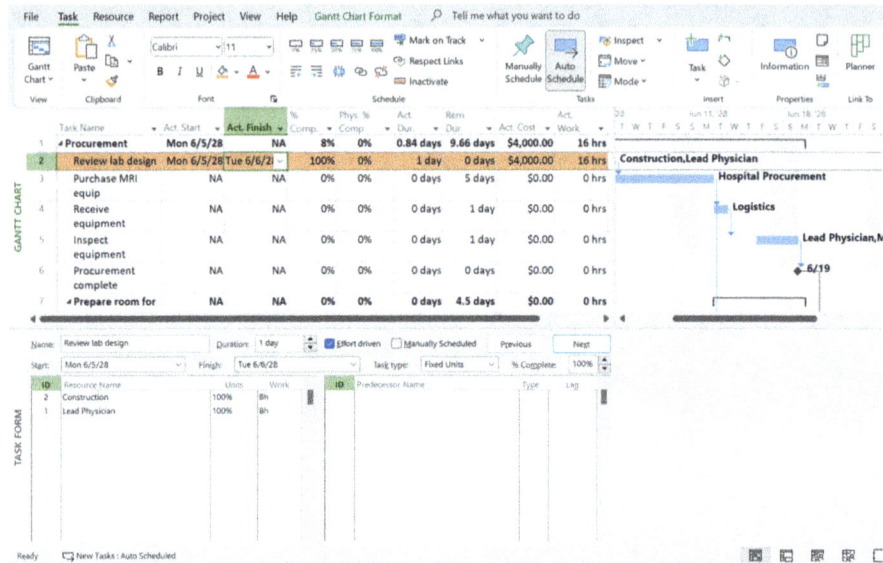

Figure 2-26. Review lab design completed 100% as it is marked as Mark on Track

Step 4: Next, update task three, **Purchase MRI equipment**, which took longer than planned and started late. Click the down arrow next to Mark on Track, and choose Update Tasks as shown in Figure 2-27.

CHAPTER 2 GETTING STARTED WITH MICROSOFT PROJECT

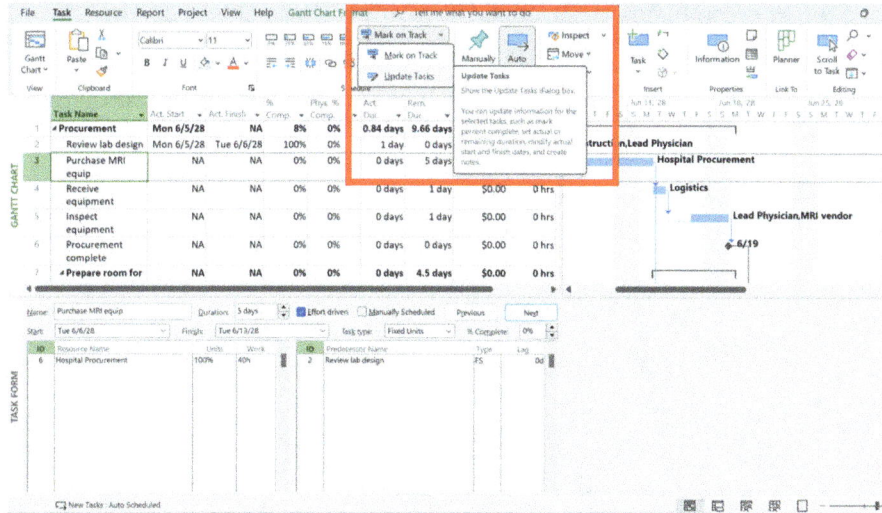

Figure 2-27. Choose Update Tasks option

Step 5: In the Update Tasks dialog box as shown in Figure 2-28, change the actual duration to seven days and adjust the start date to June 7, 2028. Set the remaining duration to zero days as shown in Figure 2-28.

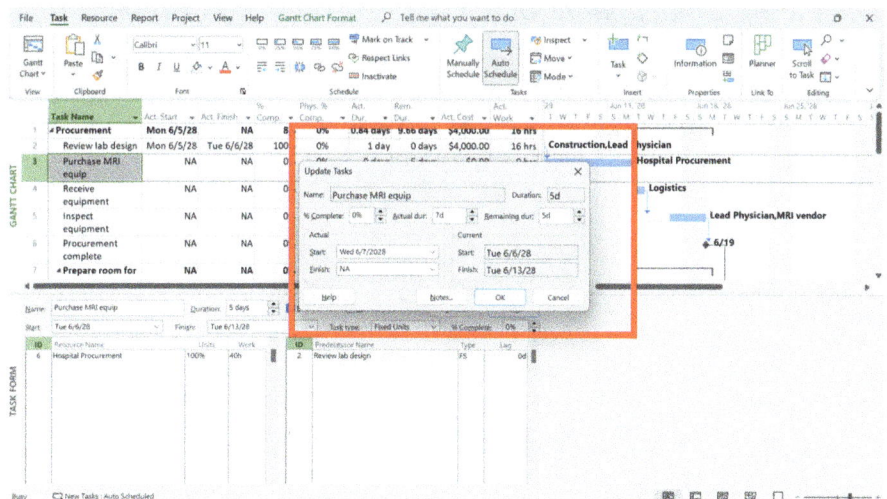

Figure 2-28. Update tasks for task "Purchase MRI equipment"

55

CHAPTER 2   GETTING STARTED WITH MICROSOFT PROJECT

Step 6: From Figure 2-28, click OK to apply these changes. The actual start date is now June 7. Project calculates the actual finish date, percent complete is 100%, and actual duration is seven days as shown in Figure 2-29.

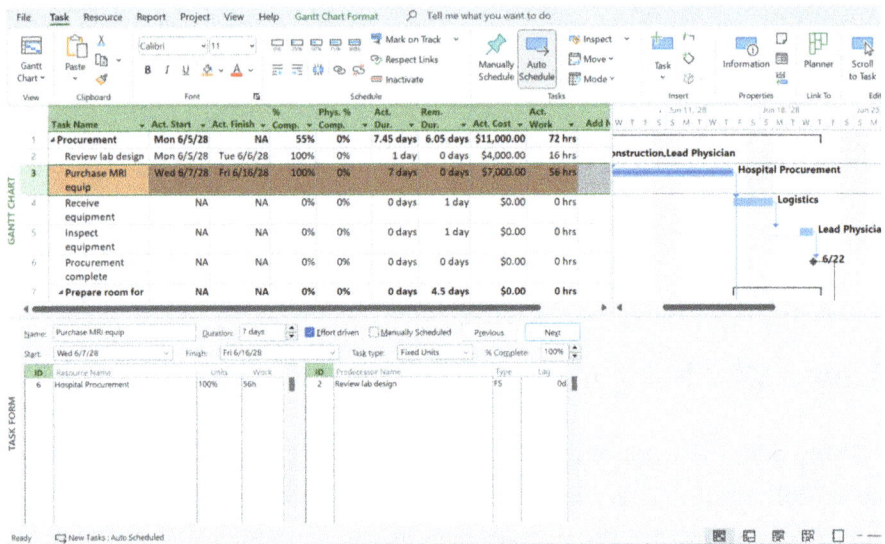

Figure 2-29. *Final update for the task "Purchase MRI equipment"*

Step 7: For simple updates, you can add values directly in the table. For task four, Receive equipment, type the actual start date in the cell, such as June 16, 2028, and the actual duration as one day as shown in Figure 2-30.

56

CHAPTER 2   GETTING STARTED WITH MICROSOFT PROJECT

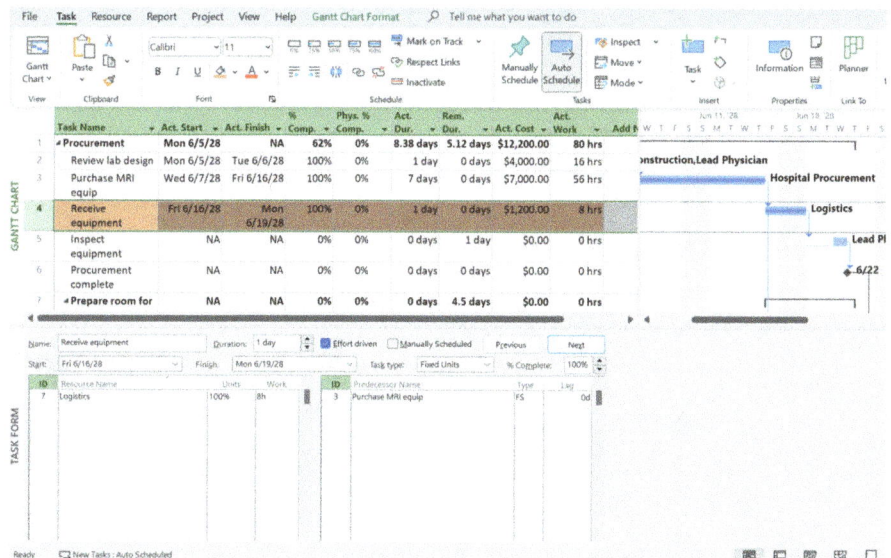

Figure 2-30. Update to the task "Receive equipment"

Project subtracts this from the remaining duration, completing the task. It fills in the finish date and percent complete.

Step 8: To update progress by work instead of duration, add the remaining work field to the table. Click Add New Column, type remaining work, and select it from the drop-down menu. Update task eight, Update power, by entering 12 hours in actual work, and Project recalculates remaining work to 12 hours as shown in Figure 2-31. If the task progresses faster than expected and only eight hours remain, update accordingly. Project recalculates percent complete based on actual work and remaining work.

57

CHAPTER 2   GETTING STARTED WITH MICROSOFT PROJECT

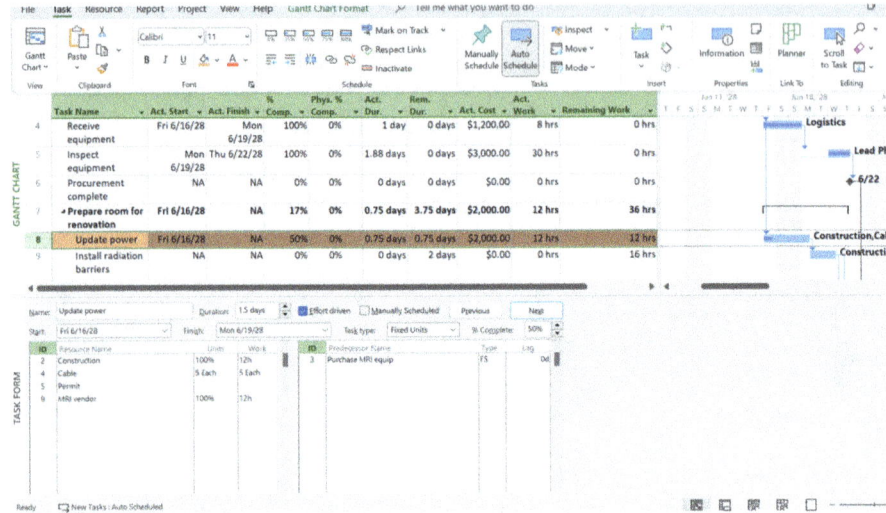

Figure 2-31. *Update to the task "Update power"*

Until now, we have seen how do we communicate using Microsoft Project by means of updating tasks in the project. Now we will communicate using different views available in the project schedule.

Communicate with the View the Project Schedule

Throughout the duration of a project, it is essential to examine various aspects of your schedule. Project offers numerous views, so let's explore a few that you will frequently use. We have already been using the Gantt chart. The Gantt chart includes a table on the left with values for your tasks and a timescale on the right that indicates when tasks occur over time – standard format for all Microsoft Project we have seen so far. Let's explore different views with below steps so we can communicate with different stakeholders using these views.

CHAPTER 2   GETTING STARTED WITH MICROSOFT PROJECT

Step 1: By selecting a task in the table, you can view the details pane in the bottom half of the window, which provides detailed information about the selected task as shown in Figure 2-32.

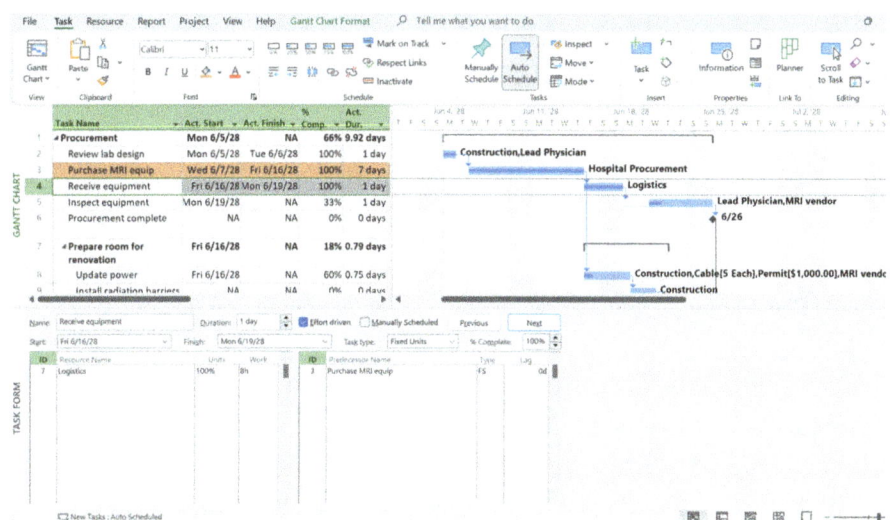

Figure 2-32. Detail view for task "Purchase MRI equip"

Step 2: The view in Figure 2-32 can be altered. In the View tab, within the Split View section, you will notice that the Details check box is enabled. Instead, enable the Timeline checkbox. This action will replace the details pane with a timeline above your primary view. The timeline provides an overview of your project, highlighting key phases and milestones as shown in Figure 2-33.

CHAPTER 2 GETTING STARTED WITH MICROSOFT PROJECT

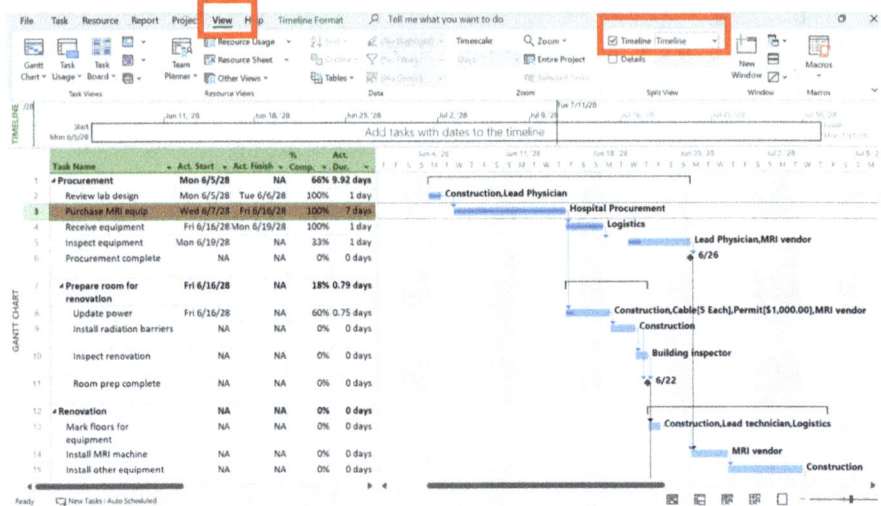

Figure 2-33. Timeline view

Step 3: For instance, selecting "Inspect equipment" and dragging its task ID cell will display the bar in the timeline, showing progress with darker and lighter blue shades on the bar as shown in Figure 2-34.

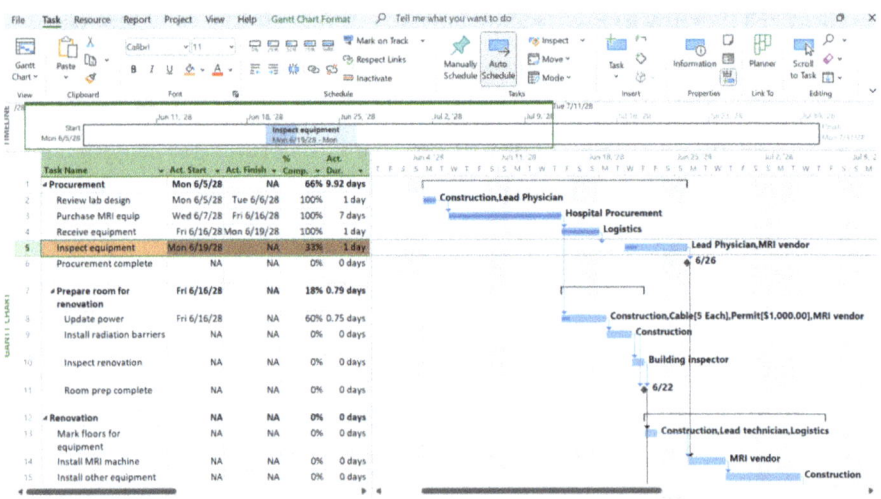

Figure 2-34. View for the task "Inspect equipment"

CHAPTER 2   GETTING STARTED WITH MICROSOFT PROJECT

Step 4: Selecting the milestone "Renovation Complete" and dragging it in the timeline will display a black diamond for the milestone, along with its name and date as a callout as shown in Figure 2-35.

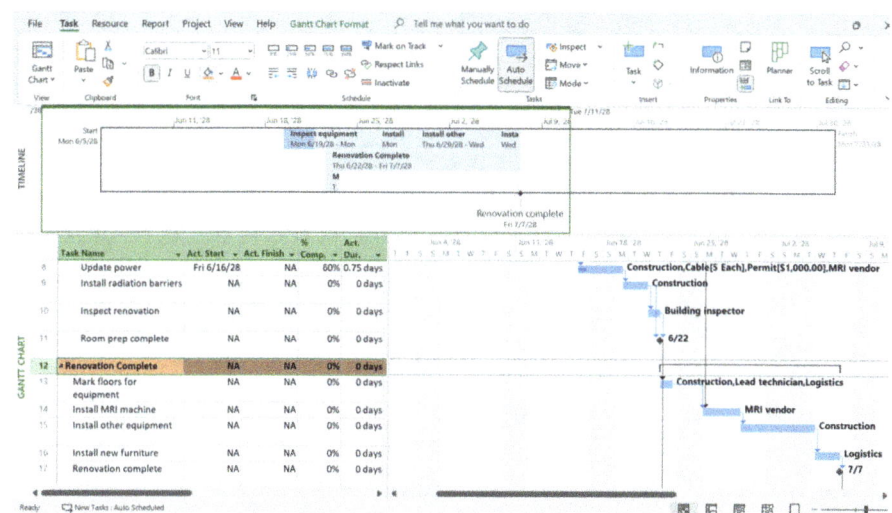

Figure 2-35. *View for the milestone "Renovation Complete"*

Step 5: Returning to the Task View section, select Task Usage as shown in Figure 2-36.

61

CHAPTER 2   GETTING STARTED WITH MICROSOFT PROJECT

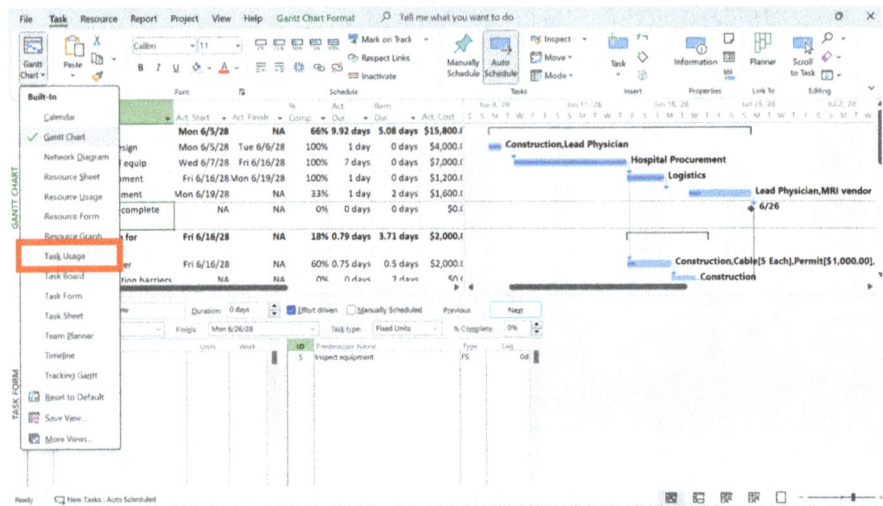

Figure 2-36. Access Task Usage view

Step 6: Task Usage displays a summary row for each task, with subrows underneath for the assignments and resources working on the task as shown in Figure 2-37.

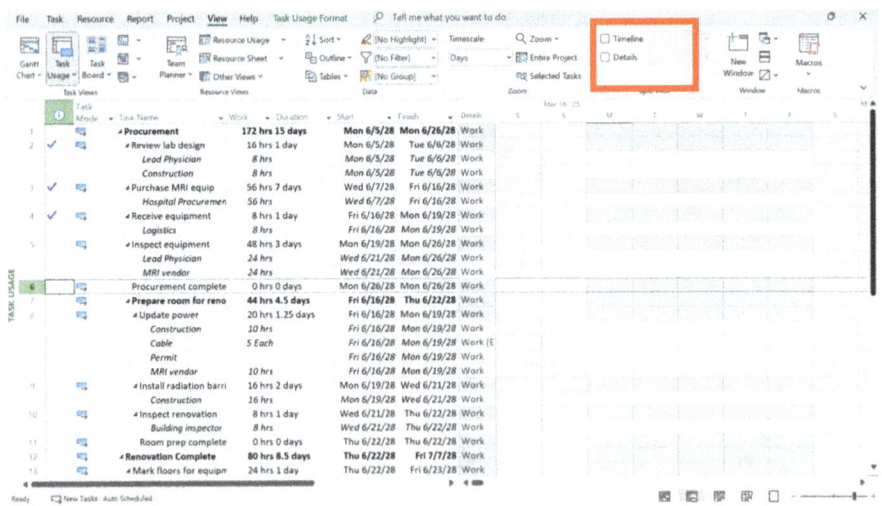

Figure 2-37. Task Usage view

CHAPTER 2   GETTING STARTED WITH MICROSOFT PROJECT

Note Uncheck Timelines and Details view for Task Usage View as shown in the outlined red box in Figure 2-37.

The Task Usage view is useful for assessing how assignments impact tasks. For example, by selecting "Inspect equipment" and clicking "Scroll to Task" on the Task tab, you can see summary information about the task, such as hours of work and resource allocation, day by day as shown in Figure 2-38.

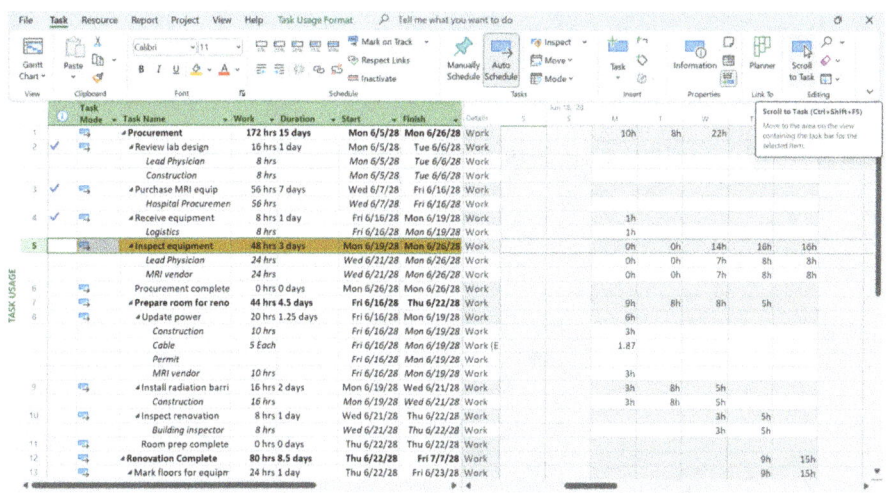

Figure 2-38. Task Usage view for "Inspect equipment"

Step 7: Next, go back to the Task tab, and then choose Tracking Gantt as shown in Figure 2-39.

63

CHAPTER 2   GETTING STARTED WITH MICROSOFT PROJECT

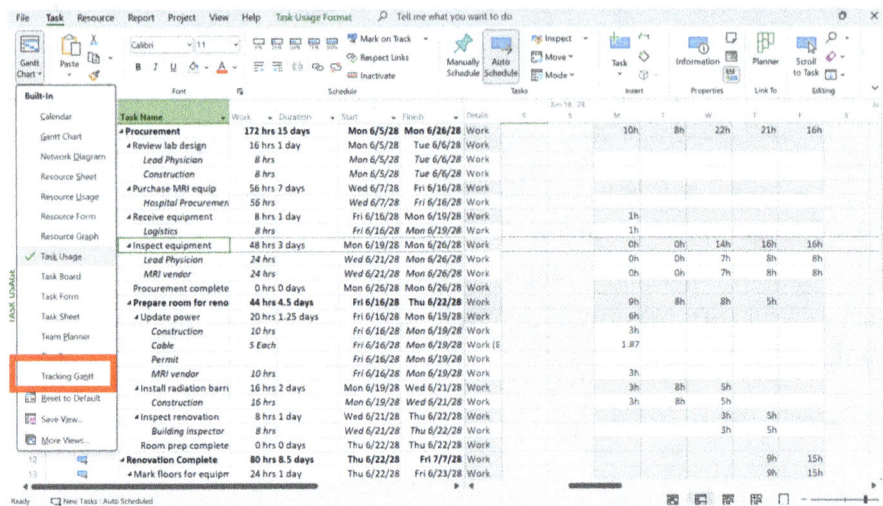

Figure 2-39. Choose Tracking Gantt view

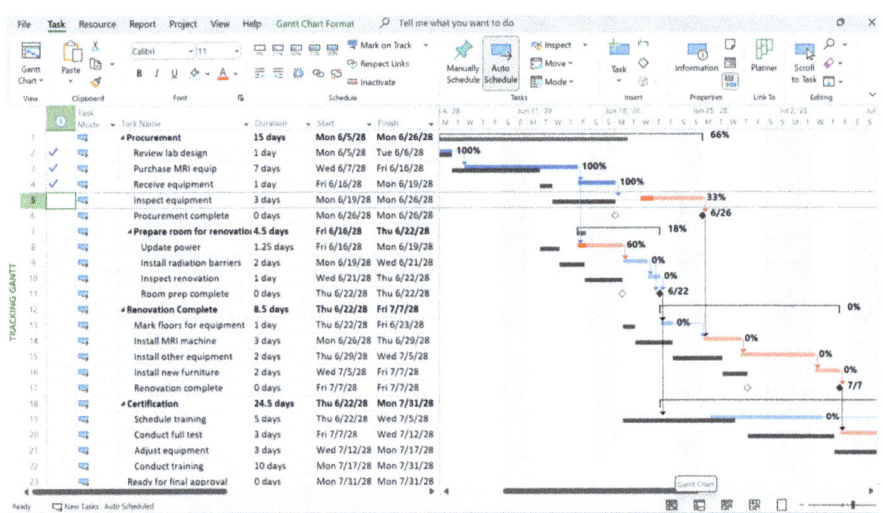

Figure 2-40. Tracking Gantt view

CHAPTER 2 GETTING STARTED WITH MICROSOFT PROJECT

Step 8: Returning to the Task tab and clicking "Scroll to Task" will reveal the Tracking Gantt view. This view differs slightly from the regular Gantt chart, featuring two sets of task bars: gray bars represent the baseline (approved schedule), while blue and red bars indicate the current schedule. Red bars denote critical tasks, while blue bars are noncritical. This view effectively highlights delays or tasks ahead of schedule.

You can also modify tables and views to display schedule dates or workload information. In the View tab's Data section, click the Tables button as shown in Figure 2-41.

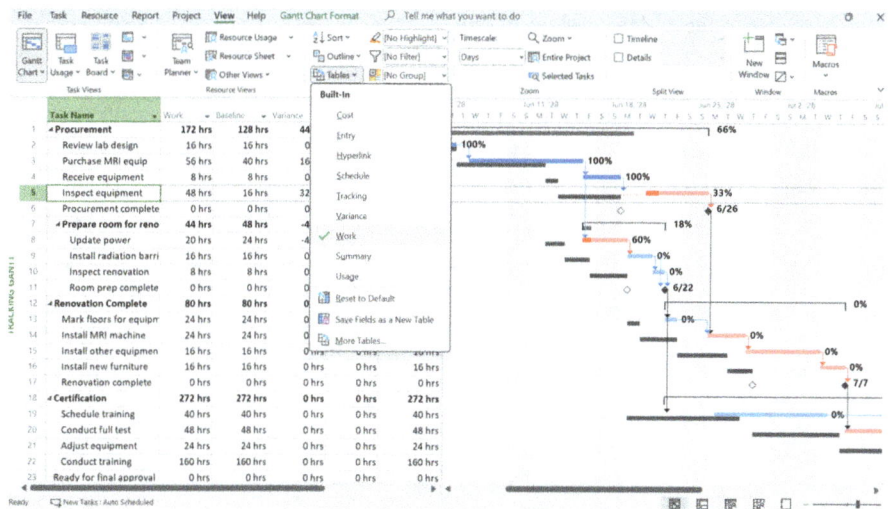

Figure 2-41. Choosing view based on Tables data

Step 9: Selecting the Work table will provide details on scheduled work, baseline work, variances, actual and remaining work, and percent work complete as shown in Figure 2-42.

65

CHAPTER 2 GETTING STARTED WITH MICROSOFT PROJECT

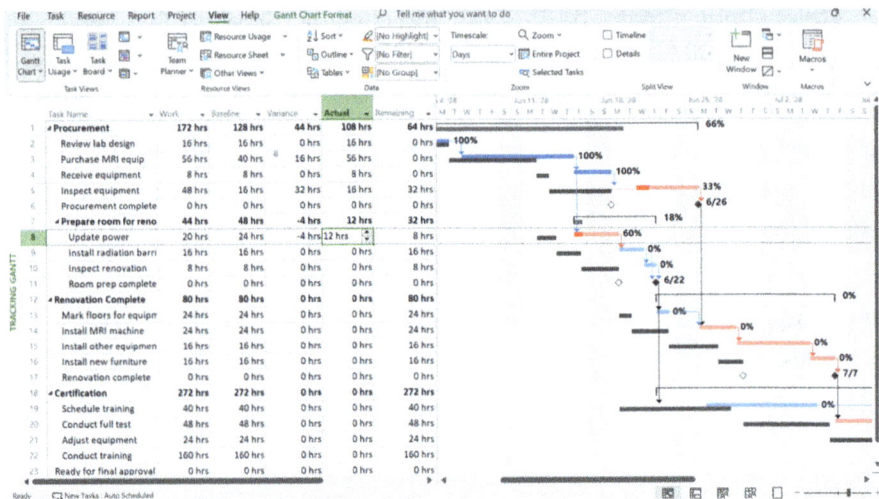

Figure 2-42. *Tables view based on Work table*

Step 10: Similarly, selecting the summary table offers key information such as start and finish dates, task duration, percent complete, cost, and work as shown in Figure 2-43.

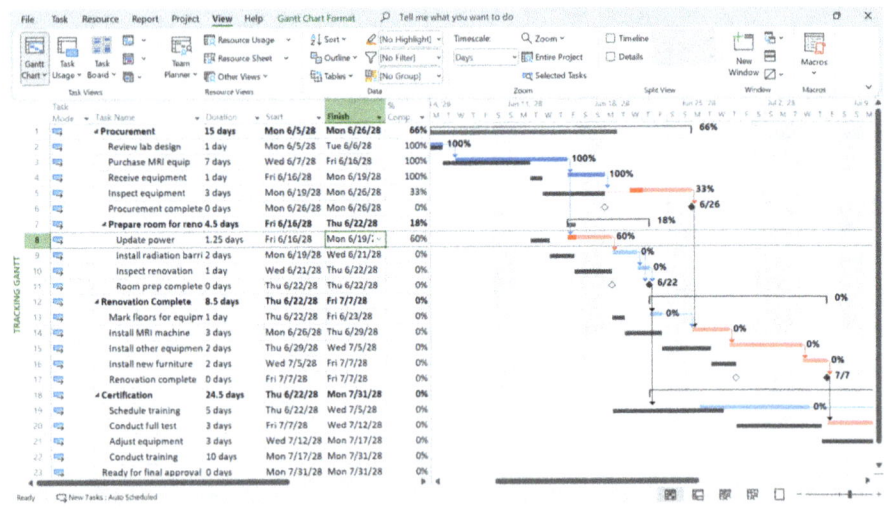

Figure 2-43. *Tables view based on Summary*

CHAPTER 2   GETTING STARTED WITH MICROSOFT PROJECT

Step 11: An additional feature is the Gantt Chart Format tab available in the ribbon when viewing any Gantt chart. Enabling the Project Summary Task option adds a new row at the top (task ID zero) displaying the project name, total project duration, start and finish dates, percent complete, cost, and work as shown in Figure 2-44. These views are invaluable tools for effectively managing your projects.

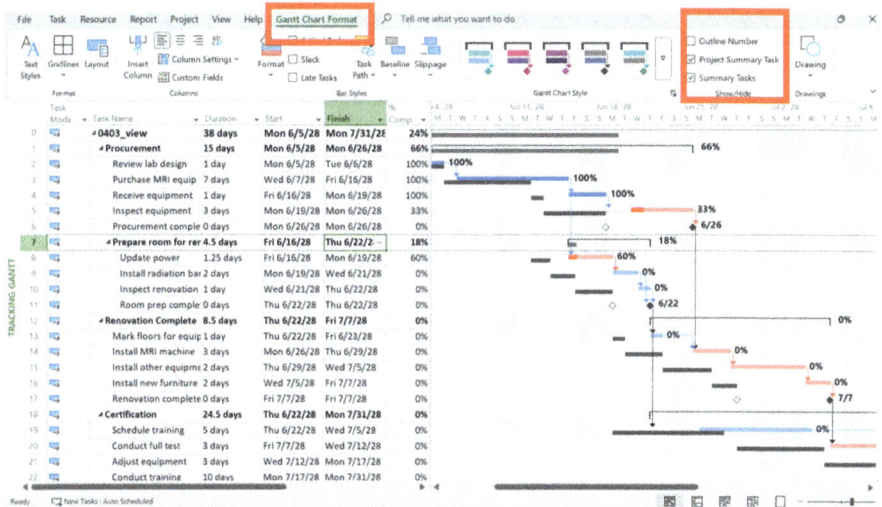

Figure 2-44. *Gantt summary view*

With this, we have come to the end of this chapter. In this chapter, we have learned how to set up a project, define project goals and objectives, and communicate with different stakeholders using Microsoft Project views. With this experience, we have established our goals of creating and communicating a project plan. In the next chapter, we will learn to create and organize tasks, work with summary tasks, add milestone, add project duration, and set task dependencies. Further, we will explore Gantt chart usage in Microsoft Project.

CHAPTER 3

Managing Tasks with Microsoft Project

In the previous chapter, we introduced setting up your project, defining project goals and objectives, and creating a project plan. In this chapter, we will learn to create and organize tasks, work with summary tasks, add milestone, add project duration, and set task dependencies. Further, we will explore Gantt chart usage in Microsoft Project. With this, we will be able to establish our goals of creating a project plan using the Microsoft Project desktop app.

> **Note** Screenshots or features described in this chapter are used from the Microsoft Project desktop app.

Introduction

Microsoft Project is a powerful tool for managing tasks, resources, and deadlines. This chapter covers creating a project task, setting up your work calendar, adding milestones, and putting tasks into a sequence. It also explains assigning resources and handling overallocation. Finally, learn to use built-in reports and visualizations to communicate your plan. This chapter aims to create and manage project files, organize tasks and milestones, and define dependencies.

CHAPTER 3   MANAGING TASKS WITH MICROSOFT PROJECT

Create and Modify Tasks

In this section, we will cover how to create and modify tasks in Microsoft Project, organize work with summary tasks, add milestones, put tasks into a sequence, add task duration, and finally, create a task plan with Microsoft Copilot.

Create Tasks

Project needs to know about the work required to complete a project. We'll start by creating tasks for a project called "Install Project Server – Project." Ensure project settings for tasks are as follows:

Step 1: Go to the File tab, click Options, and in the Project Options dialog box as shown in Figure 3-1, select Schedule and set New tasks created to Auto Scheduled, and check the box for New tasks are effort driven. This keeps task work consistent unless you change it. Click OK.

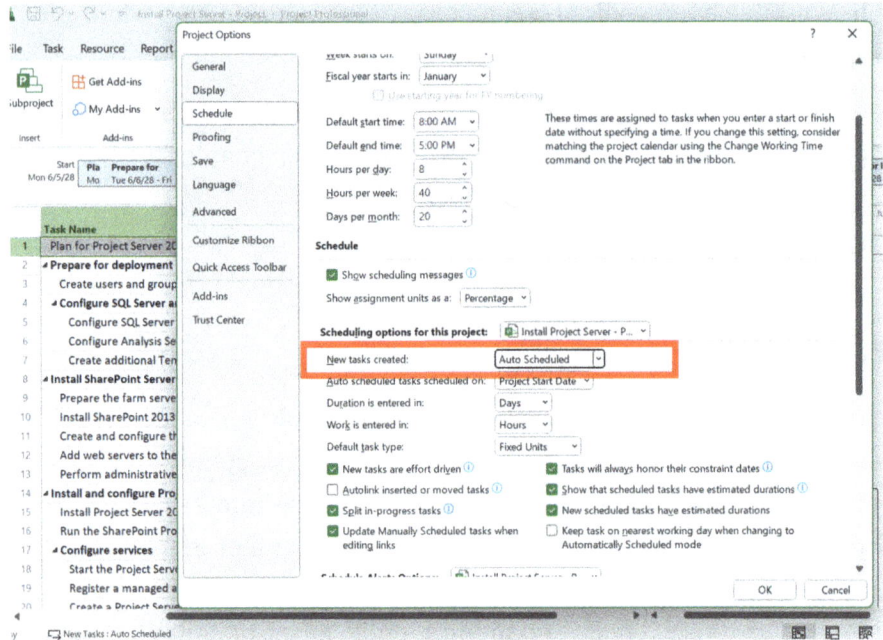

Figure 3-1. Configure settings for Auto-Schedule tasks

CHAPTER 3   MANAGING TASKS WITH MICROSOFT PROJECT

Step 2: Our project called "Install Project Server – Project" contains a list of tasks to deploy Microsoft Project Server across an organization. As shown in Figure 3-2, click the first blank task name cell, type the task name as "Plan for Project Server Deployment" as shown in Figure 3-2, and press Enter to move to the next line.

Step 3: Type the second task name "Prepare for deployment" as shown in Figure 3-2, and press Enter to other tasks. Tasks can be modified by revisiting the task's cell which needs to be modified through a click of cursor, and then, it can be edited and appended.

Step 4: If you need to insert a task, right-click "Prepare for deployment," and choose Insert Task as shown in Figure 3-3.

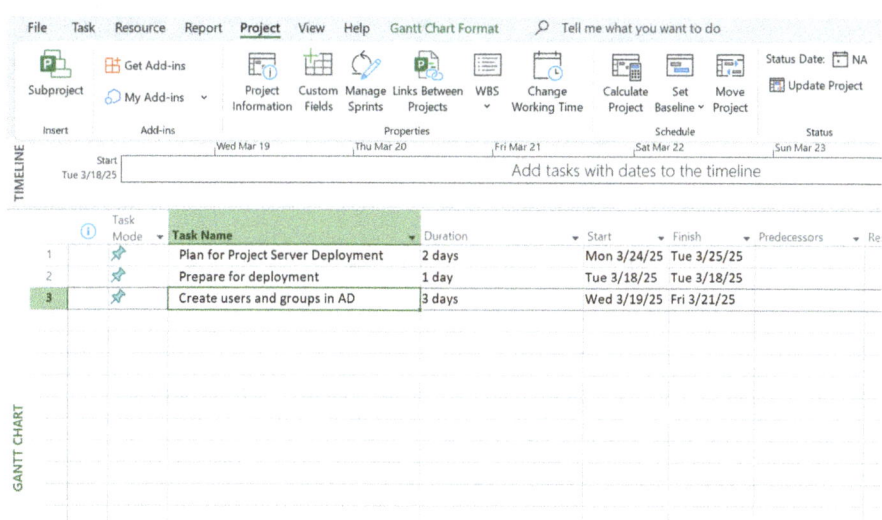

Figure 3-2. Creation of tasks in Microsoft Project

CHAPTER 3   MANAGING TASKS WITH MICROSOFT PROJECT

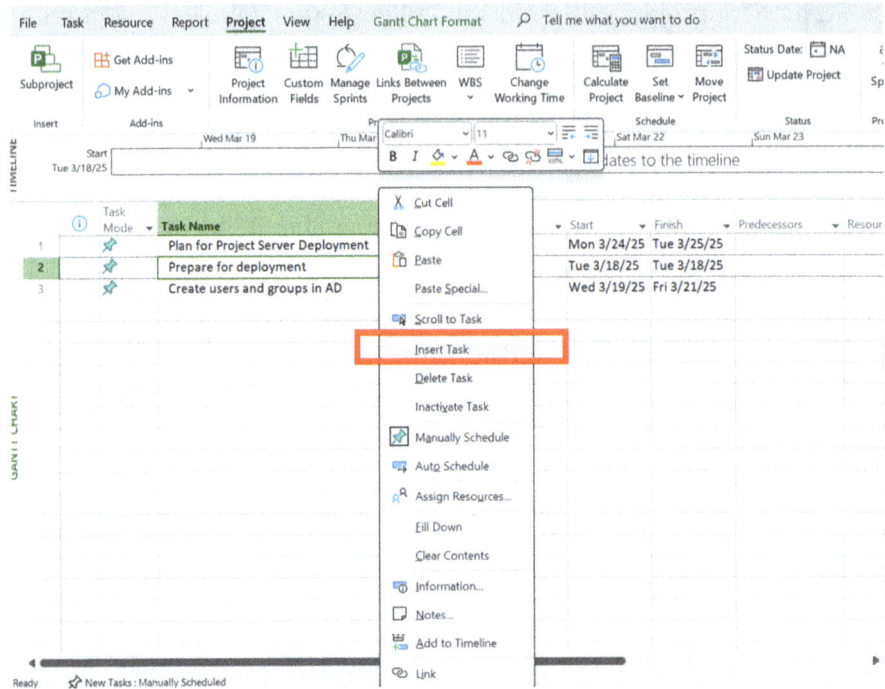

Figure 3-3. Insert tasks

Note   As shown in Figure 3-4, the task mode column shows whether tasks are auto or manually scheduled.

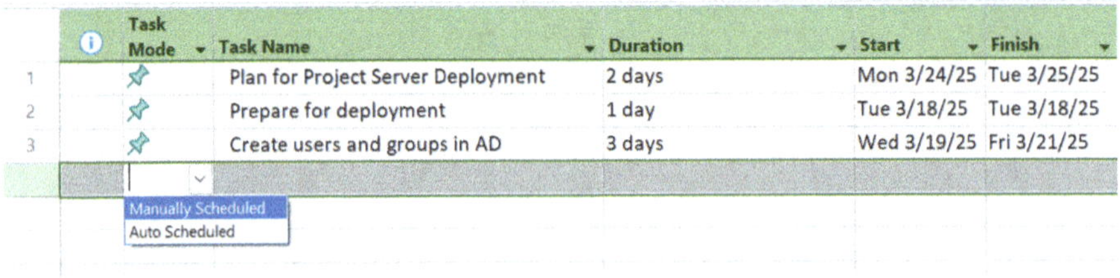

Figure 3-4. Option to choose manually scheduled tasks or auto scheduled

72

CHAPTER 3   MANAGING TASKS WITH MICROSOFT PROJECT

Manually scheduled and auto scheduled tasks are distinguished with icons shown in Figure 3-5. Manually scheduled with a pin and auto scheduled with box and arrow.

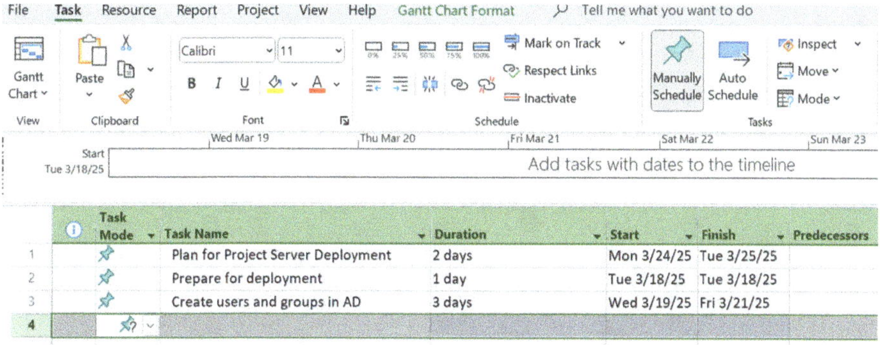

Figure 3-5. Icons for scheduled tasks or auto scheduled

In the next section, we will explore how to organize work with summary tasks.

Summary Tasks

Organize Work with Summary Tasks

Creating summary tasks within a project facilitates the delegation of work sections to team leads and allows for progress tracking. To organize tasks, start by selecting the tasks you wish to summarize by following the below steps:

Step 1: Drag over the task numbers in the first column as shown in Figure 3-6 highlighted in green.

73

CHAPTER 3   MANAGING TASKS WITH MICROSOFT PROJECT

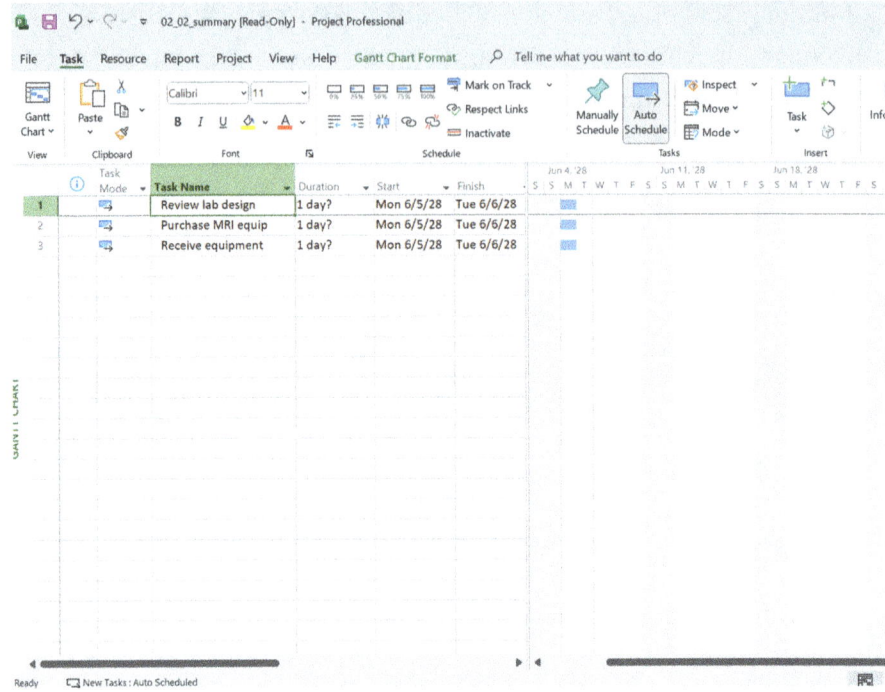

Figure 3-6. Task 1 is selected

Step 2: With the tasks selected, go to the Task tab, navigate to the Insert section, and click Summary highlighted in red in Figure 3-7. This will insert a new row with a summary task. The task name is prefilled as "New Summary Task" as shown in Figure 3-7, and the cell is selected so you can rename it. For example, you might name it "Procurement" and press Enter. The selected tasks are indented under the summary task as shown in Figure 3-8.

CHAPTER 3 MANAGING TASKS WITH MICROSOFT PROJECT

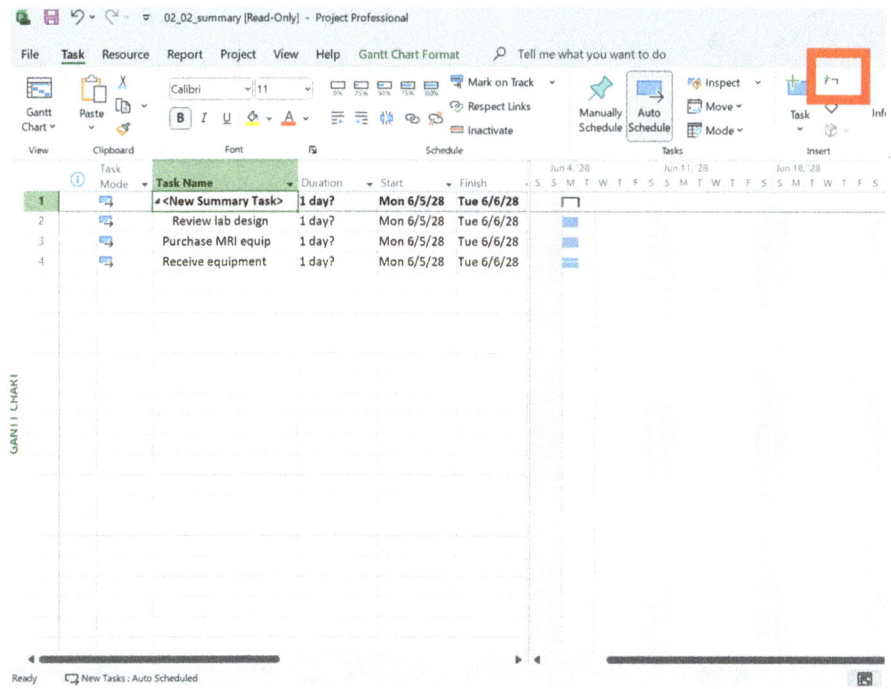

Figure 3-7. Inserting summary tasks

CHAPTER 3   MANAGING TASKS WITH MICROSOFT PROJECT

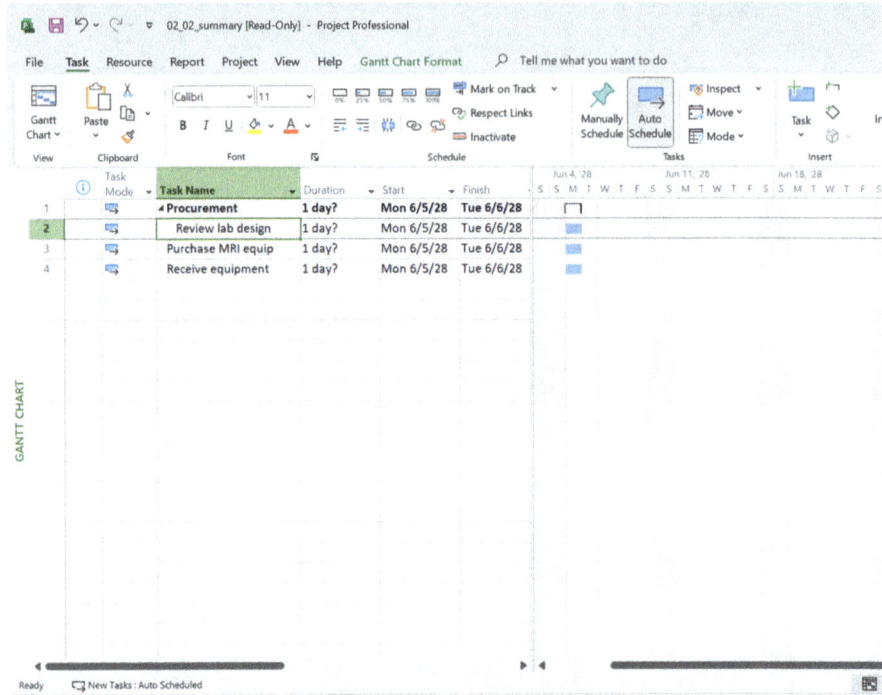

Figure 3-8. Creation of summary task called "Procurement"

Step 3: To add another task, insert a task, and it will create a blank task as shown in Figure 3-9. Then, type the task name, such as "Inspect Equipment," in the blank task name cell, and press Enter. This will show as a subtask as shown in Figure 3-10.

CHAPTER 3   MANAGING TASKS WITH MICROSOFT PROJECT

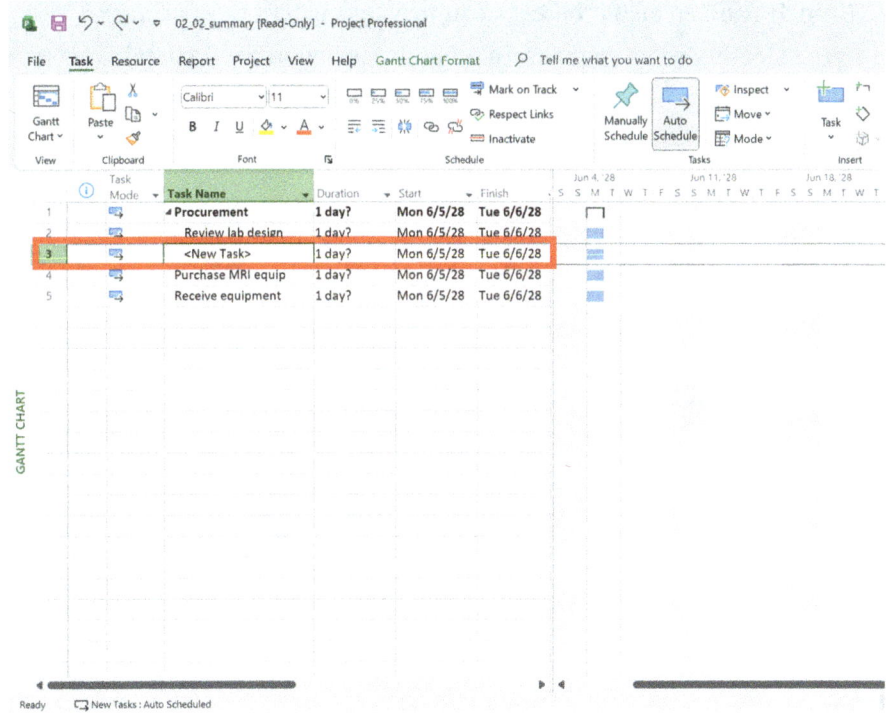

Figure 3-9.   *Insert a blank subtask*

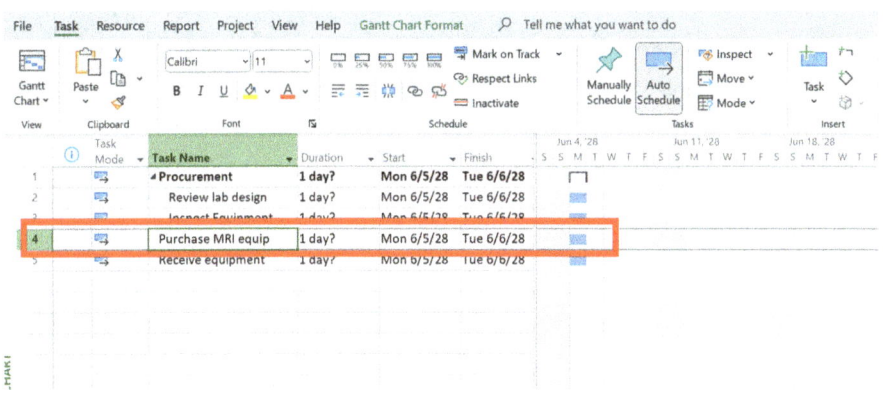

Figure 3-10.   *Creation of new subtask called "Inspect Equipment"*

CHAPTER 3   MANAGING TASKS WITH MICROSOFT PROJECT

Step 4: You can also create a summary task with a new subtask without selecting existing tasks. In a blank row, go to the Task tab and click Summary again. A new summary task row and a subtask row will be inserted as shown in Figure 3-11.

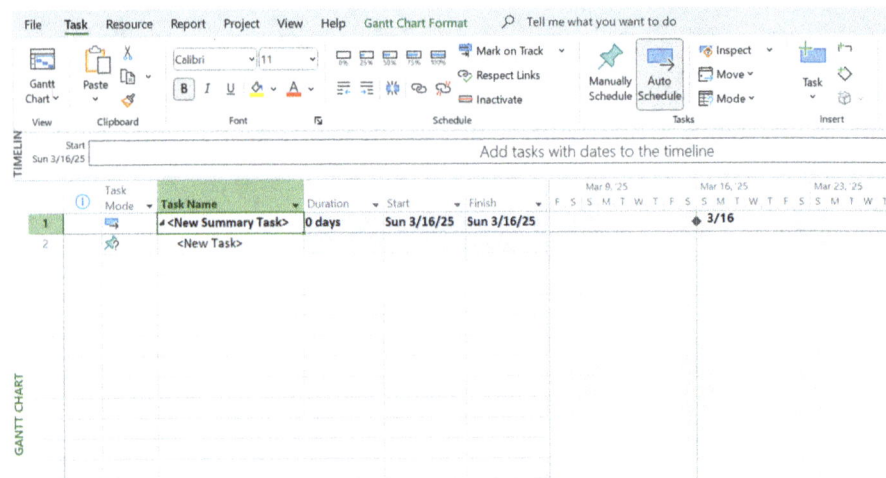

Figure 3-11. *Insert new summary task*

Step 5: Name the summary task, for example, "Prepare room for renovation," and then, enter the subtask name, such as "Update power" and "Connect cables and wires." You can continue adding additional subtasks as needed as shown in Figure 3-12.

CHAPTER 3   MANAGING TASKS WITH MICROSOFT PROJECT

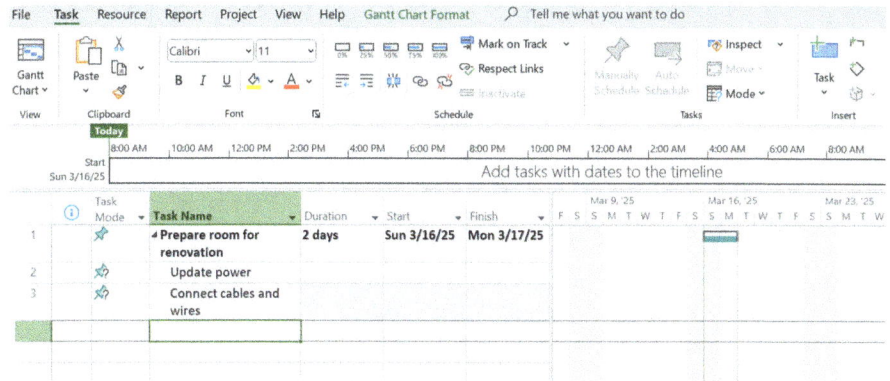

Figure 3-12. Creation of tasks and subtasks

Note   The indentation indicates hierarchy, with summary tasks appearing at higher levels than their subtasks. To change the indentation level, select the task, and use the outdent or indent icons in the Schedule section as shown in Figure 3-13. This organizes the tasks effectively within the project.

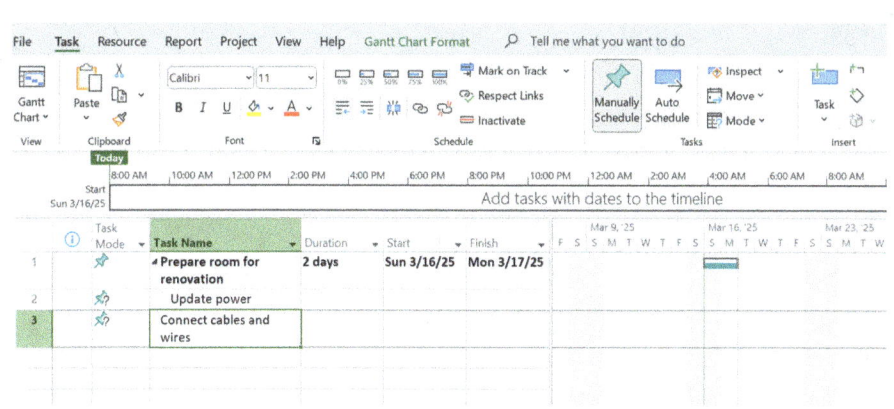

Figure 3-13. Visual view of tasks and subtasks using Gantt Chart

79

CHAPTER 3   MANAGING TASKS WITH MICROSOFT PROJECT

> **Note** "Connect cables and wires" was a subtask as per Figure 3-13. But using indentation, it is defined as separate task as shown in Figure 3-14.

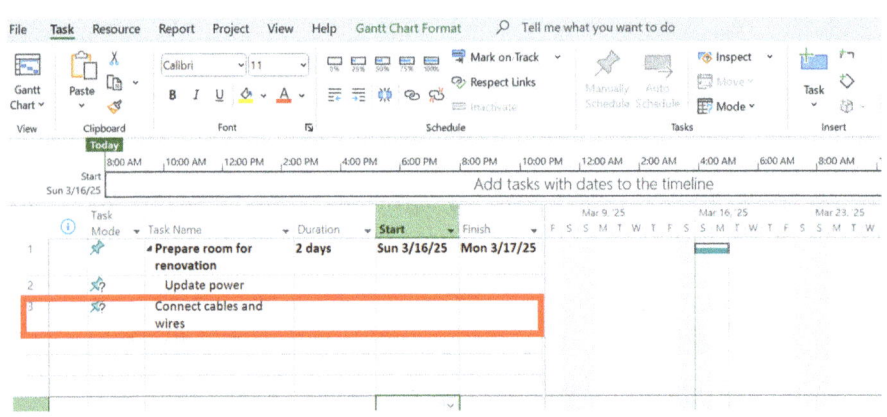

Figure 3-14. Using indentation, conversion of subtask into an independent task

In the next section, we are going to learn about adding a milestone to a project.

Add Milestone

Milestones are useful for tracking progress, decisions, payments, and other key points in a project. They motivate people by showing when targets are met. You can add milestones anywhere in your task list.

Step 1: First, select the task below where you want the milestone. For example, to add a milestone after "Inspect equipment," select task 6, "Prepare room for renovation," as shown in Figure 3-15.

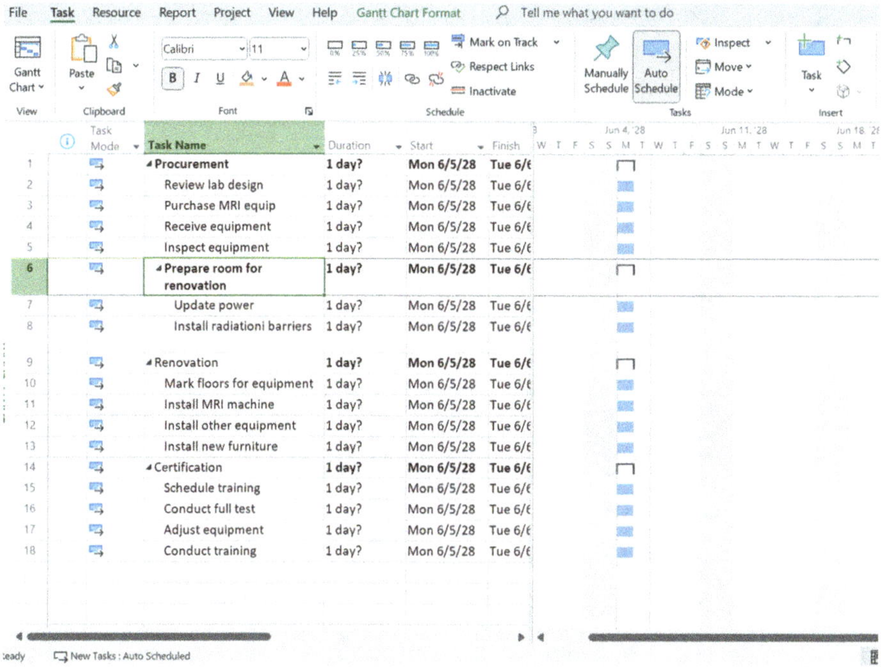

CHAPTER 3   MANAGING TASKS WITH MICROSOFT PROJECT

Figure 3-15.   Selection of task "Prepare room for renovation"

On the Task tab, click Milestone in the Insert section. This inserts a new row labeled "New Milestone" as shown in Figure 3-16. Type the name, such as "Procurement complete," and press Enter as shown in Figure 3-17.

81

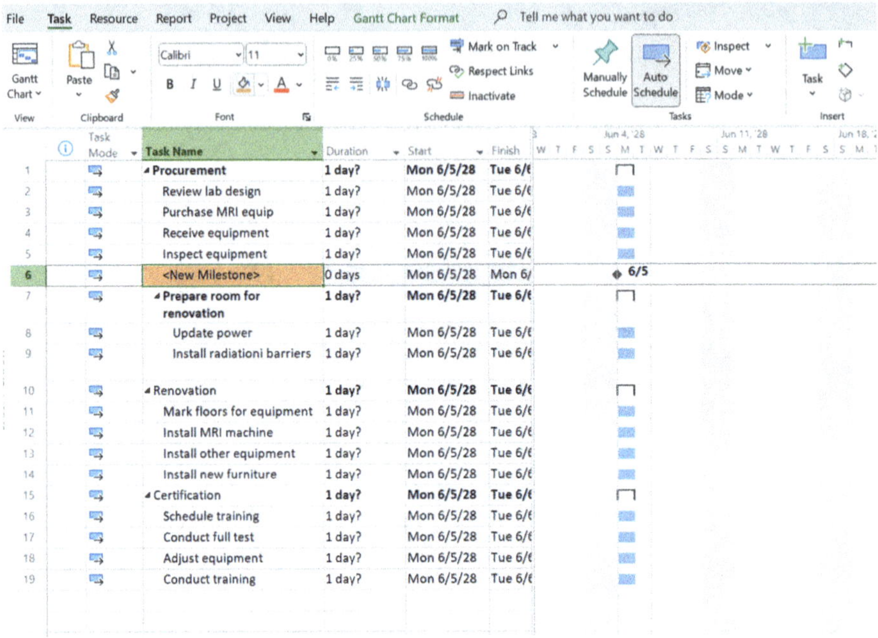

CHAPTER 3   MANAGING TASKS WITH MICROSOFT PROJECT

Figure 3-16. Insert milestone from menu

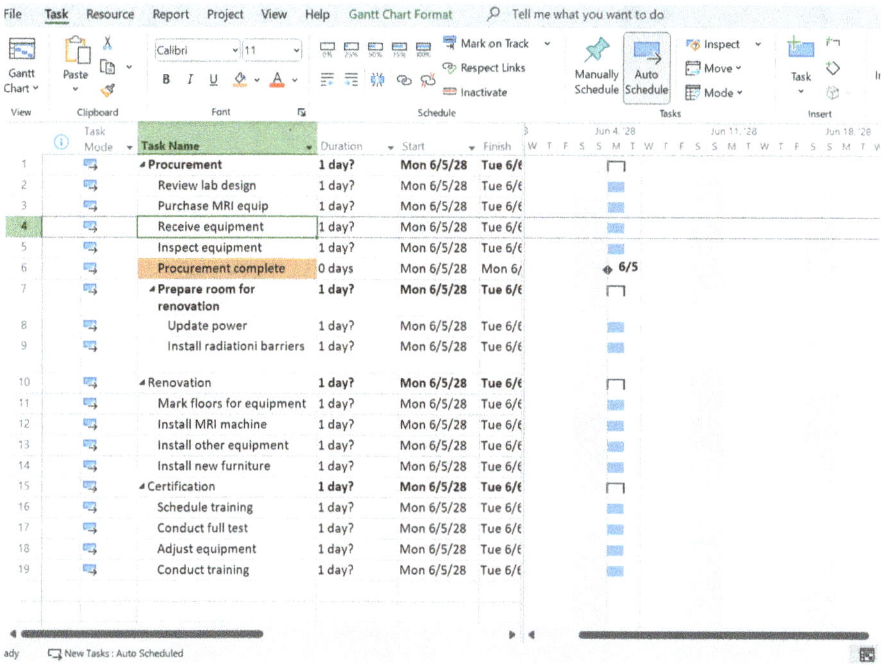

CHAPTER 3   MANAGING TASKS WITH MICROSOFT PROJECT

Figure 3-17. "Procurement complete" milestone added

Milestones have a duration of zero days and do not affect project timelines. They appear as black diamonds on the timescale. To add another milestone at the end of "Prepare room for renovation," select task 10, "Renovation," and click Milestone. Name it "Room prep complete" as shown in Figure 3-18.

83

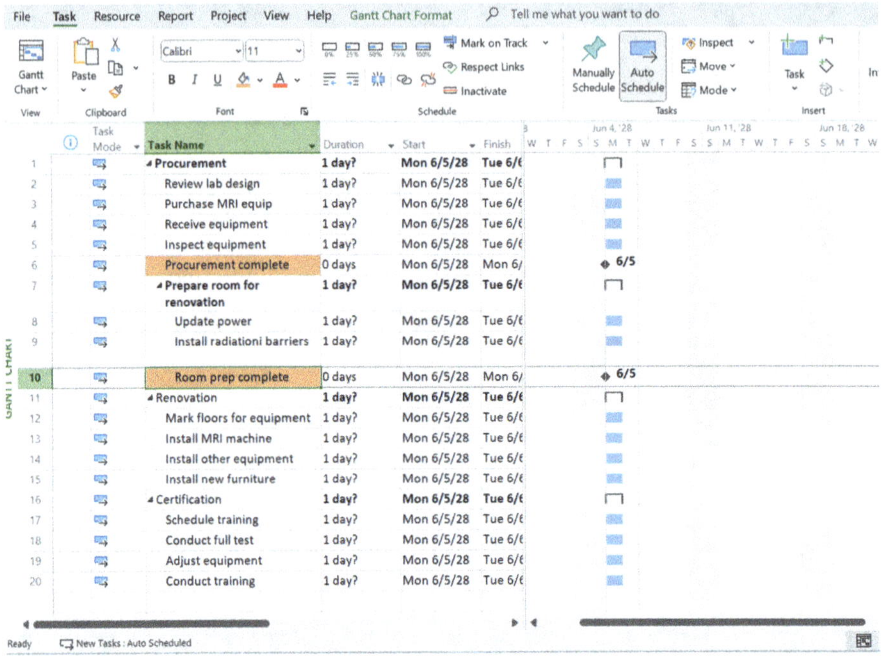

CHAPTER 3   MANAGING TASKS WITH MICROSOFT PROJECT

Figure 3-18. New milestone "Room prep complete"

To add a final milestone, select the first blank row, click Milestone, and name it "Ready for final approval" as shown in Figure 3-19. Outdent it to the correct level using the icon with horizontal lines and a left-pointing arrow in the Schedule section. This places the milestone at the top level of the outline. That's how you create milestones to track progress and key points in your project.

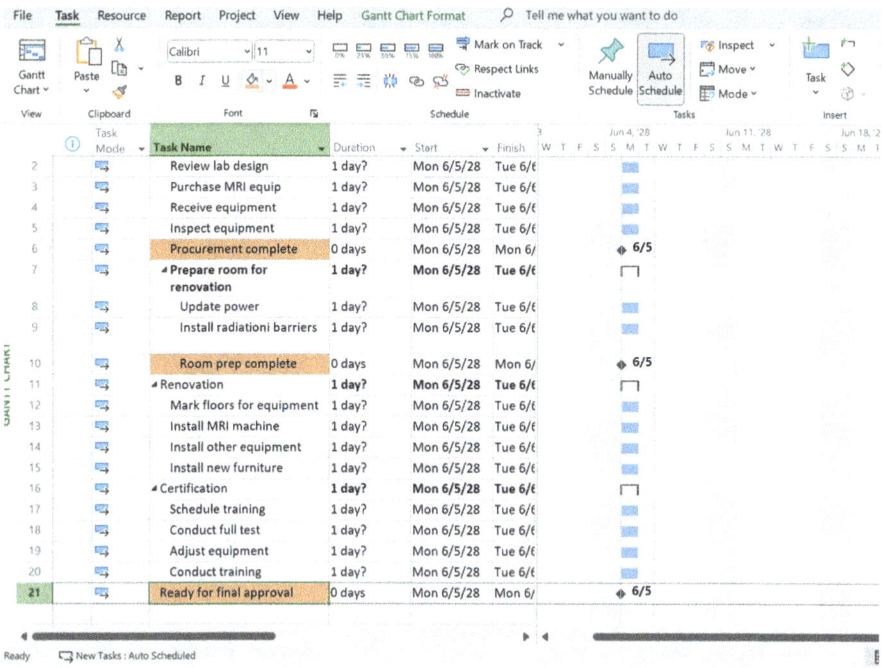

CHAPTER 3   MANAGING TASKS WITH MICROSOFT PROJECT

Figure 3-19. "Ready for final approval" outdented milestone created

Put Tasks into Sequence

With the below list of steps, you can put tasks into a sequence. Tasks need to be performed in the correct sequence for work to proceed effectively, similar to how one would open a door before attempting to walk through it. Task dependencies, also known as "task links," define the task sequence.

The initial few tasks in this project proceed from the completion of one task to the start of another, a type of dependency named "finish to start." This is the most common type. We will create links for tasks 2 through 6 by first selecting those tasks. To do this, we follow the below steps:

Step 1: Select their task ID cells (the numbers in the first column), and all these tasks will be selected as shown in Figure 3-20.

85

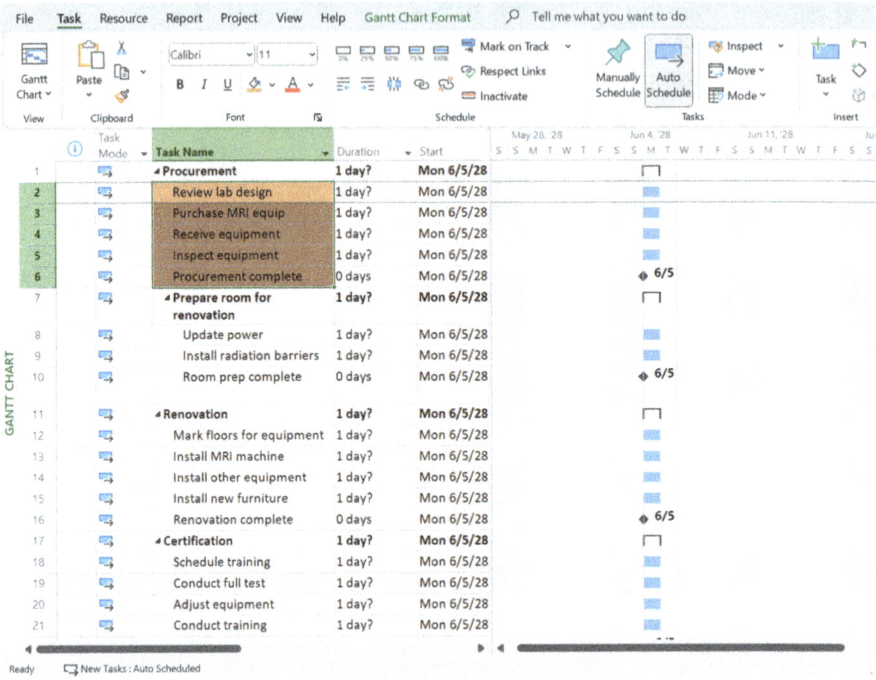

CHAPTER 3   MANAGING TASKS WITH MICROSOFT PROJECT

Figure 3-20. List of tasks selected to be put into a sequence

Step 2: Finish-to-start links for these tasks are created by navigating to the Task tab in the Schedule section and clicking "task links," which resemble two chain links. Upon clicking that, the links for those tasks will appear as shown in Figure 3-21.

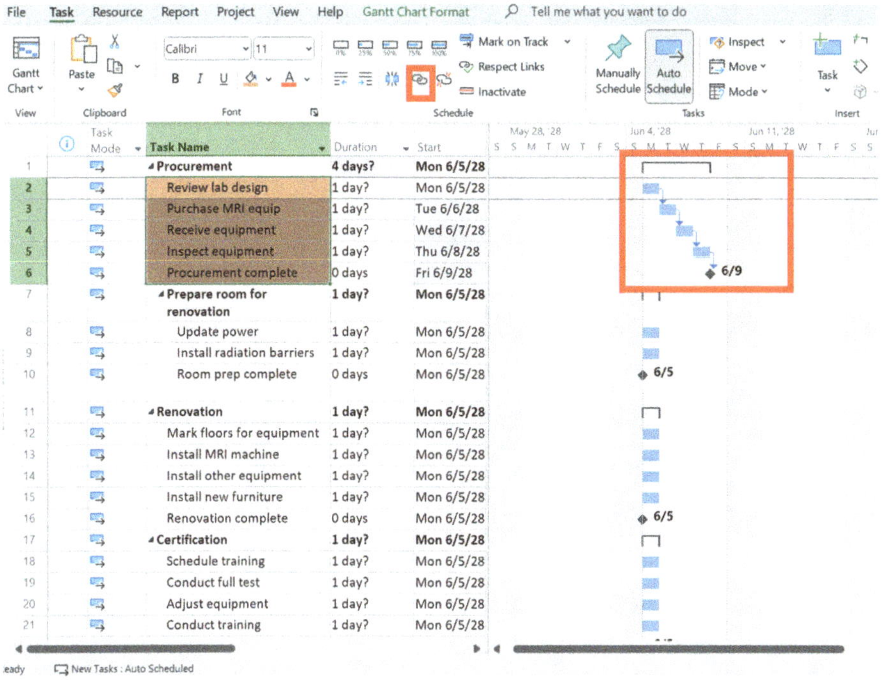

CHAPTER 3   MANAGING TASKS WITH MICROSOFT PROJECT

Figure 3-21. Tasks put into sequence

In the timescale, the task sequence is visible, and the predecessor's column shows the task ID numbers for the predecessor tasks. Before updating the power to match equipment specifications, we must purchase equipment first.

Step 3: To do this, select task 3 by clicking anywhere in the row. Then, go to task 8, "Update power." Since these tasks are not adjacent in the table, Ctrl+click in row eight for "Update power."

Select the predecessor first and the successor second, and then go to the Task tab, and click "task links" again. The link will be visible in the timescale as shown in Figure 3-22.

87

CHAPTER 3   MANAGING TASKS WITH MICROSOFT PROJECT

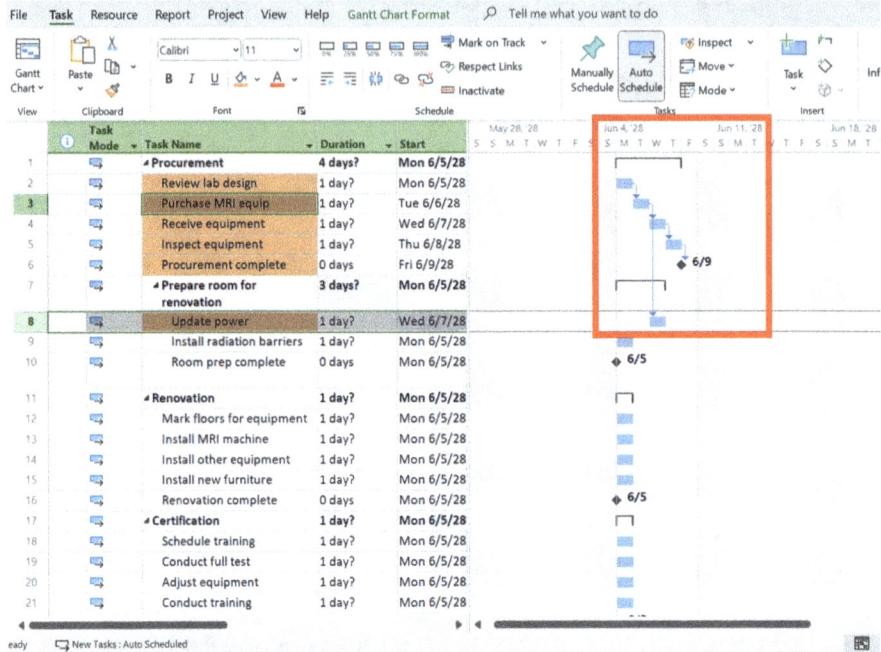

Figure 3-22. *Task 3 and task 8 are linked*

Step 4: Drag over tasks 8 through 10 – Update power through Room prep complete – and click "task links" to establish those connections as shown in Figure 3-23.

CHAPTER 3   MANAGING TASKS WITH MICROSOFT PROJECT

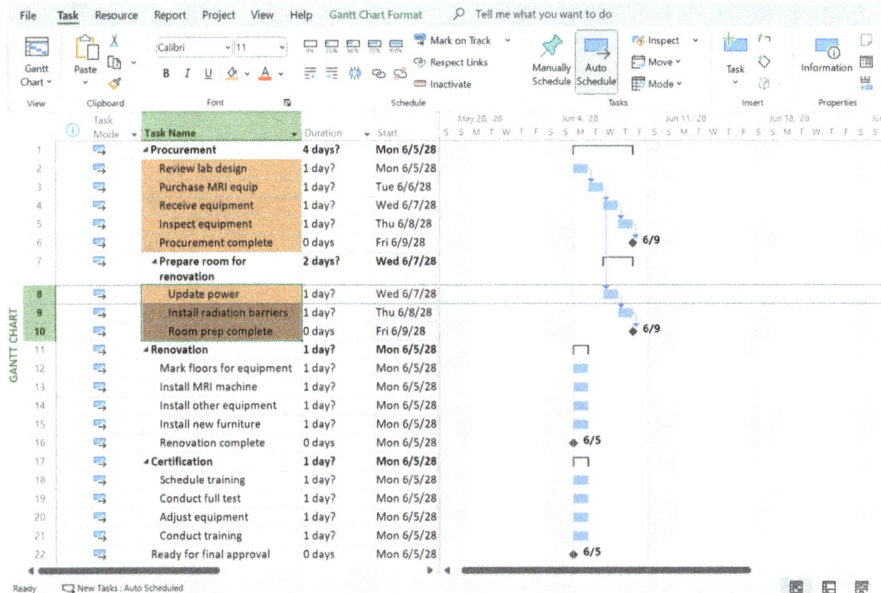

Figure 3-23. Task 8 to task 10 are put into sequence

Finally, select task 10 (Room prep complete) and Ctrl+click task 12 (Mark floors for equipment), and then link them accordingly as shown in Figure 3-24. This is the process for creating finish-to-start task links, which represent the most prevalent form of task dependency.

CHAPTER 3   MANAGING TASKS WITH MICROSOFT PROJECT

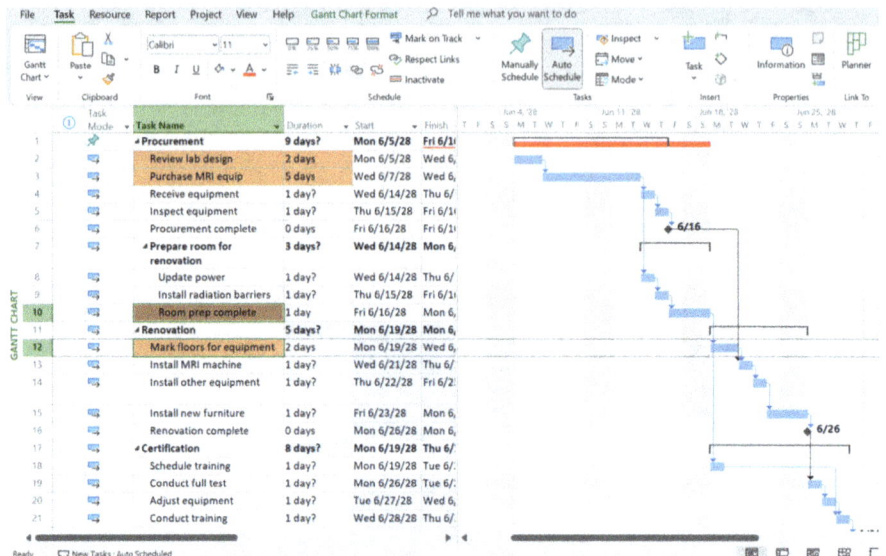

Figure 3-24. *Task 10 and task 12 are sequenced*

This demonstrates how to create finish-to-start links, which are the most common type of task dependency.

Add Task Duration to the Project

When building your project schedule, enter task durations in the duration field. Initially, Project shows "1 day?" indicating it's not filled.

For task 2, Review lab design, type 1D and press Enter. For task 3, Purchase MRI equipment, type 5D and press Enter as shown in Figure 3-25.

90

CHAPTER 3   MANAGING TASKS WITH MICROSOFT PROJECT

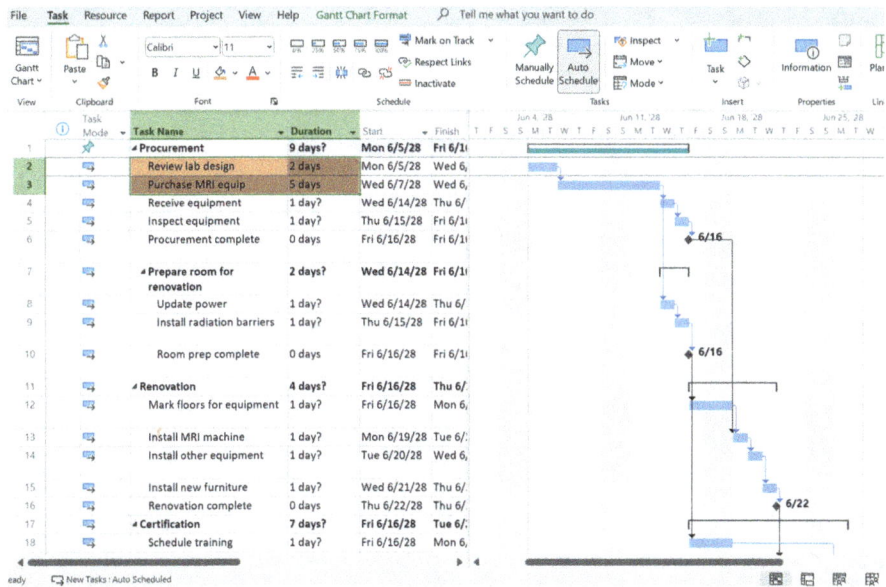

Figure 3-25. Updated duration for task 2 and task 3

Create a Task Plan Using Microsoft Copilot

It would be beneficial to save time creating a task list for a project. By describing your new project, you can utilize Microsoft Copilot to generate a list of tasks. To achieve this, you need Copilot and the Planner app in Teams. Have Teams open and have added Planner to my list of apps.

Now, proceed to the top right and click "New Plan." Then, input a name for the plan, and click "Create" as shown in Figure 3-26.

91

CHAPTER 3   MANAGING TASKS WITH MICROSOFT PROJECT

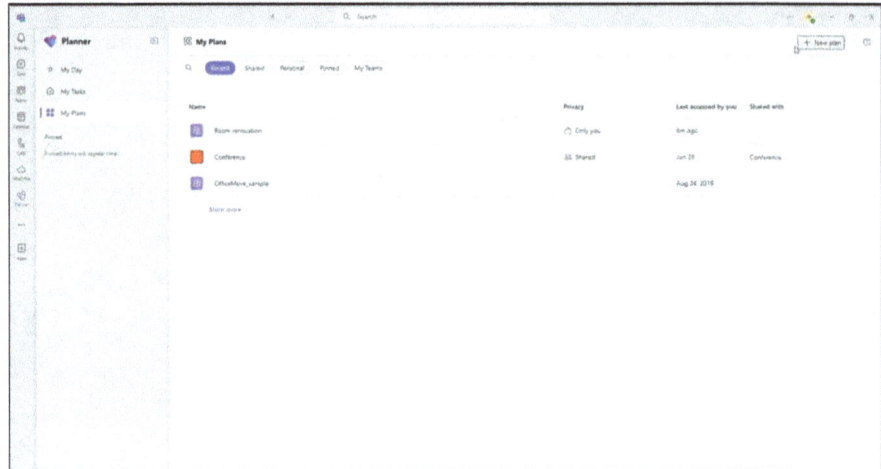

Figure 3-26. *Create a new plan using Planner inside MS Teams*

Once your plan is established, go to the top right of the ribbon and select Copilot. This action opens the Copilot panel. In the prompt box at the bottom, describe your project, which may include goals, types of tasks, and constraints as shown in Figure 3-27.

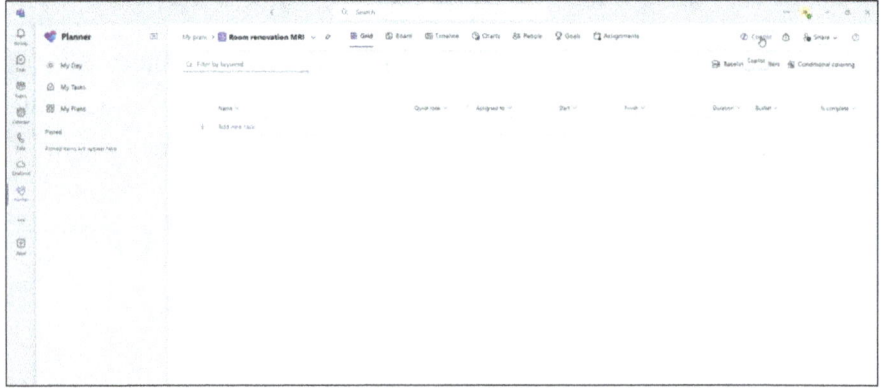

Figure 3-27. *Access Copilot to create tasks for your project*

CHAPTER 3   MANAGING TASKS WITH MICROSOFT PROJECT

For example, we requested Copilot to create tasks for remodeling an existing hospital space into an MRI testing room. Desired tasks and subtasks, approximately 25 in total. After adding your prompt as shown in Figure 3-28, click the paper airplane icon, which serves as the send icon. The panel will display the status, indicating its progress.

CHAPTER 3   MANAGING TASKS WITH MICROSOFT PROJECT

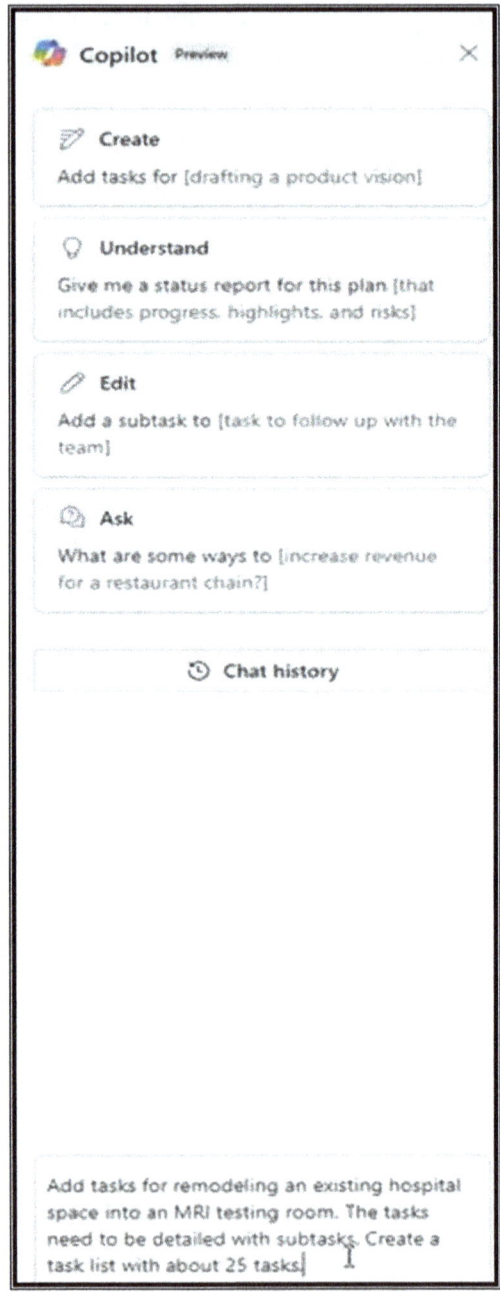

Figure 3-28.   Prompt to generate tasks for the project

CHAPTER 3   MANAGING TASKS WITH MICROSOFT PROJECT

Shortly, the task list will appear, containing information such as obtaining permits, room layout, space preparation, construction, finishing touches, equipment installation, and final inspections and approval as shown in Figure 3-29.

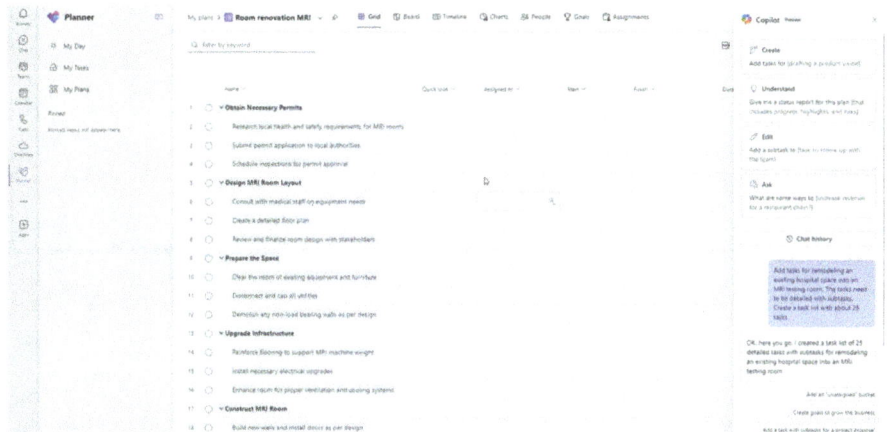

Figure 3-29. *Tasks created using Copilot*

If additional tasks are needed to close the project, you can request more tasks to be added by clicking the send icon again. For instance, tasks such as adding project documentation, conducting a postproject review, administrative closure, and celebrating success may be included.

To transfer this list into Microsoft Project, follow a two-step process from Teams: close the Copilot panel, then click the down arrow next to the plan name at the top left, and select "Export to Excel" as shown in Figure 3-30. A download pop-up for an Excel file will appear. Click the "Open File" link to view the list of tasks in Excel. Additional information can be added about the tasks, which can then be imported into a Microsoft Project Desktop Plan.

95

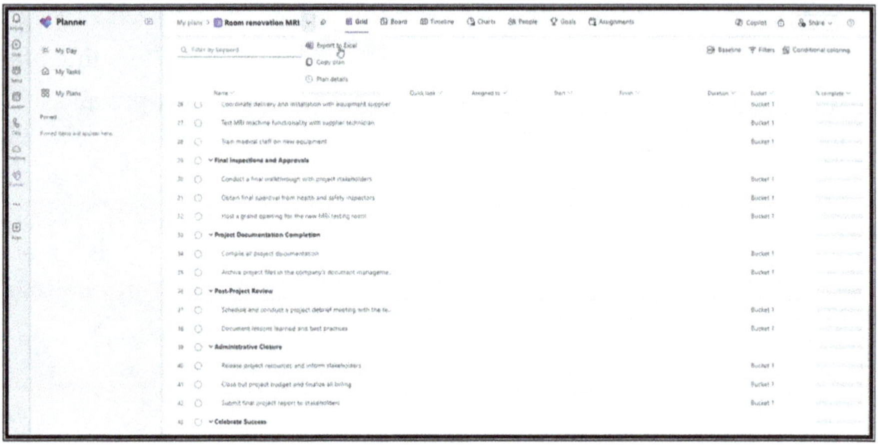

CHAPTER 3   MANAGING TASKS WITH MICROSOFT PROJECT

Figure 3-30. Export to Excel project tasks

With this, we have come to the end of this section. In this section, we have learned how to create and modify tasks, define work calendar, organize work with summary tasks, add milestones, put tasks into a sequence, and create a task plan with Microsoft Copilot. In the next section, we will explore Gantt charts in Microsoft Project.

Gantt Charts in Microsoft Project

A Gantt chart is a type of bar chart that represents a project schedule. It shows the start and end dates of tasks, their dependencies, and milestones. Gantt charts are essential for project management as they provide a clear visual representation of the project's progress and help in tracking deadlines. We already know from the previous chapter about creating a new project and saving it either on our OneDrive or SharePoint. Also, in the beginning of this chapter, we have learned how to create/modify tasks and combine tasks, add duration, add milestones, and put tasks into a sequence. So, all of these will be revised in this section. Steps to create a Gantt chart in Microsoft Project:

CHAPTER 3   MANAGING TASKS WITH MICROSOFT PROJECT

Launch Microsoft Project

- Open Microsoft Project on your computer.

- Start a new project. File ➤ New ➤ Blank Project: Create a new project by selecting these options.

- Name and Start Date: Give your project a name and choose a start date. Save the new project.

- List project tasks, subtasks, and milestones.

- Task Name Column: Begin entering tasks in the Task Name column. List all work steps that need to be completed.

- Milestones: Set the duration of a task to 0 days to convert it into a milestone, representing key events or important stages of the project.

- Subtasks: Group related tasks as subtasks by indenting them under a main task.

- Enter Task Information Duration, Start Date, and Dependencies: Enter information about each task, including their duration, start date, and dependencies. Dependencies can be set to manage sequencing, such as finish to start, start to start, finish to finish, and start to finish.

- Adjust Task Duration and Date Fine-Tuning: Review each task and adjust the duration and beginning and end dates to reflect the actual time needed.

- Define Task Relationship Dependencies: Define relationships between tasks to manage sequencing. This helps in understanding how tasks are interconnected and the impact of delays.

CHAPTER 3   MANAGING TASKS WITH MICROSOFT PROJECT

- With all above and customize the Gantt chart by changing colors, fonts, and adding notes to make it more readable and visually appealing.

- Formatting: Use the formatting options to highlight critical tasks and milestones as shown in Figure 3-31.

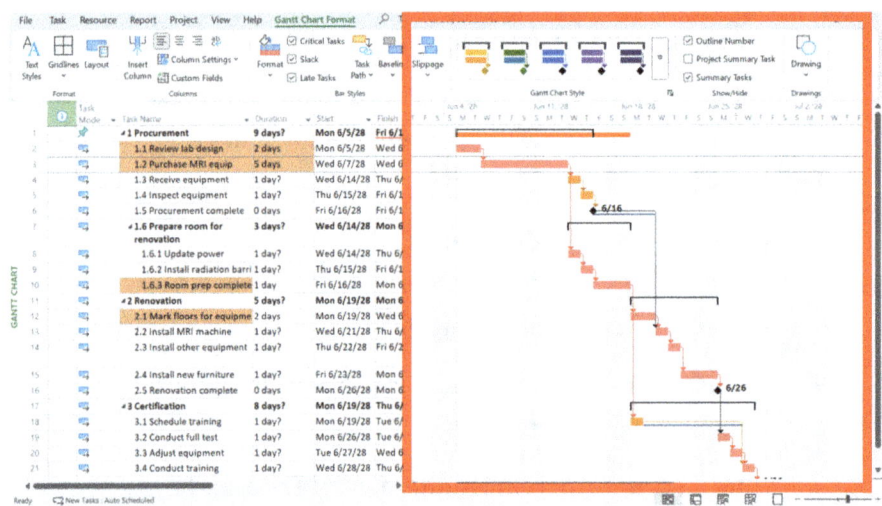

Figure 3-31. Creation of Gantt chart

- The below types of tasks are visible in Gantt charts as shown in Figure 3-32.

  - **Critical tasks** are those that directly affect the project's completion date. If any critical task is delayed, the entire project will be delayed. These tasks are part of the **critical path**, which is the sequence of tasks that determines the shortest possible duration to complete the project.

98

CHAPTER 3   MANAGING TASKS WITH MICROSOFT PROJECT

- **Slack tasks** (also known as float tasks) are tasks that have flexibility in their start and end dates without affecting the project's overall timeline. Slack time is the amount of time a task can be delayed without delaying the project

- **Late tasks** are tasks that are behind schedule compared to their baseline finish dates. Highlighting late tasks helps in identifying areas that need immediate attention to avoid further delays.

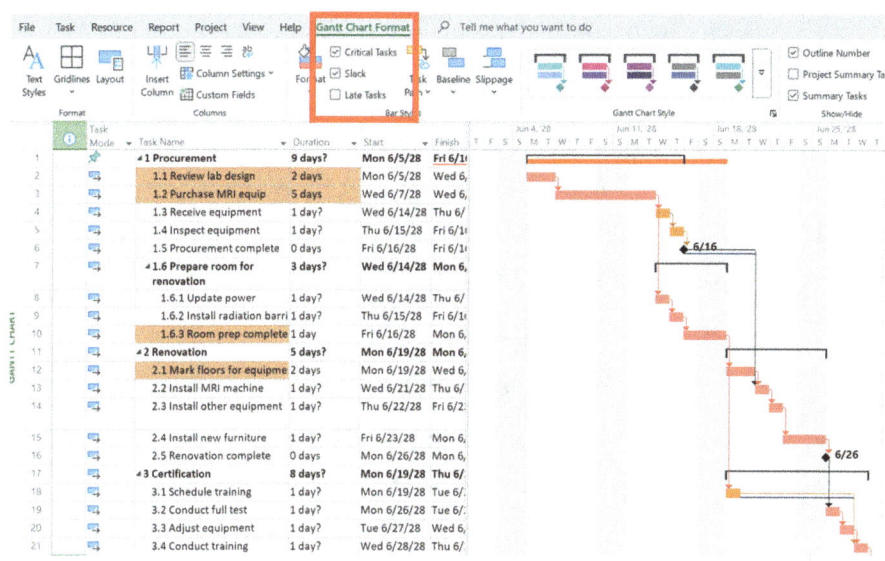

Figure 3-32. Critical tasks, slack, and late tasks

- Share the Gantt chart with your team and stakeholders to keep everyone informed. Export the Gantt chart to different formats like PDF or Excel for easy sharing and printing.

- Regular Updates: Keep the Gantt chart updated with the latest progress and changes in the project. This ensures that the project stays on track and any issues are addressed promptly.

Now, let's explore some benefits and tips on how to use Gantt charts effectively, which will help us in project management in a visual way.

Benefits of Using Gantt Charts in Microsoft Project

- **Visual Clarity**: Provides a clear visual representation of the project timeline
- **Task Management**: Helps in managing tasks and their dependencies effectively
- **Progress Tracking**: Allows tracking of project progress and identifying potential delays
- **Resource Allocation**: Assists in allocating resources efficiently and avoiding overloading
- **Stakeholder Communication**: Facilitates communication with stakeholders by providing a comprehensive view of the project

Tips for Effective Use of Gantt Charts

- **Break Down Tasks**: Break down larger tasks into smaller, manageable subtasks.
- **Set Realistic Deadlines**: Ensure that deadlines are realistic and achievable.

CHAPTER 3 MANAGING TASKS WITH MICROSOFT PROJECT

- **Monitor Progress**: Regularly monitor progress, and update the Gantt chart.

- **Use Milestones**: Use milestones to mark important stages and events in the project.

- **Collaborate**: Collaborate with your team to ensure everyone is on the same page.

Using Gantt charts in Microsoft Project can significantly enhance your project management capabilities. By following the steps outlined above, you can create dynamic and insightful Gantt charts that keep your project on track and drive your team to success.

With this, we have come to the end of this chapter. We have learned how to create and organize tasks, work with summary tasks, add milestones, add project duration, and set task dependencies. Further, we will explore Gantt chart usage in Microsoft Project. In the upcoming chapter, we will learn about resource management using Microsoft Project which covers assigning resources to tasks, managing resource availability, and optimizing resource allocation.

CHAPTER 4

Resource Management Using Microsoft Project

In the last chapter, we learned how to create and organize tasks, work with summary tasks, add milestones, add project duration, and set task dependencies. Further, we explored Gantt chart usage in Microsoft Project by showing how to access it, benefits of using Gantt charts, and tips for effective usage of Gantt charts. In this chapter, we will learn to create resources in Microsoft Project, assign resource tasks, and resolve resource overallocation.

Introduction

Resource management is a crucial aspect of project management, and Microsoft Project offers robust tools to help manage resources effectively. Resource management involves planning, allocating, and managing resources such as people, equipment, and materials to ensure project success. Microsoft Project provides a comprehensive suite of features to facilitate efficient resource management, ensuring that projects are completed on time and within budget. Below are some key features of resource management in Microsoft Project:

- **Resource Pool**: Microsoft Project allows you to create a centralized resource pool that can be shared across multiple projects. This helps in avoiding resource conflicts and ensures optimal utilization of resources.

- **Resource Allocation**: You can assign resources to tasks based on their availability and skill set. Microsoft Project provides tools to balance workloads and prevent overallocation, ensuring that resources are not overwhelmed.

- **Resource Calendars**: Customizable resource calendars allow you to define working hours, holidays, and other nonworking times for each resource. This ensures accurate scheduling and helps in managing resource availability.

- **Resource Leveling**: This feature automatically adjusts task schedules to resolve resource conflicts and overallocations. Resource leveling helps in maintaining a balanced workload and prevents bottlenecks.

- **Cost Management**: Microsoft Project enables you to track resource costs, including hourly rates, fixed costs, and overtime. This helps in budgeting and ensures that project costs are kept under control.

- **Reporting and Analytics**: The software provides various reports and dashboards to monitor resource utilization, performance, and availability. These insights help in making informed decisions and improving resource management strategies.

CHAPTER 4 RESOURCE MANAGEMENT USING MICROSOFT PROJECT

These features provide some benefits of effective resource management such as improved efficiency, enhanced collaboration, risk mitigation, and cost control.

- **Improved Efficiency**: Proper resource management ensures that resources are used optimally, reducing waste and increasing productivity.

- **Enhanced Collaboration**: By providing a clear view of resource availability and allocation, Microsoft Project fosters better collaboration among team members.

- **Risk Mitigation**: Identifying potential resource conflicts and addressing them proactively helps in minimizing risks and ensuring smooth project execution.

- **Cost Control**: Tracking resource costs and managing budgets effectively prevents cost overruns and ensures financial stability.

With resource management in Microsoft Project, one can define clear roles and responsibilities, regularly update resource information, monitor resource utilization, communicate effectively, and leverage automation.

- **Define Clear Roles and Responsibilities**: Ensure that each resource has a clear understanding of their tasks and responsibilities. This helps in avoiding confusion and ensures accountability.

- **Regularly Update Resource Information**: Keep resource information up-to-date, including availability, skills, and costs. This ensures accurate planning and allocation.

- **Monitor Resource Utilization**: Regularly monitor resource utilization to identify any issues or inefficiencies. Use the reporting tools in Microsoft Project to gain insights and make necessary adjustments.

- **Communicate Effectively**: Maintain open communication with your team to address any resource-related concerns promptly. Effective communication helps in resolving issues quickly and ensures smooth project execution.

- **Leverage Automation**: Utilize the automation features in Microsoft Project, such as resource leveling and scheduling, to streamline resource management processes and reduce manual effort.

Resource management is a vital component of successful project management, and Microsoft Project offers powerful tools to help manage resources effectively. By leveraging these features and following best practices, you can ensure optimal resource utilization, improve efficiency, and achieve project success. With this introduction of the resource management in Microsoft Project, let's start creating resources in Project.

Create Resources

Creating resources in Project involves several steps to ensure proper management of assets such as personnel, equipment, materials, and financials. You can generate resources upfront or as they become necessary during the project. The resource sheet is the optimal location for this task. Navigate to the View tab, and select Resource Sheet from the Resource Views section as shown in Figure 4-1.

CHAPTER 4   RESOURCE MANAGEMENT USING MICROSOFT PROJECT

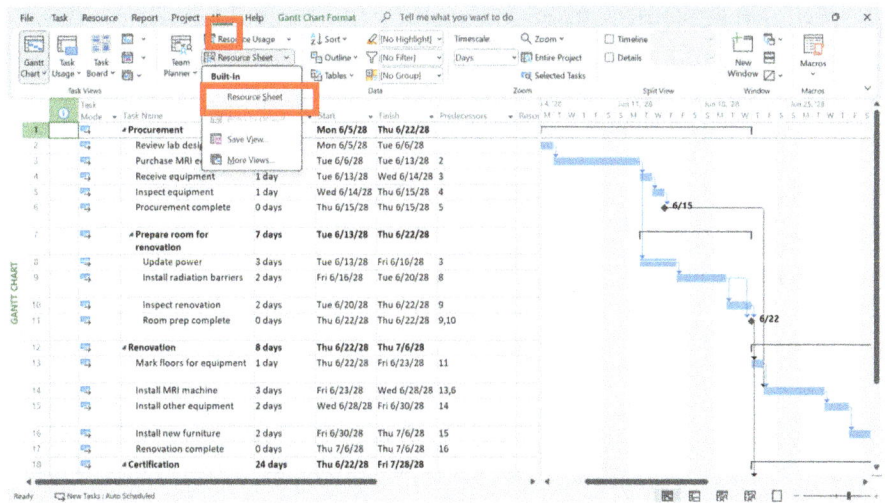

Figure 4-1. Select "Resource Sheet" from the View tab

Post selection of "Resource Sheet" from the View tab as shown in Figure 4-1, Resource Sheet appears in Microsoft Project as shown in Figure 4-2.

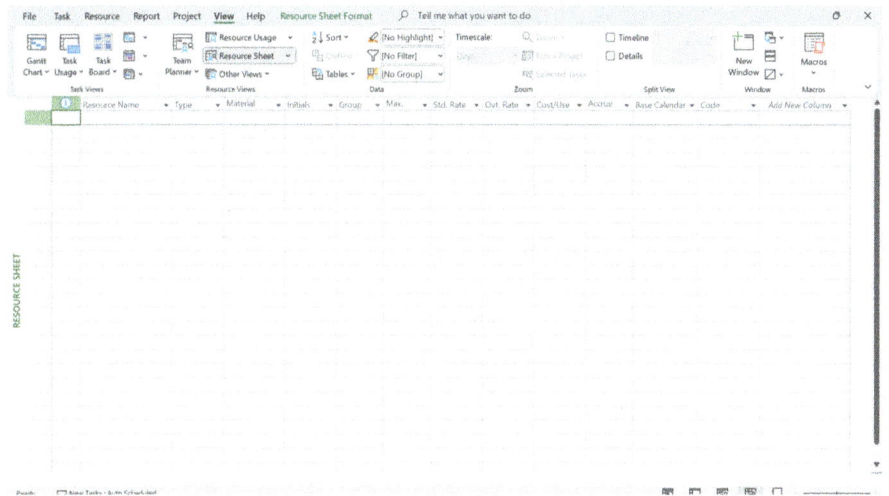

Figure 4-2. Resource Sheet in Microsoft Project

107

CHAPTER 4   RESOURCE MANAGEMENT USING MICROSOFT PROJECT

As shown in Figure 4-2, work resources, like individuals assigned by hour or day and equipment rented weekly, are categorized by their time-based assignments. These can be named using people's names, skill sets, or roles.

For example, you might name a resource "Lead Physician" and assign a standard rate of $200 per hour. Simply input "200" and press Enter; Project will automatically recognize the hourly rate as shown in Figure 4-3.

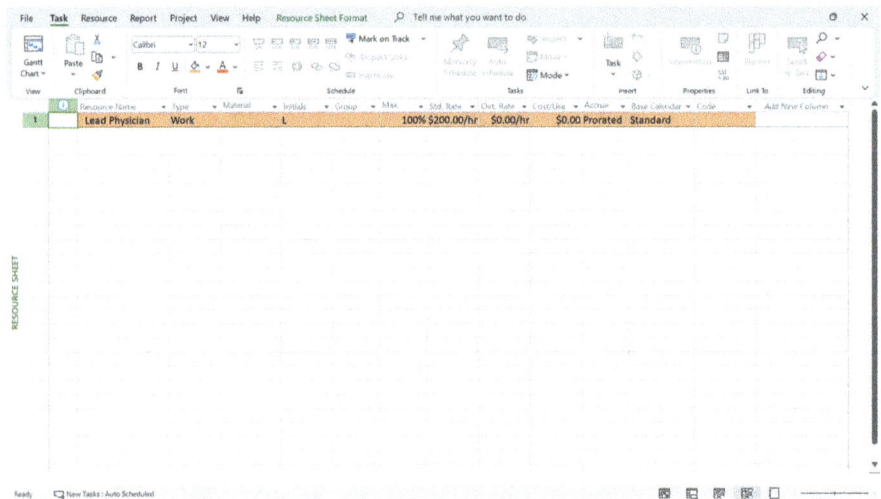

Figure 4-3. *Creation of resource name – Lead Physician*

To create a construction team resource, enter "Construction," and press Enter. Designate this as a work resource with a standard rate of $100 per hour as shown in Figure 4-4.

108

CHAPTER 4   RESOURCE MANAGEMENT USING MICROSOFT PROJECT

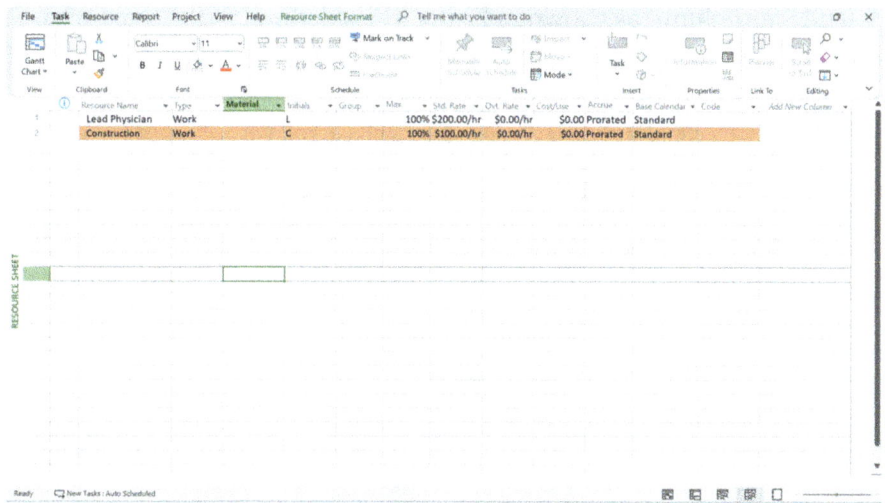

Figure 4-4. Creation of resource – "Construction"

Individual names can also be used, formatted as last name followed by first name without any additional characters. For instance, a resource could be named "Smith John" with a rate of $150 per hour as shown in Figure 4-5.

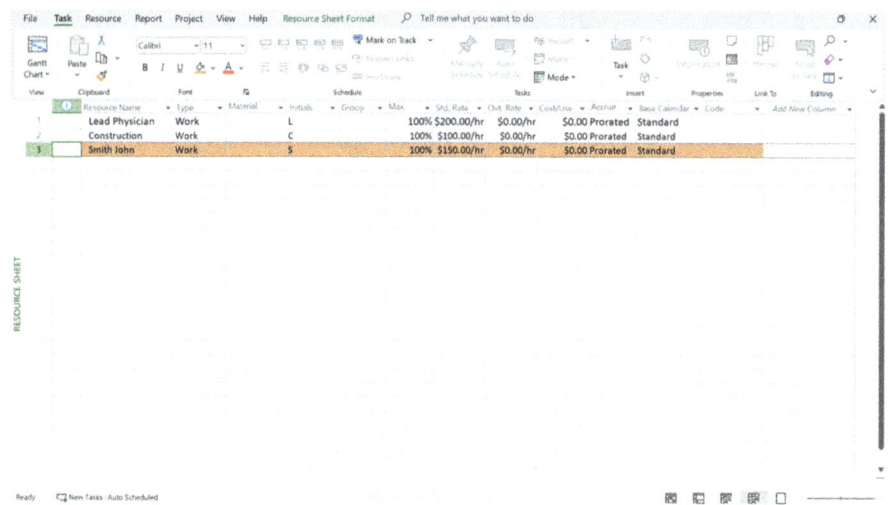

Figure 4-5. Creation of individual resource

CHAPTER 4   RESOURCE MANAGEMENT USING MICROSOFT PROJECT

The Max column as shown in Figure 4-6 is defined as the maximum availability of resources. Availability for work resources is defined by maximum units and the calendar. Maximum units represent the percentage of time the resource is available. By default, Project sets this at 100% as shown in Figure 4-6, denoting full-time availability.

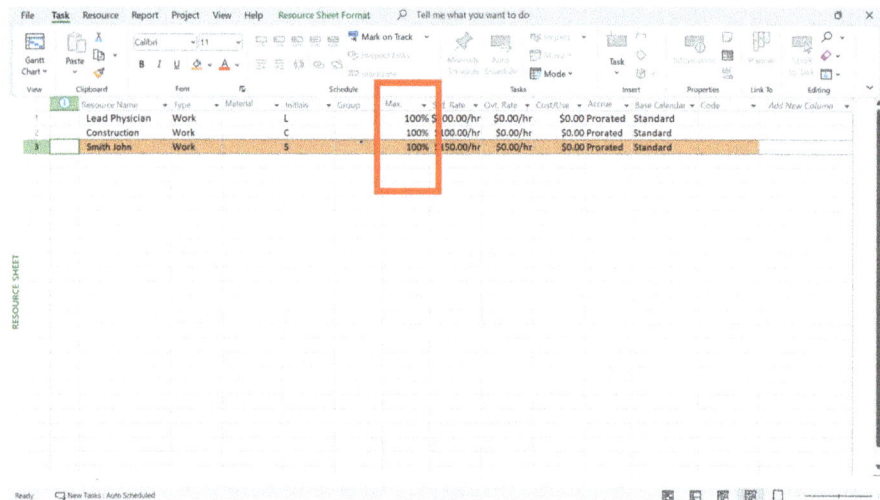

Figure 4-6. *Max column is defined as the maximum availability of resources*

Adjustments may be necessary based on resource specifics; for a construction team of three, for example, set the maximum units to 300% as shown in Figure 4-7.

CHAPTER 4   RESOURCE MANAGEMENT USING MICROSOFT PROJECT

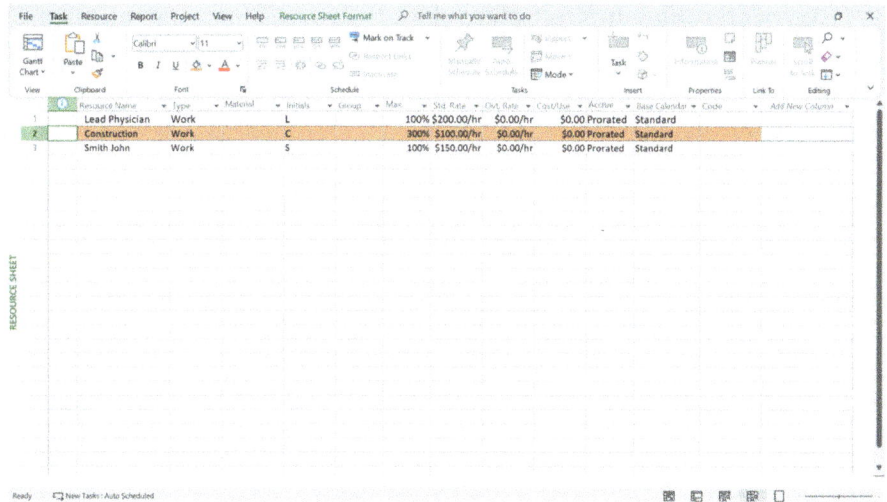

Figure 4-7. Setting up units for a team of three to 300%

Material resources, such as lumber, hardware, or gasoline, require specific details as shown in Figure 4-8.

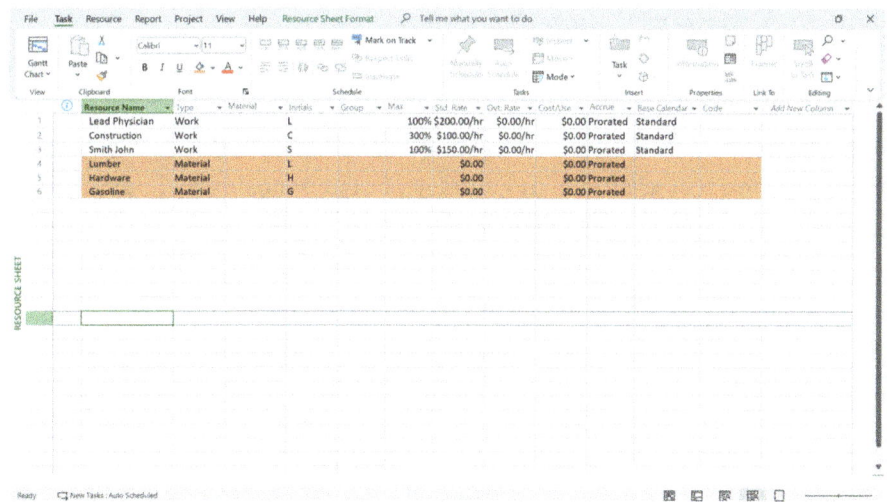

Figure 4-8. Creating material resources

111

CHAPTER 4   RESOURCE MANAGEMENT USING MICROSOFT PROJECT

If you need cables, input "Cable," designate it as a material resource by typing "M," and set the standard rate, such as $80 per unit. Labeling the unit as "ABC" in the Material column ensures clarity when assigning costs as shown in Figure 4-9.

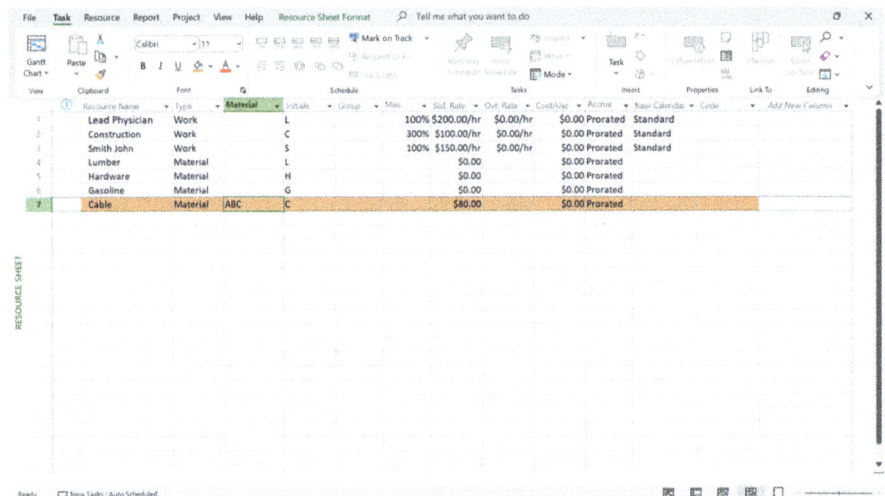

Figure 4-9. Assigning material resource a rate of 80%

For cost resources like travel and fees, simply input the resource name, such as "Permit," designate it as a cost resource by typing "C," and Project will handle the rest as shown in Figure 4-10. These costs are detailed when the resource is assigned to a task.

CHAPTER 4 RESOURCE MANAGEMENT USING MICROSOFT PROJECT

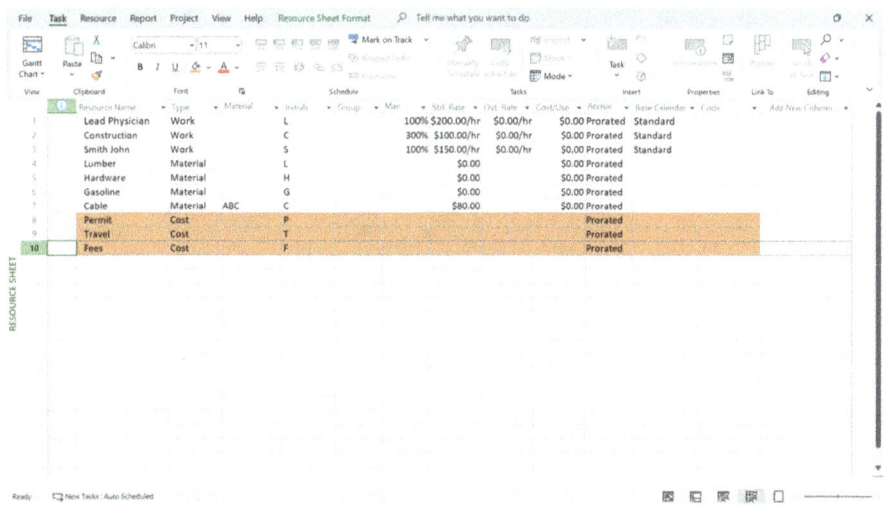

Figure 4-10. Creation of cost resources

The above overview outlines the essential steps for creating resources in Project, ensuring accurate and efficient management throughout your project's life cycle. In this section, we have seen the creation of work, material, and cost resources. In the next section, we will learn to assign resources to tasks.

Assign Resources to Tasks

As you assign resources to tasks, the project scheduling engine uses task dependencies, resource assignments, calendars, and more to calculate start and finish times. We're starting by assigning resources in the Gantt Chart view.

Go to the View tab, and click the top half of the Gantt chart button as shown in Figure 4-11.

113

CHAPTER 4　RESOURCE MANAGEMENT USING MICROSOFT PROJECT

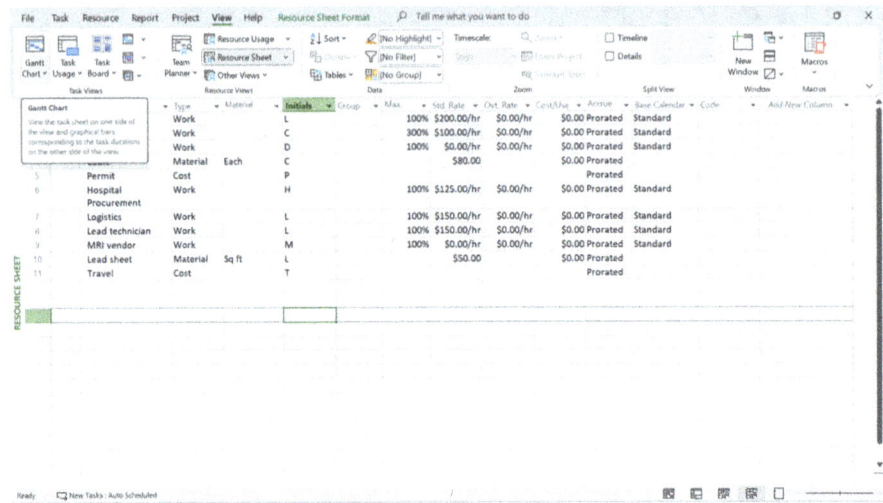

Figure 4-11. Access to Gantt Chart

Once you click the Gantt Chart option, the screen shown in Figure 4-12 appears.

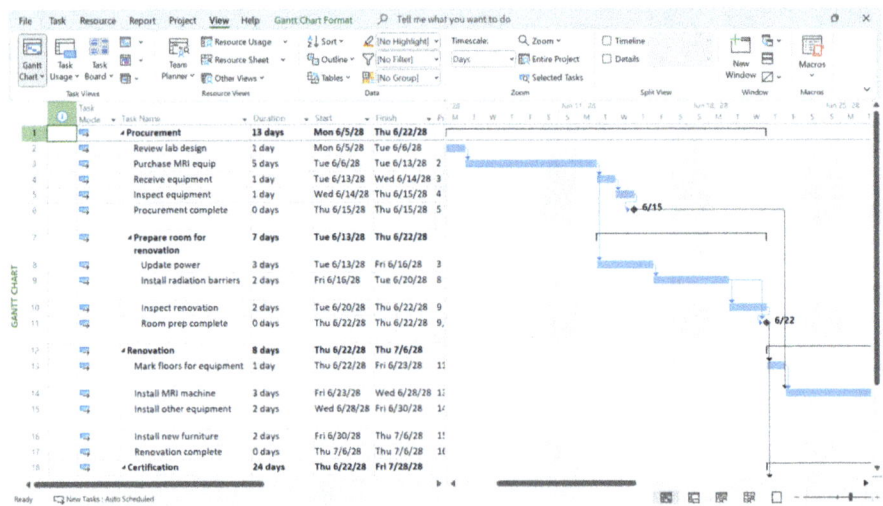

Figure 4-12. Gantt Chart view with the tasks

CHAPTER 4   RESOURCE MANAGEMENT USING MICROSOFT PROJECT

Turn on the detail's check box in the Split View section to display the task form below as shown in Figure 4-13.

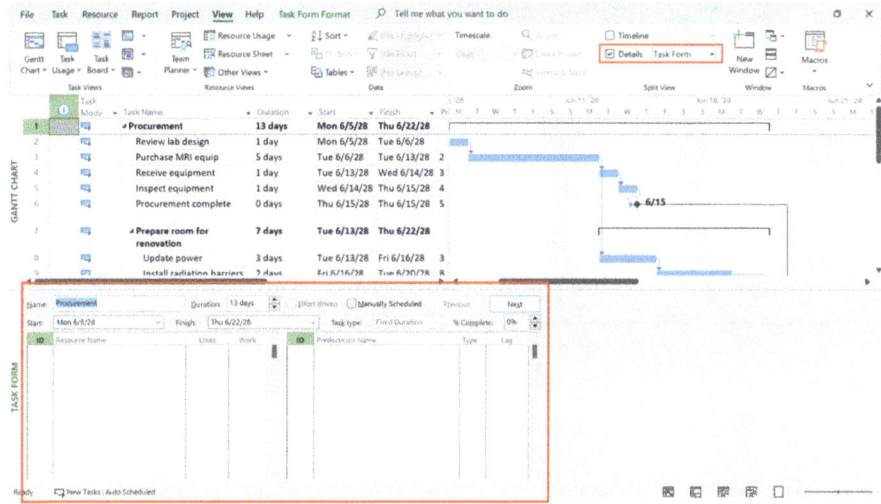

Figure 4-13. *Detail view*

In the Gantt Chart view, make sure it's active (name appears in green) as shown in Figure 4-14.

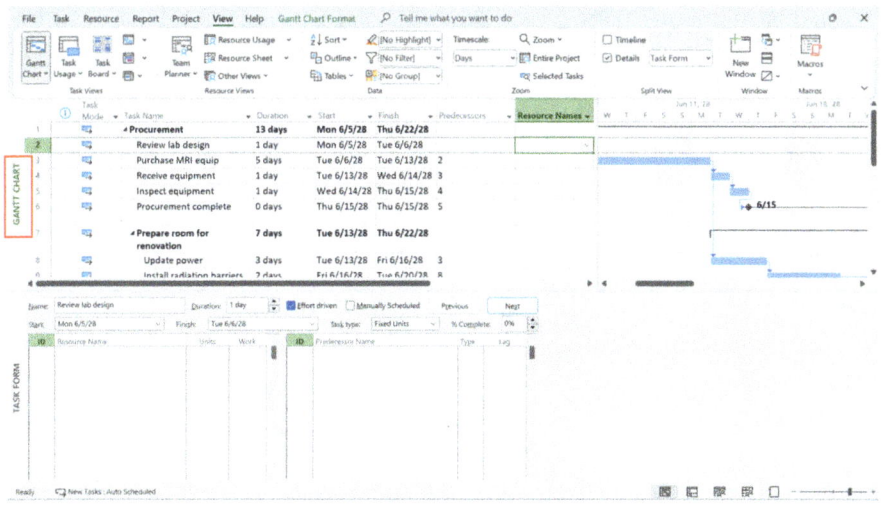

Figure 4-14. *Active Gantt Chart view*

115

CHAPTER 4   RESOURCE MANAGEMENT USING MICROSOFT PROJECT

For simple assignments, assign resources directly in the Resource Names column. Widen the table and Resource Names column as needed as shown in Figure 4-15.

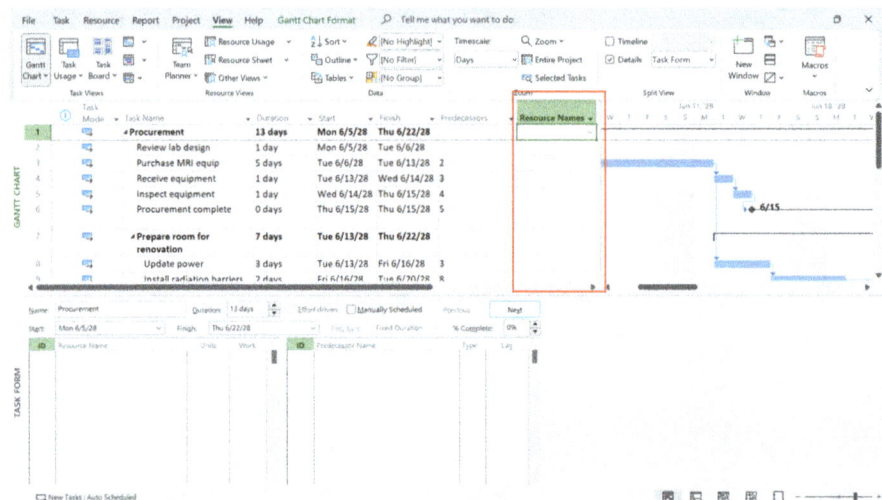

Figure 4-15. *Resource Names column made visible by widening the task table*

Select the Resource Names cell for a task, let's say "Review lab design," and click the down arrow as shown in Figure 4-16.

CHAPTER 4   RESOURCE MANAGEMENT USING MICROSOFT PROJECT

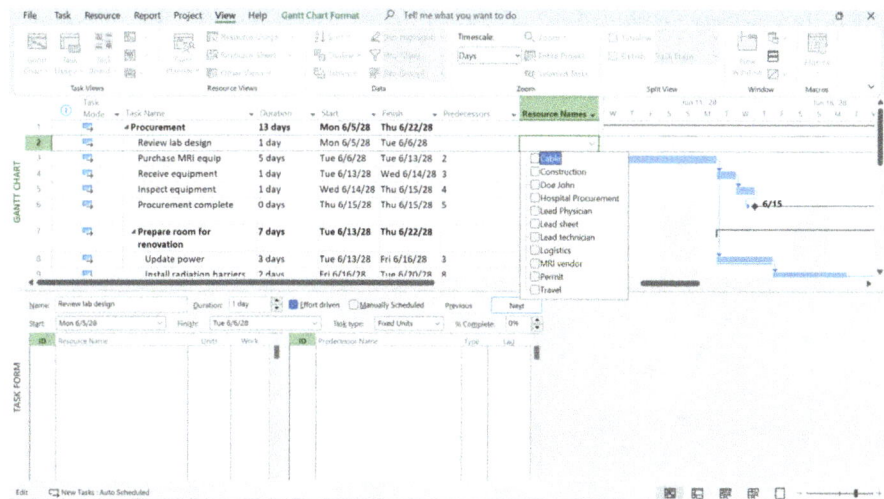

Figure 4-16. *Display of resources*

In Figure 4-16, choose the resources, let's say "Cable" and "Construction," and press Enter. Resources are added at full units (e.g., 100%) as shown in Figure 4-17.

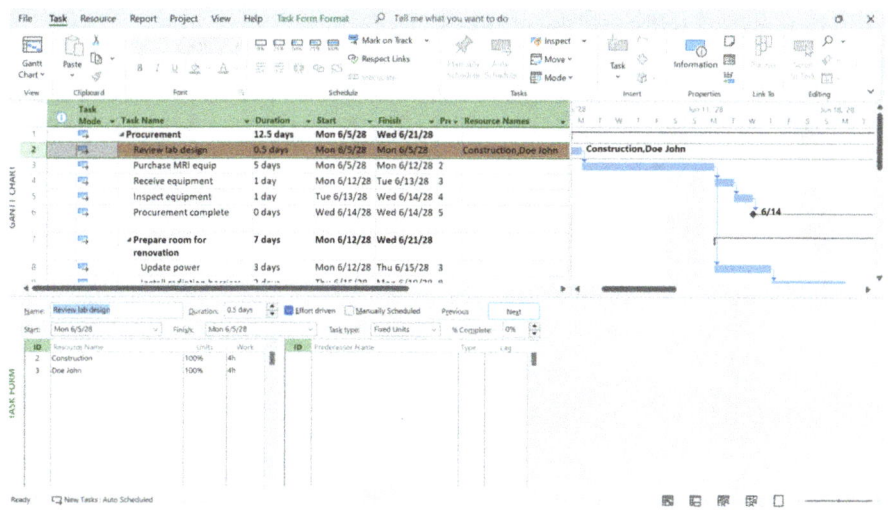

Figure 4-17. *Updating resources*

117

CHAPTER 4   RESOURCE MANAGEMENT USING MICROSOFT PROJECT

Assign resources to other tasks similarly. Click the down arrow, select the resources, and press Enter as shown in Figure 4-18.

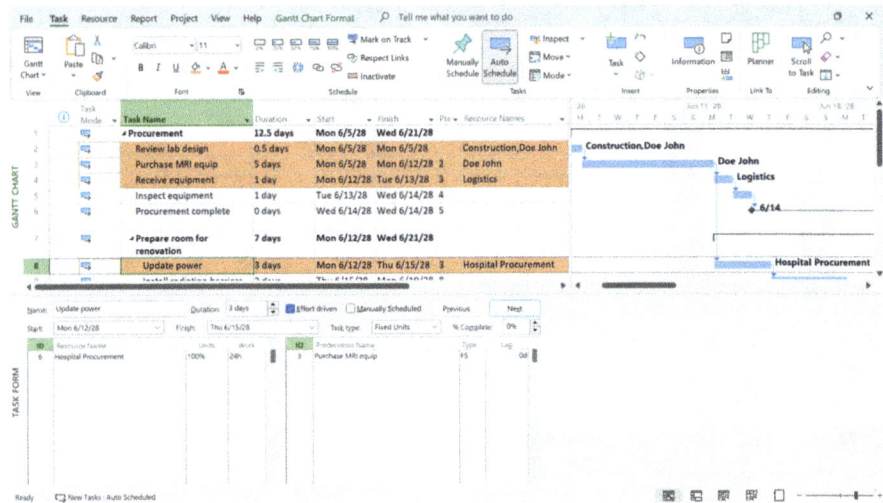

Figure 4-18. Updating resources

Use the task form as shown in Figure 4-19 for more detailed control if needed, but stick with simple assignments for now.

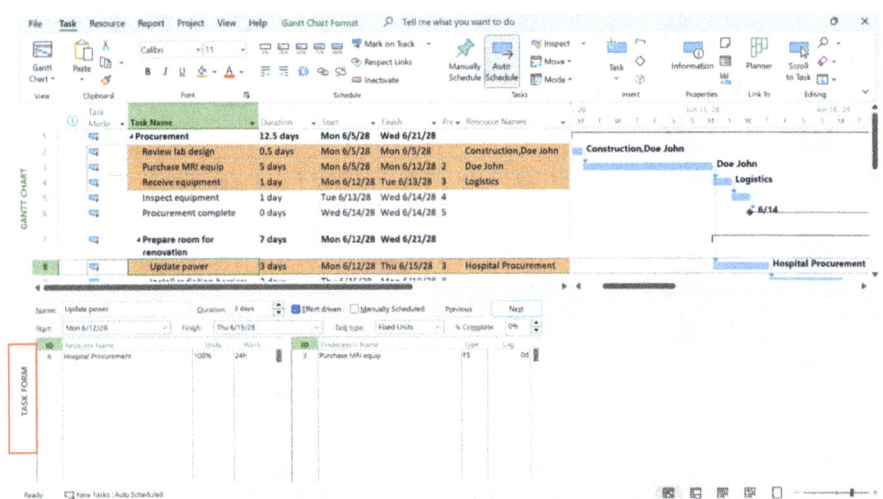

Figure 4-19. Task Form view

118

CHAPTER 4   RESOURCE MANAGEMENT USING MICROSOFT PROJECT

In the Task Form for Install radiation barriers, add material resources, and type the quantity (e.g., five cables) into the Units cell as shown in Figure 4-20.

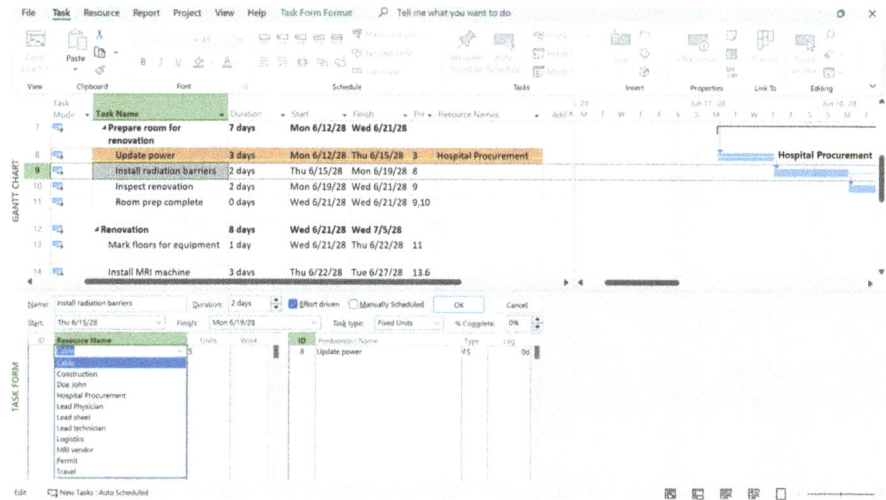

Figure 4-20. Update resources in the Task Form

After you click OK in Figure 4-20, "Cable" resources get updated against "Install radiation barriers" as shown in Figure 4-21.

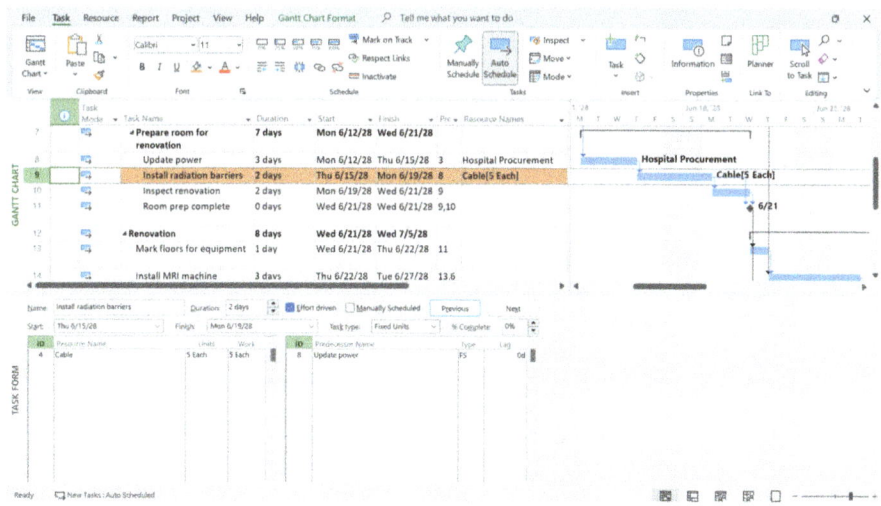

Figure 4-21. For task "Install Radiation Barriers", resource value getting updated to "Cable"

119

CHAPTER 4   RESOURCE MANAGEMENT USING MICROSOFT PROJECT

To add cost resources, click on the drop-down around the "Add New Column" field as shown in Figure 4-22.

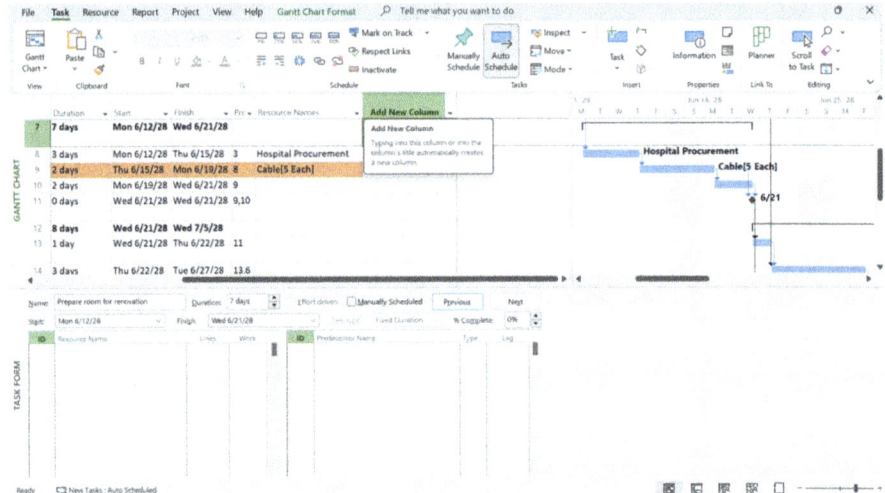

Figure 4-22. *Add a new field*

After this, add "Cost" column to the tasks as shown in Figure 4-23.

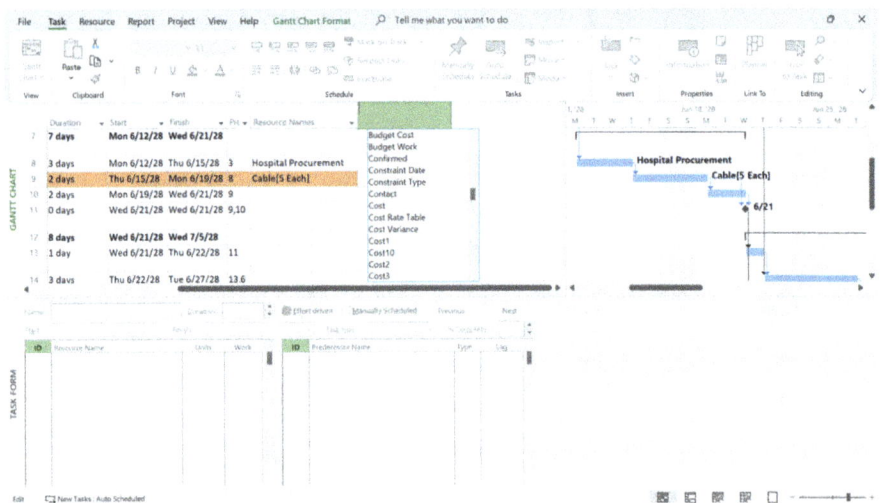

Figure 4-23. *Adding "Cost" column*

120

CHAPTER 4 RESOURCE MANAGEMENT USING MICROSOFT PROJECT

After selecting "Cost" column, it gets added successfully as shown in Figure 4-24, and cost created in Figure 4-20 is displayed.

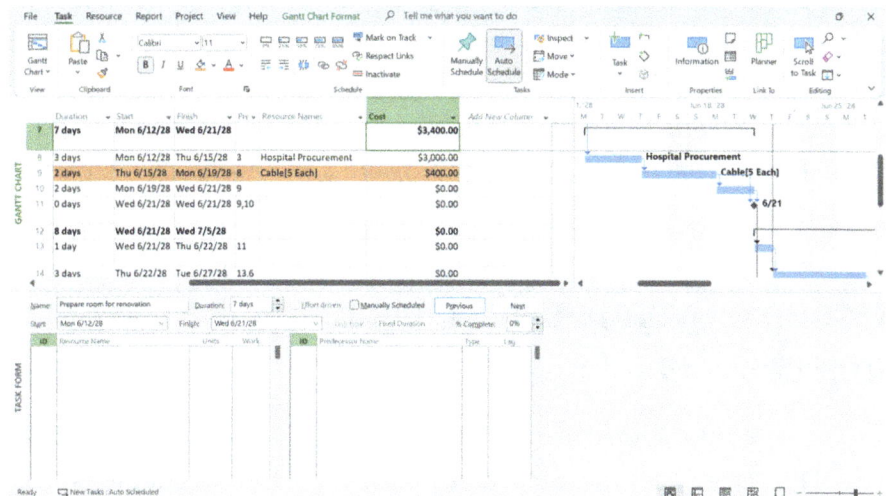

Figure 4-24. *New column "Cost" got added successfully*

Work resource costs are based on work hours and standard rate per hour. Materials cost is the quantity times the unit cost. That's a quick overview of assigning resources to tasks where we learned how to add resources to the tasks. In the next section, we will see how to resolve resource overallocation problems in Microsoft Project.

Resource Overallocation Problem

Resource overallocation occurs when resources (such as personnel, equipment, or time) are assigned more tasks or responsibilities than they can effectively manage. Overallocation of resources can result in several issues, such as reduced efficiency due to insufficient allocation, which may hinder the completion of tasks in a timely manner, thus causing delays and compromising the quality of work. Furthermore, excessive workload can significantly impact mental and physical health by increasing stress levels. Prolonged overallocation may lead to burnout, resulting in exhaustion and disengagement among resources. Constantly being overworked can also lower morale and job satisfaction, potentially contributing to higher turnover rates within the organization.

Effective resource management and realistic workload planning are essential to prevent overallocation and ensure a balanced, productive work environment.

Resource Overallocation Impact on the Overall Project Cycle

Resource overallocation can have significant impacts on the overall project cycle. This issue arises when resources, such as personnel, equipment, or time, are assigned more tasks or responsibilities than they can effectively manage. Here, we will explore the various dimensions of this problem and its implications on project management in detail.

Project Delays: One of the most immediate impacts of resource overallocation is project delays. When resources are overburdened, they struggle to complete tasks on time, leading to a cascading effect on the project schedule. Each delayed task can push subsequent tasks further down the timeline, extending the overall project duration.

Quality Issues: Overallocated resources often need to rush through their tasks to meet deadlines, which can compromise the quality of their work. This can result in errors, omissions, and substandard outputs that require rework. Rework consumes additional time and resources and affects the project's overall quality, potentially leading to client dissatisfaction.

Increased Costs: Delays and rework due to resource overallocation can lead to increased project costs. Extended project timelines mean higher labor costs, as team members need to work longer to complete their tasks. Additionally, the need for rework can consume more materials and resources, further inflating the budget. Organizations may also need to hire additional resources to manage the workload, adding to the project's financial burden.

Reduced Team Morale: Constantly overworked team members are likely to experience high levels of stress and burnout. This can lead to decreased morale, lower job satisfaction, and reduced productivity. Over time, this can result in higher turnover rates, as employees seek less stressful work environments. High turnover can disrupt the project cycle, as new team members need time to get up to speed, further delaying progress.

Risk of Project Failure: If resource overallocation is not addressed, it can jeopardize the project's success. Persistent delays, quality issues, and increased costs can lead to project failure. Stakeholders may lose confidence in the project's ability to deliver the desired outcomes, and the project may be canceled or significantly scaled back.

Impact on Stakeholder Relationships: Resource overallocation can strain relationships with stakeholders. Delays and quality issues can lead to dissatisfaction among clients and other stakeholders, who may feel that their expectations are not being met. This can damage the organization's reputation and lead to a loss of future business opportunities.

Compromised Scope: To manage the workload and meet deadlines, project managers may need to reduce the project's scope. This means cutting back on features, functionalities, or deliverables, which can affect the project's overall value and effectiveness. Compromising the scope can result in a final product that does not fully meet the stakeholders' needs or expectations.

Resource Conflicts: Overallocation can lead to conflicts among team members, as they compete for limited resources. This can create a stressful work environment and hinder collaboration and teamwork. Resource conflicts can also lead to inefficiencies, as team members spend time resolving disputes instead of focusing on their tasks.

Long-Term Organizational Impact: The effects of resource overallocation can extend beyond the immediate project. Persistent overallocation can lead to a culture of overwork within the organization, where employees are regularly expected to take on more than they can handle. This can result in long-term issues such as chronic stress, high turnover, and a negative organizational reputation.

Mitigation Strategies: To mitigate the impacts of resource overallocation, project managers can employ several strategies:

1. **Resource Levelling**: Adjusting the project schedule to balance the workload more evenly across resources. Tasks may be rescheduled to ensure that no resource is overburdened at any given time.

   - **Resource Allocation Tools**: Utilizing project management software and tools to help managers track resource usage and identify overallocation early. These tools can provide insights into resource availability and help in planning more effectively.

   - **Prioritization and Delegation**: Prioritizing tasks and delegating responsibilities to ensure that critical tasks are completed on time. This can help in managing the workload more effectively and preventing overallocation.

   - **Hiring Additional Resources**: If the workload is consistently high, hiring additional resources to help distribute the tasks more evenly. This can prevent burnout and ensure that the project stays on track.

   - **Training and Development**: Investing in training and development to enhance the skills and efficiency of the existing team, enabling them to handle their tasks more effectively and reducing the risk of overallocation.

Conclusion

Resource overallocation presents a significant challenge in project management that can impact the project cycle. From delays and quality issues to increased costs and reduced team morale, the effects of overallocation can jeopardize a project's success. By employing effective resource management strategies and tools, project managers can mitigate these impacts and ensure a balanced, productive work environment. Addressing resource overallocation proactively is essential for maintaining project timelines, quality, and stakeholder satisfaction.

Crucial to Resolve Resource Overallocation

Resource overallocation can arise from various factors related to project management practices and organizational dynamics. Here are some crucial reasons to address them:

- Simultaneous projects often vie for the same resources, leading to overallocation as managers struggle to balance demands.

- Manually managing capacity with spreadsheets can be error-prone and inefficient, resulting in inaccurate resource allocation.

- Setting unrealistic schedules and budgets can pressure managers to overallocate tasks, straining resources.

- Poor forecasting causes imbalances, leading to overcommitment of resources without understanding their capabilities and future needs.

- Projects dependent on specific resources may face bottlenecks and overallocation if those resources are limited or unavailable.

- Poor communication among teams can result in misunderstandings about resource availability, leading to overallocation.

- Inadequate planning leads to haphazard task assignments and an uneven workload distribution.

- High demand coupled with limited resources pressures teams, causing overallocation and overburdened team members.

- Cultures prioritizing high productivity over well-being often lead to overworked resources and burnout.

- Unexpected tasks disrupt planned allocation, creating stressful environments and difficulty managing workloads.

- Without proper tools, tracking and allocating resources efficiently becomes challenging, leading to overallocation.

- Resources lacking skills take longer to complete tasks, leading to overallocation. Investing in training mitigates this risk.

- Stakeholders demanding quick results can cause unrealistic deadlines and excessive workloads, leading to overallocation.

- Conflicts over limited resources create stress and hinder collaboration, contributing to overallocation.

- Rigid project plans that don't allow adjustments lead to overburdened resources. Flexibility in planning is essential.

CHAPTER 4 RESOURCE MANAGEMENT USING MICROSOFT PROJECT

Resource overallocation arises from various factors like competing projects, manual processes, and unrealistic expectations. Effective resource management, communication, and realistic planning are key to preventing overallocation and ensuring successful projects.

Demonstration to Fix a Resource Overallocation Problem

To create a realistic schedule, team members should be engaged without being overallocated. It is essential to identify and resolve resource overallocations.

We are currently viewing the Gantt chart for our project. In the indicator's column, there are icons resembling red people. Hovering over these icons reveals the message "This task has overallocated resources," as shown in Figure 4-25, indicating that we have some overallocations to address.

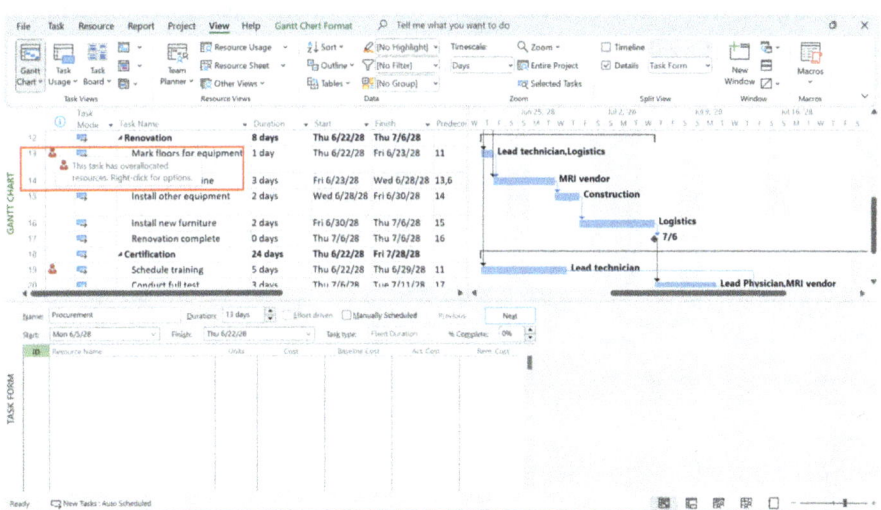

Figure 4-25. Overallocated tasks

To address this, first, navigate to the Resource tab as shown in Figure 4-26.

127

CHAPTER 4   RESOURCE MANAGEMENT USING MICROSOFT PROJECT

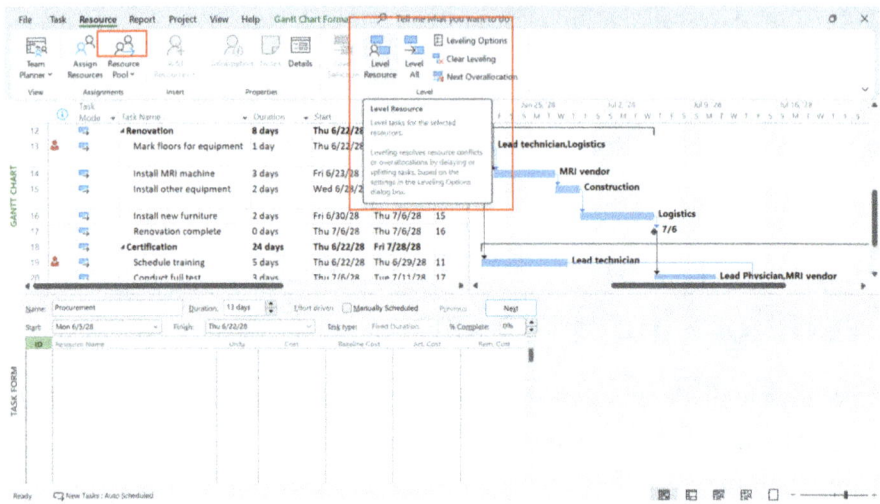

Figure 4-26. Level Resource option

Click the overallocated resource task, and in the menu, select Resource ➤ "Level Resource," and this opens the resource leveling dialog box as shown in Figure 4-27. In this image, we see that the task "Mark floors for equipment" is overallocated by resources "Lead technician" and "Logistics."

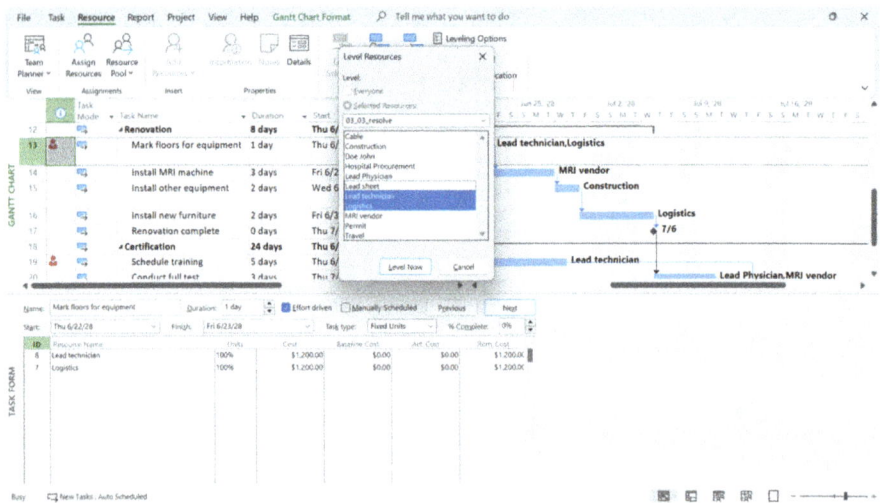

Figure 4-27. Resource leveling dialog box

128

CHAPTER 4   RESOURCE MANAGEMENT USING MICROSOFT PROJECT

In Figure 4-27, to resolve the resource allocation problem, click "Level Now" button as shown in Figure 4-28. Also, in the Gantt Chart view, there is enough gap between the end of the task "Schedule training" and start of the task "Conduct full test." The start date of the "Schedule training" is "6/22/28."

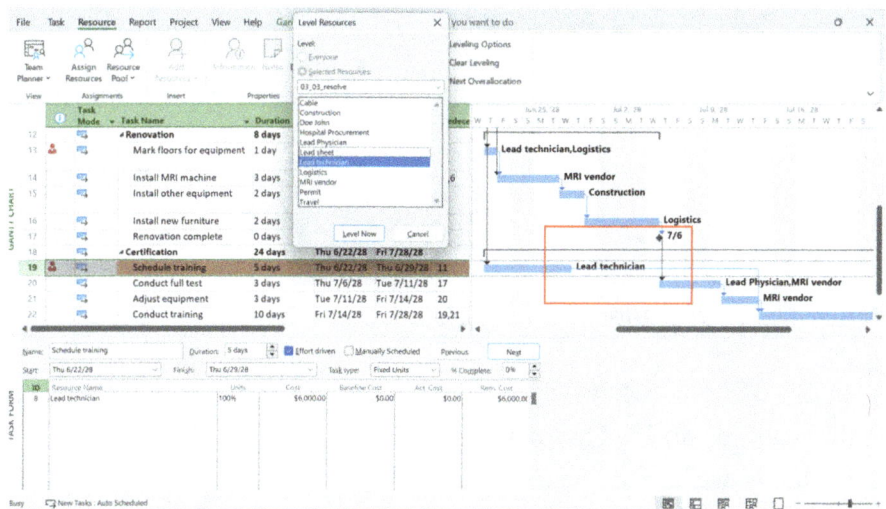

Figure 4-28. Apply Level Now feature

Once we apply Level Now feature, all overallocated tasks vanishes, and the lags in the Gantt chart disappears. To overcome overallocation problem, the start date of the "Schedule training" is adjusted to "6/23/28" as shown in Figure 4-29.

CHAPTER 4 RESOURCE MANAGEMENT USING MICROSOFT PROJECT

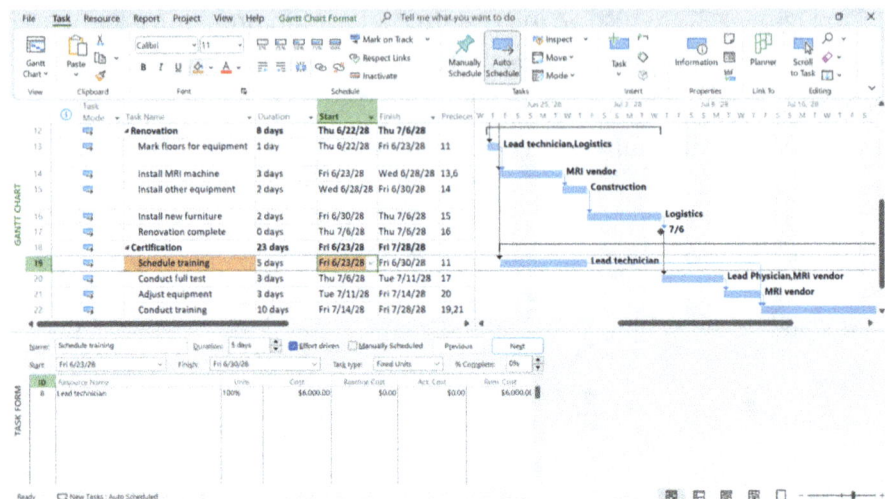

Figure 4-29. Overallocation problem is resolved

In this section, we have learned how resource overallocation problems are highlighted and fixed in Microsoft Project with a few clicks.

With this, we have come to the end of this chapter. In this chapter, we have learned how to create work, material, and cost resources in Microsoft Project, assign resource tasks, and resolve resource overallocation. In the next chapter, we will be creating a project schedule in Microsoft Project, which involves developing project schedules, managing deadlines and milestones, and the critical path method.

CHAPTER 5

Fine-Tuning a Project Schedule

In the last chapter, we have learned how to create Work, Material, and Cost resources in Microsoft Project, assign resource tasks, and resolve resource overallocation. In this chapter, we will be fine-tuning a project schedule in Microsoft Project which involves reviewing the critical path, identifying schedule issues with Task Inspector, delaying a task or assignment and managing inactive tasks, and finally identifying project scheduling problems.

Introduction

Creating a project schedule in Microsoft Project is a crucial step in project management. It helps you plan, execute, and monitor your project's progress effectively. Microsoft Project is a powerful tool designed to assist project managers in planning, scheduling, and managing projects. It provides a comprehensive platform to create detailed project schedules, allocate resources, track progress, and manage budgets. Below are some key features of Microsoft Project:

- **Task Management**: You can break down your project into smaller tasks, assign durations, and set dependencies between tasks.

- **Resource Allocation**: Allocate resources such as team members, equipment, and materials to tasks, ensuring optimal utilization.

- **Timeline Visualization**: Visualize your project timeline with Gantt charts, which provide a clear view of task sequences and durations.

- **Progress Tracking**: Monitor the progress of tasks and the overall project, identifying any deviations from the plan.

- **Budget Management**: Track costs and manage budgets, ensuring your project stays within financial constraints.

- **Reporting**: Generate various reports to communicate project status to stakeholders.

Consider the learnings we had in Chapter 3 on task management such as how to create and organize tasks, work with summary tasks, add milestone, add project duration, and set task dependencies. Further, we will explore Gantt chart usage in Microsoft Project. Below are some steps to create a project schedule:

- **Define Project Scope**: Start by defining the scope of your project. Identify the main objectives, deliverables, and milestones.

- **Break Down Tasks**: Divide the project into smaller, manageable tasks. Each task should have a clear start and end date.

- **Set Dependencies**: Determine the dependencies between tasks. Some tasks may need to be completed before others can start.

CHAPTER 5 FINE-TUNING A PROJECT SCHEDULE

- **Allocate Resources**: Assign resources to each task. Ensure that resources are not overallocated and are used efficiently.

- **Create a Timeline**: Use Gantt charts to visualize the project timeline. Adjust task durations and dependencies to optimize the schedule.

- **Monitor Progress**: Regularly update the project schedule with actual progress. Identify any delays and adjust the schedule accordingly.

- **Generate Reports**: Use Microsoft Project's reporting features to create status reports, resource reports, and budget reports.

Microsoft Project is an essential tool for project managers looking to create detailed and effective project schedules. By leveraging its features, you can ensure that your project is well-planned, resources are optimally utilized, and progress is closely monitored. This leads to successful project completion within the defined scope, time, and budget.

Review of the Critical Path

The critical path is the longest linked sequence of tasks in a project. Changes to the critical path also change the project finish date. Project makes it easy to see the critical path, allowing you to keep your project on time or shorten the schedule. Let's review the critical path using the below steps:

Step 1: Start by navigating to the Gantt Chart Format tab. In the Bar Styles section, there is a Critical Tasks check box, and check this box as shown in Figure 5-1.

CHAPTER 5 FINE-TUNING A PROJECT SCHEDULE

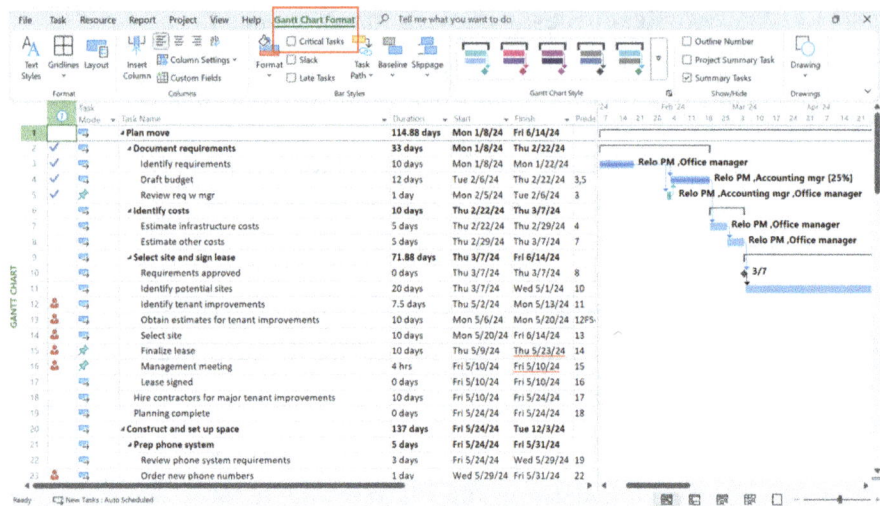

Figure 5-1. *Critical Tasks option under Gantt Chart Format*

Step 2: After ticking Critical Tasks, observe the timescale, and note the color of the bars. Turn on Critical Tasks, and some of the bars will turn red, indicating they are critical as shown in Figure 5-2. Critical tasks have no slack, meaning any delay in these tasks delays the project.

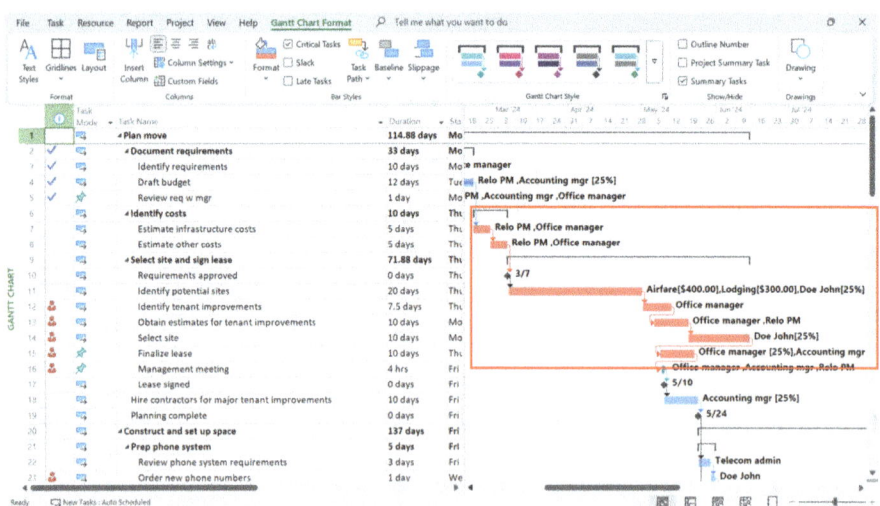

Figure 5-2. *Critical path*

CHAPTER 5   FINE-TUNING A PROJECT SCHEDULE

Step 3: There are two ways to view slack. Go to the Format tab, and click the Slack check box to enable it as shown in Figure 5-3.

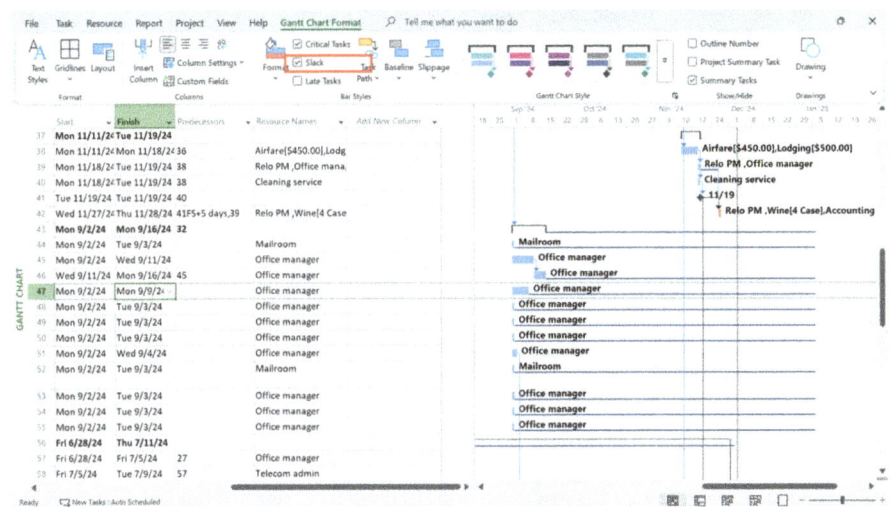

Figure 5-3. *Slack feature under Gantt Chart Format*

Step 4: After putting a tick under Slack tick box to see slack tasks, check out the task list, and look at a specific task, such as task 47, "Arrange external maintenance," as shown in Figure 5-4. Use the Scroll to Task option in the Quick Access Toolbar to see the bars in the timescale. Notice the narrow red lines coming off the finish date of those tasks, indicating slack as shown in Figure 5-4.

135

CHAPTER 5 FINE-TUNING A PROJECT SCHEDULE

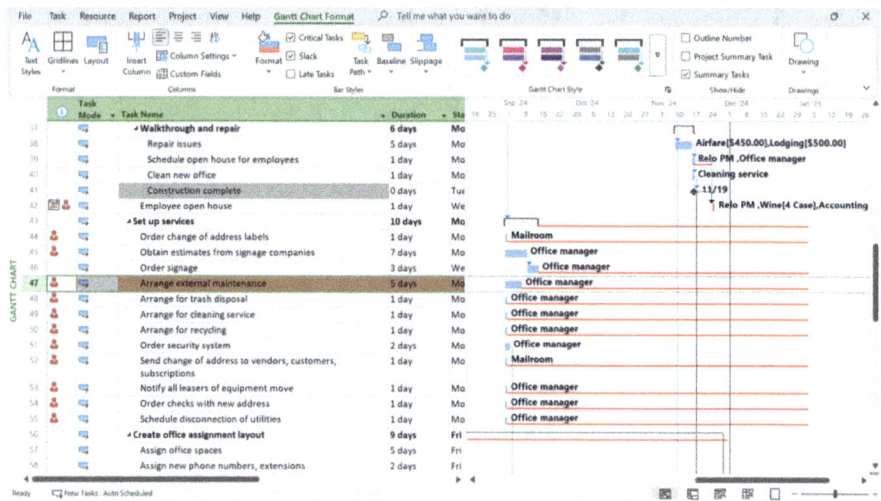

Figure 5-4. View slack task "Arrange external maintenance"

Step 5: To see the actual value for slack, insert total slack into a table by right-clicking the Duration column as shown in Figure 5-5.

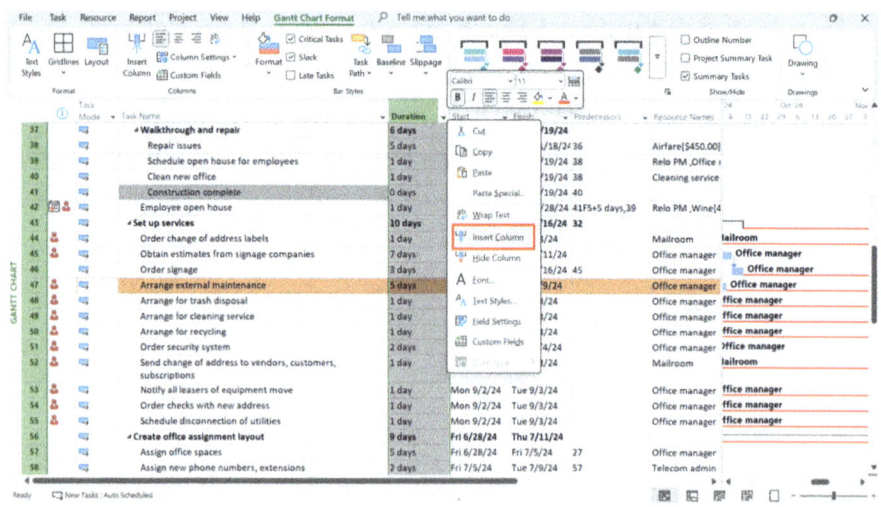

Figure 5-5. Right-click the Duration column to Insert Column

136

CHAPTER 5   FINE-TUNING A PROJECT SCHEDULE

Step 6: Choose the Insert Column type "Total Slack," and select it to add to the table as shown in Figure 5-6.

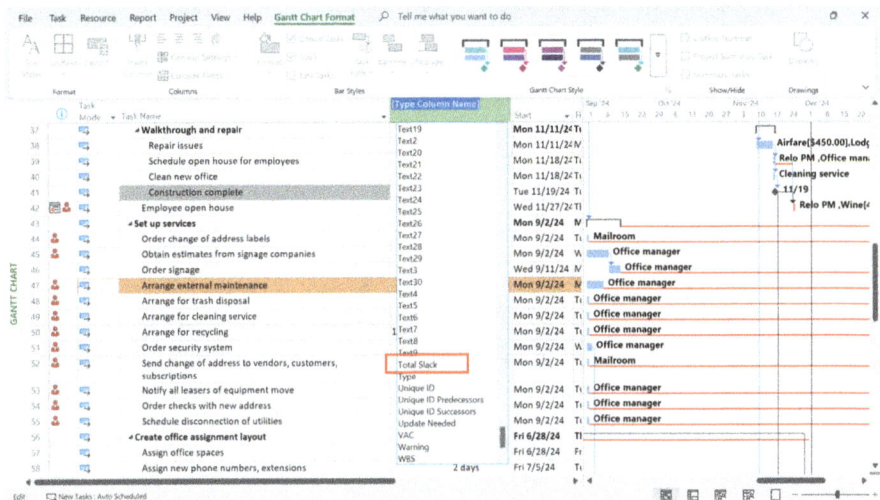

Figure 5-6. *Insert "Total Slack" column*

Step 7: Check if the "Total Slack" column got added successfully as shown in Figure 5-7.

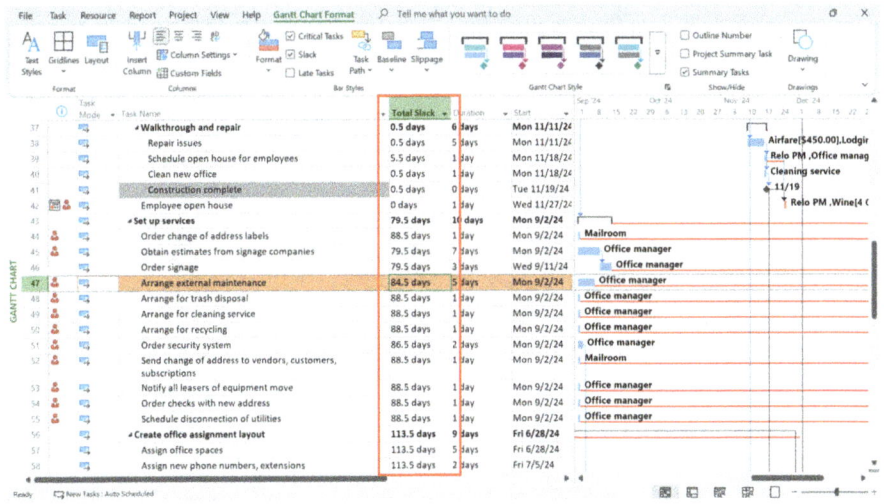

Figure 5-7. *"Total Slack" column got added successfully*

137

CHAPTER 5   FINE-TUNING A PROJECT SCHEDULE

Step 8: For instance, consider task 28, "Prepare drawings." Click Scroll to Task in the Quick Access Toolbar to view the bars in the timescale. This task has a duration of 5 days, but if it takes longer – say 12 days – press Enter to update the duration as shown in Figure 5-8.

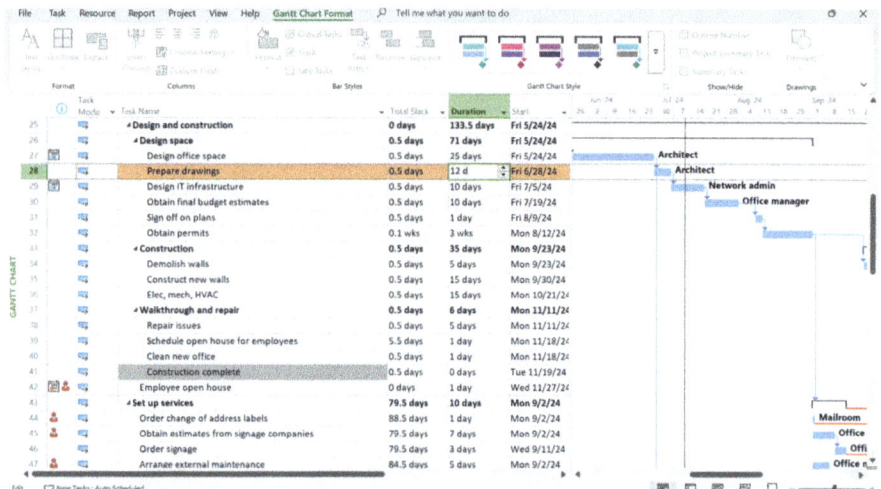

Figure 5-8. Update task 28, "Prepare drawings," to 12 days

Step 9: The Planning Wizard will warn you about a scheduling conflict; choose Continue, and then click OK as shown in Figure 5-9.

CHAPTER 5   FINE-TUNING A PROJECT SCHEDULE

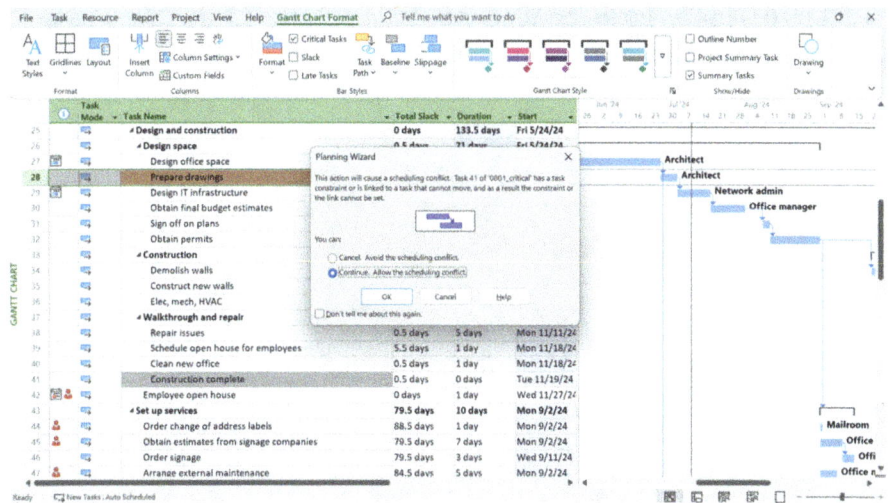

Figure 5-9. Planning Wizard will warn you about a scheduling conflict

Step 9: After accepting the conflict, the delay will place the task on the critical path, affecting the project finish date as shown in Figure 5-10.

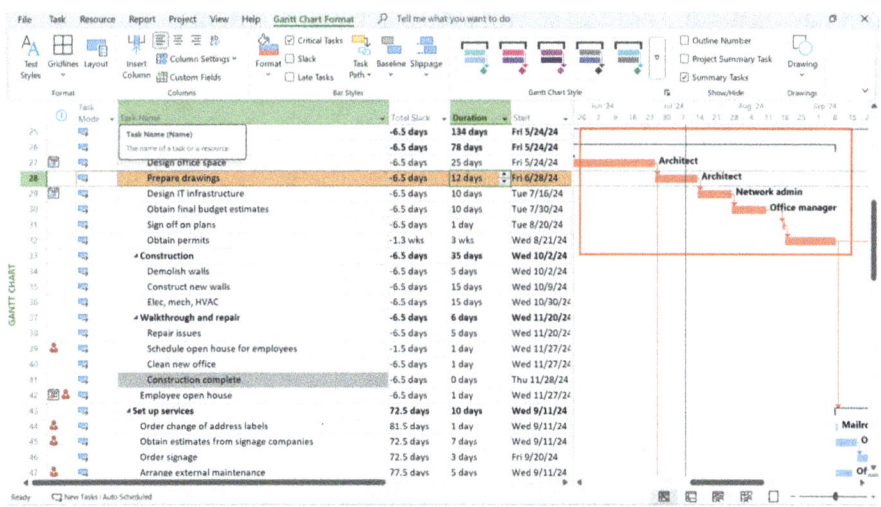

Figure 5-10. "Prepare drawings" task got added to critical path after its duration was increased to 12 days

139

CHAPTER 5   FINE-TUNING A PROJECT SCHEDULE

Step 10: Finally, go to the View tab, and apply the Critical filter as shown in Figure 5-11.

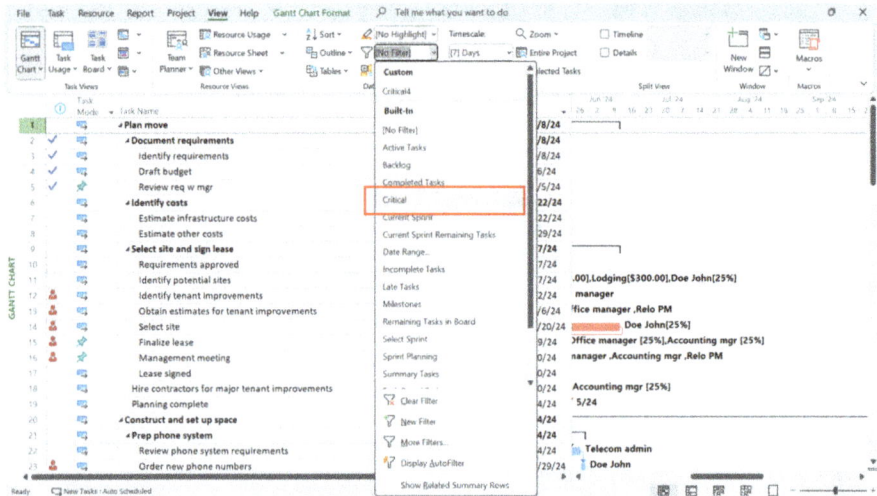

Figure 5-11.   Critical filter under View tab

Step 5.11: In the Filter box, choose Critical. The list will show both summary tasks and subtasks, with total slack being zero or negative, and everything listed is on the critical path as shown in Figure 5-12.

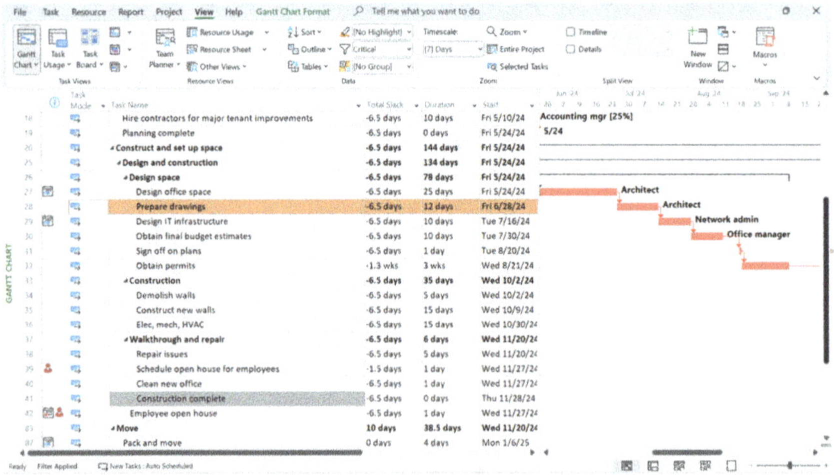

Figure 5-12.   Slack being zero or negative for Critical filter

CHAPTER 5   FINE-TUNING A PROJECT SCHEDULE

Step 12: When done, remove the filter. This is how to display the critical path in the timescale and filter the task list to show only critical tasks (Figure 5-13).

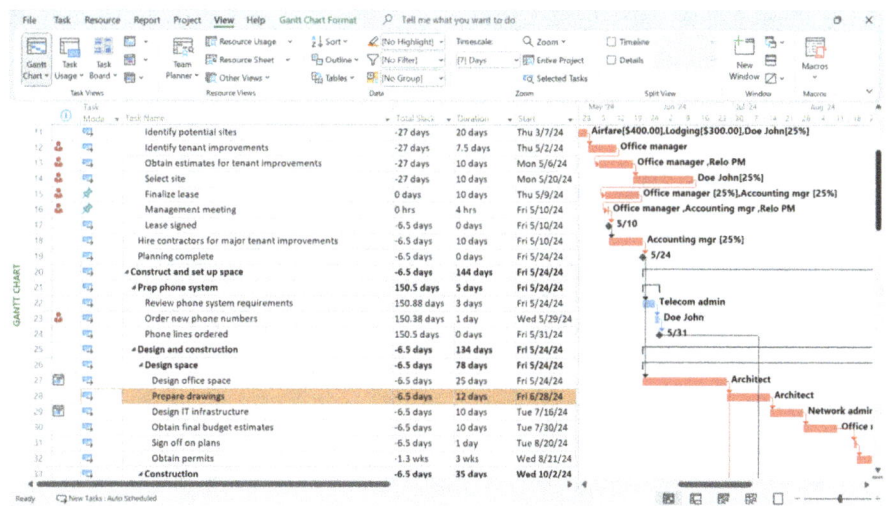

Figure 5-13. Critical path view after the removal of critical filter

In this section, while fine-tuning a project schedule, we have learned how to review the critical path in Microsoft Project. In the next section, we will identify schedule issues with Task Inspector.

Identify Schedule Issues with Task Inspector

Task Inspector assists you in identifying factors that influence a task's start date and any issues requiring resolution. We will understand the Task Inspector through the below steps.

Step 1: When opening any Microsoft Project file, if prompted by the Planning Wizard, select Continue to permit the scheduling conflict, and then click OK as shown in Figure 5-14.

141

CHAPTER 5   FINE-TUNING A PROJECT SCHEDULE

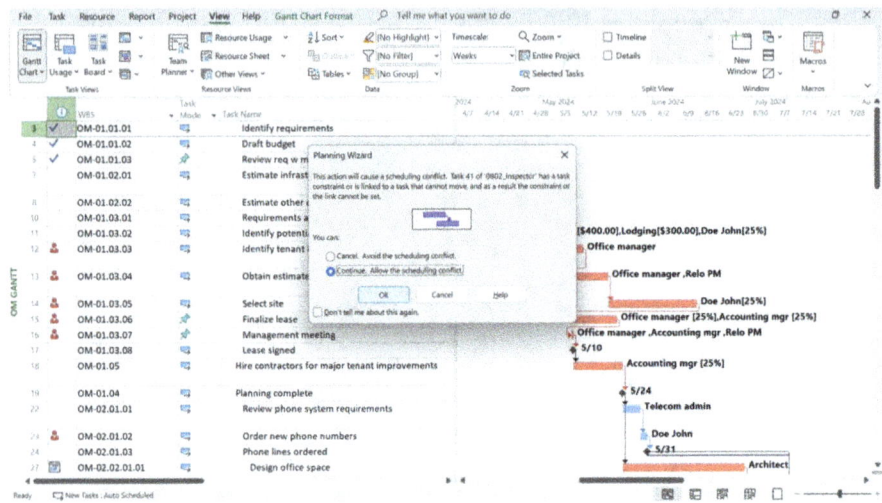

Figure 5-14. *Accept the conflict*

Step 2: Let's examine task 15, Finalize lease. Notice there is a red squiggly line under the date within the Finish cell for this task as shown in Figure 5-15. This indicates a scheduling issue.

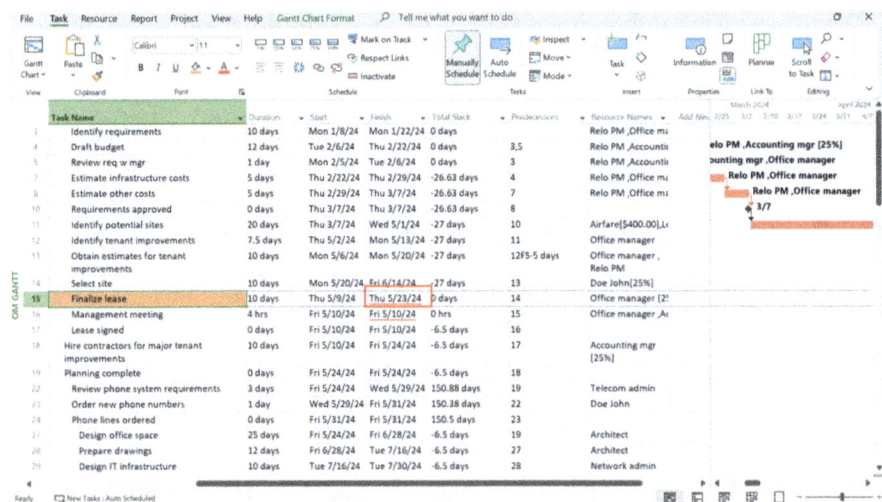

Figure 5-15. *Scheduling issue for task 15 "Finalize lease"*

142

CHAPTER 5   FINE-TUNING A PROJECT SCHEDULE

Step 3: Right-click the task. From the top of the shortcut menu, select Fix in Task Inspector to open the Inspector pane on the left side of the screen as shown in Figure 5-16.

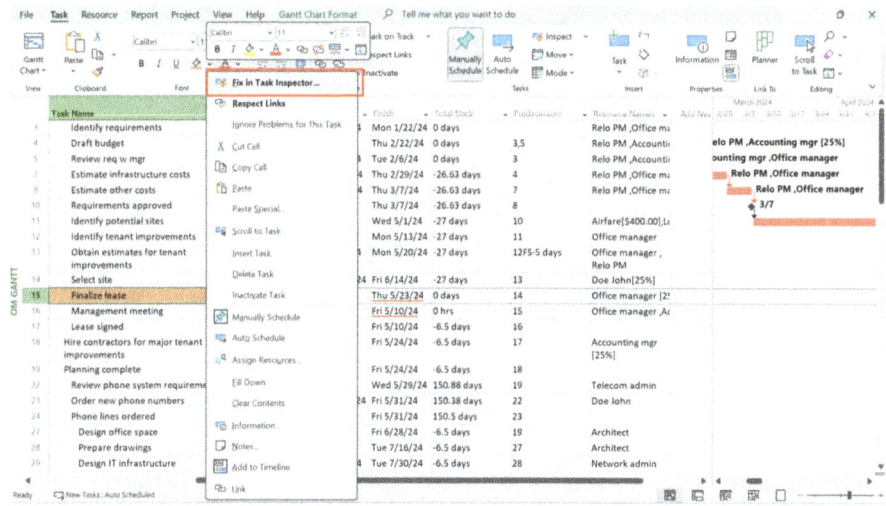

Figure 5-16. *Access "Fix in Task Inspector"*

Step 4: At the left-hand side of the page, details about the task and potential fixes are displayed. Various buttons offer methods for addressing issues as shown in Figure 5-17. Additionally, an information section at the bottom shows factors affecting the task's start date, such as manual scheduling, predecessors, calendar, and assigned resources, as shown in Figure 5-18.

143

CHAPTER 5   FINE-TUNING A PROJECT SCHEDULE

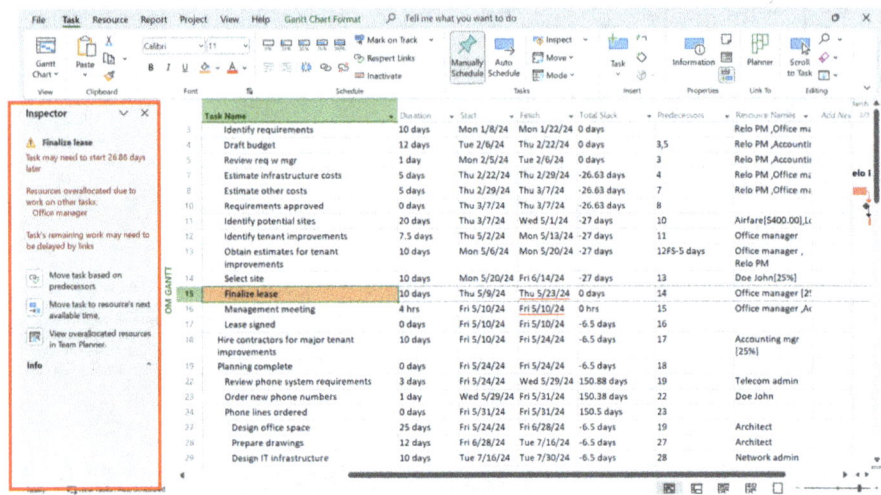

Figure 5-17. *As an example, for Task – Finalize Lease*

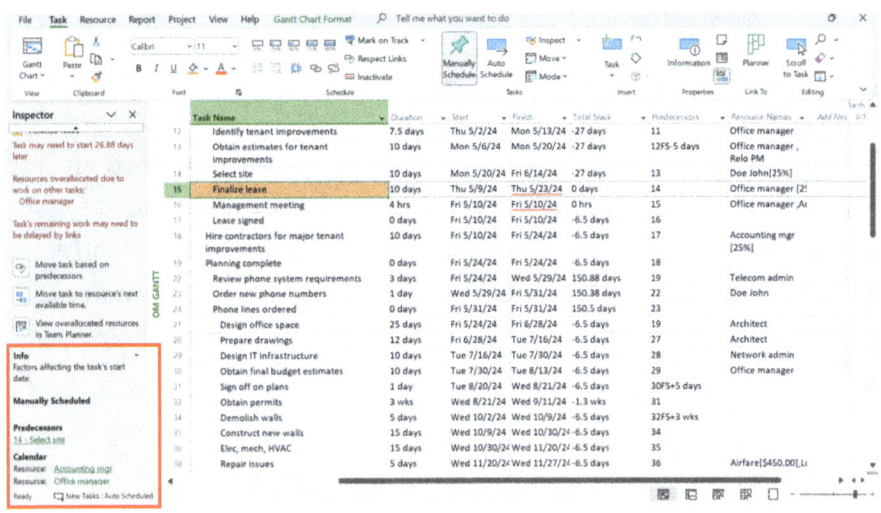

Figure 5-18. *Additional information for the task "Finalize lease"*

144

CHAPTER 5   FINE-TUNING A PROJECT SCHEDULE

Step 5: Before proceeding with the Inspector, let's review the timescale. Point at the vertical divider between the table and the timescale, and drag it to the left. This reveals the issue: Finalize lease, a manually scheduled task, is occurring before site selection completion, which is incorrect as shown in Figure 5-19.

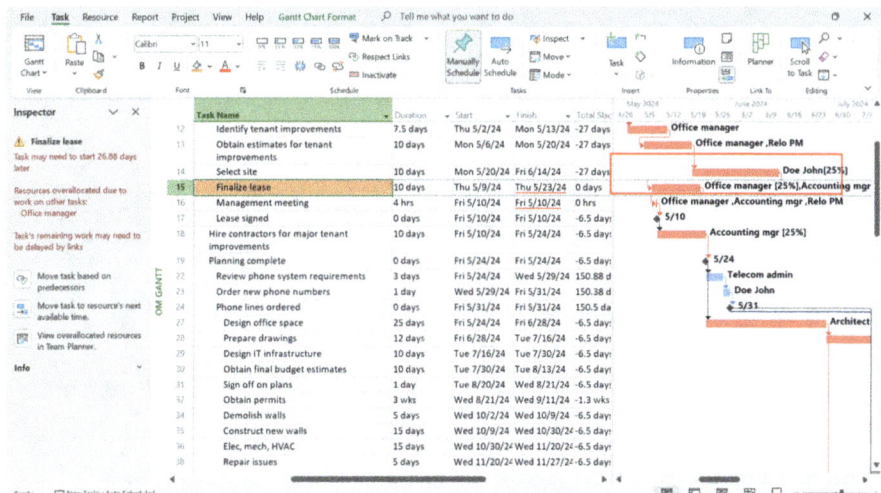

Figure 5-19. *Finalize lease, a manually scheduled task, is occurring before site selection completion*

Step 9: In the Inspector, select Move task based on predecessors to ensure it respects the links as shown in Figure 5-20. As a result, the finish-to-start relationship is now maintained.

145

CHAPTER 5   FINE-TUNING A PROJECT SCHEDULE

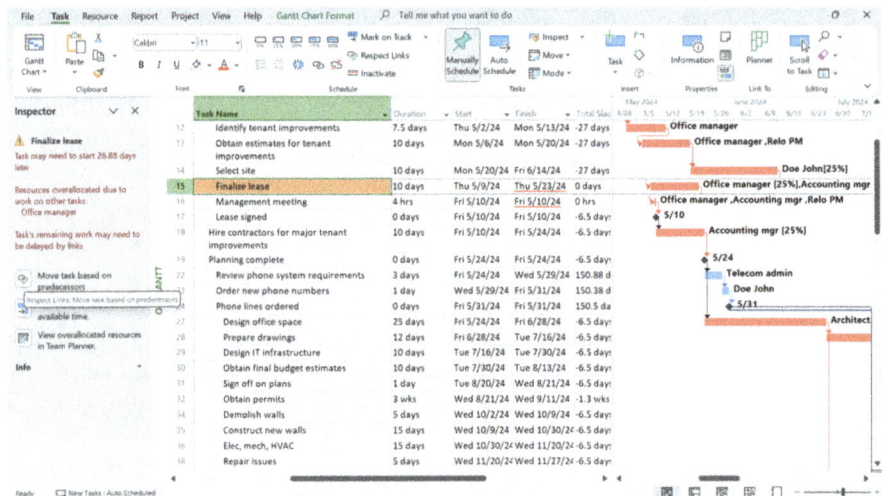

Figure 5-20. Select Move task based on predecessors

Step 10: Moreover, there is no red squiggly line under the finish date when scrolling through the table, indicating the scheduling problem has been resolved as shown in Figure 5-21.

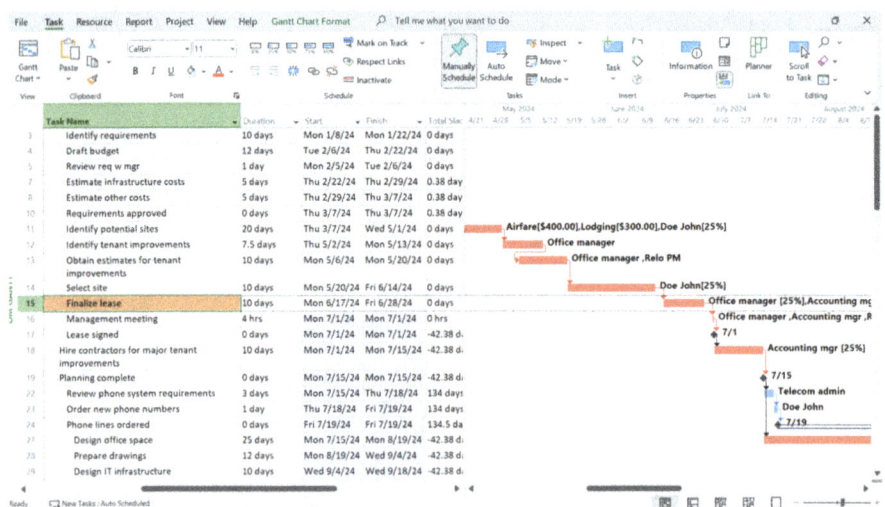

Figure 5-21. Scheduling problem has been resolved

146

CHAPTER 5   FINE-TUNING A PROJECT SCHEDULE

This overview demonstrates how to utilize the Task Inspector to investigate and resolve scheduling problems effectively. In the next section, we learn how to delay a task or an assignment to resolve project scheduling problems.

Delay a Task or Assignment

If resources are overallocated due to being assigned multiple concurrent tasks, you can delay specific tasks or assignments to resolve these overallocations. We will demonstrate this through below steps mentioned in this section.

Step 1: Scroll down the task list and observe that starting with task 45, several tasks display red resource overallocation icons in the indicators column as shown in Figure 5-22.

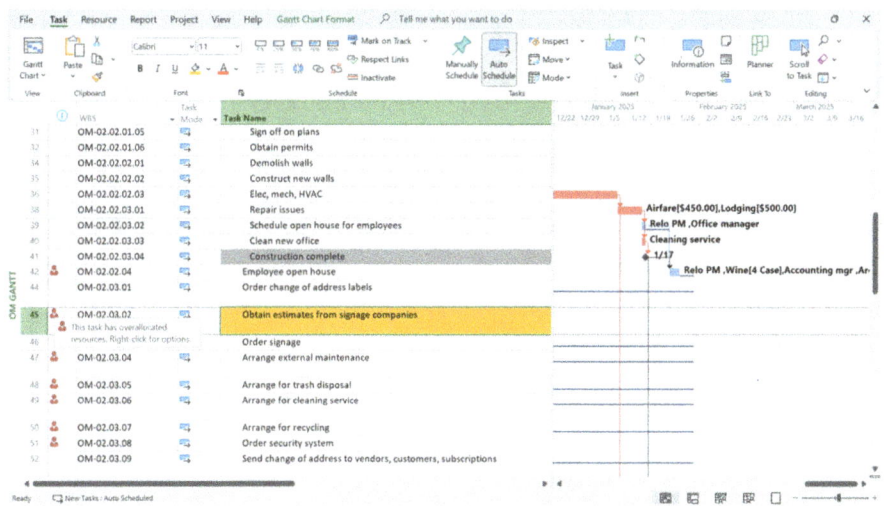

Figure 5-22. *Task 45 with overallocation problem*

147

CHAPTER 5   FINE-TUNING A PROJECT SCHEDULE

Step 2: Moreover, in the Resource Names column, most of these tasks are assigned to the office manager as shown in Figure 5-23. These tasks do not need to be performed in a specific sequence, so no links were added to put them in order.

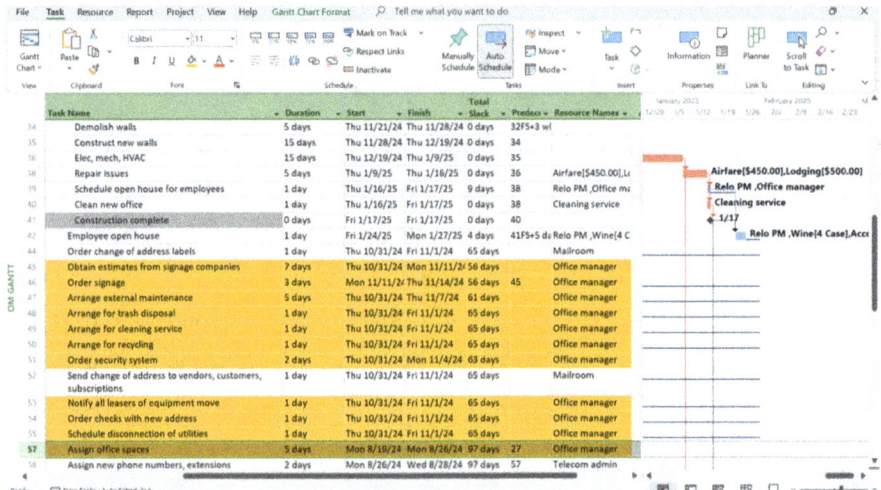

Figure 5-23. Tasks assigned to the office manager

Step 3: To add delays to reschedule the tasks for when the resource "Office manager" is available, navigate to the View tab, click on the Gantt Chart button, and then select More Views from the bottom of the menu as shown in Figure 5-24.

CHAPTER 5   FINE-TUNING A PROJECT SCHEDULE

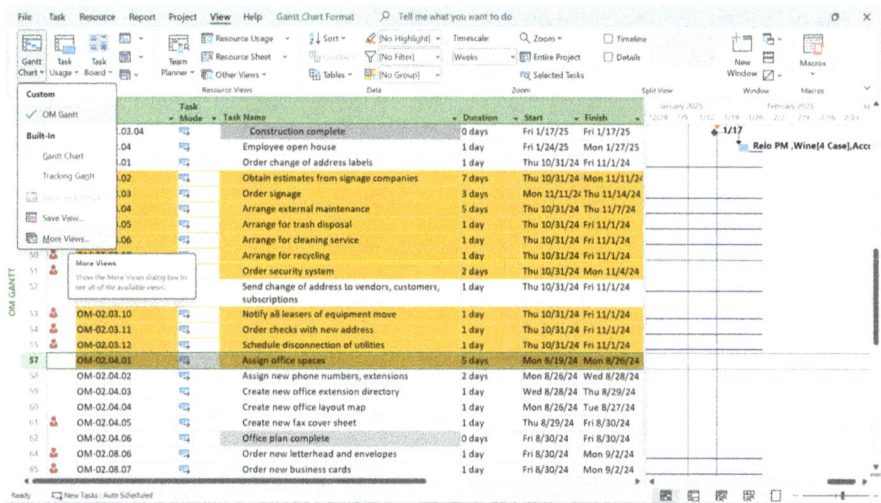

Figure 5-24. *Click Gantt Chart ➤ More Views under View tab*

Step 4: After clicking the More Views option, in the More Views dialog box, choose Leveling Gantt and then click Apply as shown in Figure 5-25.

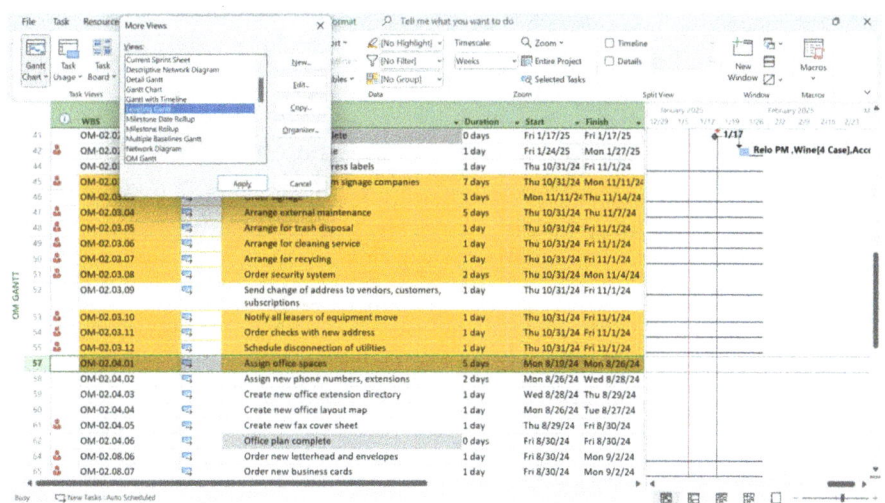

Figure 5-25. *Choose Leveling Gantt*

149

CHAPTER 5   FINE-TUNING A PROJECT SCHEDULE

Step 5: First, widen the column for the task names to better view the names. Next, examine the Leveling Delay column, which we will use to add delays to our tasks. Note that the duration may appear different as it uses "edays" instead of days, meaning elapsed time, inclusive of weekends and nonworking days as shown in Figure 5-26.

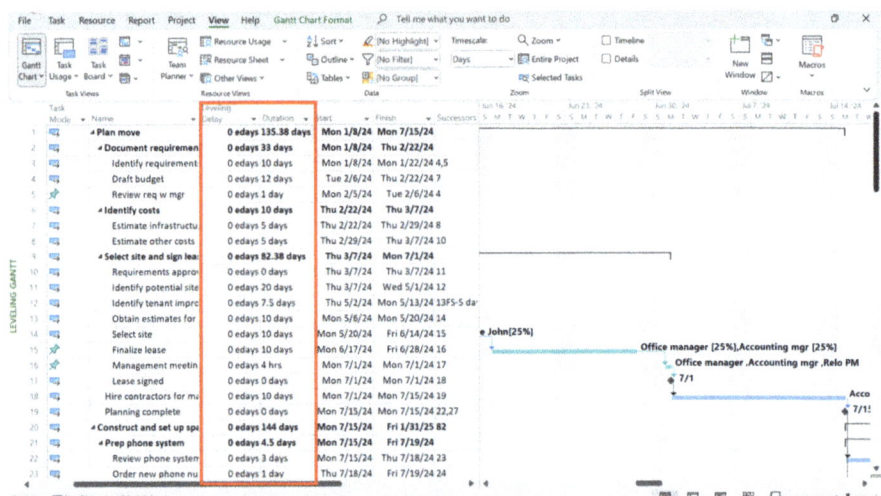

Figure 5-26. Leveling Gantt view

Step 6: Consider task 47 "Arrange external maintenance." Select it in the list, and then, at the right end of the Task tab, click Scroll to Task to view the task bars in the timescale as shown in Figure 5-27.

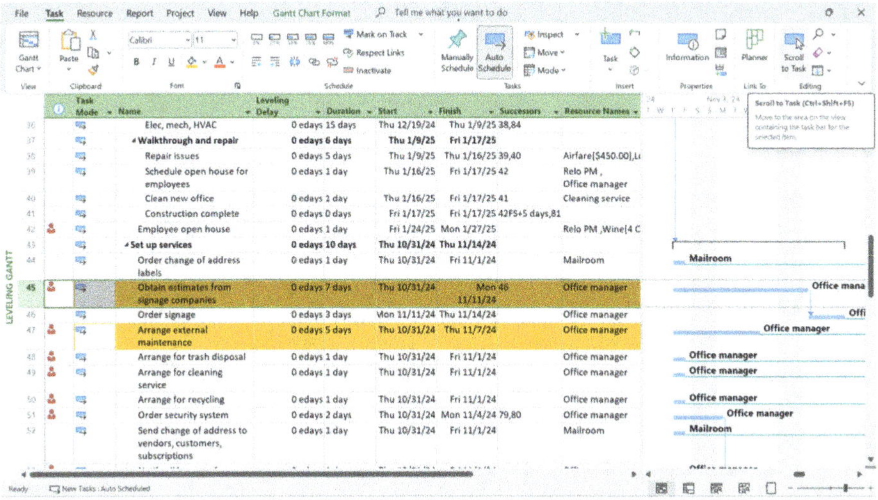

CHAPTER 5   FINE-TUNING A PROJECT SCHEDULE

Figure 5-27. Task 47 "Arrange external maintenance"

Step 7: Refer to Figure 5-27, where overallocation occurs because tasks 45 and 47 overlap; both are assigned to the resource name "Office manager" and they are both happening at the same time. We need to delay task 47, "Arrange external maintenance," until after the preceding two tasks that span 10 working days plus two weekends, totaling 14 elapsed days. Enter 14 edays in the Leveling Delay cell for task 47, and press Enter as shown in Figure 5-28.

151

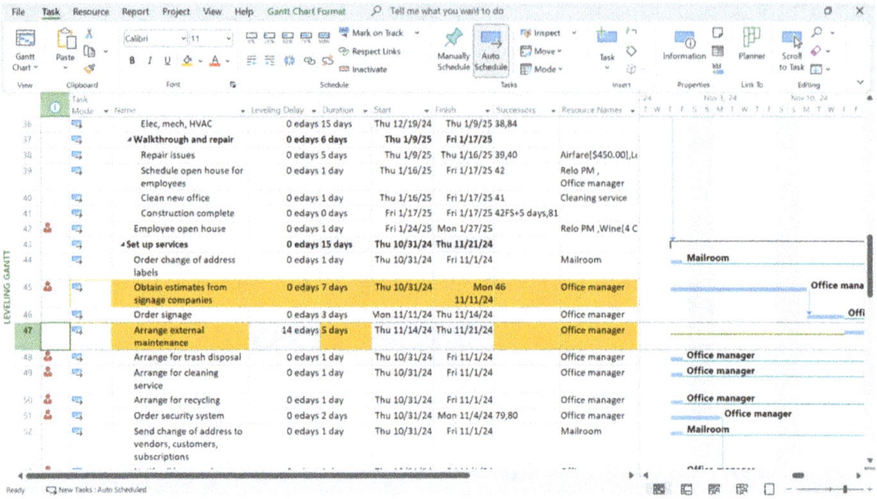

CHAPTER 5   FINE-TUNING A PROJECT SCHEDULE

Figure 5-28.   Update 14 ed in the Leveling Delay cell for task 47

In Figure 5-28, notice that the red overallocation icon disappears, indicating success. The task bar in the timescale also moves to start after "Order signage" finishes, represented by the narrow olive green bar at the beginning of the task bar signifying the leveling delay. This is how you delay a task to resolve resource overallocations. In the next section, we will discuss how to tackle inactive tasks.

Inactive Tasks in Microsoft Project

Inactive tasks available in Microsoft are useful for exploring alternative approaches for the same work or recording change requests that have not been approved. Inactive tasks appear in the schedule but are not considered in dates, cost, or resource workloads. Let's understand inactive tasks with the below steps.

Step 1: Go to the top-left corner of the table, right-click all cells box, and choose Summary on the shortcut menu as shown in Figure 5-29.

CHAPTER 5   FINE-TUNING A PROJECT SCHEDULE

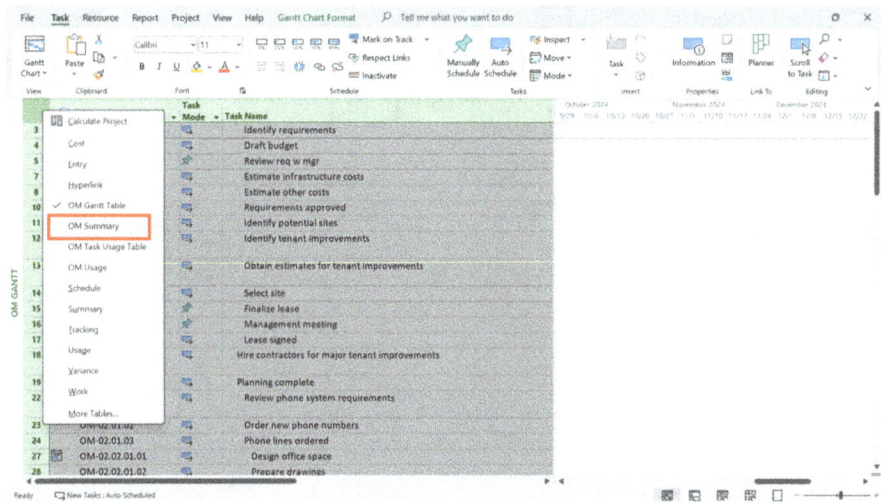

Figure 5-29. *Click on Summary shortcut*

Step 2: Then, go to the Gantt Chart Format tab, and turn on Project Summary Task and Summary Tasks in the Show/Hide section on the right side of the ribbon to see all tasks in the project as shown in Figure 5-30.

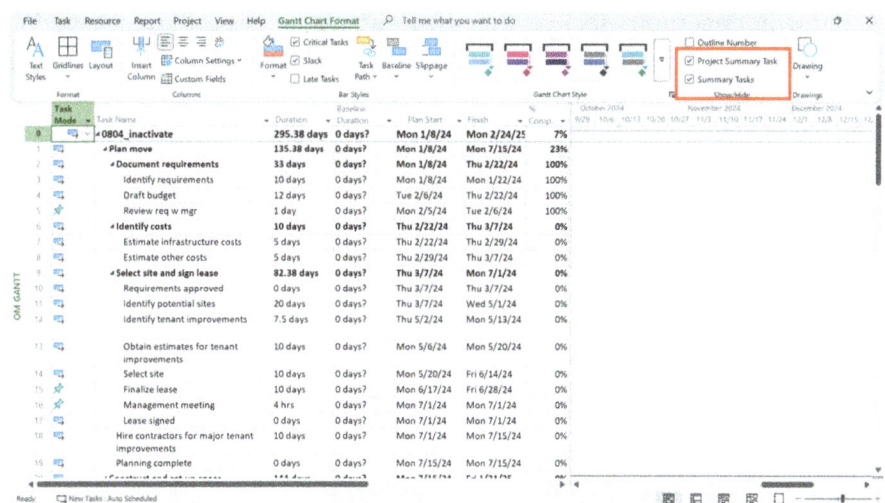

Figure 5-30. *Enable Project Summary Task and Summary Tasks*

153

CHAPTER 5   FINE-TUNING A PROJECT SCHEDULE

Widen a couple of columns to view the values. As of now, the project cost is about $222,000, the work is 2,056 hours, and the finish date is scheduled for February 24 as shown in Figure 5-31.

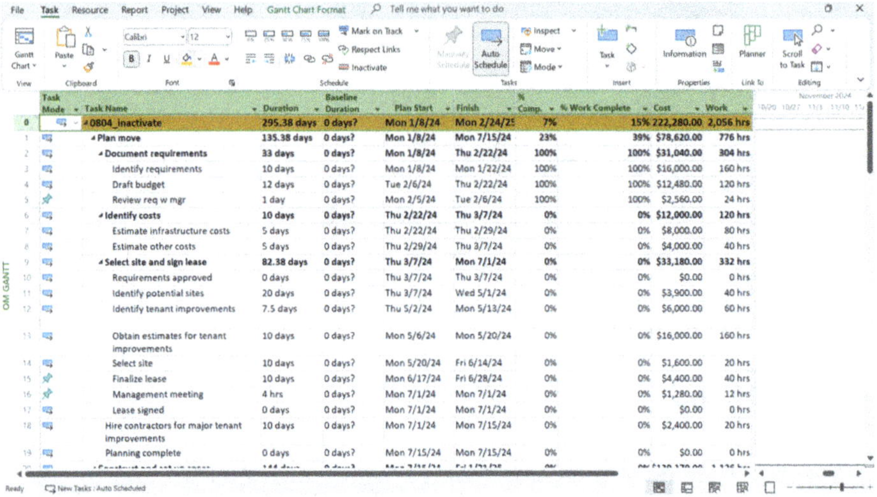

Figure 5-31.   Project details in row 0

If the management decides that the new space does not require major improvements, it will impact task 18, which involves hiring contractors for major improvements.

Step 3: Select task 18, and click Scroll to Task in the Quick Access Toolbar to view the task bar in the timescale as shown in Figure 5-32.

CHAPTER 5   FINE-TUNING A PROJECT SCHEDULE

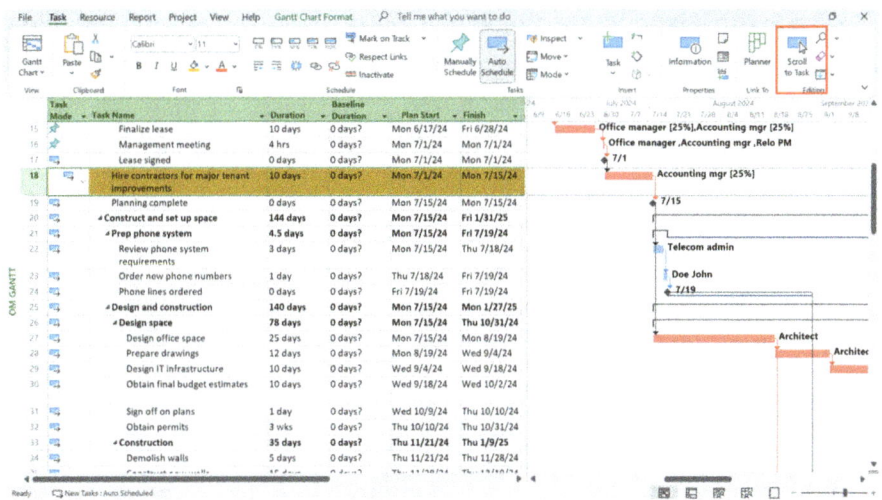

Figure 5-32. *View task 18 in the timescale*

Step 4: Make task 18 inactive to observe the changes it makes to the project. Go to the Task tab, and access Inactivate in the Schedule section as shown in Figure 5-33.

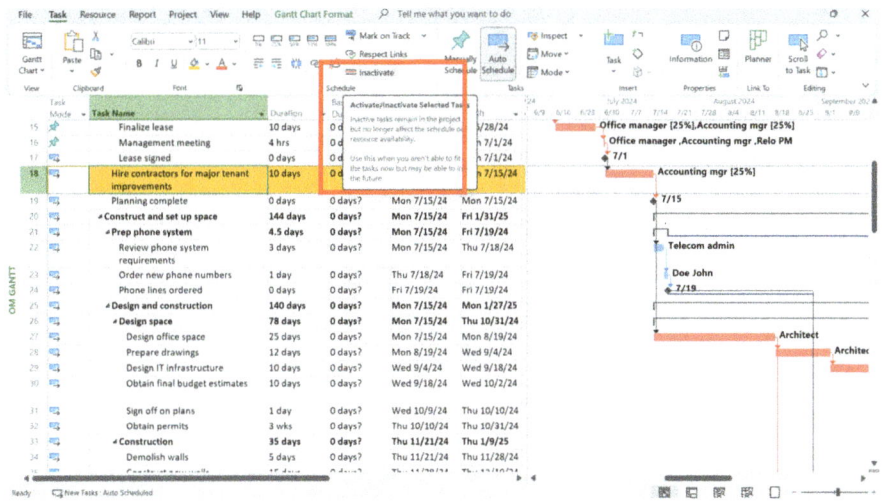

Figure 5-33. *Access Inactive option*

155

CHAPTER 5   FINE-TUNING A PROJECT SCHEDULE

Step 5: Click Inactivate as shown in Figure 5-34. The text in the table will turn gray with strikethrough, and the task bar in the timescale will be white with a gray border. Successors to the inactive task called "Planning complete" will be rescheduled earlier as if the task is no longer present.

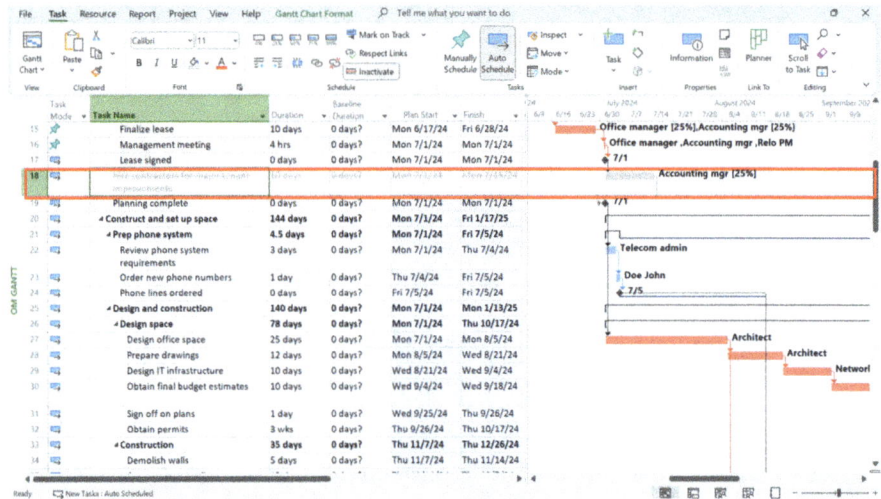

Figure 5-34.   Inactive task 18

The project summary task will show a decrease in cost by a couple thousand dollars, the work reduced to 2,036 hours, and the finish date moved up to February 10 as shown in Figure 5-35.

156

CHAPTER 5   FINE-TUNING A PROJECT SCHEDULE

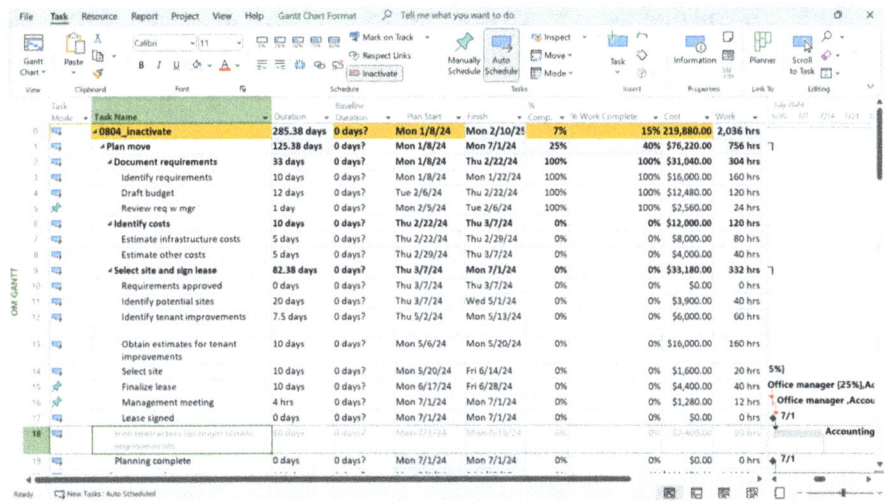

Figure 5-35. Updated Project Summary Task

Step 6: Inactive tasks can still be edited while inactive. For example, the duration of hiring contractors can be reduced from ten days to five days as shown in Figure 5-36.

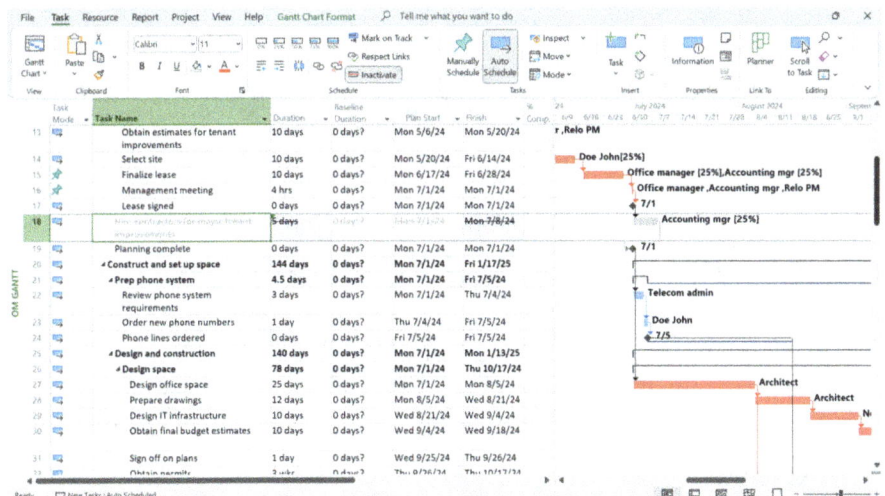

Figure 5-36. Update to the inactive task 18

157

CHAPTER 5   FINE-TUNING A PROJECT SCHEDULE

Step 7: If you decide to reactivate the task, select it again, go to the Task tab, and click Inactivate in the Schedule section. The task will become active again, retaining any changes made to its duration as shown in Figure 5-37.

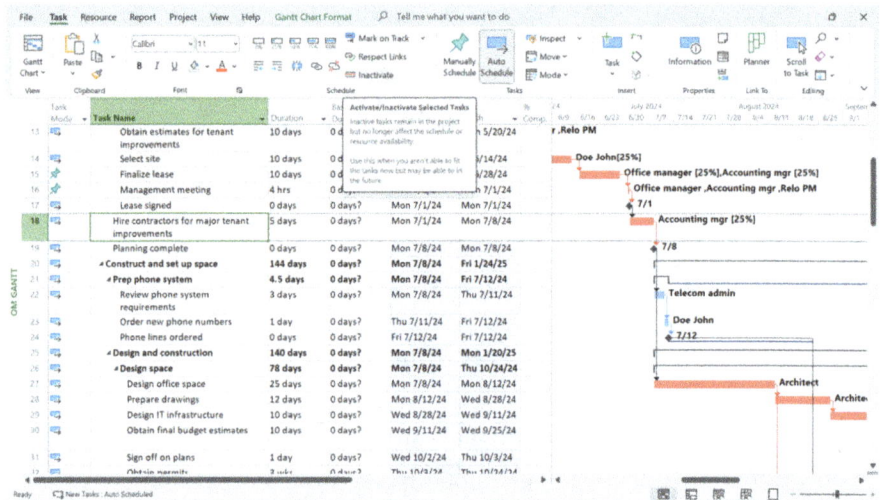

Figure 5-37. *Task 18 reactivated successfully*

This is how tasks can be inactivated when they are not meant to affect your schedule. In the next and final section, let's identify schedule problems.

Identify Project Schedule Problems

Project offers several tools to help identify potential issues that could delay the schedule. By utilizing these tools, you can develop strategies to address problems before they escalate. Let us start by examining the Tracking Gantt.

158

CHAPTER 5 FINE-TUNING A PROJECT SCHEDULE

Step 1: First, navigate to the bottom half of the Gantt Chart button as shown in Figure 5-38, click, and then select Tracking Gantt as shown in Figure 5-39.

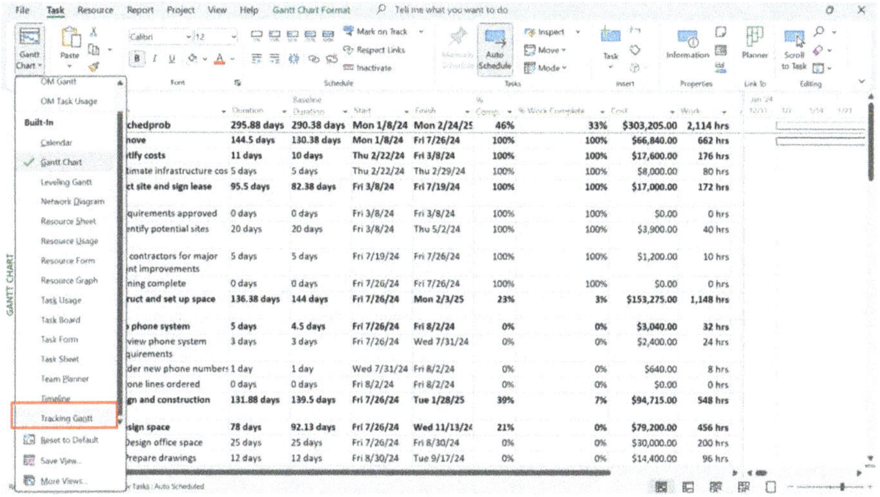

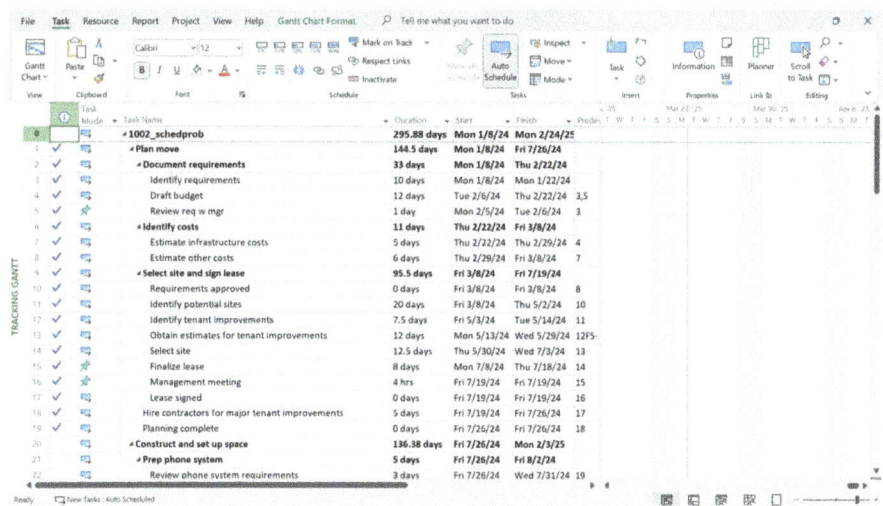

Figure 5-38. *Navigate to the Tracking Gantt*

Figure 5-39. *Tracking Gantt view*

159

CHAPTER 5   FINE-TUNING A PROJECT SCHEDULE

Step 2: Next, choose the Project Summary Task, and use the "Scroll to Task" option available on the Quick Access Toolbar as shown in Figure 5-40. This action will allow you to view the project from the beginning.

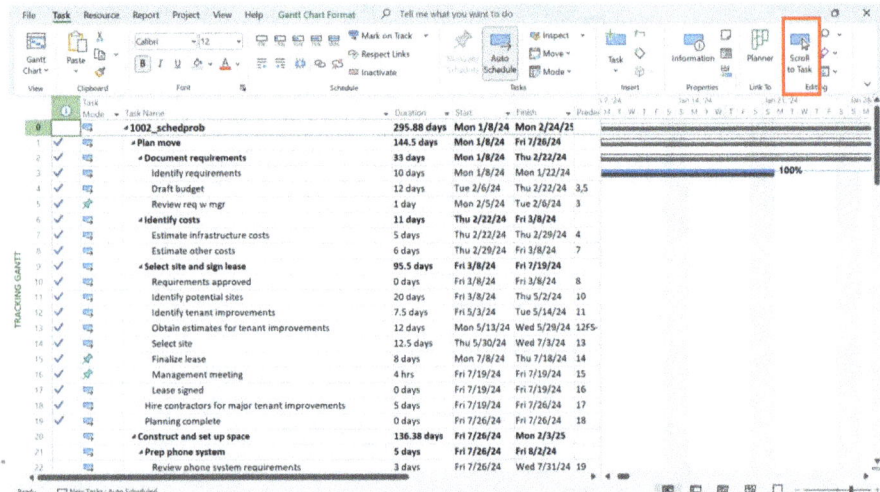

Figure 5-40. *To view the project schedule from the beginning*

Step 4: Now, adjust the timescale units from days to weeks. On the View tab, within the Timescale section, click the down arrow, and select weeks as shown in Figure 5-41. This change will display the task bars more compactly. In this view, the dark gray bars represent the baseline, while the blue bars indicate the current schedule as shown in Figure 5-42.

160

CHAPTER 5   FINE-TUNING A PROJECT SCHEDULE

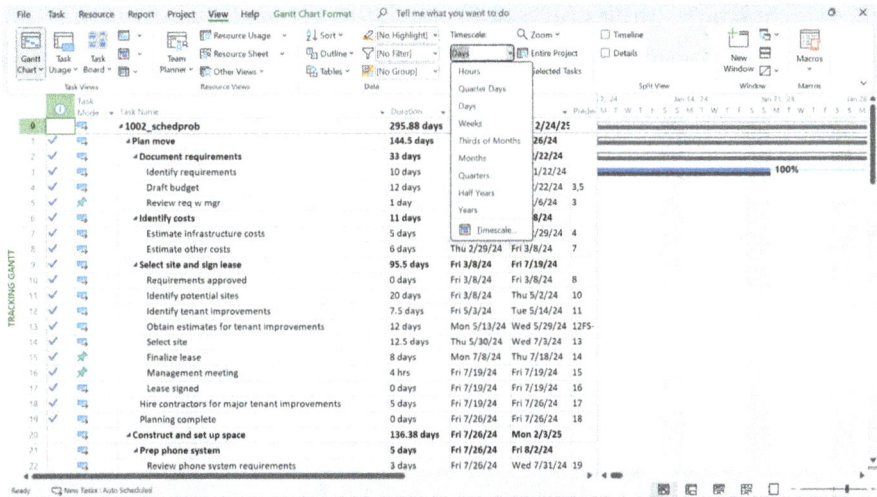

Figure 5-41. Change timescale from days to weeks

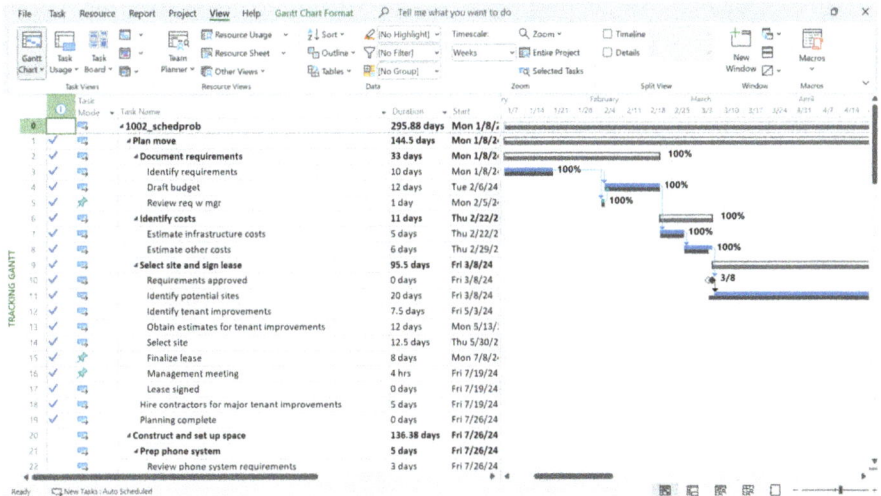

Figure 5-42. Task bars become more compact

Initially, the project appears to be on track, with tasks starting and finishing as planned. However, some tasks introduce delays, causing the gray bars to precede the current schedule on the timescale. To identify

CHAPTER 5 FINE-TUNING A PROJECT SCHEDULE

tasks starting late, apply a filter by going to the View tab, selecting the Filter box, clicking the down arrow, and choosing More Filters as shown in Figure 5-43.

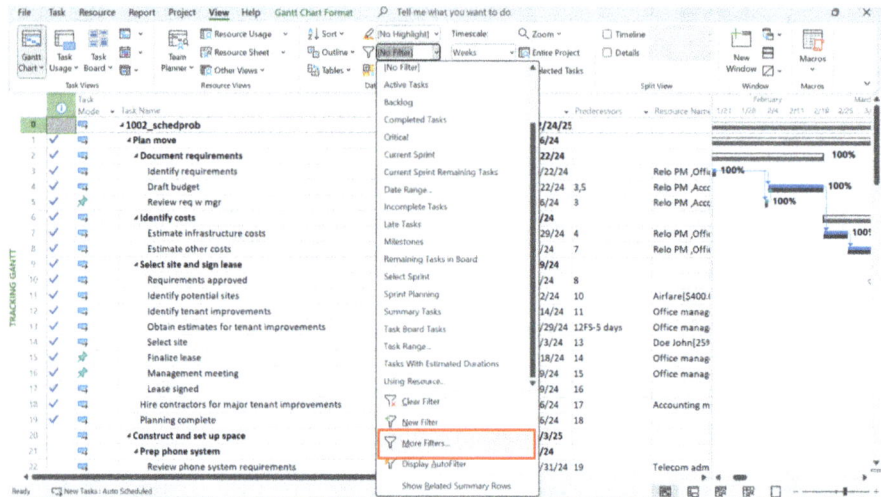

Figure 5-43. *Select More Filters*

Step 5: Select the "Should Start By" filter as shown in Figure 5-44 and click Apply. Enter the comparison date, for instance, July 28, 2024, and confirm as shown in Figure 5-45.

CHAPTER 5   FINE-TUNING A PROJECT SCHEDULE

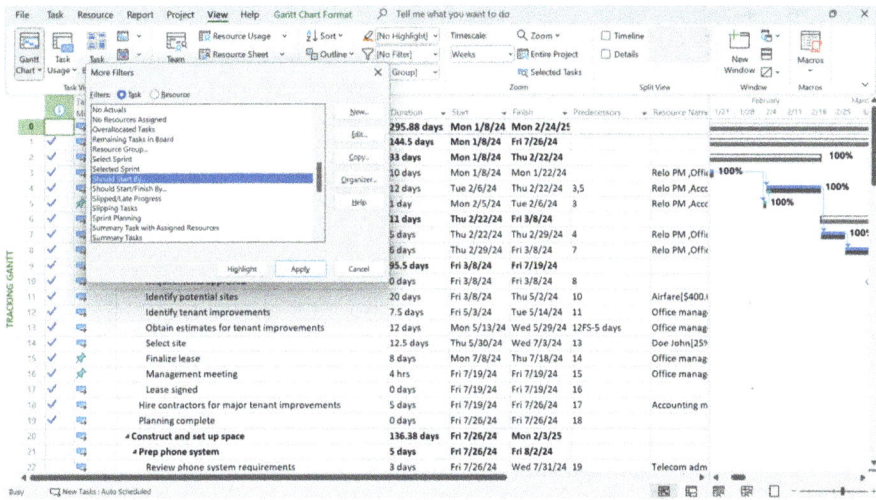

Figure 5-44. Select "Should Start by" filter

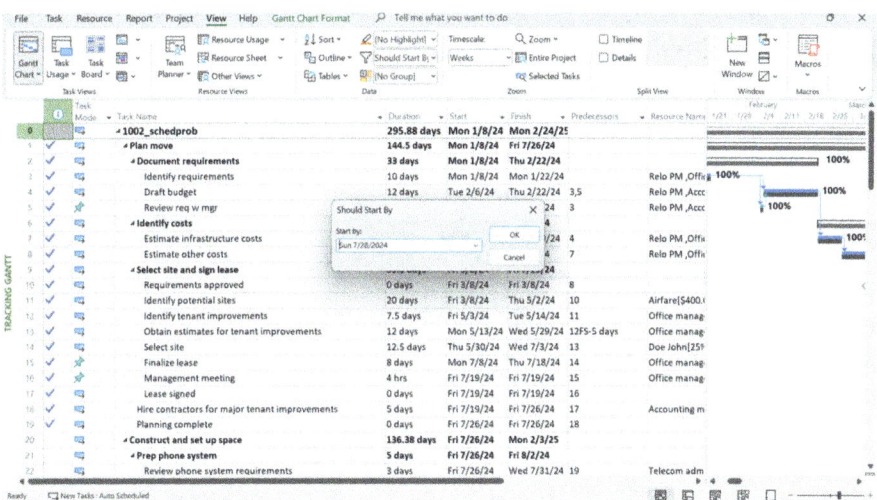

Figure 5-45. Apply date July 28, 2024

The filter will highlight tasks without actual start dates that should have commenced by the specified date as shown in Figure 5-46. Assigned resources to determine the reasons for the delays, which may be due to preceding tasks running late.

163

CHAPTER 5   FINE-TUNING A PROJECT SCHEDULE

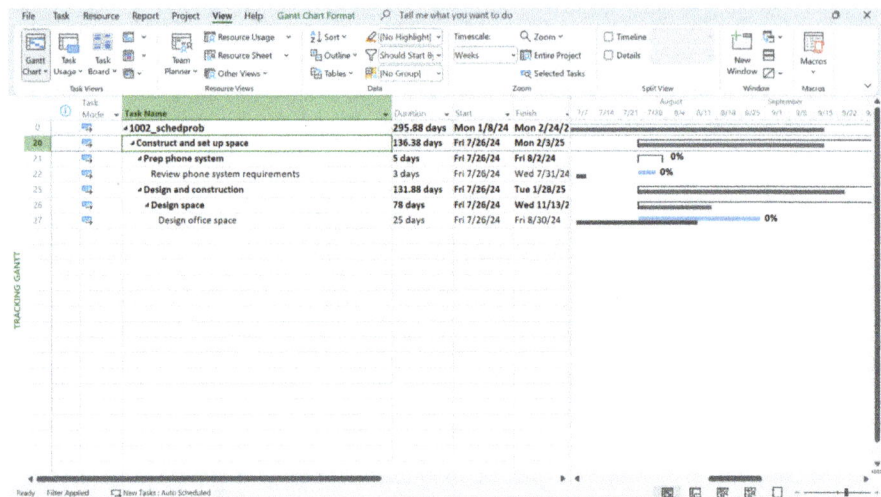

Figure 5-46. Only tasks that "Should Start By" July 28, 2024

Step 6: Next, apply another filter by repeating the previous steps and choosing "Slipping Tasks" as shown in Figure 5-47.

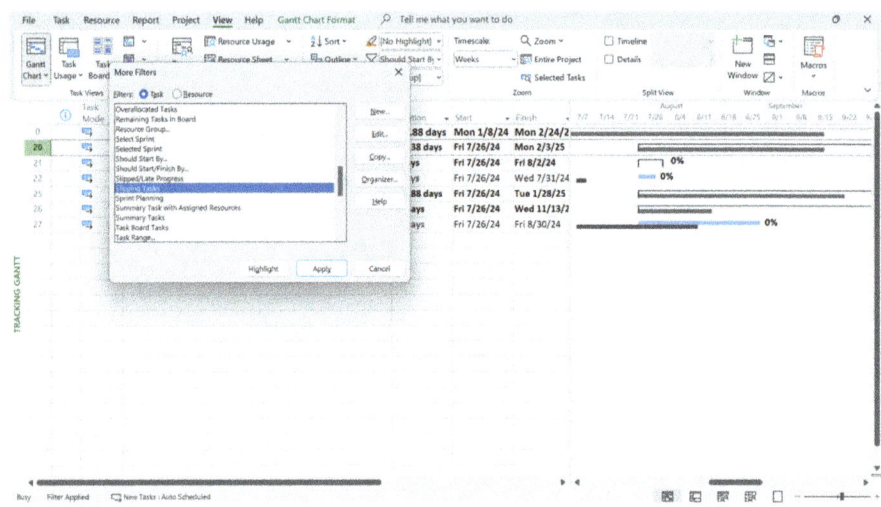

Figure 5-47. Apply filter Slipping Tasks

CHAPTER 5   FINE-TUNING A PROJECT SCHEDULE

This Slipping Task filter identifies tasks that started late or are scheduled to start late or are taking longer than anticipated. For additional clarity, go to the Gantt Chart Format tab and click the Slippage button, and then select the baseline as shown in Figure 5-48 to compare the slippage. Narrow black bars will indicate slippage from the baseline start date to the scheduled start date as shown in Figure 5-49.

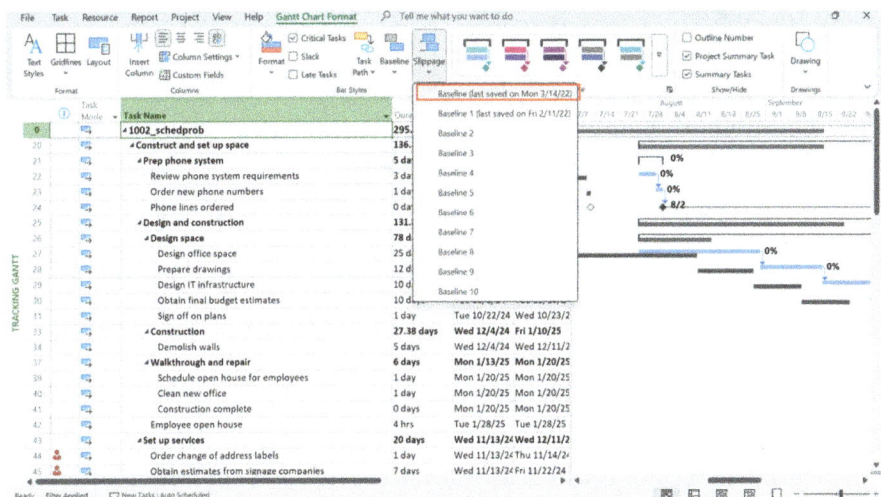

Figure 5-48. Access baseline Slippage

165

CHAPTER 5 FINE-TUNING A PROJECT SCHEDULE

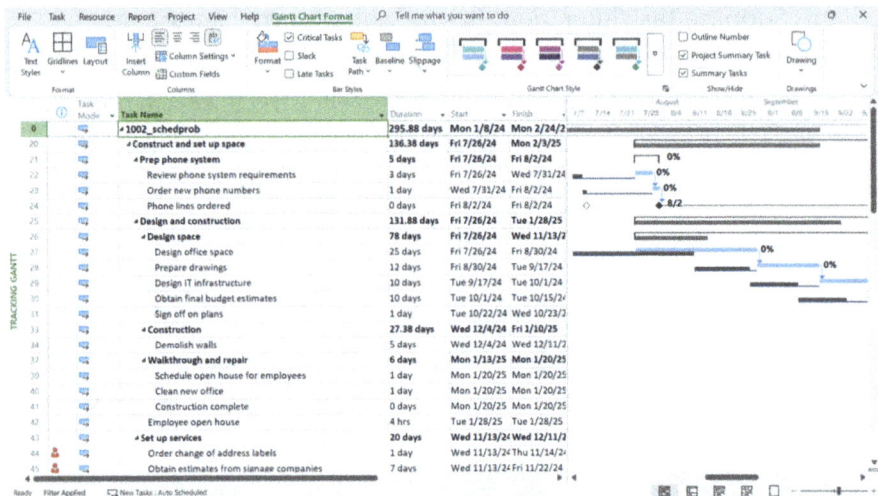

Figure 5-49. *Slippage from the baseline start date to the scheduled start date*

These are some ways that Microsoft Project features collectively assist in identifying scheduling issues.

Finally, we have to come to the end of this chapter. In this chapter, we have learned fine-tuning a project schedule in Microsoft Project which involves reviewing the critical path, identifying schedule issues with Task Inspector, delaying a task or assignment and managing inactive tasks, and finally identifying project scheduling problems. In the upcoming chapter, we will take a deep dive into budget and cost management in Microsoft Project to estimate project costs, track expenses, and manage budgets.

CHAPTER 6

Budget and Cost Management Using Microsoft Project

In the last chapter, we have seen how to fine-tune a project schedule in Microsoft Project, which involves reviewing the critical path, identifying schedule issues with Task Inspector, delaying a task or assignment and managing inactive tasks, and finally identifying project scheduling problems. This chapter covers budget and cost management in project management, dealing with challenging project costs, and managing work and resource costs. It includes setting up work resources; handling resource capacities, pay rates, and working calendars; and setting resource costs.

Introduction

Budget and cost management are crucial aspects of project management, ensuring that projects are completed within the allocated budget and resources. Microsoft Project is a powerful tool that helps project managers plan, track, and manage budgets and costs effectively. Here's a detailed explanation of how to use Microsoft Project for budget and cost management.

Setting Up Your Project

- **Define Project Scope and Objectives**: Start by clearly defining the scope and objectives of your project. This includes identifying the deliverables, milestones, and tasks required to complete the project.

- **Create a Work Breakdown Structure (WBS)**: Break down the project into smaller, manageable tasks. This hierarchical decomposition helps in organizing and planning the project effectively.

Budget Planning

- **Estimate Costs**: For each task in the WBS, estimate the costs associated with labor, materials, equipment, and other resources. Microsoft Project allows you to input these cost estimates directly into the task details.

- **Define Resource Rates**: Set up resource rates for different types of resources (e.g., hourly rates for labor, unit costs for materials). This helps in calculating the total cost for each task based on the resources assigned.

- **Create a Budget**: Use the cost estimates and resource rates to create a project budget. Microsoft Project provides tools to aggregate these costs and generate a comprehensive budget for the entire project.

Cost Tracking

- **Assign Resources to Tasks**: Allocate resources to specific tasks in the project. Microsoft Project will automatically calculate the cost based on the resource rates and the duration of the tasks.

- **Track Actual Costs**: As the project progresses, track the actual costs incurred for each task. Microsoft Project allows you to input actual costs and compare them with the estimated costs.

- **Monitor Variances**: Use the built-in reporting tools to monitor variances between the estimated and actual costs. This helps in identifying any deviations from the budget and taking corrective actions.

Cost Control

- **Baseline Budget**: Set a baseline budget at the beginning of the project. This serves as a reference point for comparing actual costs throughout the project life cycle.

- **Earned Value Management (EVM)**: Utilize EVM techniques to measure project performance and progress. Microsoft Project supports EVM calculations, providing insights into cost performance and schedule performance.

- **Adjustments and Forecasting**: Based on the variances and EVM analysis, make necessary adjustments to the project plan. Microsoft Project allows you to forecast future costs and make informed decisions to keep the project within budget.

Reporting and Analysis

- **Generate Reports**: Microsoft Project offers a variety of reporting options to visualize cost data. Generate reports on budget status, cost variances, resource utilization, and more.

- **Analyze Trends**: Use the reporting tools to analyze trends in cost performance. Identify patterns and areas where costs are consistently higher or lower than expected.

- **Stakeholder Communication**: Share the reports with stakeholders to keep them informed about the budget status and any potential issues. Effective communication helps in managing expectations and ensuring transparency.

Best Practices

- **Regular Monitoring**: Continuously monitor costs and budget throughout the project. Regular updates and reviews help in keeping the project on track.

- **Proactive Management**: Be proactive in managing costs. Identify potential risks and take preventive measures to avoid budget overruns.

- **Use Templates**: Microsoft Project offers templates for different types of projects. Utilize these templates to streamline budget and cost management processes.

- **Training and Support**: Ensure that project team members are trained in using Microsoft Project effectively. Utilize available support resources and documentation to enhance your skills.

In conclusion, budget and cost management are essential for the success of any project. Microsoft Project provides robust tools and features to help project managers plan, track, and control costs effectively. By following best practices and leveraging the capabilities of Microsoft Project, you can ensure that your projects are completed within budget and deliver the desired outcomes

Handle Tricky Project Costs

With inflation, costs usually increase over time. If you're managing a long-term project, you must account for cost increases mid-project. Let's see how to set up changing costs in a project.

First, open the Resource Sheet as shown in Figure 6-1, and look at the network admin's rate, $150 per hour, and the network tech's rate, $125 per hour, as shown in Figure 6-2.

CHAPTER 6   BUDGET AND COST MANAGEMENT USING MICROSOFT PROJECT

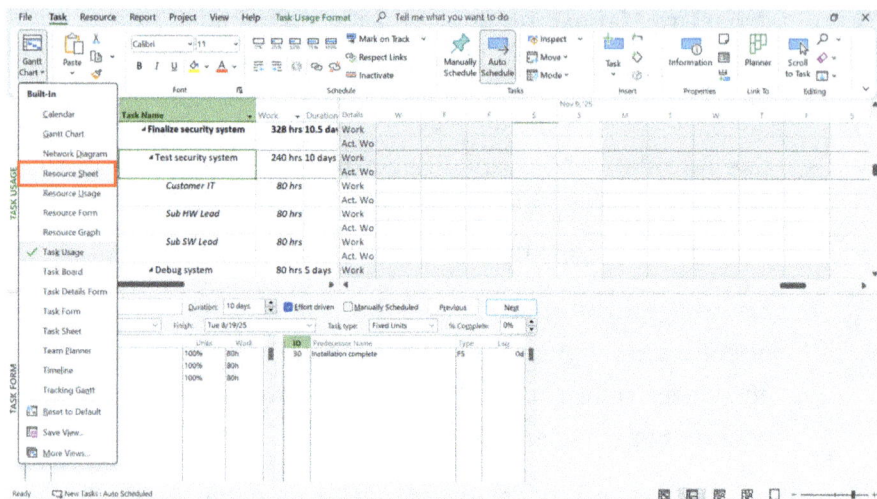

Figure 6-1. *Access to Resource Sheet*

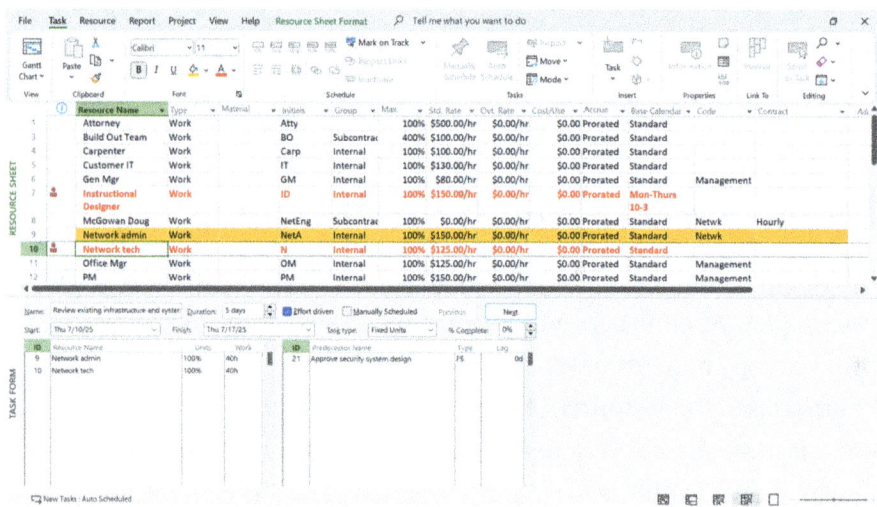

Figure 6-2. *Network admin and tech rates*

If these rates rise on August 1, 2025, double-click the Network admin row to open the Resource Information dialog box, and go to the Cost tab as shown in Figure 6-3.

172

CHAPTER 6   BUDGET AND COST MANAGEMENT USING MICROSOFT PROJECT

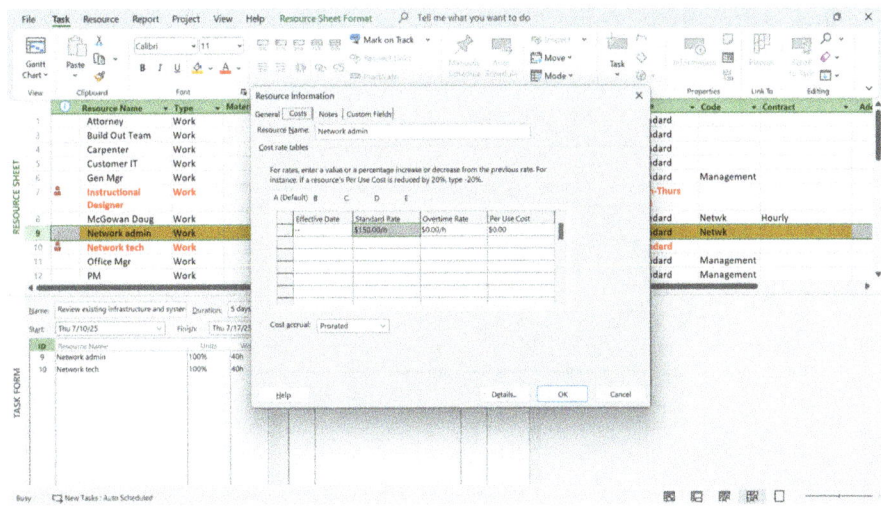

Figure 6-3. Cost tab

In Cost table A, add the new rate effective from August 1, 2025, increasing by 10% (enter "10%" to automatically calculate $165 per hour), and click OK to save changes as shown in Figure 6-4.

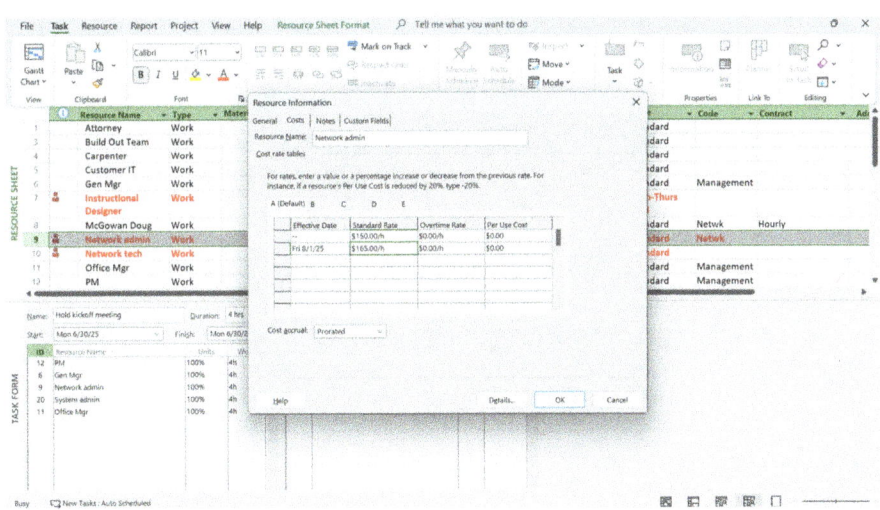

Figure 6-4. Update cost to $165

173

CHAPTER 6   BUDGET AND COST MANAGEMENT USING MICROSOFT PROJECT

Now, switch to the Gantt Chart as shown in Figure 6-5.

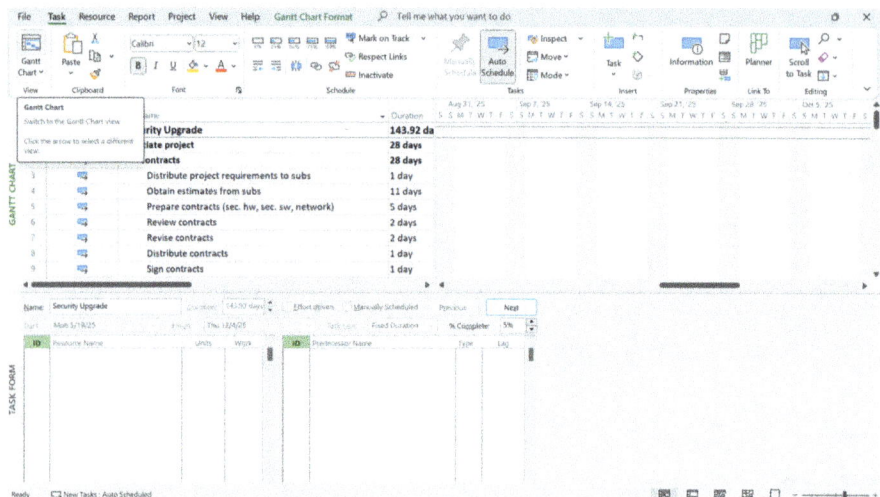

Figure 6-5. Gantt Chart view

Check task 39 ("Review existing infrastructure and system requirements") before August 1 at $150 per hour as shown in Figures 6-6, 6-7, and 6-8.

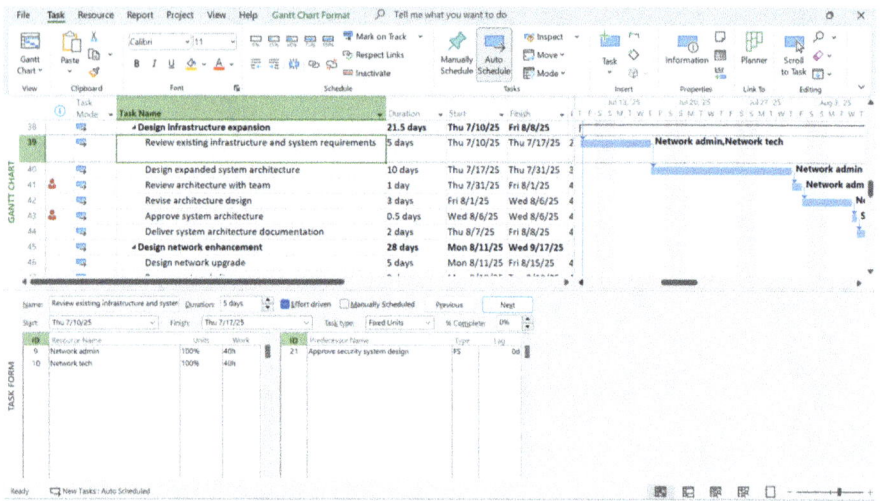

Figure 6-6. Task 39 runs before August 1 as per start date

CHAPTER 6   BUDGET AND COST MANAGEMENT USING MICROSOFT PROJECT

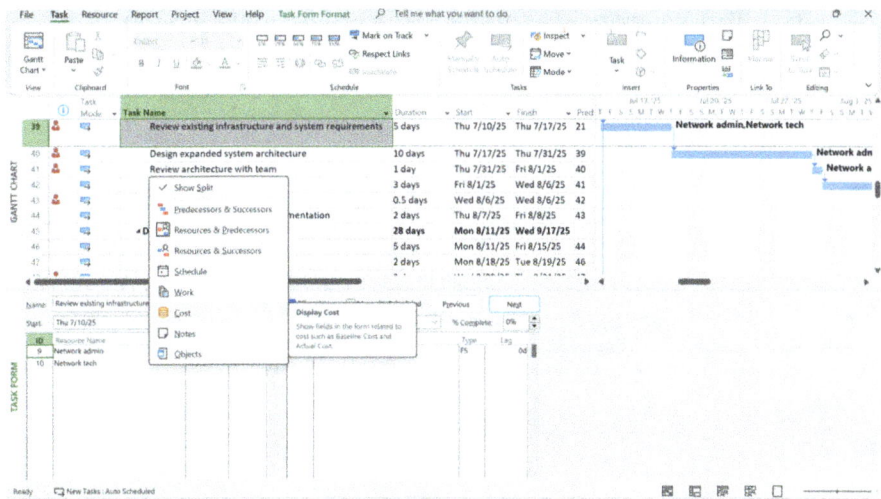

Figure 6-7. Access Cost table for task 39

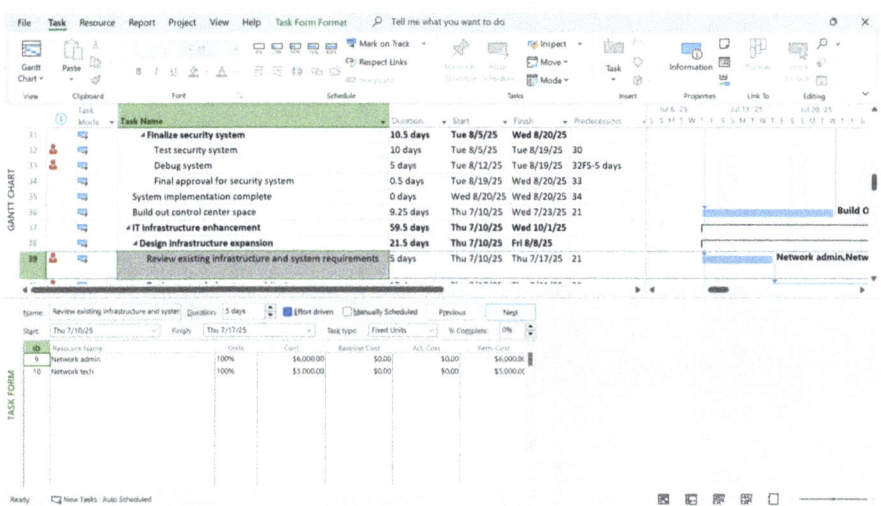

Figure 6-8. Task 39 runs at $150

175

CHAPTER 6   BUDGET AND COST MANAGEMENT USING MICROSOFT PROJECT

For task 39, total work is 40 hours, i.e., 150x40 = 6000 @ $150.

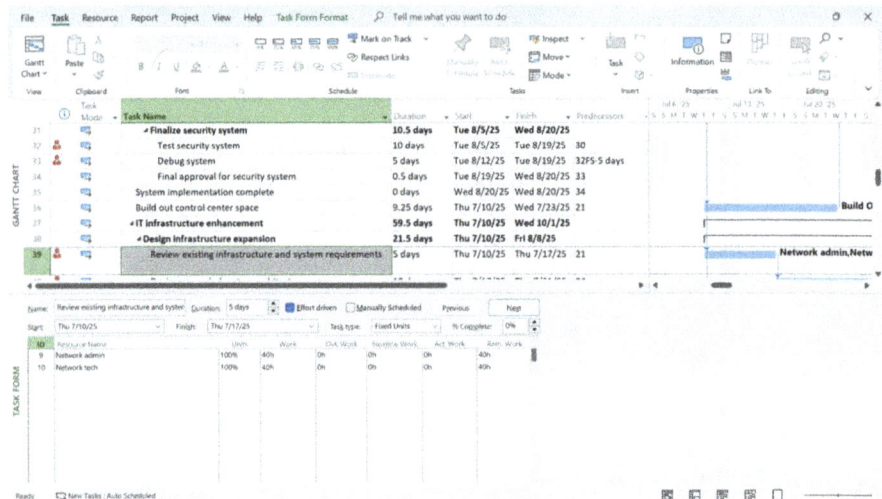

Figure 6-9. *Work View for Task 39*

For Task 49 - "Review network design" estimated cost after August 1st is $165 per hour shown through Figures 6-10 to 6-12 respectively.

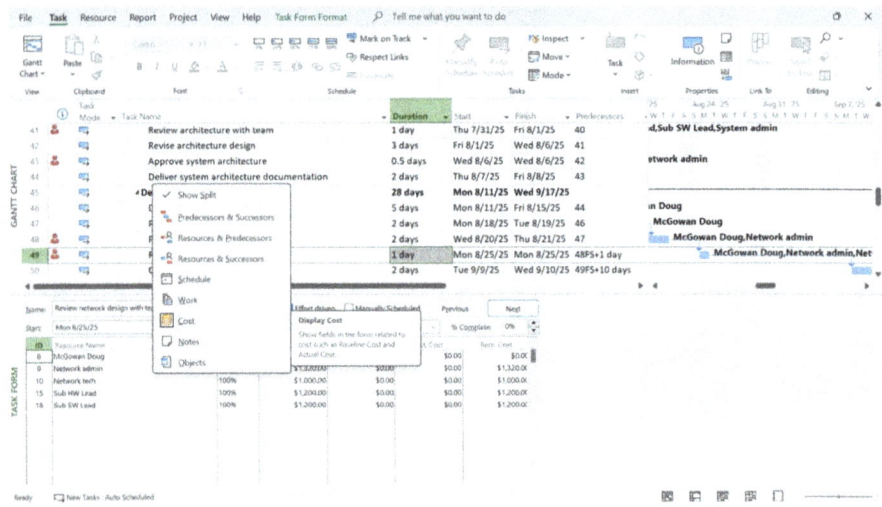

Figure 6-10. *Cost view of task 49*

CHAPTER 6   BUDGET AND COST MANAGEMENT USING MICROSOFT PROJECT

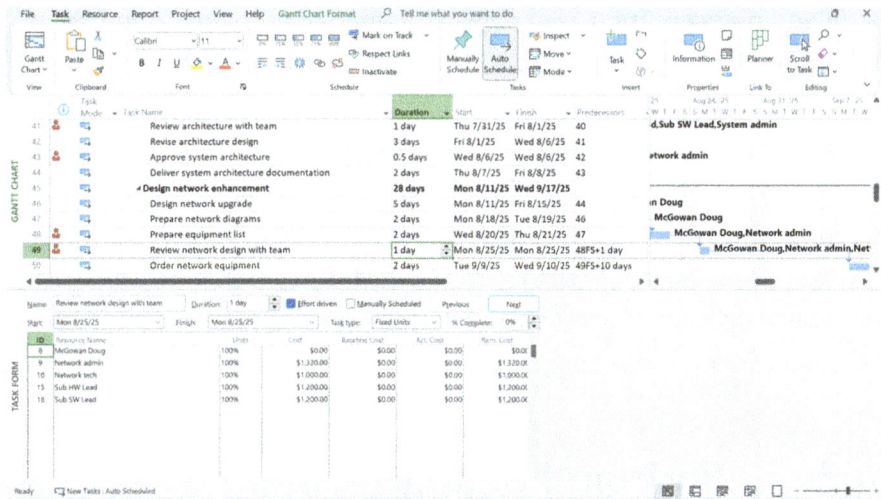

Figure 6-11. *Task 49 at the Rate of $165*

For task 49, total work is 40 hours, i.e., 165x8 hours = 1320 @ $165.

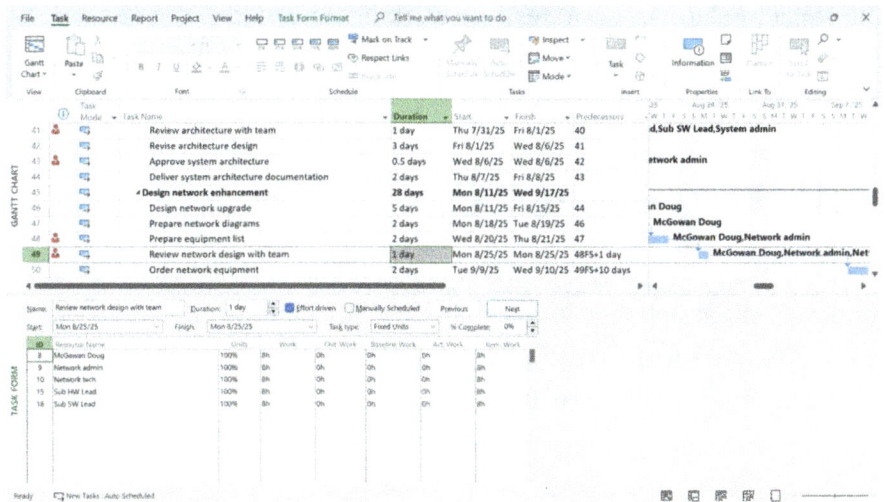

Figure 6-12. *Work view of task 49*

177

CHAPTER 6   BUDGET AND COST MANAGEMENT USING MICROSOFT PROJECT

In Summary, we increased network administration rate from $150 to $165 thus, it has impacted tasks 39 and 49 respectively which demonstrates Microsoft Project capabilities to handle to tricky costs. Apply Cost tables changes similarly to overtime rates, per-use costs, and material resources and experience how Microsoft Project handles tricky cost.

For practice, try changing the cost rate for another resource. E.g., set the network tech's rate to $130 per hour starting August 1st, 2025, and reduce the exterior cameras' cost to $80 starting May 5th, 2025, to experience tricky cost management experience with Microsoft Project.

Budget Work and Resource Cost

In this section, we will comprehensively cover budgeting for work and cost resources. The section begins with instructions on how to compile a list of personnel required for your project. We will then enhance this list with capacity settings, pay rates, and working times. Subsequently, we will transition to cost resources, providing guidance on how to document various types of project expenses.

Set Up Work Resources

For planning, identifying the individuals required to complete tasks is an important initial step in resource planning. You enter your resource list on the resource sheet, but how do you get there? Let's use the View tab instead as shown in Figure 6-13.

CHAPTER 6 BUDGET AND COST MANAGEMENT USING MICROSOFT PROJECT

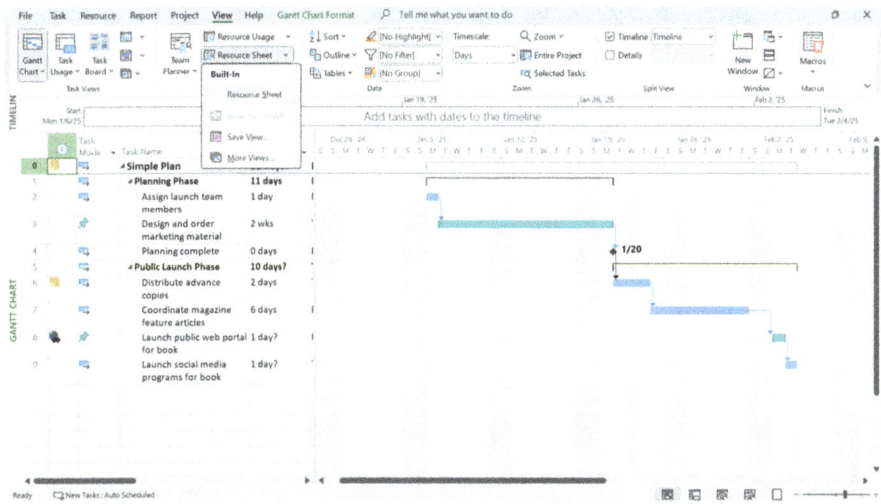

Figure 6-13. Navigation to Resource Sheet

You may have noticed a Gantt Chart button here that looks similar to the one on the Task tab, but there's a key difference. When you click the down arrow here, the list is long as shown in Figure 6-14, but on the View tab, it is short as shown in Figure 6-15.

179

CHAPTER 6   BUDGET AND COST MANAGEMENT USING MICROSOFT PROJECT

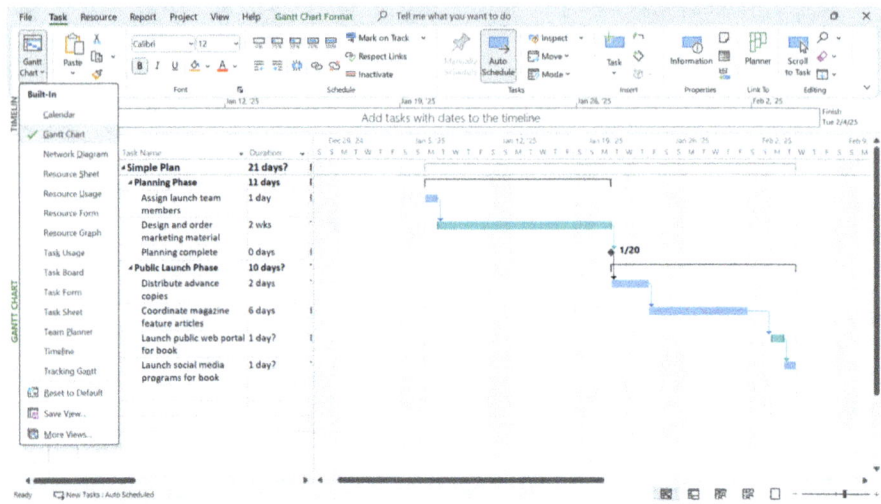

Figure 6-14. *Navigation of Gantt Chart under Task tab*

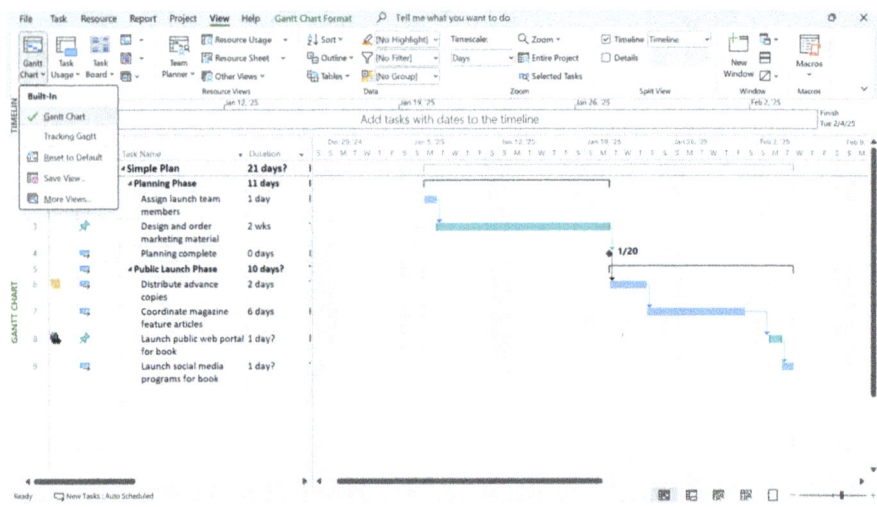

Figure 6-15. *Navigation of Gantt Chart under View tab*

Above Gantt Charts described in the Figures 6-14 and 6-15 choice ensures that all other view options are now buttons you can click, such as the Resource Sheet.

180

CHAPTER 6   BUDGET AND COST MANAGEMENT USING MICROSOFT PROJECT

If you get confused about the Gantt chart drop-down not displaying everything, just return to the Task tab. I am clicking "Resource Sheet" and it appears blank as shown in Figures 6-16 and 6-17, respectively.

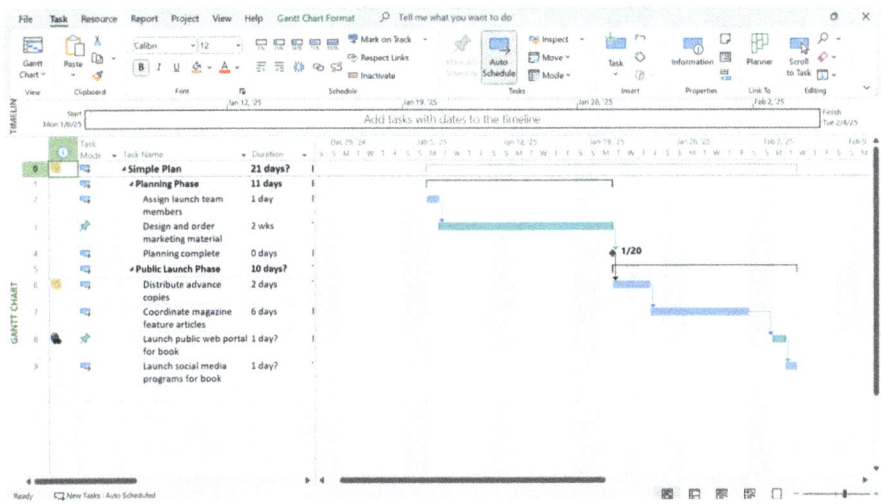

Figure 6-16.   Navigation of Resource Sheet through Task tab

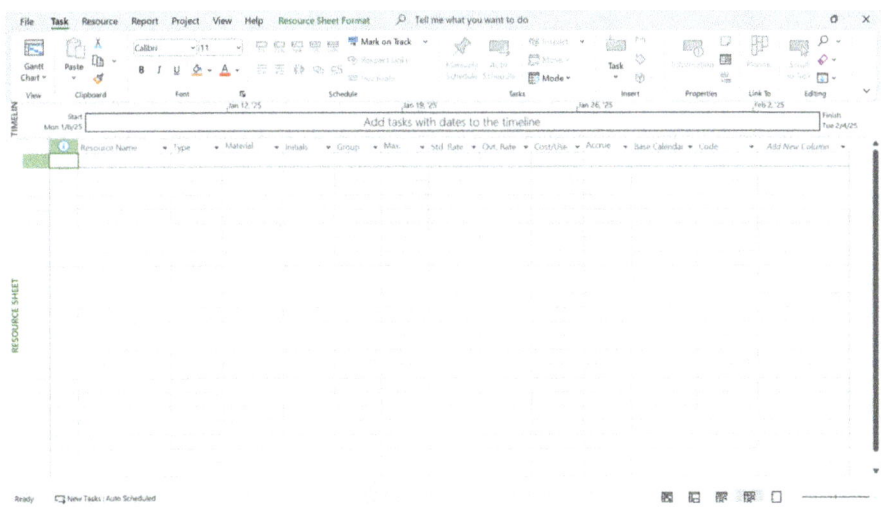

Figure 6-17.   Resource Sheet appears blank

181

CHAPTER 6   BUDGET AND COST MANAGEMENT USING MICROSOFT PROJECT

Let us enter names as the first resource by pressing "Enter" to automatically fill in some items in the blank sheet shown in Figure 6-17.

You might notice the type is Work. There are three types: Work (typically a person), Material (something purchased by unit), and Cost (expenses with variable amounts, such as travel) as shown in Figure 6-18. We will mostly focus on work and cost resources.

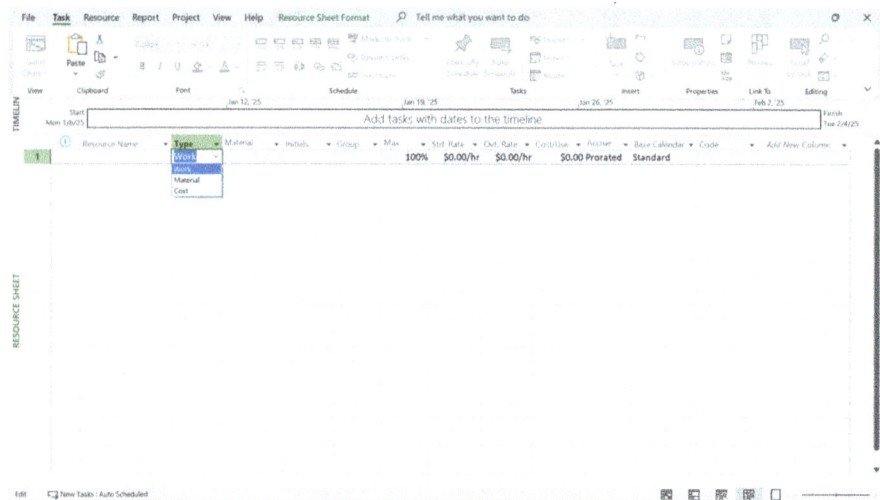

Figure 6-18. Different work types

The Material type "Material" as shown in Figure 6-19 will be selected for Material resource as it will contain unit of measurement for the material resources such as cubic yards, tons or boxes. Referring to Figure 6-18, the Initials column can be customized for easier display or abbreviation of multiple resources on a task. The Group can represent departments or locations, and we will cover other fields later. The Code column currently lacks a built-in purpose, so you can use it as needed.

Now, let's add a few more resources. Note that sorting by Microsoft Project will be based on the first initial it sees; for sorting by last name, enter the last name first. Enter real names, but for planning, you may need generic placeholders. For example, you could use "Copyeditor 1,"

CHAPTER 6   BUDGET AND COST MANAGEMENT USING MICROSOFT PROJECT

"Copyeditor 2," etc., or simply "Copyeditor" as shown in Figure 6-19. Consider whether specific roles or generalized skill sets better suit your planning needs.

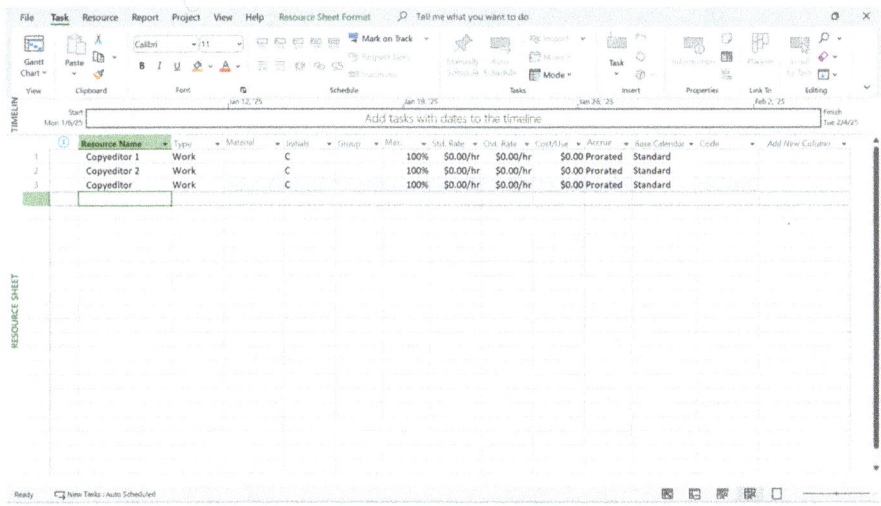

Figure 6-19.   Updating few resource names

Think about the job types or skill sets needed for tasks, and list these when planning resources for your plan.

Enter the Maximum Capacity for Work Resources

You can determine when Project considers a resource overbooked by adjusting max units. Access the Max Units column as shown in Figure 6-20.

183

CHAPTER 6   BUDGET AND COST MANAGEMENT USING MICROSOFT PROJECT

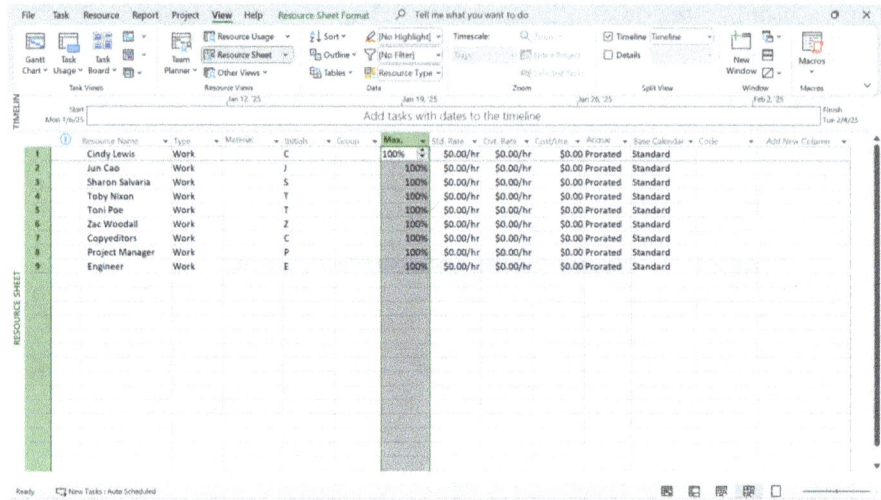

Figure 6-20. Maximum column

This setting informs you and Project about resource overallocation. By default, it is set to 100%, which typically represents an eight-hour workday. You can represent multiple individuals, such as four copyeditors, by setting this value to 400% as shown in Figure 6-21.

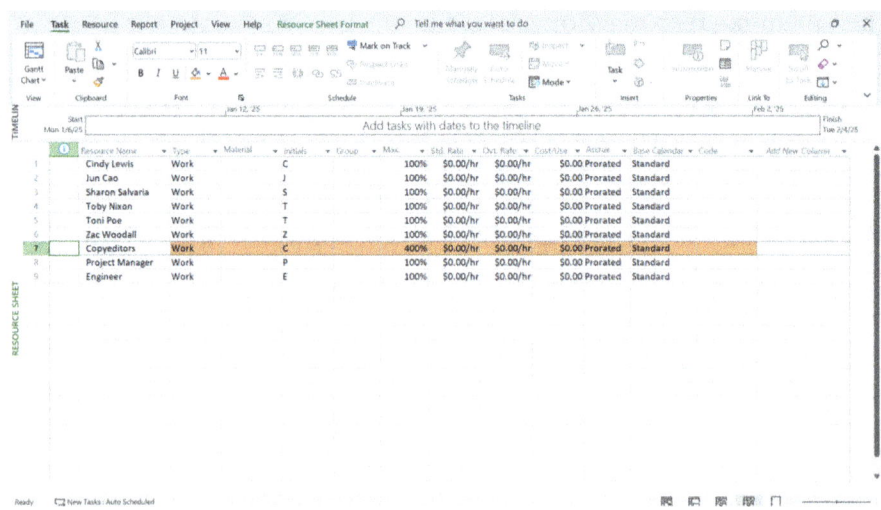

Figure 6-21. Copyeditors represents four people with 400% availability

CHAPTER 6   BUDGET AND COST MANAGEMENT USING MICROSOFT PROJECT

Another example, a botanical garden, uses volunteers for various tasks, like ticket taking or cleaning. They list volunteers collectively with a value such as 1,000% to represent ten volunteers.

However, changing this value might not always be realistic. For instance, setting an individual's capacity to 200% would imply a 16-hour workday, which may not be feasible. The system does not differentiate between a generic placeholder and an actual person. You could also reduce the value to 50%, indicating a part-time role as shown in Figure 6-22.

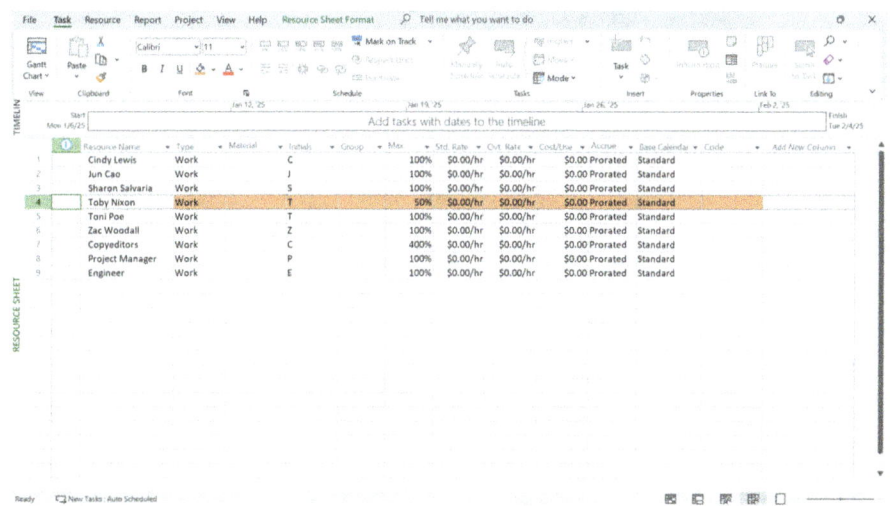

Figure 6-22. *Part-time role for Toby Nixon*

The max units setting establishes the overallocation threshold. Exceeding this threshold triggers a notification, whereas staying below it indicates resource availability. You can adjust the display of max units to show either decimal values or percentages. This option is located under File options in the Schedule section as shown in Figures 6-23 and 6-24, respectively.

185

CHAPTER 6   BUDGET AND COST MANAGEMENT USING MICROSOFT PROJECT

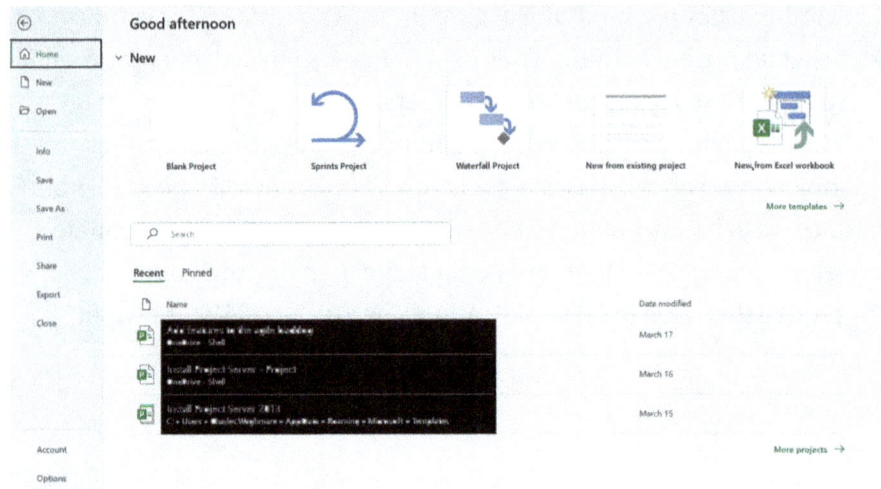

Figure 6-23. *Navigation to Options*

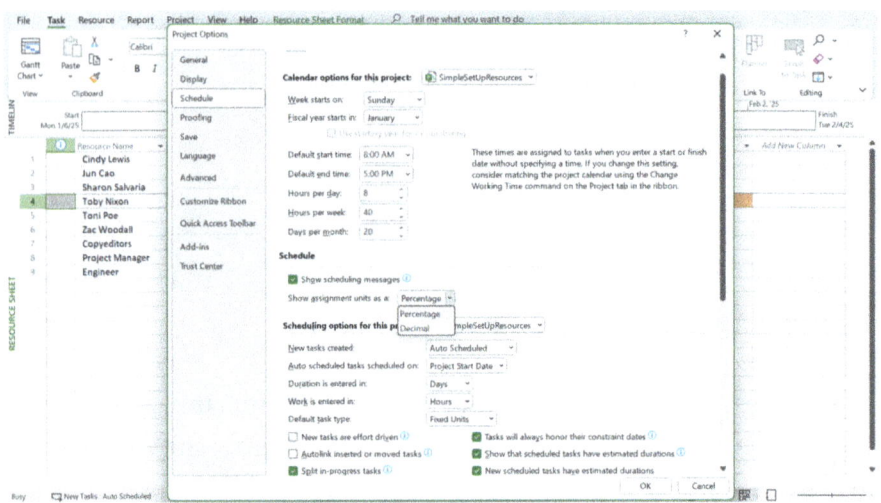

Figure 6-24. *Assignment unit in percentage and decimal*

This setting shown in Figure 6-24 is specific to each computer, so another computer might display the values differently. Use max units to control overallocation triggers in Project and specify resource capacity.

186

CHAPTER 6 BUDGET AND COST MANAGEMENT USING MICROSOFT PROJECT

Enter Work Resource Pay Rates

Standard rates are the rate at which the resources are paid for their regular nonovertime work as shown in Figure 6-25. Standard rates are the budget cost of the project.

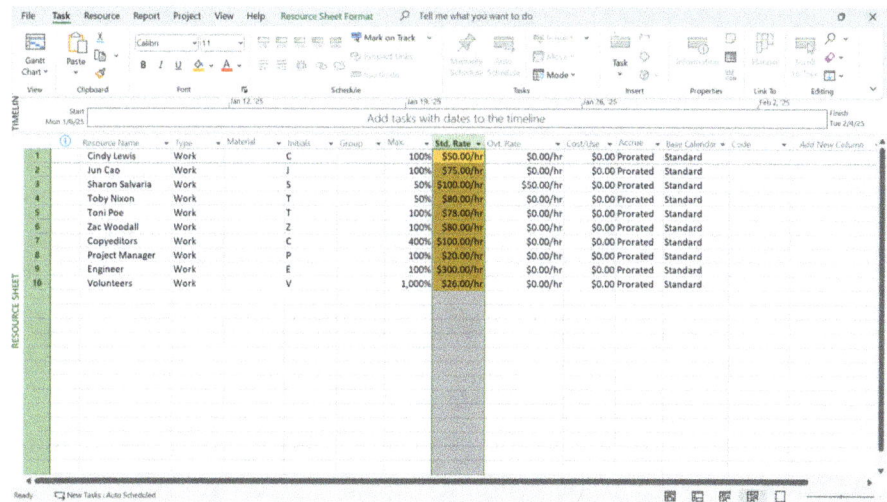

Figure 6-25. *Standard rates of the resources*

A nice benefit to your team is you can update their pay rates when needed. If you're following along, feel free to give yourself a pay raise. Entering a rate is simple: just type in the amount. Set up with US dollars, and press "Enter" in the Overtime Rate column as shown in Figure 6-26.

CHAPTER 6   BUDGET AND COST MANAGEMENT USING MICROSOFT PROJECT

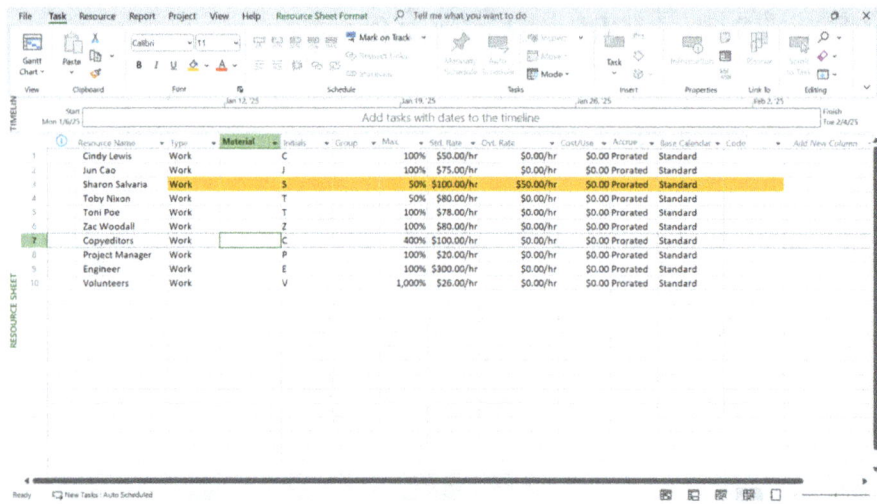

Figure 6-26. Update in Overtime Rate column

But if your overtime rate is time and a half, you'll need to do that calculation yourself. Note that Microsoft Project will only use the overtime rate if you designate hours as overtime.

You can also double-click on a resource to change their rate. Navigate to Costs to set an effective date for a new rate. For example, you could adjust rates annually or for specific projects. The program will apply the new rate from the designated date. You can input a percentage increase too, like 15%, to automatically calculate the raise. Different rate tables allow for various pay rates based on client type, but remember to assign the rate table to the task. For example, resource Toby Nixon has standard rate of $80 per hour and $0 of overtime as shown in Figure 6-27. Let's increase the standard rate by 15% and overtime by $20 per hour as of April 1, 2025, as shown in Figure 6-28.

CHAPTER 6   BUDGET AND COST MANAGEMENT USING MICROSOFT PROJECT

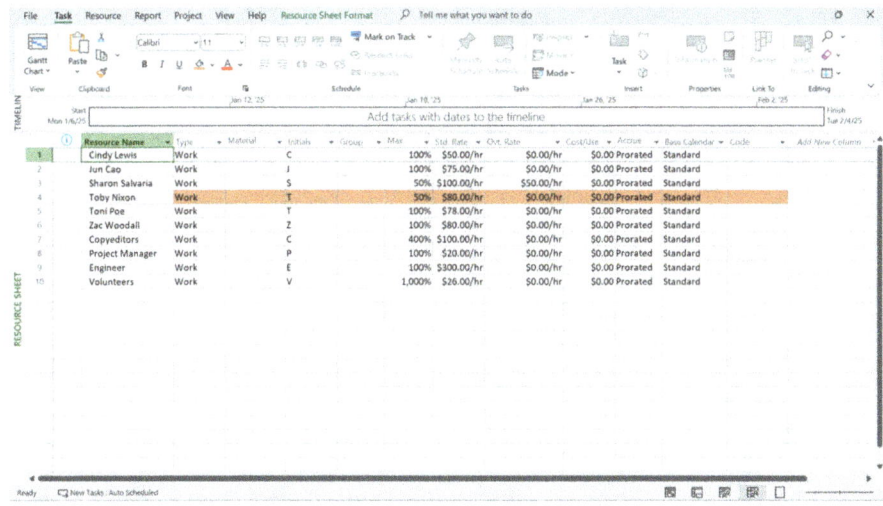

Figure 6-27. Resource " Toby Nixon" standard and overtime cost

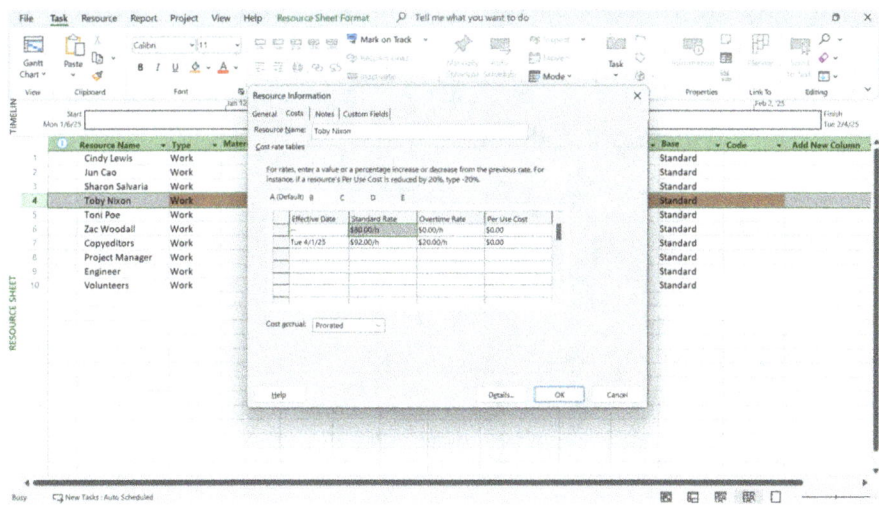

Figure 6-28. Increase the standard rate by 15% and overtime by $20 per hour for Toby Nixon

Finally, resource Toby Nixon rates updated in the Resource Sheet as shown in Figure 6-29.

189

CHAPTER 6 BUDGET AND COST MANAGEMENT USING MICROSOFT PROJECT

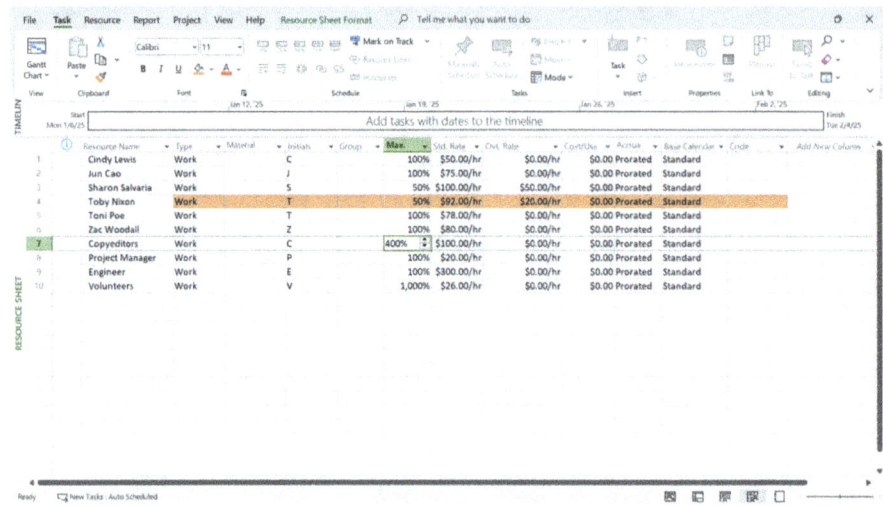

Figure 6-29. Updated rates for Toby Nixon

Similarly, we can do budgeting of the project by adjusting working time in the resource work calendar as shown in Figures 6-30 and 6-31 and while setting up resource cost as shown in Figure 6-32. Double-click any resource to find these two options.

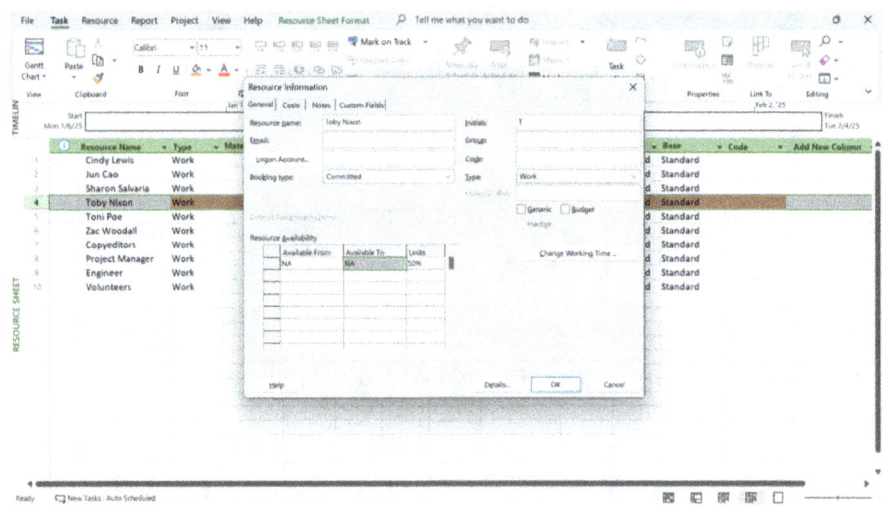

Figure 6-30. General ➤ Change Working Time

CHAPTER 6   BUDGET AND COST MANAGEMENT USING MICROSOFT PROJECT

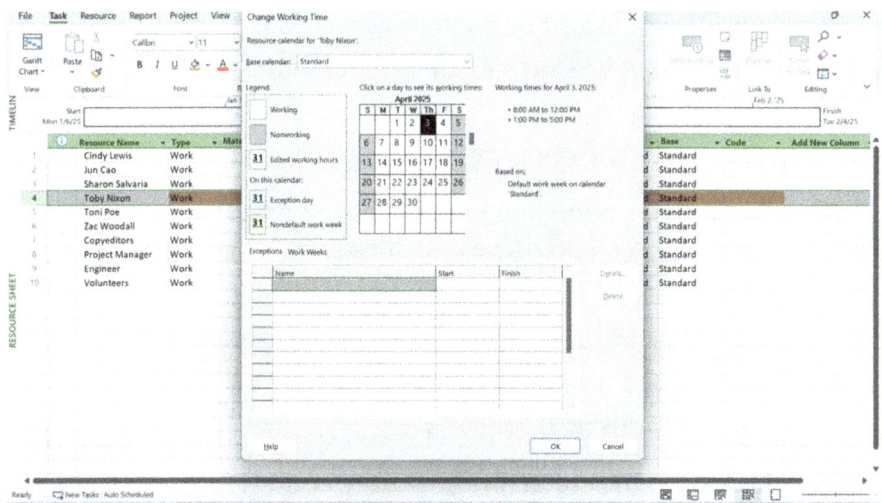

Figure 6-31. *Update working times*

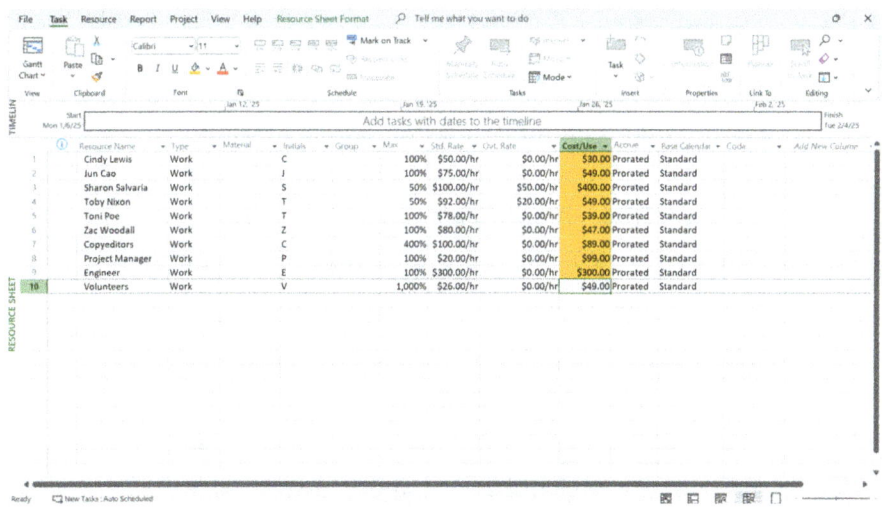

Figure 6-32. *Cost/Use column in the Resource Sheet*

191

CHAPTER 6   BUDGET AND COST MANAGEMENT USING MICROSOFT PROJECT

In conclusion, not using Microsoft Project can lead to several cost implications for businesses such as inefficiency and time loss, increased risk of errors, higher administrative costs, reduced productivity, training and integration costs, and opportunity costs. This is explained as below:

- **Inefficiency and Time Loss**: Without a robust project management tool like Microsoft Project, teams may struggle with organizing tasks, tracking progress, and managing timelines. This inefficiency can lead to missed deadlines and increased project durations, ultimately raising labor costs.

- **Increased Risk of Errors**: Manual tracking and management of projects can result in higher chances of errors and miscommunication. These errors can lead to costly rework, project delays, and potential loss of client trust.

- **Higher Administrative Costs**: Without automated features for scheduling, resource allocation, and reporting, businesses may need to invest more in administrative support. This can include hiring additional staff or spending more time on manual processes, increasing operational costs.

- **Reduced Productivity**: Microsoft Project offers tools for efficient collaboration and resource management. Not using it can lead to fragmented communication and poor resource utilization, reducing overall productivity and increasing costs associated with inefficiencies

- **Training and Integration Costs**: While Microsoft Project has a learning curve, its integration with other Microsoft tools can streamline processes. Without it, businesses might need to invest in training for alternative tools and face challenges in integrating various software solutions, leading to additional cost.

- **Opportunity Costs**: The lack of advanced project management capabilities can hinder a business's ability to take on complex projects or scale operations effectively. This can result in lost opportunities and potential revenue.

In summary, not using Microsoft Project can lead to increased labor and administrative costs, higher risk of errors, reduced productivity, and missed opportunities, all of which can significantly impact a business's bottom line.

With this, we have come to the end of this chapter. In the next chapter, we will explore the seamless integration of Microsoft Project with Microsoft 365 products like MS Teams and SharePoint Online, best practices for Microsoft Project, and keyboard shortcuts. While Microsoft Project and Microsoft 365 differ in appearance, they offer a unified experience in collaboration and communication.

CHAPTER 7

Seamless Integration of Microsoft Project with Microsoft 365 Family

In the previous chapter, we took a deep dive into budget and cost management using Microsoft Project by exploring project parameters such as estimating project costs, tracking expenses, and managing budgets. In this chapter, we are going to explore seamless integration of Microsoft Project with Microsoft 365 family of products such as Microsoft or MS Teams and SharePoint Online, Microsoft Project best practices, and Microsoft Project keyboard shortcuts. In this chapter, we are going to study how Microsoft Project and Microsoft 365 products are different in terms of look or feel; however, when it comes to collaboration and communication, they all provide seamless experiences to the user community.

CHAPTER 7   SEAMLESS INTEGRATION OF MICROSOFT PROJECT WITH MICROSOFT 365 FAMILY

Introduction

Microsoft Project is a powerful tool for project management, offering a range of features that facilitate collaboration and communication among team members. Microsoft Project is a project management software that helps project managers plan, execute, and control projects. It provides tools for scheduling, resource management, and tracking project progress. The software is available in different versions, including Project Online, Project for the Web, and Project Professional, each catering to different collaboration needs as explained below.

Microsoft Project Versions and Their Features

- **Project Online**: A cloud-based solution that offers flexibility and scalability. It supports real-time collaboration, allowing multiple users to work on the same project file simultaneously.

- **Project for the Web**: A web-based version that integrates seamlessly with Microsoft Teams and other Microsoft 365 tools. It is designed for simplicity and ease of use, making it ideal for smaller projects.

- **Project Professional or Microsoft Project Desktop**: A desktop application that provides advanced project management features. It is suitable for complex projects that require detailed planning and resource management.

Collaboration and Communication Using Microsoft Project

Effective collaboration and communication are crucial for the success of any project. They ensure that all team members are aligned with the project goals, tasks are completed on time, and any issues are promptly addressed. Poor communication can lead to misunderstandings, delays, and increased project costs.

Collaboration involves working together toward a common goal, while communication is the exchange of information between team members. Both are essential for coordinating efforts, sharing knowledge, and making informed decisions. In project management, collaboration and communication help in

- **Aligning Team Members**: Ensuring everyone understands their roles and responsibilities
- **Facilitating Problem-Solving**: Allowing team members to share ideas and find solutions to challenges
- **Enhancing Productivity**: Streamlining workflows and reducing duplication of efforts
- **Improving Stakeholder Engagement**: Keeping stakeholders informed and involved in the project

Projects with strong collaboration and communication practices are more likely to succeed. They experience fewer delays, better resource utilization, and higher stakeholder satisfaction. Conversely, projects with poor communication often face issues such as missed deadlines, budget overruns, and low team morale.

Collaboration Features in Microsoft Project

Microsoft Project offers several features that facilitate collaboration among team members. These features help in coordinating efforts, sharing information, and working together efficiently.

Coauthoring

Project for the Web and Project Online support coauthoring, allowing multiple users to work on the same project file simultaneously. This feature is particularly useful for large projects where different team members need to update their tasks in real time.

Resource Pooling

Microsoft Project allows you to create a shared resource pool, which can be used across multiple projects. This ensures that resources are allocated efficiently and helps in avoiding overallocation.

Integration with Microsoft Teams

Microsoft Project integrates seamlessly with Microsoft Teams, providing a centralized platform for communication and collaboration. Team members can discuss project updates, share files, and hold virtual meetings without leaving the Teams environment.

Shared Resource Pool

A shared resource pool allows multiple projects to draw from a common pool of resources. This helps in optimizing resource allocation and ensures that resources are used efficiently across all projects.

In the next section, we will provide an overview of communication and collaboration with Microsoft Project which covers aspects such as project communication plan, status reports, notifications and alerts, integration with other Microsoft 365 tools, best practices for collaboration and communication, defining roles and responsibilities, regular meetings, and using collaboration tools, monitoring, and adjusting.

CHAPTER 7   SEAMLESS INTEGRATION OF MICROSOFT PROJECT WITH MICROSOFT 365 FAMILY

Overview of Communication and Collaboration with Microsoft Project

Effective communication is essential for keeping all stakeholders informed about the project's progress. Microsoft Project provides several tools to facilitate communication among team members and stakeholders.

Project Communication Plan

A well-defined communication plan is essential for keeping all stakeholders informed about the project's progress. Microsoft Project allows you to create and share communication plans, ensuring that everyone knows when and how updates will be provided.

Status Reports

Regular status reports are crucial for keeping stakeholders informed about the project's progress. Microsoft Project provides various reporting tools, including Gantt charts, burndown charts, and dashboards, which can be customized to meet the needs of different stakeholders.

Notifications and Alerts

Microsoft Project can send automatic notifications and alerts to team members about upcoming deadlines, task assignments, and changes to the project schedule. This helps in keeping everyone on the same page and ensures that important updates are not missed.

Integration with Other Microsoft 365 Tools

Microsoft Project integrates with other Microsoft 365 tools, such as Outlook, SharePoint, and OneDrive, to facilitate communication and collaboration. This integration allows team members to access project information and communicate seamlessly across different platforms.

Best Practices for Collaboration and Communication

Implementing best practices for collaboration and communication can significantly improve the efficiency and success of your projects. Here are some key practices to consider:

Defining Roles and Responsibilities

Clearly define the roles and responsibilities of each team member at the beginning of the project. This helps in avoiding confusion and ensures that everyone knows what is expected of them.

Regular Meetings

Hold regular meetings to discuss project updates, address any issues, and ensure that everyone is aligned with the project goals. Use Microsoft Teams for virtual meetings to facilitate communication among remote team members.

Using Collaboration Tools

Leverage the collaboration tools available in Microsoft Project, such as coauthoring, resource pooling, and integration with Microsoft Teams. These tools can help in improving communication and collaboration among team members.

Monitoring and Adjusting

Regularly monitor the project's progress and make adjustments as needed. Use the reporting tools in Microsoft Project to track the project's status and identify any.

Conclusion

The importance of real-time collaboration is allowing multiple users to work on the same project file simultaneously which can significantly improve efficiency and reduce delays. Integrating Microsoft Project with other Microsoft 365 tools can enhance communication and collaboration across different platforms. Regularly monitoring the project's progress and making necessary adjustments can help in identifying and addressing potential issues early on.

Microsoft Project offers a range of features that can enhance collaboration and communication within your projects. By leveraging these tools and following best practices, you can ensure that your projects are completed on time, within budget, and to the satisfaction of all stakeholders.

Seamless Integration of Microsoft Project with Microsoft Teams

Use the Project apps in Microsoft Teams to manage tasks and projects within your channels. These apps integrate with Project for the Web and Roadmap, allowing you to add projects and road maps as channel tabs accessible to anyone in the channel. Sync your work between Teams and the Web seamlessly. In this section, we will discuss how to add a Project tab to a Teams channel.

Work on a Project in Teams

By using the Project or Roadmap app to add a tab, you have the option to either include an existing project or create a new one as shown in the below steps:

Step 1: In your Teams channel, select Add a tab + as shown in Figure 7-1.

Figure 7-1. Click on tab +

Step 2: In the Add a tab dialog box, select Project. You may need to use Search to find them as shown in Figure 7-2.

CHAPTER 7 SEAMLESS INTEGRATION OF MICROSOFT PROJECT WITH MICROSOFT 365 FAMILY

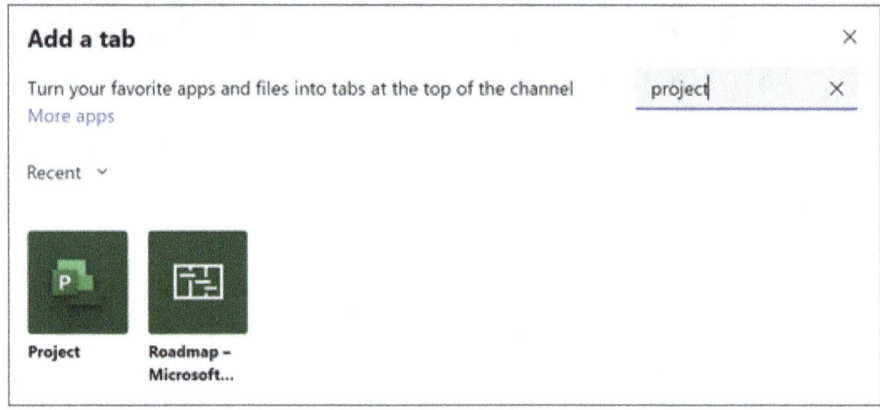

Figure 7-2. *Select Project app*

Step 3: Within the **Project** dialog box, please proceed with one of the following actions shown in Figure 7-3.

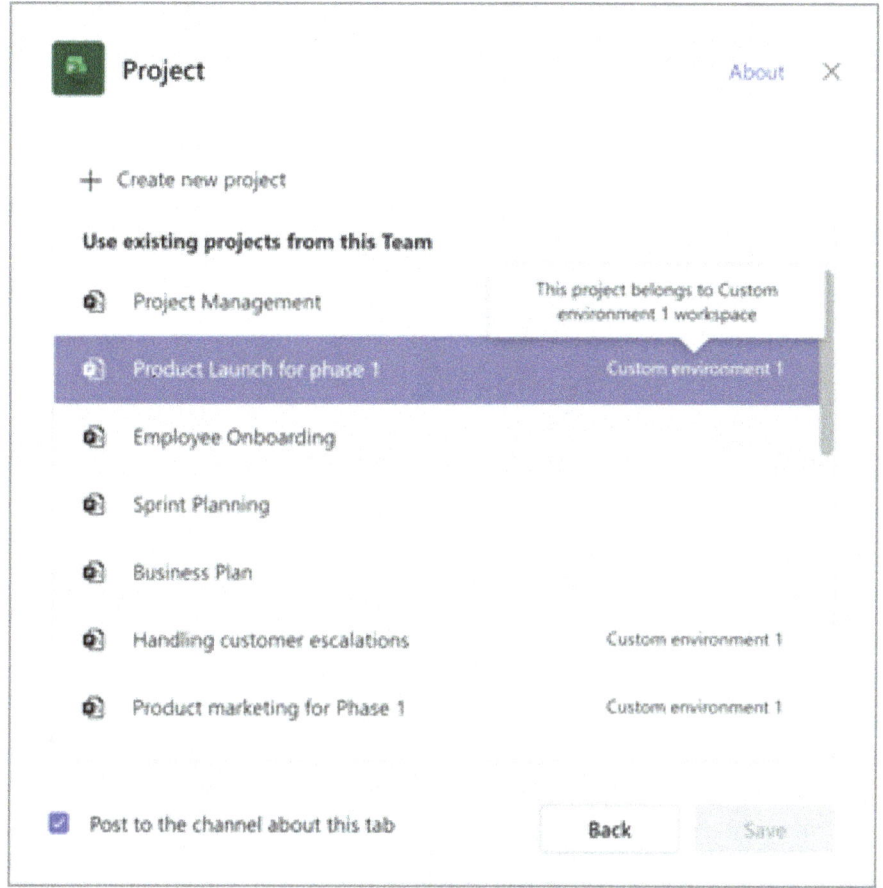

Figure 7-3. Choose option for your project

Step 5: To initiate a new venture, select either "Create new project" or "Create new roadmap," and then enter a name for your project or road map as shown in Figure 7-4. All newly created projects will be automatically assigned to the default environment.

CHAPTER 7   SEAMLESS INTEGRATION OF MICROSOFT PROJECT WITH MICROSOFT 365 FAMILY

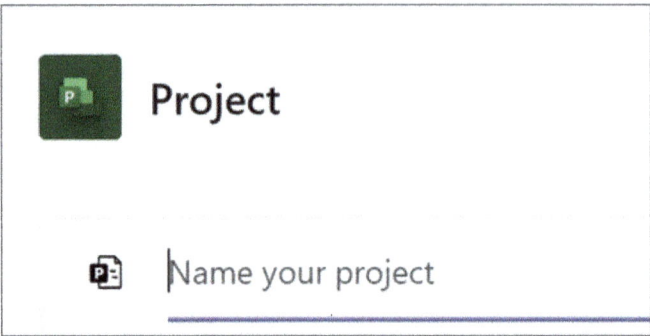

Figure 7-4. Add project name

Step 6: Select an existing project from the list, where the environment is shown in brackets as shown in Figure 7-5. Decide whether to post about the tab, and then select Save. The tab will be added to your team channel tabs, ready for use.

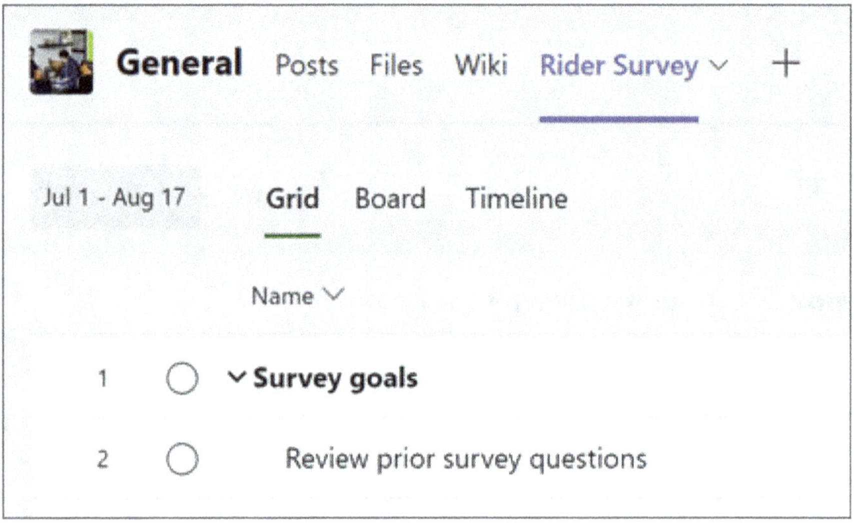

Figure 7-5. Selecting an existing project

CHAPTER 7   SEAMLESS INTEGRATION OF MICROSOFT PROJECT WITH MICROSOFT 365 FAMILY

Repeat this procedure to add multiple projects or road maps to your channel.

Remove a Project Tab

You can remove a Project tab from your Teams channel without deleting the project or road map itself.

In the team channel, choose the Project tab to be removed, click the arrow next to the tab name, and then click **Remove** as shown in Figure 7-6.

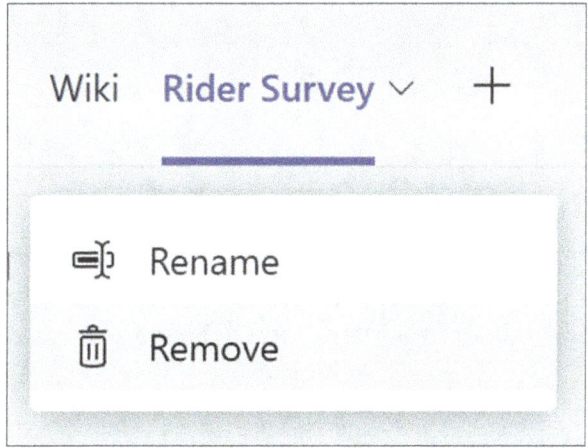

Figure 7-6. *Selecting Remove to remove project*

In the **Remove** dialog box, choose **Remove**. To access your project or road map after its tab has been removed from your Teams channel, you can either re-add it as a tab or locate it at project.microsoft.com.

CHAPTER 7 SEAMLESS INTEGRATION OF MICROSOFT PROJECT WITH MICROSOFT 365 FAMILY

Delete a Project

To delete both the Project or Roadmap tab in Teams and the underlying project or road map, follow these steps.

To delete a project:

- Go to the Project tab in your team channel.

- Click **Settings** in the top right corner.

- Click the ellipses (**…**), and select **Delete project** as shown in Figure 7-7.

Figure 7-7. *Delete project*

With the above-described steps, we will definitely have seamless experience between Microsoft Project and Microsoft Teams. In the next section, we will experience seamless integration between Microsoft Project and SharePoint Online.

CHAPTER 7   SEAMLESS INTEGRATION OF MICROSOFT PROJECT WITH MICROSOFT 365 FAMILY

Seamless Integration of Microsoft Project with Microsoft SharePoint Online

Microsoft Project can sync tasks with SharePoint. Team members update their work in SharePoint, and changes also appear in Project, and vice versa. Let's sync Microsoft Project with a SharePoint site.

Sync with a New SharePoint Site

These steps assume that you have a project open in Project, but you have not yet created a SharePoint site for it.

- In Project, select **File ➤ Save** as shown in Figure 7-8.

- Choose **Sync with SharePoint**, and in the **Sync with** list, select **New SharePoint Site** as shown in Figure 7-9.

- Enter a name in the **Project name** box as shown in Figure 7-9.

- Add the address of the SharePoint tasks list to which you will sync in the **Site address** list as shown in Figure 7-9.

CHAPTER 7   SEAMLESS INTEGRATION OF MICROSOFT PROJECT WITH MICROSOFT 365 FAMILY

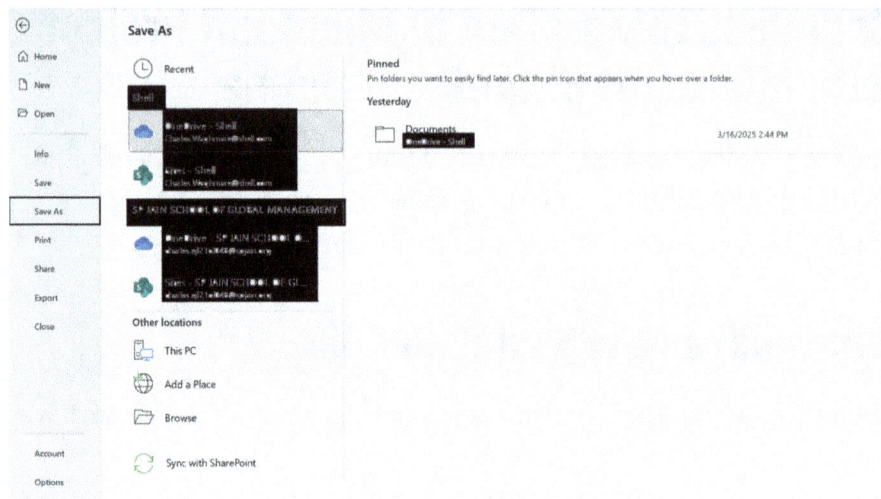

Figure 7-8. *Click on File ➤ Save As to sync with SharePoint*

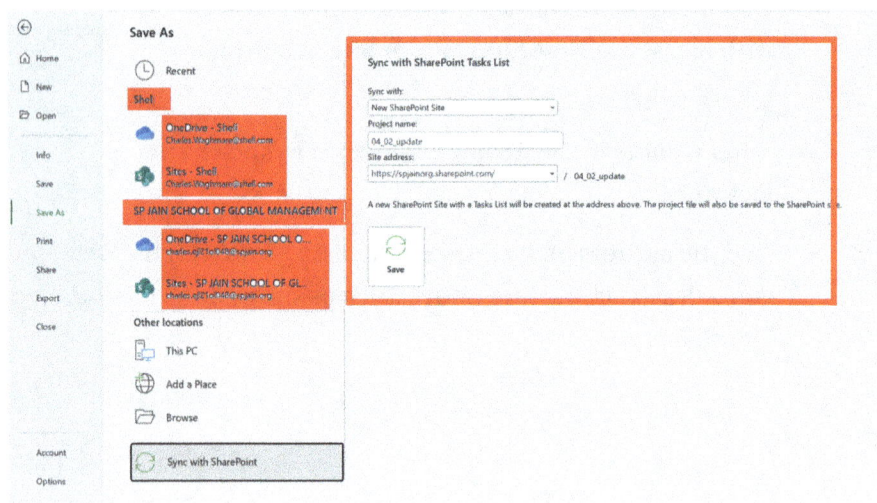

Figure 7-9. *Sync project with a SharePoint site by adding details*

CHAPTER 7   SEAMLESS INTEGRATION OF MICROSOFT PROJECT WITH MICROSOFT 365 FAMILY

Sync with an Existing SharePoint Site

These steps assume that you have an empty schedule open in Project, with all the tasks to be synchronized located on a SharePoint site.

- In Project, go to File ➤ Save As as shown in Figure 7-10.

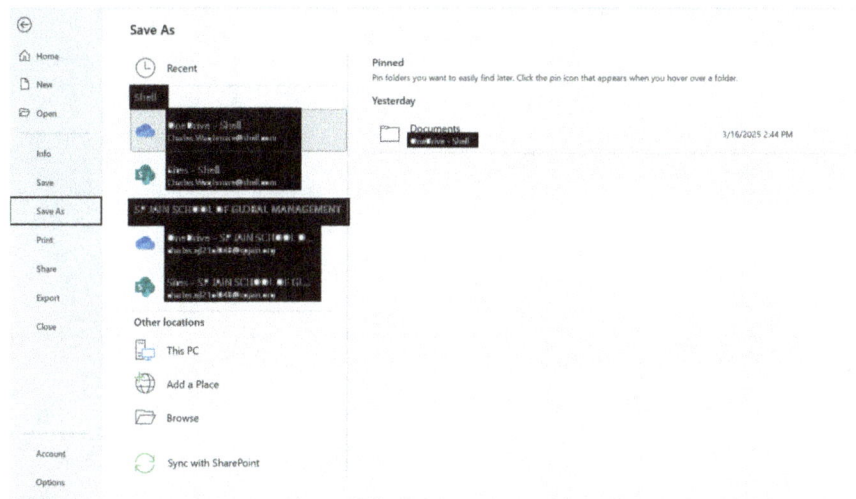

Figure 7-10. *Click on File ➤ Save As to sync with SharePoint*

- In the Sync with SharePoint, select Existing SharePoint Site as shown in Figure 7-11.

209

CHAPTER 7   SEAMLESS INTEGRATION OF MICROSOFT PROJECT WITH MICROSOFT 365 FAMILY

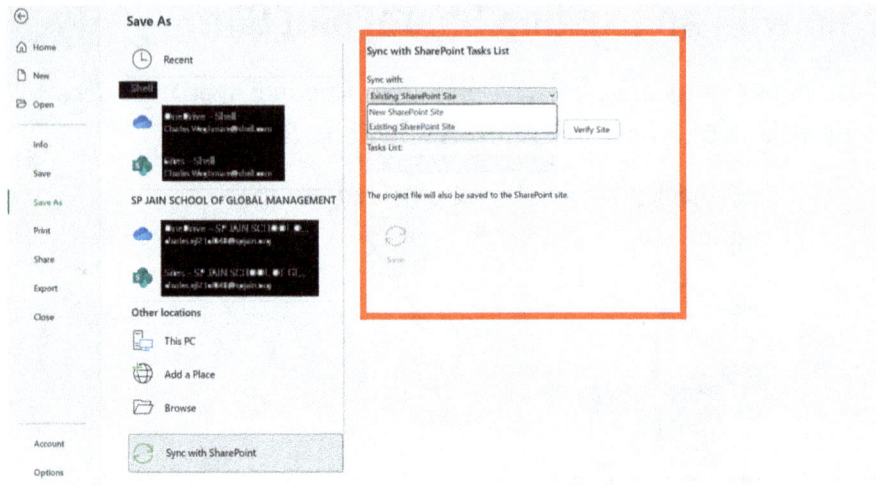

Figure 7-11. *Select Sync with SharePoint option*

- In the Site address box, enter the address of the SharePoint tasks list that you want to import as shown in Figure 7-12.

- Select Verify Site as shown in Figure 7-12.

- In the Tasks List box, enter or select a name for the tasks list that you want to sync with your project as shown in Figure 7-12.

- When you select **Save**, the SharePoint tasks list will sync with Project. Changes in Project or SharePoint will update in both as shown in Figure 7-12.

CHAPTER 7   SEAMLESS INTEGRATION OF MICROSOFT PROJECT WITH MICROSOFT 365 FAMILY

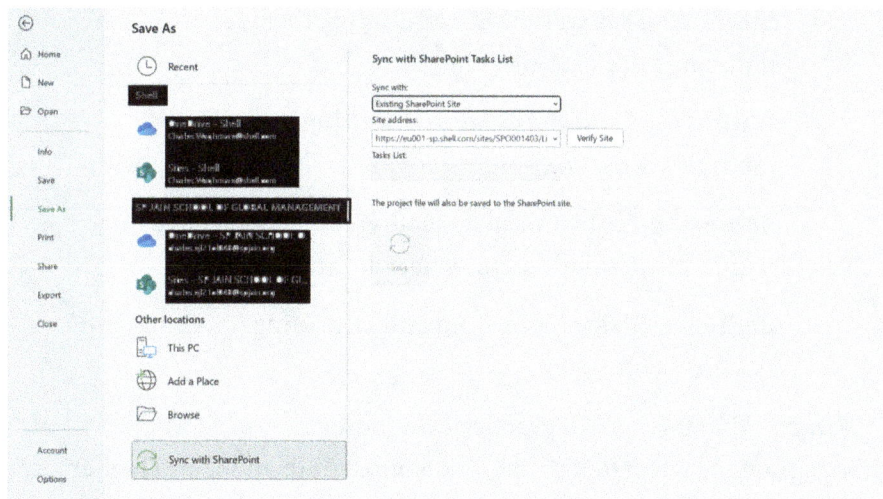

Figure 7-12.   Update site details to sync Project with SharePoint Online

With this, we have come to the end of seamless integration of Microsoft Project with Microsoft Teams and SharePoint Online. In the next section, we will explore some best practices around Microsoft which will help to do project management effectively.

Best Practices Around Microsoft Project

Implementing best practices in project management is crucial for ensuring the success of your projects. These practices help in optimizing workflows, improving communication, and achieving project goals within the defined constraints. Best practices are standardized methods or techniques that have been proven to yield successful results. In project management, best practices help in

- **Enhancing Efficiency**: Streamlining processes and reducing duplication of efforts

- **Improving Communication**: Ensuring that all team members and stakeholders are informed and engaged

- **Achieving Project Goals**: Meeting project objectives within the defined scope, schedule, and budget

- **Reducing Risks**: Identifying and mitigating potential risks early on

Projects that follow best practices are more likely to succeed. They experience fewer delays, better resource utilization, and higher stakeholder satisfaction. Conversely, projects that do not adhere to best practices often face issues such as missed deadlines, budget overruns, and low team morale.

Best Practices for Using Microsoft Project

Before diving into advanced features, it's important to familiarize yourself with the basics of Microsoft Project. This includes understanding how to create a project, set up tasks, assign resources, and track progress as described below:

- **Utilizing Templates**: Microsoft Project offers various templates that can help you quickly set up your project. These templates are designed for different types of projects and can save you time by providing a structured starting point.

- **Implementing Task Dependencies Wisely**: Task dependencies define the relationships between tasks. Properly setting up dependencies ensures that tasks are completed in the correct order and helps in identifying the critical path of the project. Use finish-to-start, start-to-start, finish-to-finish, and start-to-finish dependencies as needed.

- **Regularly Updating the Project Schedule**: Keeping your project schedule up-to-date is crucial for accurate tracking and forecasting. Regular updates help in identifying potential delays and making necessary adjustments to keep the project on track.

- **Leveraging Reporting Tools**: Microsoft Project provides various reporting tools, including Gantt charts, burndown charts, and dashboards. These tools can offer valuable insights into the project's progress and help in communicating status updates to stakeholders.

- **Managing Project Scope**: Managing project scope involves defining what your project will do – and just as importantly – what it won't do. Use capabilities in Project Web App for Project Online to help manage scope changes and ensure project goals are met.

- **Risk Management**: Develop a risk management plan to identify and plan for risks that could potentially affect your project. Track risks in Project Online and use techniques such as SWOT analysis to examine strengths, weaknesses, opportunities, and threats.

- **Resource Management**: Efficient resource management is key to avoiding overallocation and ensuring that resources are used effectively. Create a shared resource pool in Microsoft Project to optimize resource allocation across multiple projects

- **Integration with Other Tools**: Integrate Microsoft Project with other Microsoft 365 tools, such as Teams, Outlook, SharePoint, and OneDrive, to facilitate communication and collaboration. This integration allows team members to access project information and communicate seamlessly across different platforms.

- **Regular Meetings**: Hold regular meetings to discuss project updates, address any issues, and ensure that everyone is aligned with the project goals. Use Microsoft Teams for virtual meetings to facilitate communication among remote team members.

- **Monitoring and Adjusting**: Regularly monitor the project's progress and adjust as needed. Use the reporting tools in Microsoft Project to track the project's status and identify any potential issues early on.

- **Training and Support**: Ensure that all team members are trained in using Microsoft Project. Provide ongoing support and resources to help them utilize the software effectively.

- **Feedback and Continuous Improvement**: Encourage feedback from team members and stakeholders to identify areas for improvement. Continuously refine your project management practices based on this feedback.

During the Project Management phase, there is a regular need to update Project tasks therefore in order to become efficient it is useful to learn Microsoft Project Keyboard shortcuts to quickly update project tasks.

CHAPTER 7   SEAMLESS INTEGRATION OF MICROSOFT PROJECT WITH MICROSOFT 365 FAMILY

Microsoft Project Keyboard Shortcuts

Keyboard shortcuts can significantly enhance your efficiency when using Microsoft Project. They allow you to perform tasks quickly without relying on a mouse, which can be particularly useful for users with mobility or vision disabilities. Here's a detailed guide to the most useful keyboard shortcuts in Microsoft Project, organized by functionality.

Frequently Used Shortcuts

These shortcuts are commonly used for basic operations in Microsoft Project:

- **Open a project file (display the Open dialog box)**: Ctrl+F12

- **Open a project file (display the Open tab in the File menu)**: Ctrl+O

- **Save a project file**: Ctrl+S

- **Create a new project**: Ctrl+N

- **Activate the entry bar to edit text in a field**: F2

- **Activate the menu bar**: F10 or Alt

- **Activate the project control menu**: Alt+Hyphen (-) or Alt+Spacebar

Navigate Views and Windows

These shortcuts help you navigate through different views and windows within Microsoft Project:

- **Activate the entry bar to edit text in a field**: F2

- **Activate the menu bar**: F10 or Alt

- **Activate the project control menu**: Alt+Hyphen (-) or Alt+Spacebar
- **Activate the split bar**: Shift+F6
- **Close the program window**: Alt+F4
- **Display all filtered tasks or all filtered resources**: F3
- **Display the Field Settings dialog box**: Alt+F3
- **Open a new window**: Shift+F11
- **Reduce a selection to a single field**: Shift+Backspace
- **Reset sort order to ID order and turn off grouping**: Shift+F3
- **Select a drawing object**: F6
- **Display task information**: Shift+F2
- **Display resource information**: Shift+F2
- **Display assignment information**: Shift+F2
- **Turn on or off the Add To Selection mode**: Shift+F8
- **Turn on or off Auto Calculate**: Ctrl+F9
- **Turn on or off the Extend Selection mode**: F8
- **In the Print window, move left, right, up, or down to view different pages in the print preview pane**: Alt+Arrow keys

Use the Main Window

These shortcuts are useful for managing the main window in Microsoft Project:

- **Switch between active dialog boxes and the main app**: Alt+F6

- **Open the context menu for the selected item (the right-click menu)**: Shift+F10 or the Windows Menu key

- **Activate the ribbon**: F10

- **Activate the view splitter**: Alt+Shift+F6

- **Display the autofilter drop-down menu for the selected column**: Alt+Down Arrow

Use the Timeline View

These shortcuts help you navigate and manage the Timeline view:

- **Move to the next task**: Tab

- **Move to the previous task**: Shift+Tab

- **Move to the next milestone**: Down Arrow

- **Move to the previous milestone**: Up Arrow

- **Select the current task or milestone**: Enter

- **Open the task information dialog box**: Shift+F2

- **Open the milestone information dialog box**: Shift+F2

Outline a Project

These shortcuts are useful for outlining tasks and resources in your project:

- **Indent a task or resource**: Alt+Shift+Right Arrow
- **Outdent a task or resource**: Alt+Shift+Left Arrow
- **Move a task or resource up**: Alt+Shift+Up Arrow
- **Move a task or resource down**: Alt+Shift+Down Arrow
- **Expand a task or resource**: Alt+Shift+Plus (+)
- **Collapse a task or resource**: Alt+Shift+Minus (-)

Select and Edit in a Dialog Box

These shortcuts help you select and edit items within dialog boxes:

- **Move to the next field**: Tab
- **Move to the previous field**: Shift+Tab
- **Select the current field**: Enter
- **Open the drop-down menu for the current field**: Alt+Down Arrow
- **Close the drop-down menu for the current field**: Alt+Up Arrow

Select and Edit in a Sheet View

These shortcuts are useful for selecting and editing items in a sheet view:

- **Move to the next cell**: Tab
- **Move to the previous cell**: Shift+Tab

- **Select the current cell**: Enter
- **Open the drop-down menu for the current cell**: Alt+Down Arrow
- **Close the drop-down menu for the current cell**: Alt+Up Arrow

Use a Network Diagram

These shortcuts help you navigate and manage a network diagram:

- **Move to the next box**: Tab
- **Move to the previous box**: Shift+Tab
- **Select the current box**: Enter
- **Open the task information dialog box**: Shift+F2
- **Open the resource information dialog box**: Shift+F2

Use Office Art Objects

These shortcuts are useful for managing Office Art objects within Microsoft Project:

- **Select the next object**: Tab
- **Select the previous object**: Shift+Tab
- **Move the selected object up**: Up Arrow
- **Move the selected object down**: Down Arrow
- **Move the selected object left**: Left Arrow
- **Move the selected object right**: Right Arrow
- **Resize the selected object**: Shift+Arrow keys

Conclusion

Keyboard shortcuts can greatly enhance your productivity when using Microsoft Project. By familiarizing yourself with these shortcuts, you can perform tasks more efficiently and navigate the software with ease. Whether you're managing tasks, resources, or timelines, these shortcuts will help you streamline your workflow and improve your project management experience

In this chapter, we explored seamless integration of Microsoft Project with Microsoft 365 family of products such as Microsoft or MS Teams and SharePoint Online, Microsoft Project best practices, and Microsoft Project keyboard shortcuts. In the next chapter, we will discover Agile project management using Microsoft Project which will contain an introduction to Agile methodology, using Agile features in Microsoft Project, and managing Agile projects using Microsoft Project.

CHAPTER 8

Agile Project Management Using Microsoft Project

In the earlier chapter, we discussed the integration of Microsoft Project with the Microsoft 365 suite, including MS Teams and SharePoint Online. We also covered best practices for using Microsoft Project and provided keyboard shortcuts for efficiency. In this chapter, we will be learning Agile project management using Microsoft Project features. We will provide an introduction to Agile (Agile is a mindset and philosophy that guides the way teams work together) in Microsoft Project context and set up an Agile project in Microsoft Project application. In the set up an Agile project we have covered, turn on Agile feature for a project, add features to the agile backlog, and create sprints.

Introduction

Do you handle agile projects, or use both agile and traditional waterfall methodologies? Microsoft Project Online Desktop Client offers tools for managing agile projects. It includes features like defining sprints, a task board view for Scrum or Kanban work, and reports to show agile progress.

CHAPTER 8   AGILE PROJECT MANAGEMENT USING MICROSOFT PROJECT

Upcoming sections will demonstrate how to manage an agile project in a Microsoft Project file, helping you plan, track, and manage agile and hybrid projects efficiently.

Before we get started, there are a few things you should know:

- This chapter is easier if you're familiar with Microsoft Project basics like ribbon tabs, switching views, creating tasks, and filling in values.

- We'll focus on using Project Online Desktop Client to manage agile and hybrid projects, which requires a Project Online Plan 3 or Plan 5 subscription. These tools support Scrum and Kanban approaches.

- You should already be familiar with the agile methodology you plan to use. For detailed steps outside of Microsoft Project, refer to courses on Microsoft Project, Agile methodology, and hybrid agile waterfall projects.

An Introduction to Agile in Microsoft Project

Agile approaches are highly effective when an organization seeks to achieve benefits sooner or when business needs frequently change. This mindset allows work to be conducted based on the current understanding of business requirements. Should these requirements shift, they can simply be added to the backlog or incorporated into the next iteration.

Agile project management is the structured process utilized to oversee and execute agile projects. Two prominent methodologies within agile are Scrum and Kanban. In Scrum projects, tasks are executed in short bursts referred to as iterations or sprints. The objective is to deliver value promptly in small, frequent increments and to adapt to changes with greater ease. All sprints within a project maintain a consistent duration established at the project's inception. Sprint lengths typically range from 2 weeks, in some cases, up to 12 weeks.

Unlike traditional projects, sprint durations do not extend if work takes longer than anticipated. Instead, unfinished tasks are transferred to the backlog or the subsequent sprint. Agile projects emphasize delivering business value over exhaustive documentation. Consequently, team members are committed full-time to the project. They collaborate closely, utilizing face-to-face communication or advanced collaboration tools. The product owner partners with the team to determine which features will be delivered during each sprint. Documentary outputs in an agile project may include design documents, user stories, and a prioritized features list known as the backlog. Documentation that is part of the project deliverables, like a user guide, might also be included. Unnecessary documentation is not created just to check a box.

Kanban manages project work like an assembly line, which makes sense because Toyota created Kanban to streamline manufacturing. Kanban focuses on maintaining a steady workflow pace. In IT projects, Kanban is effective for managing ongoing software maintenance or regularly releasing new features, like those in cloud-based software products. A Kanban board allows easy visual tracking of work progress through the workflow. Teams focus on work in progress, reducing multitasking and increasing productivity. The product owner can reprioritize work at any time, allowing the team to pick the next item from the backlog once a task is completed. The goal is to optimize cycle time, which is the time for work to move through the workflow.

Roles within Kanban teams are flexible to eliminate bottlenecks. There are similarities among Scrum, Kanban, and traditional projects. You still start by developing a project vision. Requirements for deliverables are developed but not simultaneously as in traditional projects. Although agile methods differ from traditional ones, the team follows agreed-upon processes throughout the project. Lastly, communication with stakeholders remains essential.

CHAPTER 8   AGILE PROJECT MANAGEMENT USING MICROSOFT PROJECT

Project Online Desktop Client includes built-in agile tools, which come with a subscription to Project Online Plan 3 or Plan 5. To check if you have the correct software, follow the below steps:

Steps:

- Go to the File tab and click Account as shown in Figure 8-1.

- On the right side, under Product Information, look for Subscription Product and then Microsoft Project Online Desktop Client as shown in Figure 8-1. Make sure you are using Project Online, not the on-premises project server.

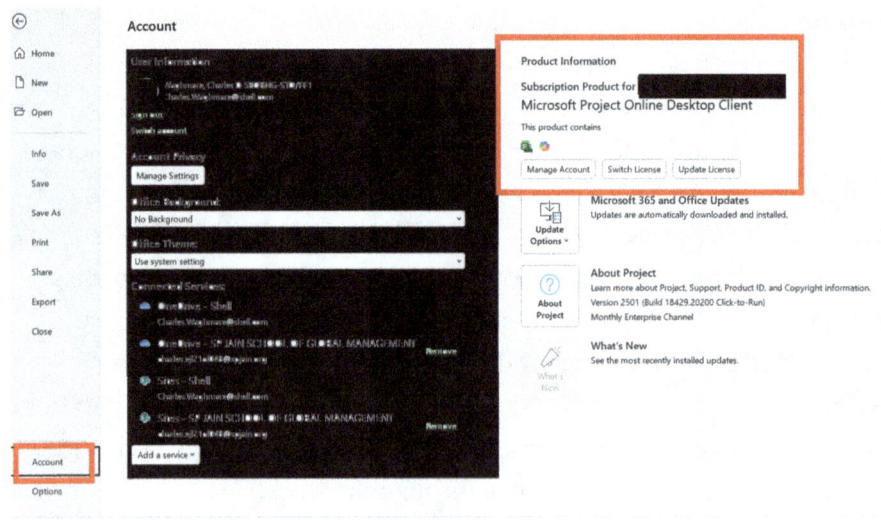

Figure 8-1. *Microsoft Project Product Information*

Microsoft Project agile tools support Scrum and Kanban. Follow the below steps to view them.

CHAPTER 8   AGILE PROJECT MANAGEMENT USING MICROSOFT PROJECT

Steps:

- Go to the File tab and click New, and you'll see an option to create a Sprints Project as shown in Figure 8-2.

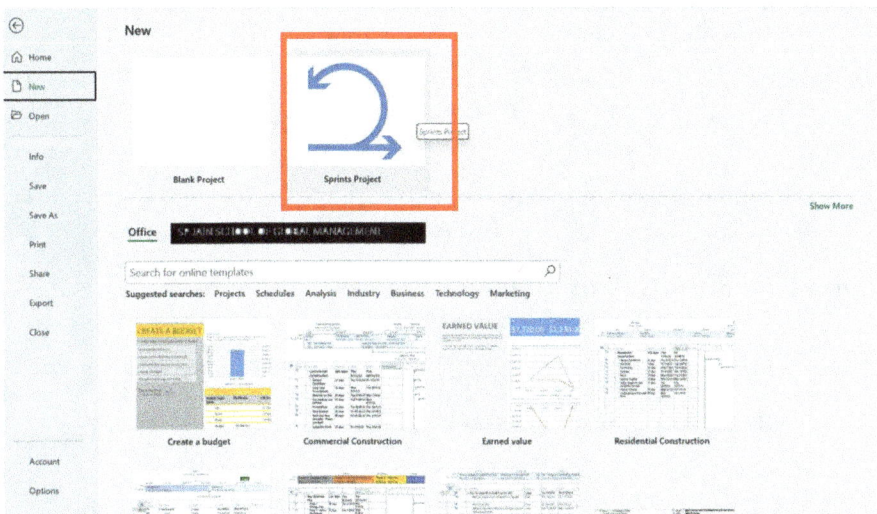

Figure 8-2. *Option to create Sprints Project*

- Clicking this opens a blank project in the Sprints Planning Board view as shown in Figure 8-3.

225

CHAPTER 8 AGILE PROJECT MANAGEMENT USING MICROSOFT PROJECT

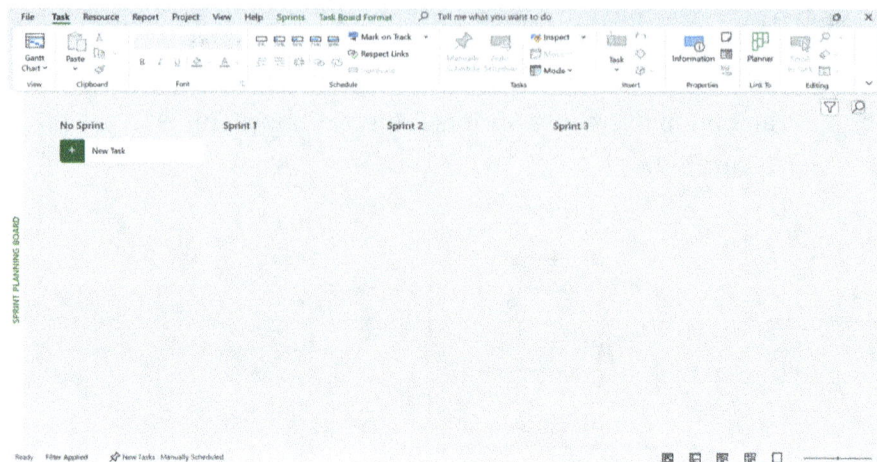

Figure 8-3. Sprints Planning Board view

- The ribbon will display the Sprints tab and the Task Board Format tab as shown in Figure 8-4.

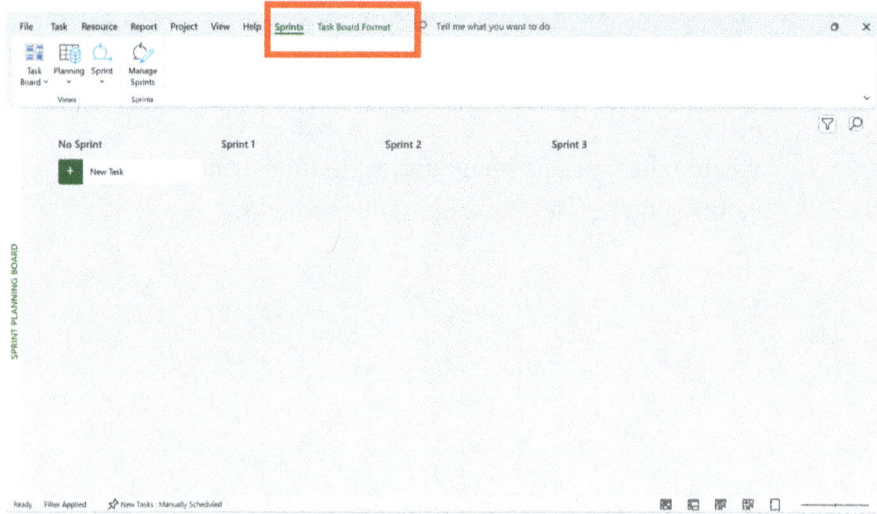

Figure 8-4. Sprints tab and the Task Board

CHAPTER 8 AGILE PROJECT MANAGEMENT USING MICROSOFT PROJECT

- Specialized views for task boards are available. On the Sprints tab, you can click Planning and choose either Sprint Planning Board or Sprint Planning Sheet as shown in Figure 8-5, which shows a table including agile fields like Board Status and Sprint field for tasks assigned to Scrum sprints shown in Figure 8-6 for Sprint Planning Board and Figure 8-7 for Sprint Planning Sheet.

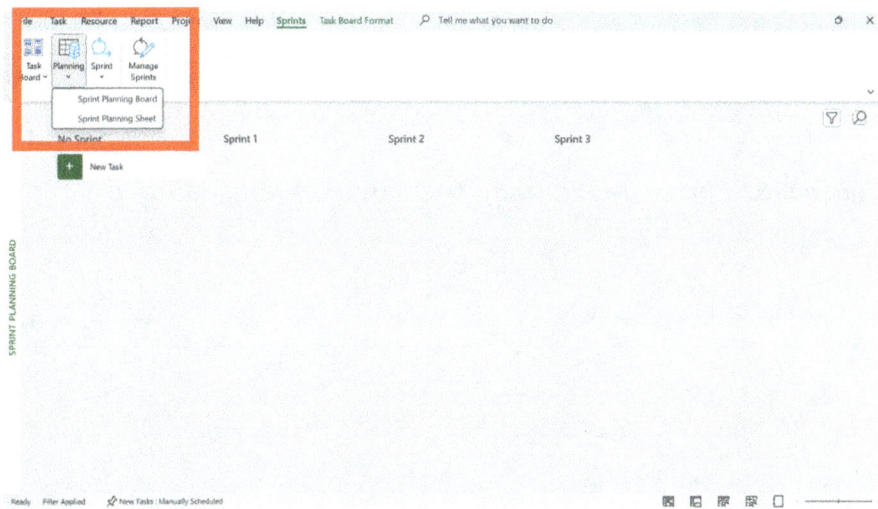

Figure 8-5. *Sprints ➤ Planning ➤ Sprint Planning Board and Sprint Planning Sheet*

227

CHAPTER 8   AGILE PROJECT MANAGEMENT USING MICROSOFT PROJECT

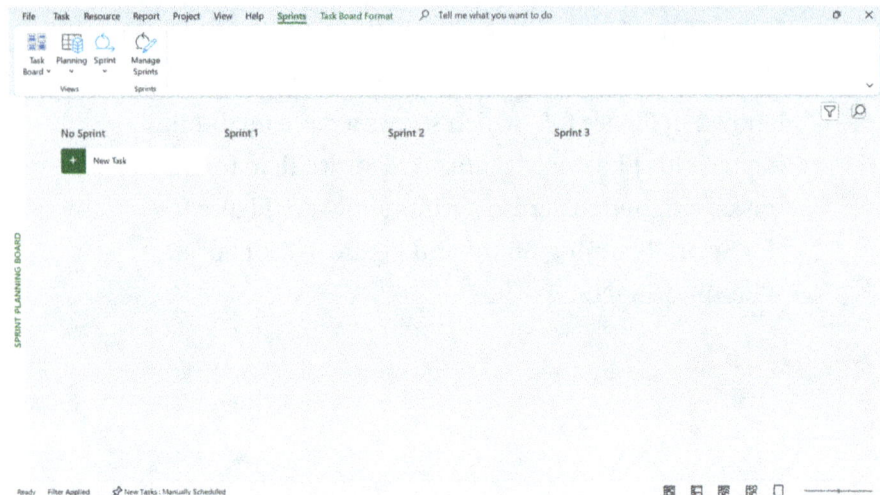

Figure 8-6. Sprints ➤ Planning ➤ Sprint Planning Board

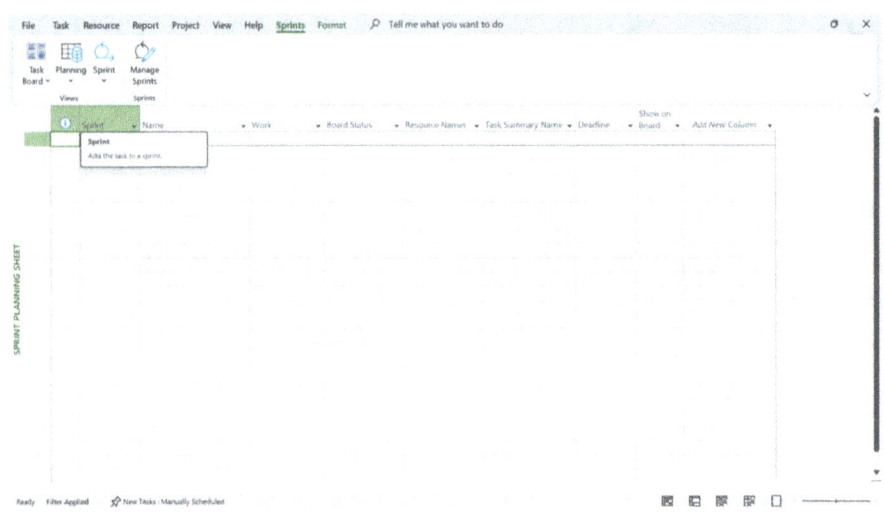

Figure 8-7. Sprints ➤ Planning ➤ Sprint Planning Sheet

228

CHAPTER 8   AGILE PROJECT MANAGEMENT USING MICROSOFT PROJECT

- By clicking Task Board and choosing Task Board as shown in Figure 8-8, columns similar to Kanban will be displayed as shown in Figure 8-9.

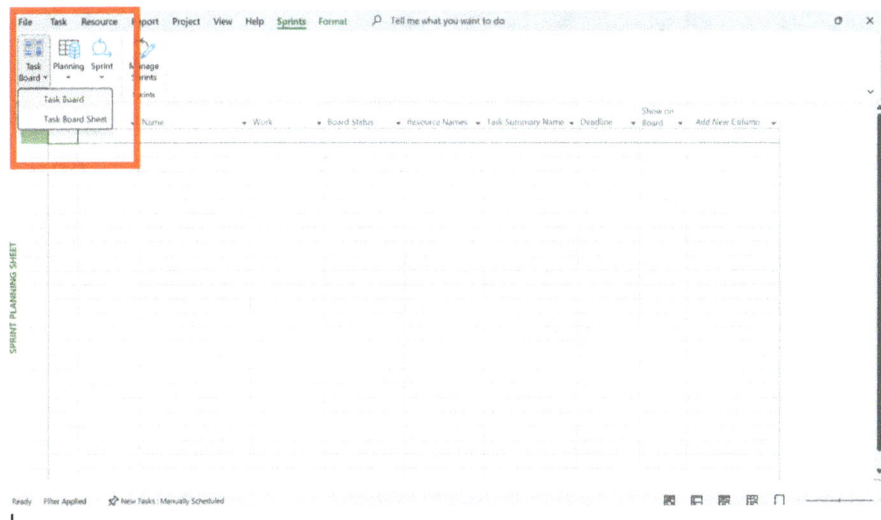

Figure 8-8. *Task Board ▶ Task Board and Task Board Sheet*

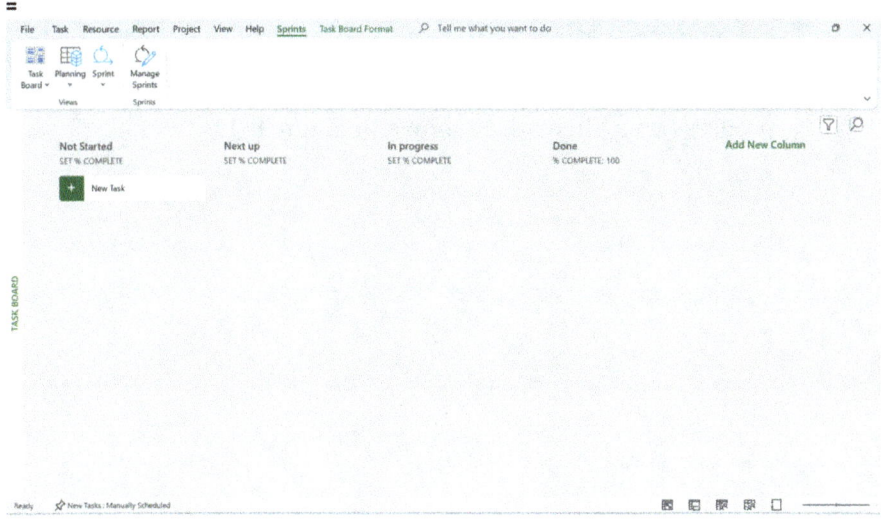

Figure 8-9. *Task Board ▶ Task Board*

229

CHAPTER 8 AGILE PROJECT MANAGEMENT USING MICROSOFT PROJECT

- In the View tab, you can use built-in filters for current sprint, current sprint remaining tasks, and more as shown in Figure 8-10.

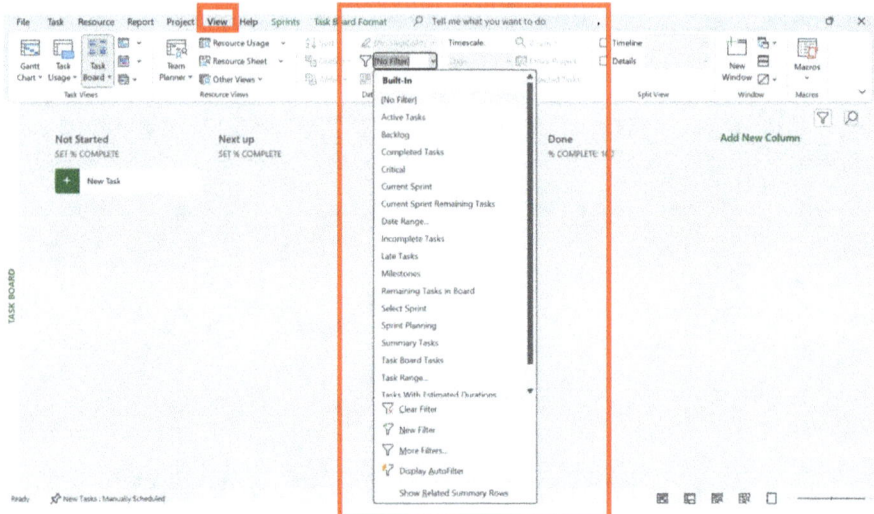

Figure 8-10. *Built-in filters*

- On the Report tab, there's an icon for Task Boards, providing agile-oriented graphical reports to show progress on agile work as shown in Figure 8-11.

230

CHAPTER 8   AGILE PROJECT MANAGEMENT USING MICROSOFT PROJECT

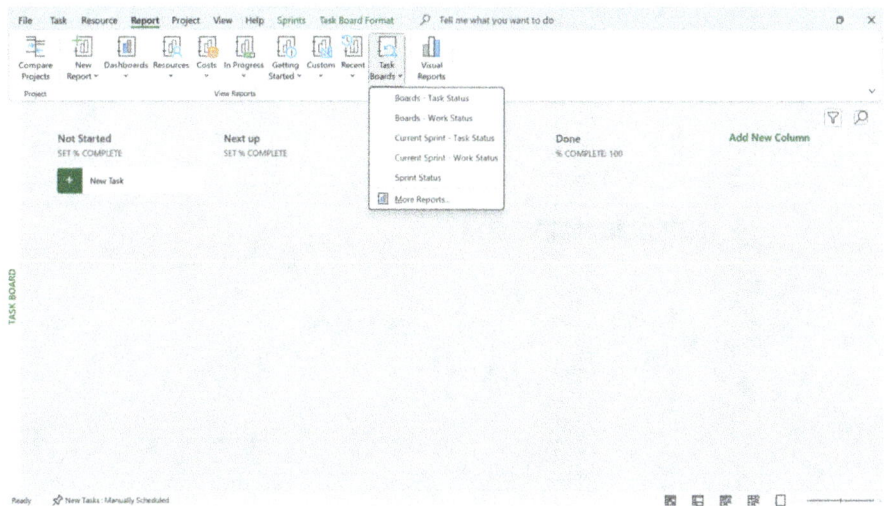

Figure 8-11. *Task Boards reports*

Until now, we have seen different features of Agile Project management in the Microsoft Project application. In the next section, we will set up an agile project in Microsoft and convert an existing project into an Agile one.

Set Up an Agile Project

In this section, we will cover how to turn on an Agile feature for a project, add features to the agile backlog, record feature information, create sprints, create a view to manage the backlog, and assign features to sprint. With Project Online Desktop Client, you can create an agile project from scratch or add agile features to an existing one.

Turn on Agile Feature for a Project

To start a new project, go to the File tab and click New as shown in Figure 8-12.

231

CHAPTER 8   AGILE PROJECT MANAGEMENT USING MICROSOFT PROJECT

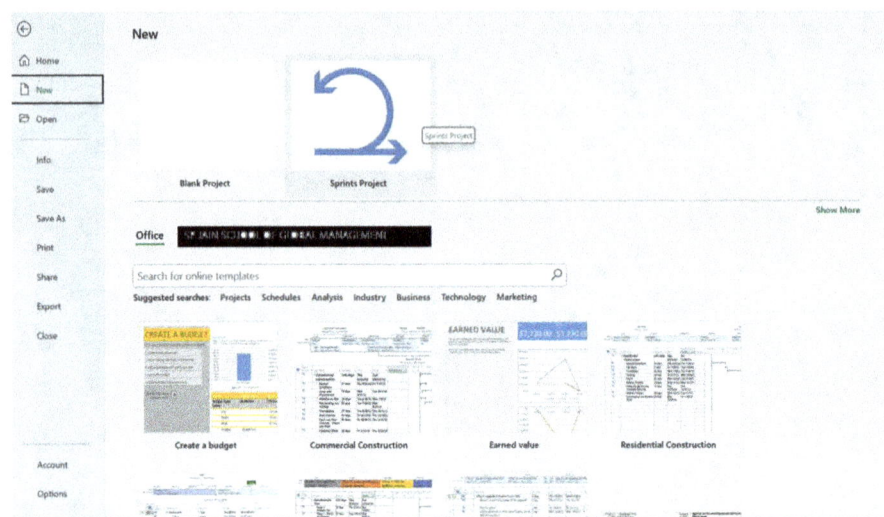

Figure 8-12.   Click New and choose Sprints Project

Choose the Sprints Project icon as shown in Figure 8-12 to enable agile features. This will add the Sprints tab to the ribbon and display the Sprint Planning Board View, ready for task addition as shown in Figure 8-13.

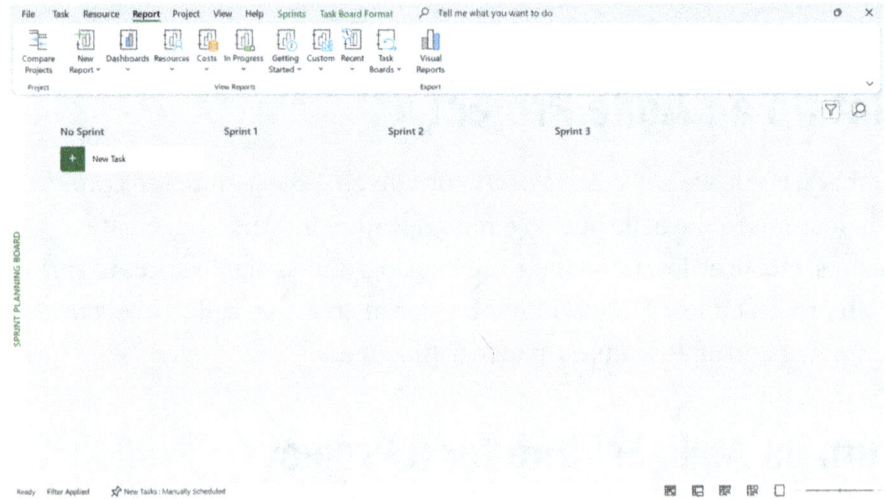

Figure 8-13.   Sprint project with Sprint Planning Board view

CHAPTER 8   AGILE PROJECT MANAGEMENT USING MICROSOFT PROJECT

For an existing project, go to the Project tab and click Manage Sprints in the Properties section. In the Manage Sprints dialog box, check the duration (default is two weeks), and correct the sprint's start date if needed as shown in Figure 8-14.

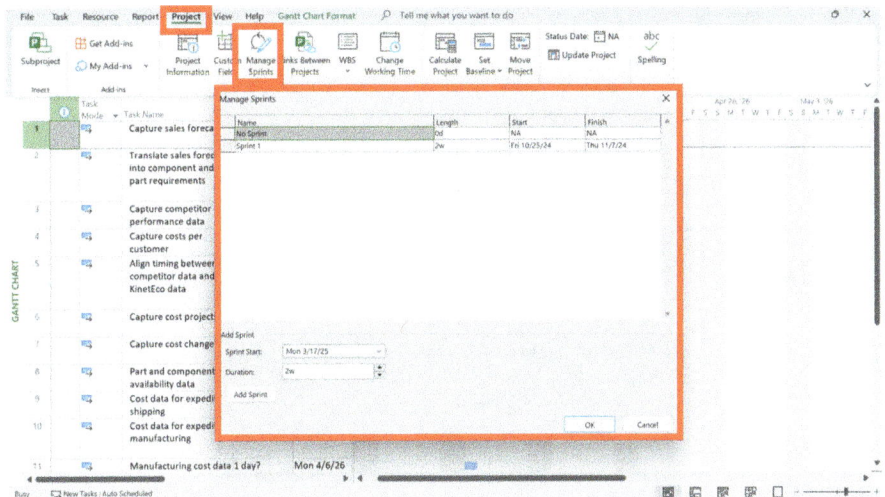

Figure 8-14. *Add sprint to an existing project*

Add another sprint to activate agile tools by clicking Add Sprint. This sets the dates automatically as shown in Figure 8-15. Click OK to see the Sprints tab indicating agile features are enabled as shown in Figure 8-16.

233

CHAPTER 8   AGILE PROJECT MANAGEMENT USING MICROSOFT PROJECT

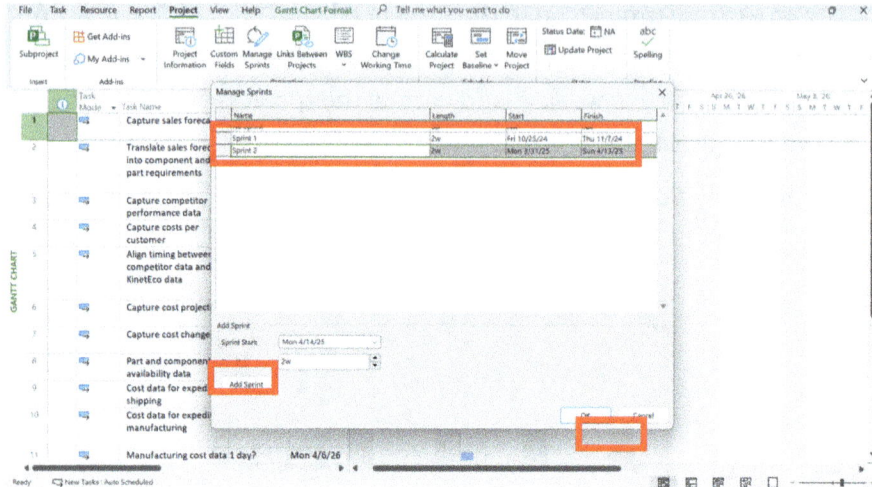

Figure 8-15. *Add a new Sprint, which creates Sprint 2*

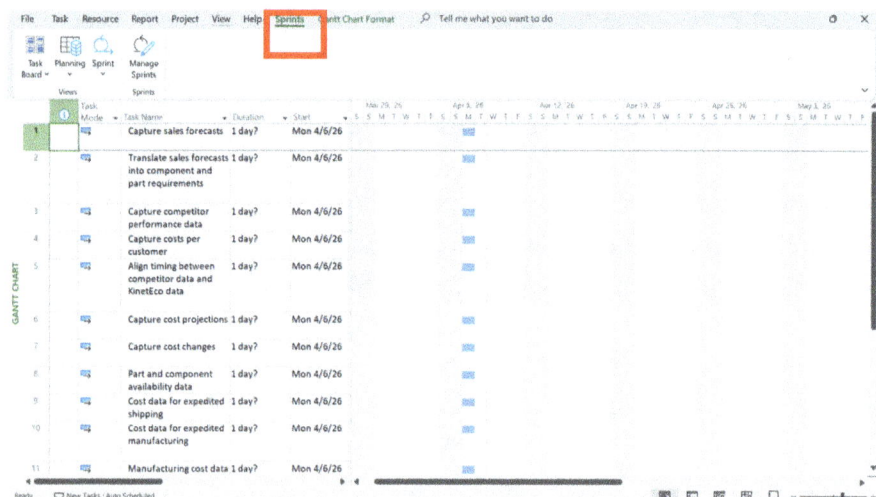

Figure 8-16. *Sprint added to an existing project*

The above explanation shows how you set up a project with agile tools in Project Online Desktop Client. Now we will add features to the agile backlog.

234

CHAPTER 8　AGILE PROJECT MANAGEMENT USING MICROSOFT PROJECT

Add Features to the Agile Backlog

Upon completing the initial agile planning, including the product vision, road map, and release planning, you will compile a list of features to be developed over the project's life cycle. This compilation is referred to as the backlog.

Begin by creating a new agile project, and on the new screen, select the Sprints Project icon as shown in Figure 8-17.

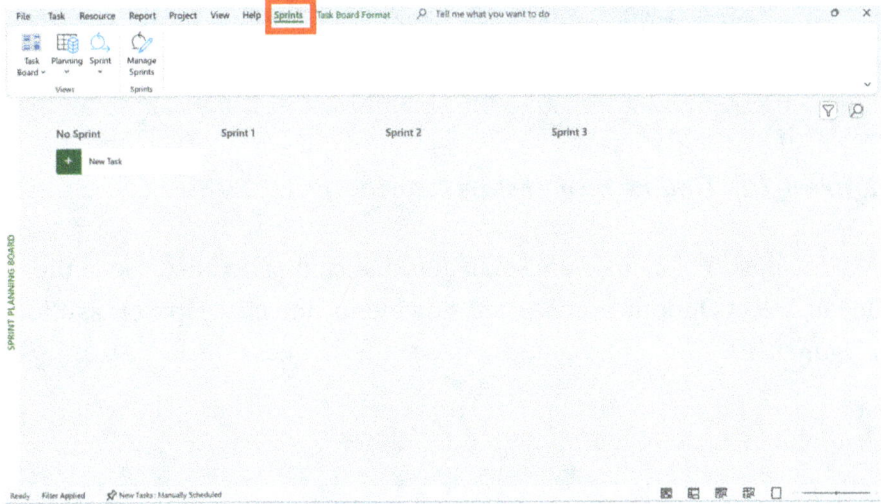

Figure 8-17. *New sprint project*

Navigate to the Project tab on the ribbon and select Project Information. Set the start date to April 6, 2026, as shown in Figure 8-18, and confirm by clicking OK.

235

CHAPTER 8   AGILE PROJECT MANAGEMENT USING MICROSOFT PROJECT

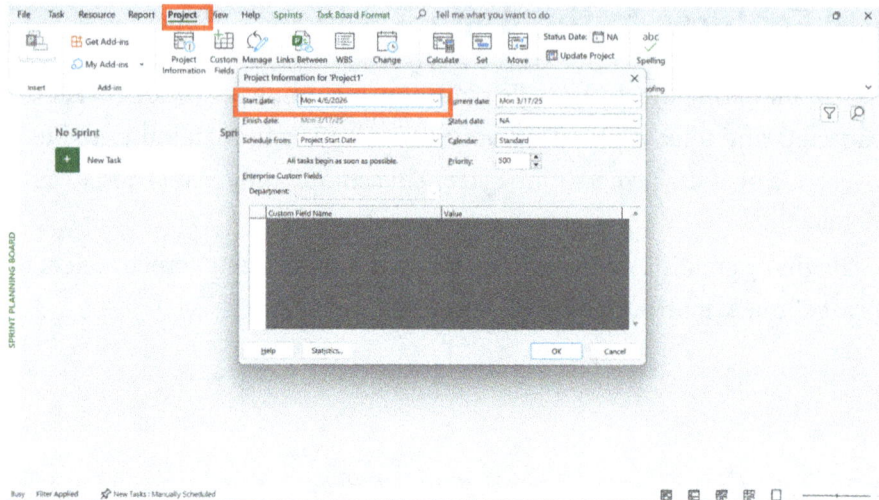

Figure 8-18. *Update project start date to April 6, 2026*

Next, ensure that tasks are set to automatically scheduled. Go to the File tab, select Options from the left side menu, and click Options as shown in Figure 8-19.

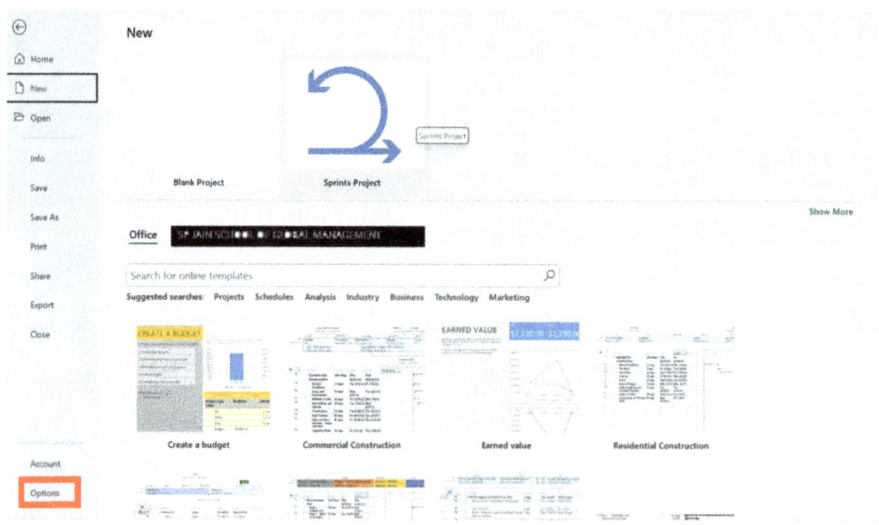

Figure 8-19. *Access Microsoft Project Options feature for configuration*

CHAPTER 8   AGILE PROJECT MANAGEMENT USING MICROSOFT PROJECT

Once you click Options, in the Project Options dialog box, click the Schedule category. Under Scheduling options for this project, change New tasks created from Manually Scheduled to Auto Scheduled as shown in Figure 8-20, and then click OK.

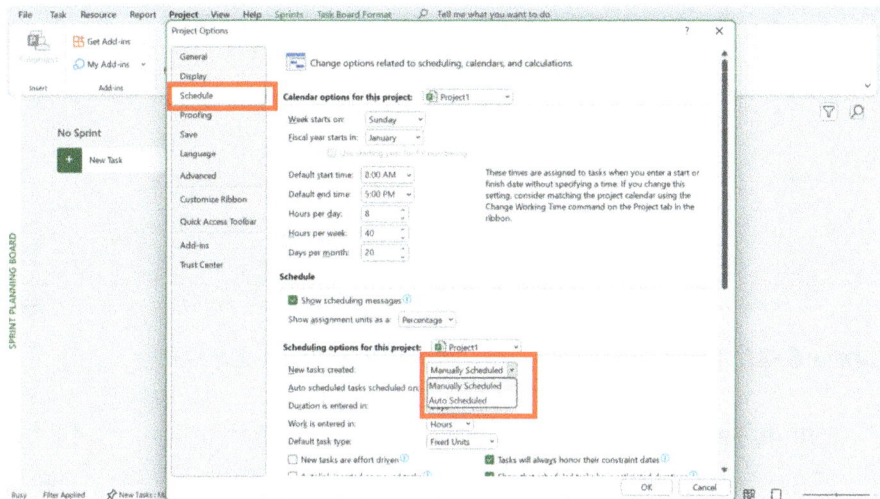

Figure 8-20. *Change New tasks created from Manually Scheduled to Auto Scheduled*

You are now prepared to add features to the list. In the Sprint Planning Board, click where it says New Task; enter the task name, such as Capture Sales Forecasts, as shown in Figure 8-21; and click Add.

237

CHAPTER 8   AGILE PROJECT MANAGEMENT USING MICROSOFT PROJECT

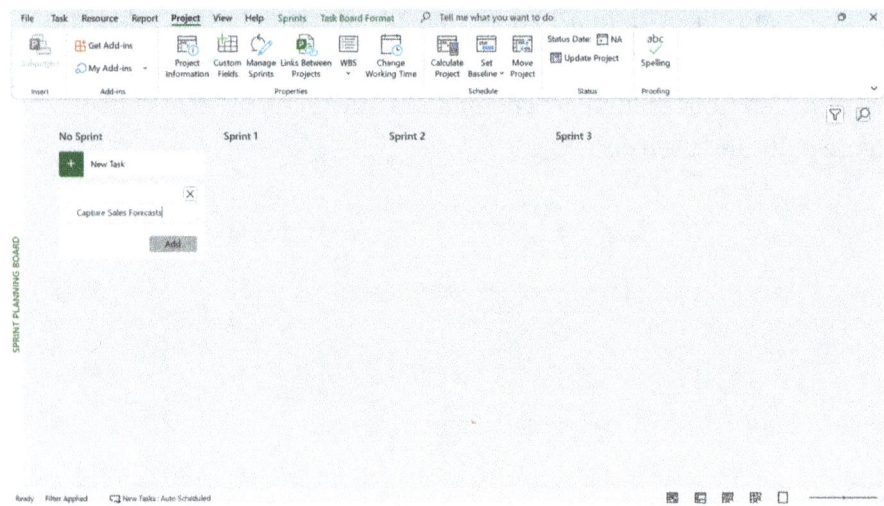

Figure 8-21.   Add "Capture Sales Forecasts" task

Continue adding all your features this way as shown in Figure 8-22.

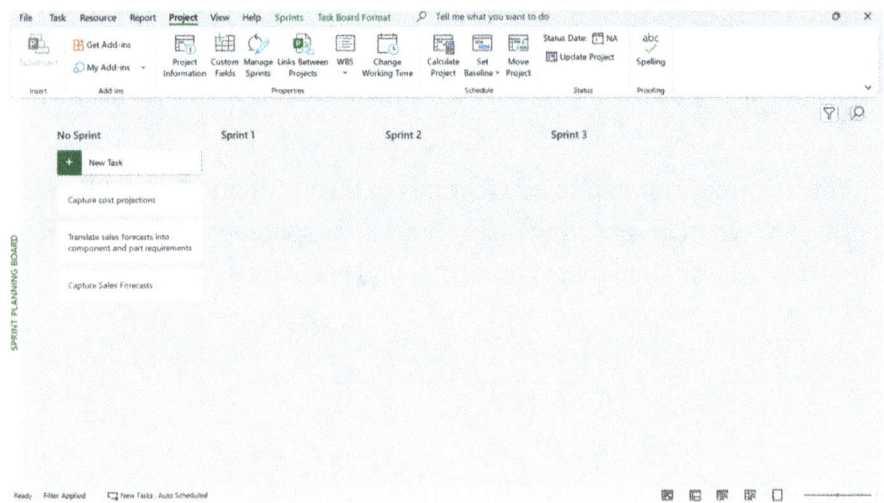

Figure 8-22.   Add features to the Sprint Planning Board

CHAPTER 8   AGILE PROJECT MANAGEMENT USING MICROSOFT PROJECT

If you have features listed in another file, like Word, they can be copied and pasted into the project. For easier management, use a task table. Go to the Sprints tab in the ribbon, select Planning as shown in Figure 8-23, and then click Sprint Planning Sheet to display a table. You will see the first feature already listed as shown in Figure 8-24.

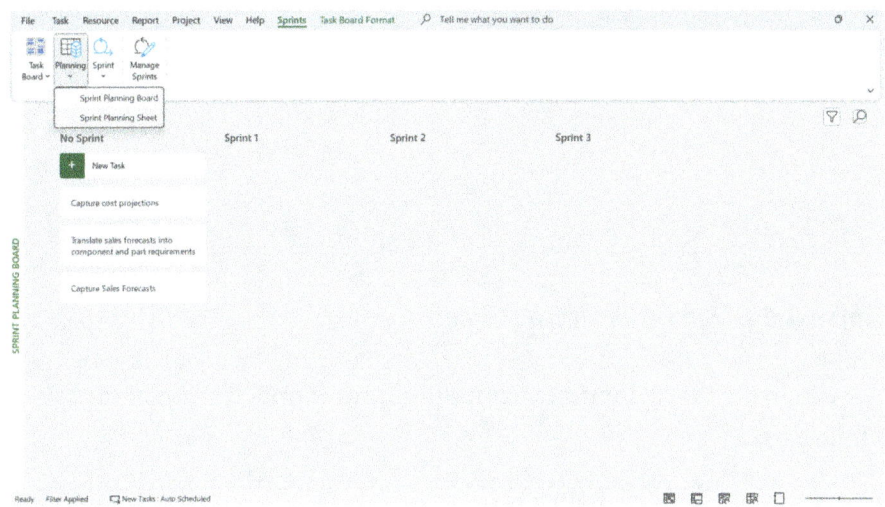

Figure 8-23. Access Sprint Planning Sheet

CHAPTER 8   AGILE PROJECT MANAGEMENT USING MICROSOFT PROJECT

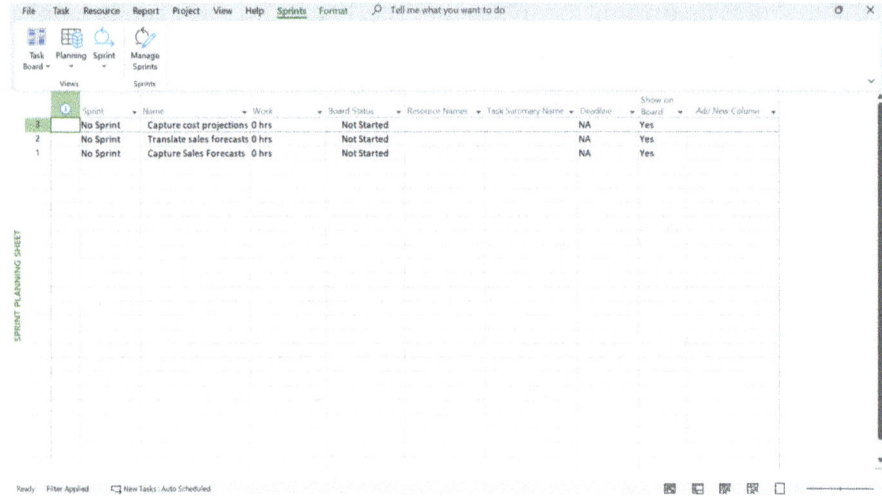

Figure 8-24. Sprint Planning Sheet

Switch to a Word document containing additional feature names such as follows:

- Capture cost changes
- Refactoring of prior features as needed
- Part and component availability data
- Cost data for expedited shipping
- Cost data for expedited manufacturing
- Capture competitor performance data
- Capture costs per customer
- Align timing between competitor and KinetEco data for data integrity
- Manufacturing cost data per shift per week
- Calculate cost from staffing changes

CHAPTER 8   AGILE PROJECT MANAGEMENT USING MICROSOFT PROJECT

And copy the remaining features to the clipboard, return to the project file, and paste them into the Name column by selecting the first blank name cell and pressing Ctrl+V as shown in Figure 8-25.

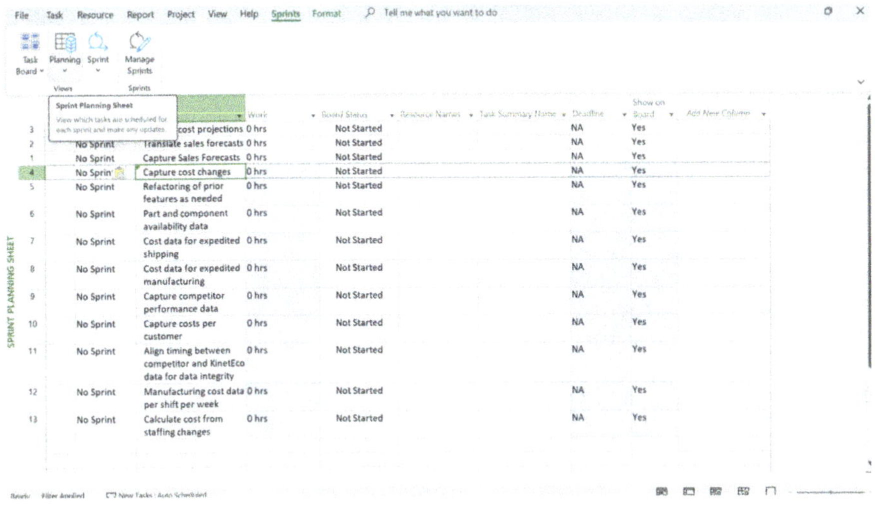

Figure 8-25. *Features from a Word file updated in the Sprint Planning Sheet*

For any additional tasks, click the first blank name cell, and insert a new task, such as Dashboard Closeout, which includes a comprehensive retrospective, lessons learned, and a technical review to identify potential enhancements as shown in Figure 8-26. Right-click the task, select Information from the shortcut menu, change the duration to five days (5d) as shown in Figure 8-27, and click OK.

CHAPTER 8   AGILE PROJECT MANAGEMENT USING MICROSOFT PROJECT

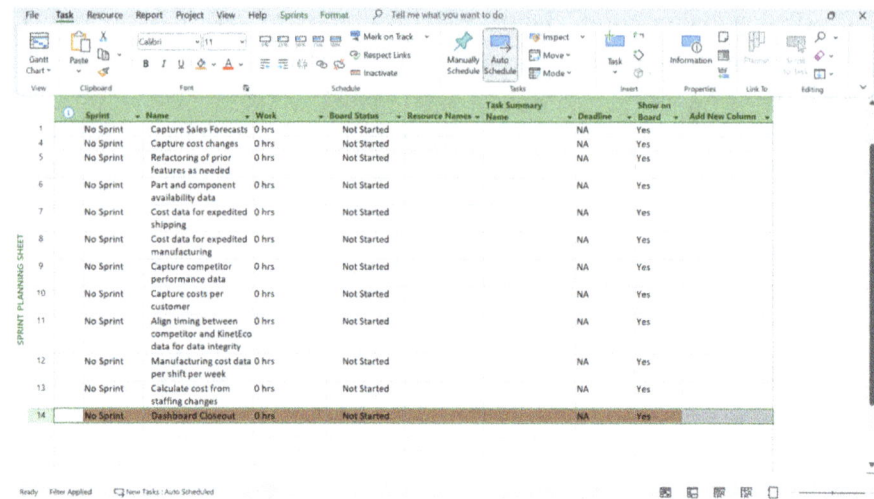

Figure 8-26. Addition of new task "Dashboard Closeout"

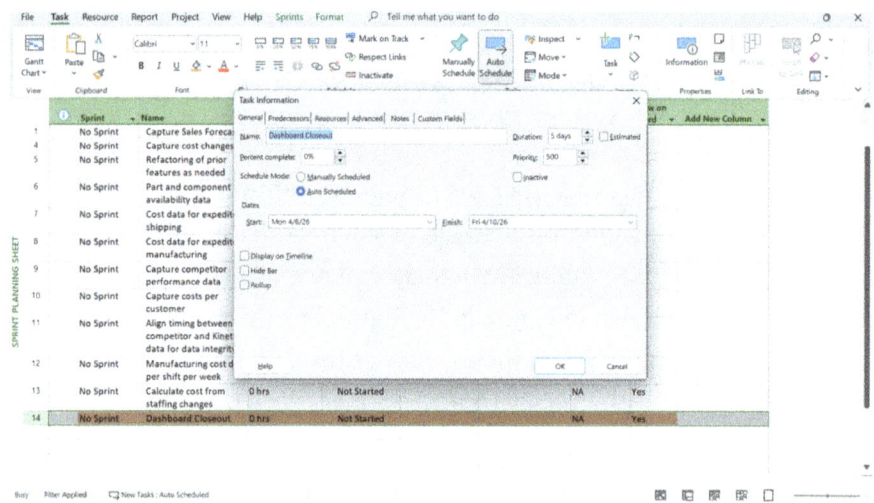

Figure 8-27. Duration updated to 5 days

To manage nonfeature tasks, adjust their visibility on Task Boards. For Dashboard Closeout, change Show on Board from yes to no, preventing its display in Task Boards view as shown in Figure 8-28.

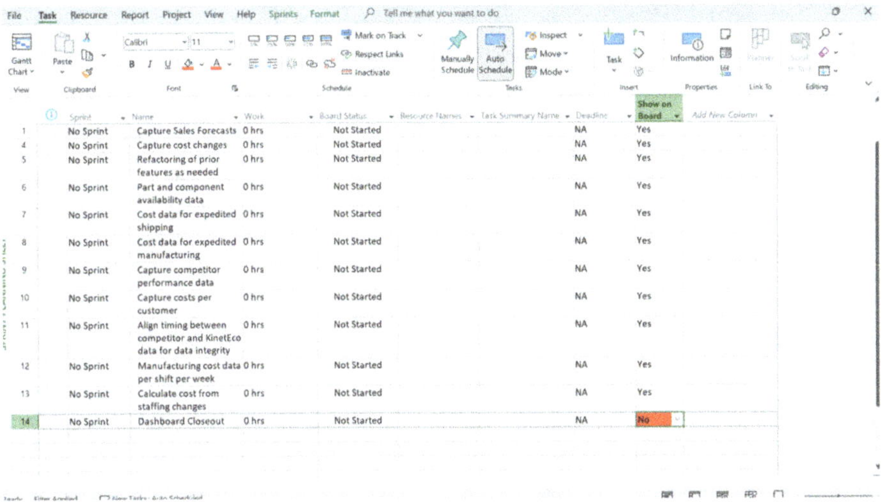

CHAPTER 8   AGILE PROJECT MANAGEMENT USING MICROSOFT PROJECT

Figure 8-28.   Changed Show on Board from yes to no

Finally, save the project with an appropriate name as "Add features to the agile backlog." These steps outline how to add tasks for features to the backlog in Project.

Create Sprint

In agile projects, the sprint length is standardized across all sprints, with the project duration established during high-level planning by the owner and the team. Within Microsoft Project, you can specify the sprint length for your project, determine the total number of sprints, and set their start dates.

To manage sprints, navigate to the Sprints tab and select Manage, which opens the Manage Sprints dialog box as shown in Figure 8-29.

243

CHAPTER 8   AGILE PROJECT MANAGEMENT USING MICROSOFT PROJECT

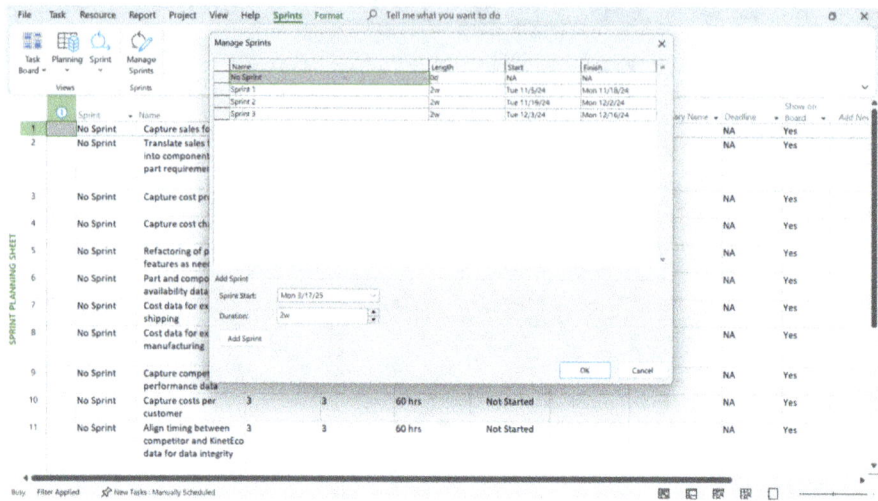

Figure 8-29. Manage Sprints dialog box

In this scenario, Project has prepopulated some sprints; however, the dates are incorrect. We will delete these three sprints and begin anew. Select the three rows, right-click, and choose Delete Sprint. This action will prompt a message box indicating tasks will move to No Sprint as shown in Figure 8-30. Since no sprints have been assigned yet, click OK.

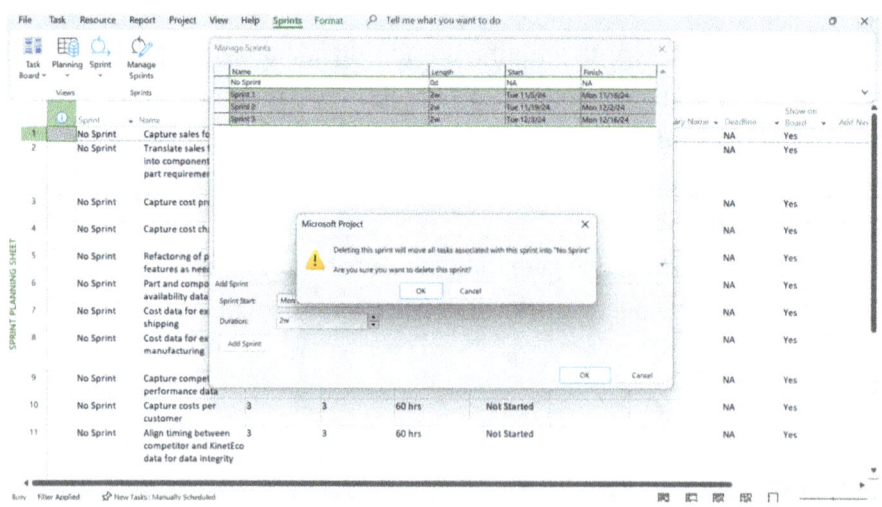

Figure 8-30. Delete existing sprints

CHAPTER 8   AGILE PROJECT MANAGEMENT USING MICROSOFT PROJECT

Next, enter the desired start date for the first sprint in the Sprint Start box, which in this case is April 6, 2026. The duration is set to two weeks, which aligns with our requirements as shown in Figure 8-31.

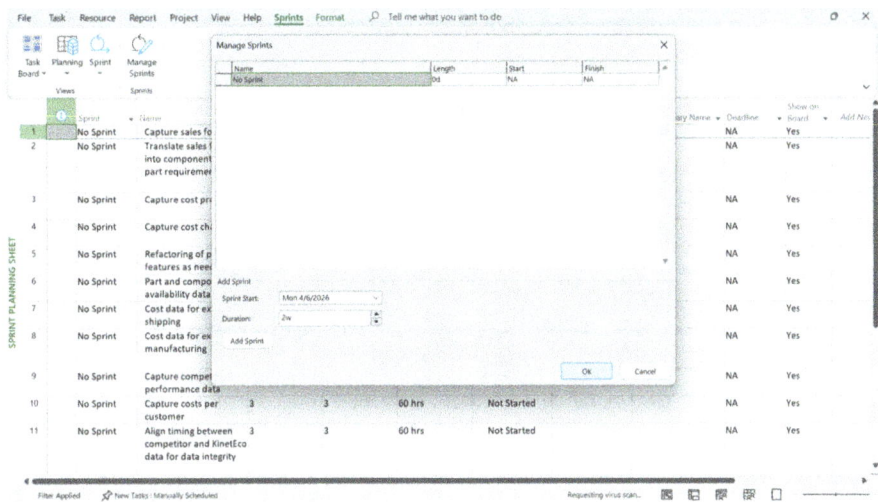

Figure 8-31. *Create new sprints*

Click Add Sprint to create Sprint 1, and then repeat this process two more times to establish the first three sprints for Release 1, as shown in Figure 8-32.

245

CHAPTER 8   AGILE PROJECT MANAGEMENT USING MICROSOFT PROJECT

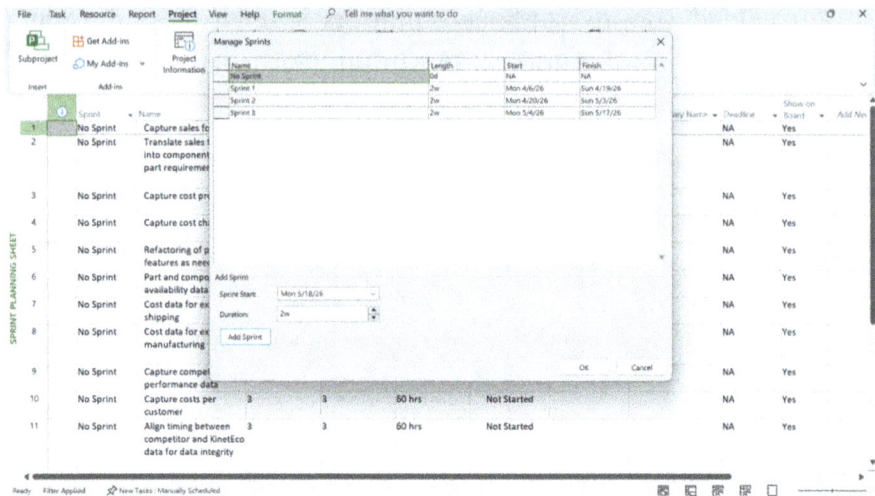

Figure 8-32. *Creation of Sprints 1, 2, and 3*

This method effectively defines sprints in Microsoft Project, including intervals for release activities.

With this, we have come to the end of this chapter. In this chapter, we have provided an introduction to Agile in Microsoft Project and setting up an Agile project. In the set up of the Agile project. In the set-up of the Agile project, we covered turning Agile features on for a project, add new product features to be developed to the agile backlog and create Sprints. In the next chapter, we will be analyzing Microsoft Project reports which includes New reports, Dashboards, resources, costs, in-progress and other reports.

CHAPTER 9

Microsoft Project Reports and Analytics

In the previous chapter, we provided an introduction to Agile in Microsoft Project and how to set up an Agile project. In setting up an Agile project, we covered topics such as enabling the Agile feature for a project, adding features to the Agile backlog, and creating sprints. In the chapter, we will be exploring our learning of Microsoft project with its reports and analytics features. In this chapter, we will be learning how to play with a Microsoft Project report by choosing its different set fields and focusing on the key results in a graphical report. Since we have already explored different types of reports in Microsoft Project in the first chapter of this book under the section "Reporting and Analytics," new learnings in this chapter about Microsoft Project report will be valuable from the practical application perspective.

Introduction

Microsoft Project offers powerful reporting and analytics to monitor project performance. Users can create custom reports to check project status, spot trends, and make informed decisions. This helps identify improvement areas and apply best practices. These features keep stakeholders updated on progress and performance, as shown in Figure 9-1.

CHAPTER 9 MICROSOFT PROJECT REPORTS AND ANALYTICS

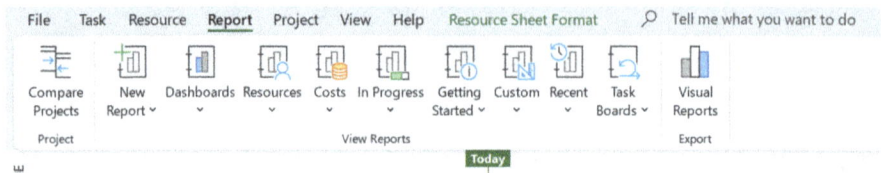

Figure 9-1. *Reports in MS Project*

Microsoft Project offers a variety of reports to help you manage and visualize your project data effectively. Here are some of the key types of reports you can generate and we have learned in the first chapter under the section "Reporting and Analytics":

Overview Reports: These reports provide a high-level summary of your project, including key metrics and overall progress. Examples include

- **Project Overview**: Summarizes the project's status, including start and finish dates, percentage complete, and key milestones
- **Burndown**: Shows the work remaining over time, helping you track progress against your schedule

Task Reports: Task reports focus on the details of individual tasks within your project. Examples include

- **Critical Tasks**: Lists tasks that are on the critical path and must be completed on time to avoid delaying the project
- **Late Tasks**: Identifies tasks that are behind schedule
- **Milestones**: Highlights key milestones and their status

CHAPTER 9 MICROSOFT PROJECT REPORTS AND ANALYTICS

Resource Reports: Resource reports provide insights into how resources are being utilized in your project. Examples include

- **Resource Overview**: Summarizes the allocation and workload of resources
- **Resource Work**: Details the amount of work assigned to each resource
- **Resource Cost**: Shows the cost associated with each resource

Cost Reports: Cost reports help you track and manage the financial aspects of your project. Examples include

- **Cost Overview**: Provides a summary of the project's costs, including actual, remaining, and baseline costs
- **Cash Flow**: Displays the projected cash flow over time
- **Earned Value**: Combines cost and schedule performance to provide a comprehensive view of project health

Progress Reports: Progress reports focus on tracking the progress of tasks and the overall project. Examples include

- **Task Progress**: Shows the percentage complete for each task
- **Project Progress**: Summarizes the overall progress of the project

Custom Reports: Microsoft Project allows you to create custom reports tailored to your specific needs. You can choose the data to include, the layout, and the formatting to create reports that best suit your project requirements.

249

Visual Reports: Visual reports use charts and graphs to present project data in a more digestible format. Examples include

- **Resource Allocation**: Displays resource usage in a graphical format
- **Task Status**: Uses charts to show the status of tasks

Timeline Reports: Timeline reports provide a visual representation of your project schedule. Examples include

- **Gantt Chart**: A classic timeline view showing tasks, durations, and dependencies
- **Timeline View**: A simplified timeline that highlights key tasks and milestones

Workload Reports: Workload reports help you manage and balance the workload across resources. Examples include

- **Resource Usage**: Shows the amount of work assigned to each resource over time
- **Resource Availability**: Displays the availability of resources for future tasks

Variance Reports: Variance reports compare planned versus actual performance. Examples include

- **Task Variance**: Shows the difference between planned and actual task durations
- **Cost Variance**: Highlights discrepancies between planned and actual costs

These reports can be customized and tailored to meet the specific needs of your project, providing valuable insights and helping you make informed decisions.

CHAPTER 9   MICROSOFT PROJECT REPORTS AND ANALYTICS

Choosing the Fields in a Graphical Report

Project includes several built-in graphical reports, but additional customized reports may be required to meet specific company needs. This section explains how to choose fields in a graphical report, whether replacing existing ones or adding new ones.

Step 1: To edit reports, navigate to the Report tab, and click Dashboards ➤ More Reports option as shown in Figure 9-2.

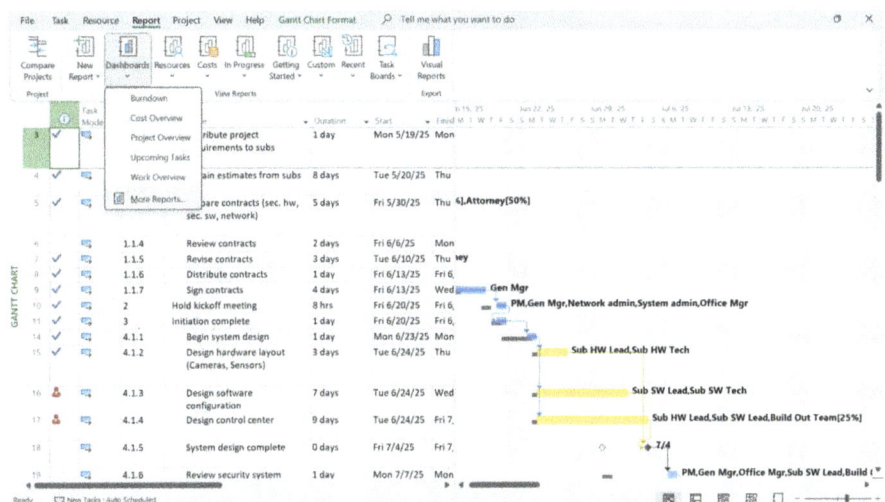

Figure 9-2. Access Dashboards reports

Step 2: Choose value "Dashboards" and "Project Overview," and click the Select button as shown in Figure 9-3.

251

CHAPTER 9   MICROSOFT PROJECT REPORTS AND ANALYTICS

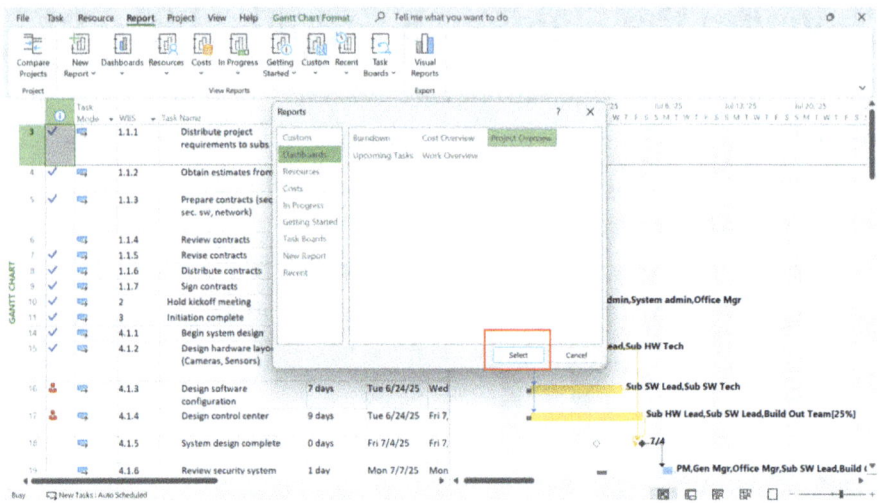

Figure 9-3.   Choose Project Overview report from Dashboards reports

Step 3: Project Overview report is displayed as shown in Figure 9-4.

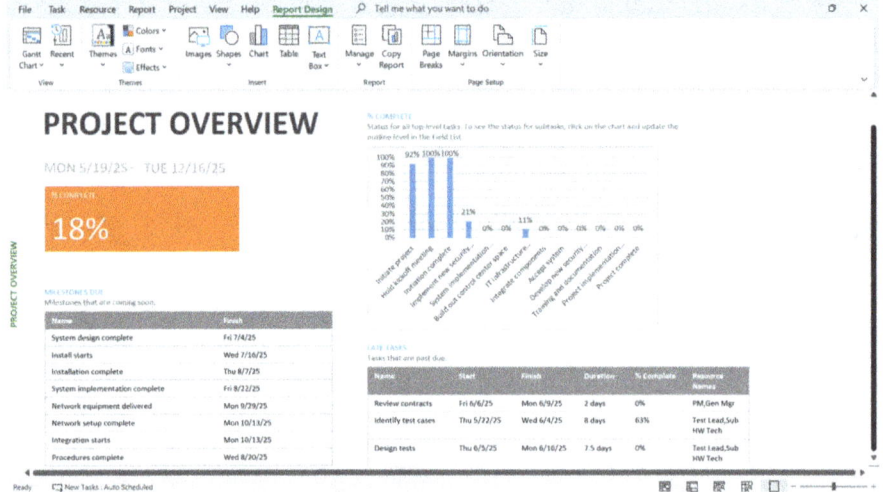

Figure 9-4.   Project Overview report

CHAPTER 9   MICROSOFT PROJECT REPORTS AND ANALYTICS

Step 4: In the Report Design tab, select Manage ➤ Rename Report as shown in Figure 9-5, to create a copy with a new name, such as Project at a Glance.

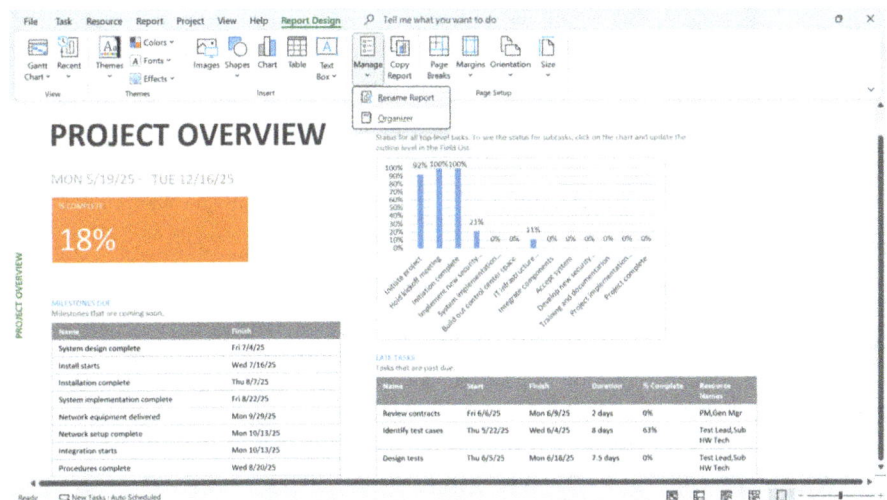

Figure 9-5.   Rename Report option

Step 5: Update report name as Project at a Glance, and click OK as shown in Figure 9-6.

253

CHAPTER 9   MICROSOFT PROJECT REPORTS AND ANALYTICS

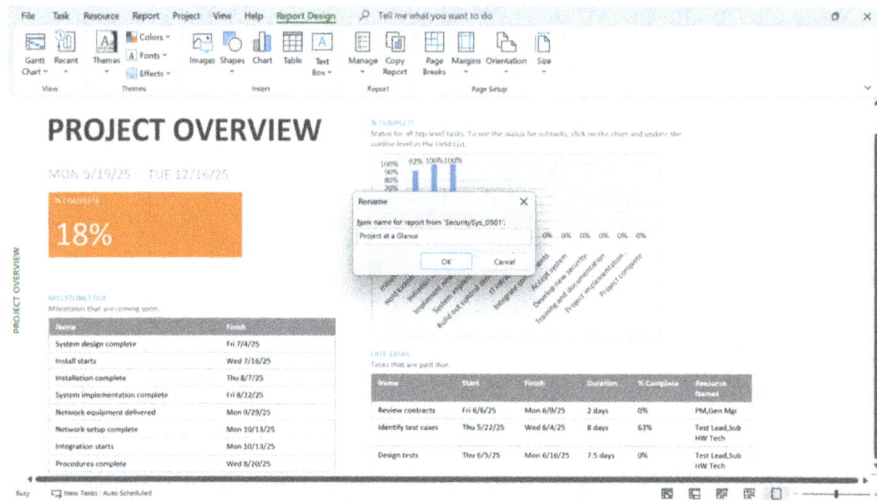

Figure 9-6. Rename project

Step 6: Updated report name appears as shown in Figure 9-7.

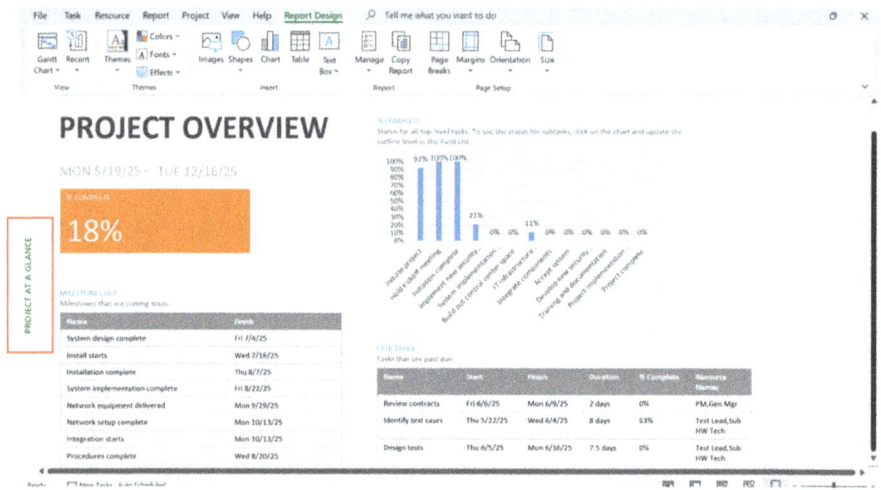

Figure 9-7. Report name changed to "Project at a Glance"

Now, we will change the title of the report from Project Overview to Project at a Glance by following the below steps.

CHAPTER 9   MICROSOFT PROJECT REPORTS AND ANALYTICS

Step 1: The first step is to change the name in the report to reflect its new title, Project at a Glance, as shown in Figure 9-8.

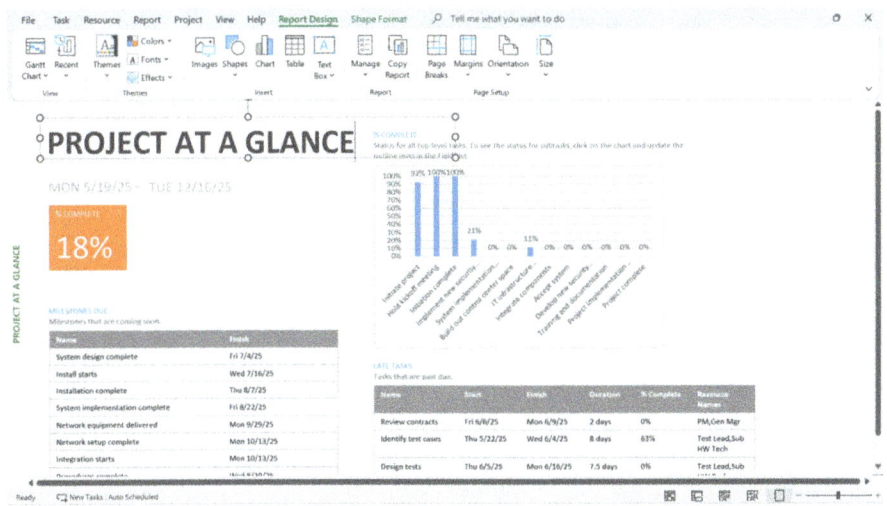

Figure 9-8. *Update project title to "Project at a Glance"*

Step 2: Next, update the field in the text box from % Complete to % Work Complete. As shown in Figure 9-9, right-click the box to display the Field List on the right-hand side.

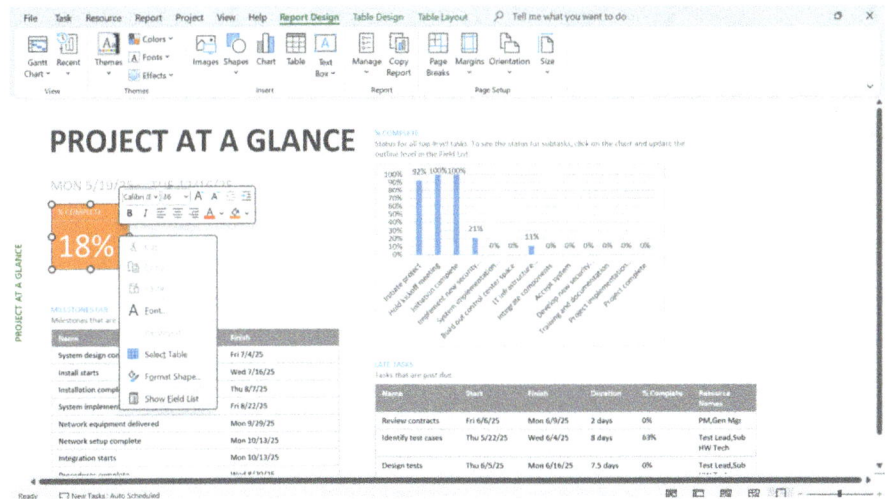

Figure 9-9. *Access Field List*

CHAPTER 9   MICROSOFT PROJECT REPORTS AND ANALYTICS

Step 3: Turn on % Work Complete and turn off % Complete as shown in Figure 9-10.

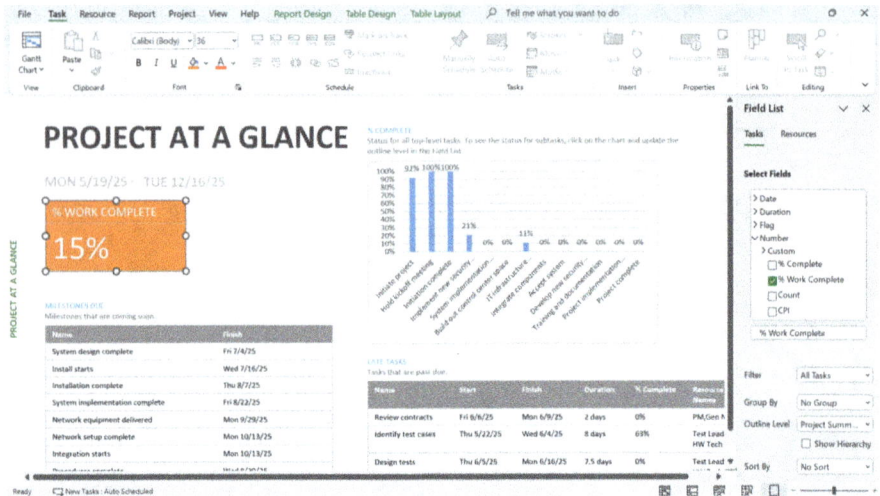

Figure 9-10. % Work Complete updated

For charts, similar steps apply.

Step 1: Use the % Complete chart; right-click the chart to display the Field List panel on the right-hand side as shown in Figure 9-11.

CHAPTER 9   MICROSOFT PROJECT REPORTS AND ANALYTICS

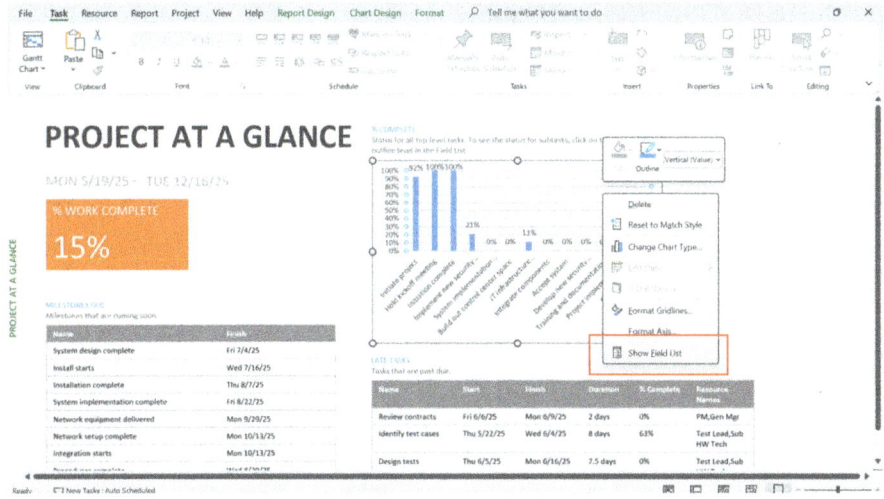

Figure 9-11. Right-click the chart

Step 2: From the Field List on the right-hand side, select % Work Complete, and turn off % Complete as shown in Figure 9-12. Also, update chart report title to % Work Complete.

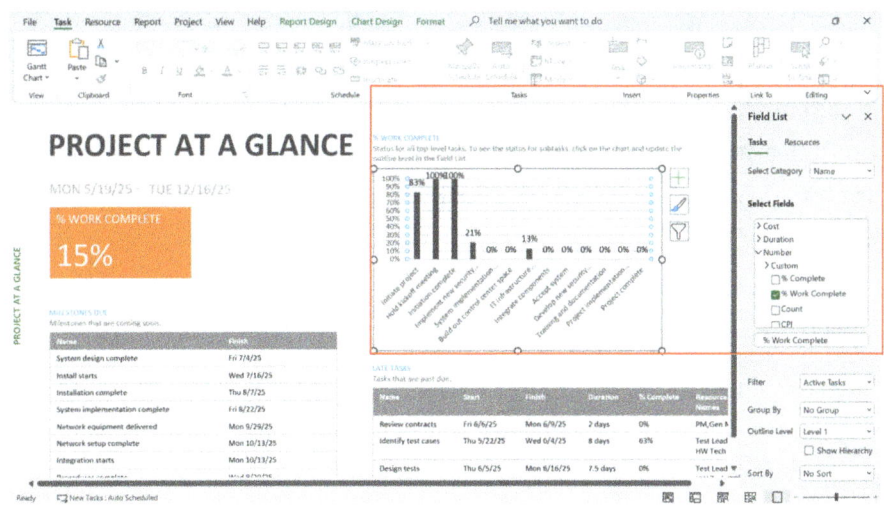

Figure 9-12. Select % Work Complete

257

CHAPTER 9   MICROSOFT PROJECT REPORTS AND ANALYTICS

Changing fields in tables follows the same process.

Step 1: Select the Late Tasks table, and right-click on it to display the Field List as shown in Figure 9-13.

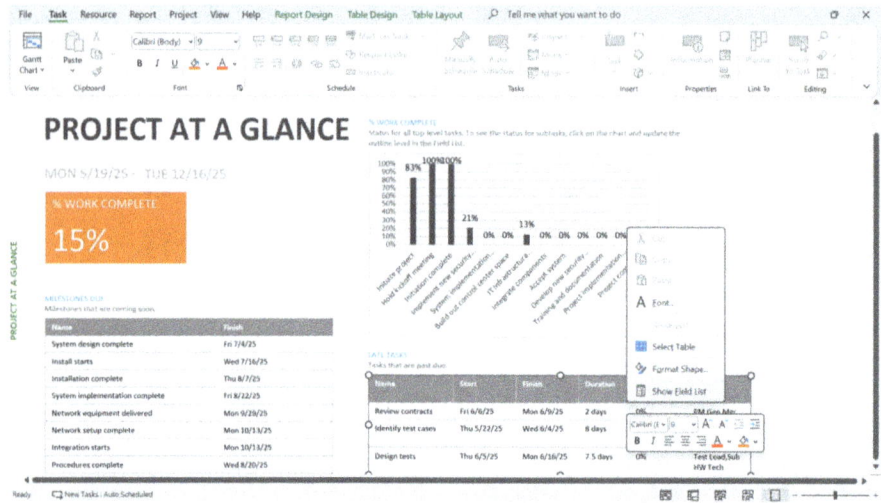

Figure 9-13. Right-click the Late Tasks table to access Show Field List option

Step 2: Add % Work Complete as shown in Figure 9-14. Navigate through the list by collapsing higher-level categories like Date and Duration, and then find the relevant fields under the Number category. Turn on % Work Complete, and adjust the order if necessary by dragging it next to % Complete.

CHAPTER 9   MICROSOFT PROJECT REPORTS AND ANALYTICS

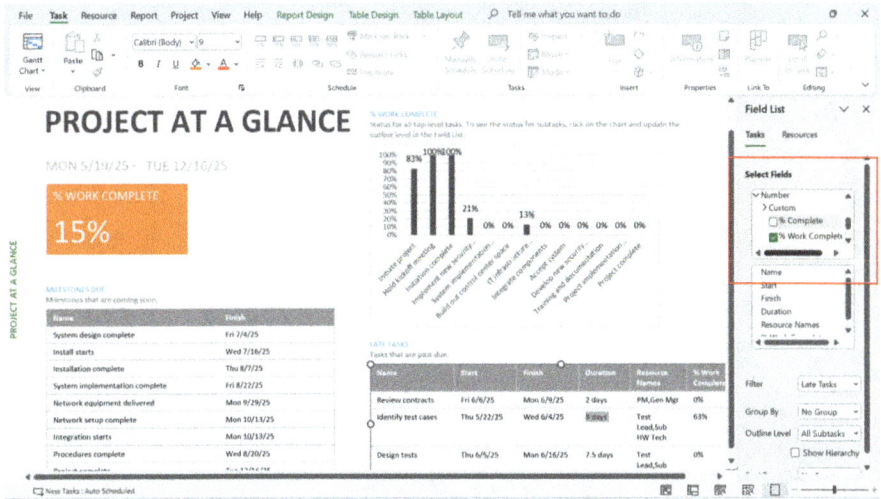

Figure 9-14. *Add % Work Complete*

The challenging part of choosing fields is locating them in the Field List. Add the Actual Work field to the Late Tasks table; it can be found in the Work category, just below the Number category as shown in Figure 9-15.

259

CHAPTER 9   MICROSOFT PROJECT REPORTS AND ANALYTICS

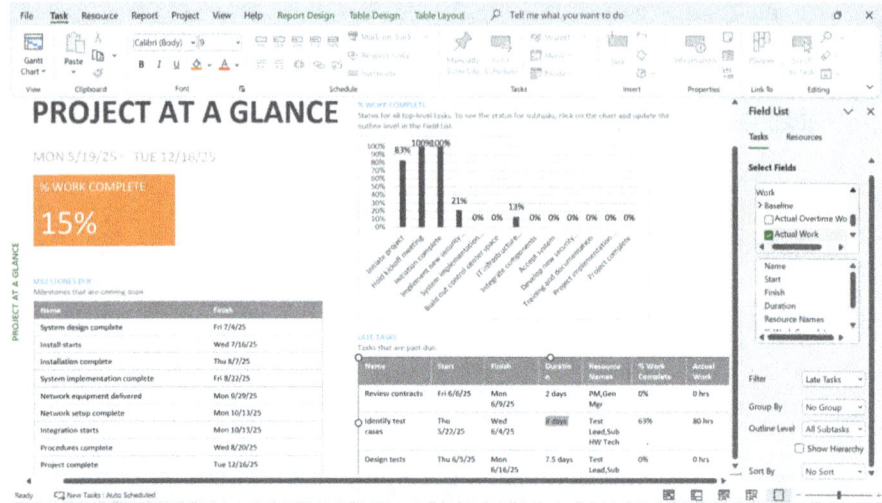

Figure 9-15. Add Actual Work field

Focusing on Key Results in a Graphical Report

The most effective reports emphasize crucial information. In Project, important data can be highlighted by filtering and grouping results in tables and charts. We will continue working on our custom report. Remember that you can access your custom reports by going to the Report tab and clicking Custom. Let us begin by filtering the % Complete Chart as shown in the below steps.

Step 1: Clicking on the chart opens the Field List pane on the right-hand side as shown in Figure 9-16.

CHAPTER 9   MICROSOFT PROJECT REPORTS AND ANALYTICS

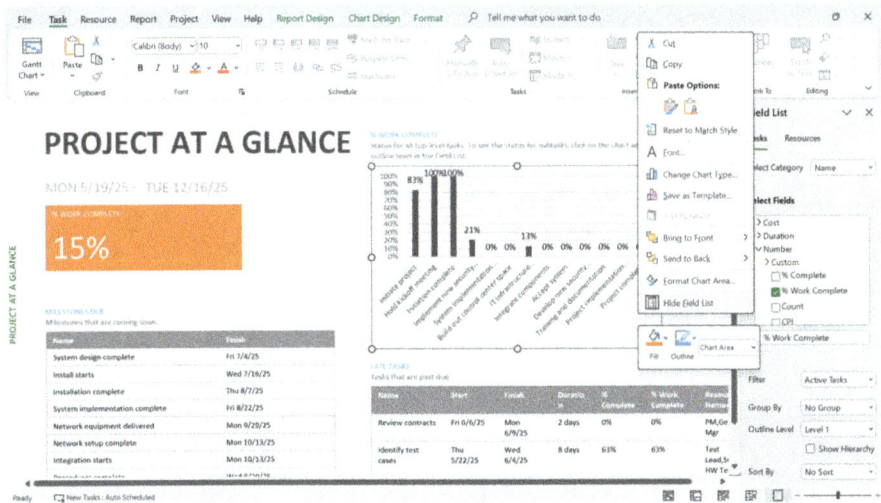

Figure 9-16. Access Field List to modify the chart

Step 2: In the lower half of the Field List pane, you will find the Filter box. By clicking the down arrow, you can view all available filters in the project and select one as needed. For instance, to filter by date range, click it in the list as shown in Figure 9-17.

CHAPTER 9   MICROSOFT PROJECT REPORTS AND ANALYTICS

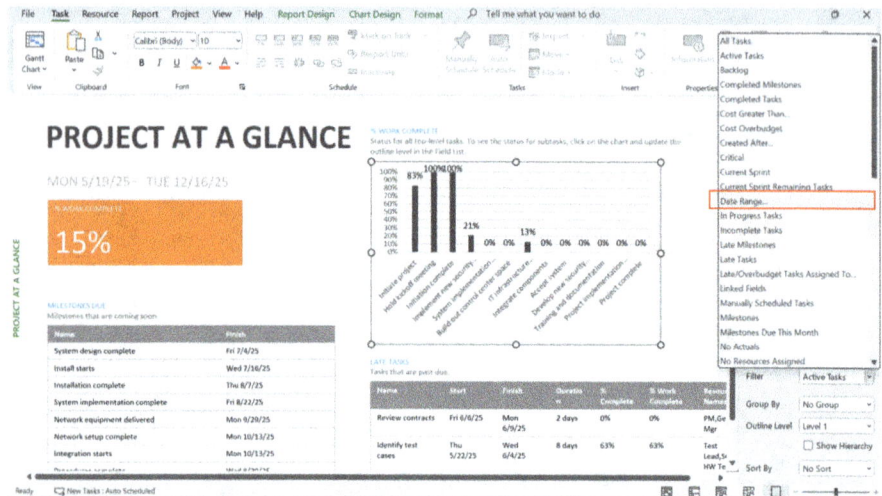

Figure 9-17. Select Date Range filter

Step 3: Enter dates, such as June 15, 2025, and August 15, 2025, in Figures 9-18 and 9-19, respectively.

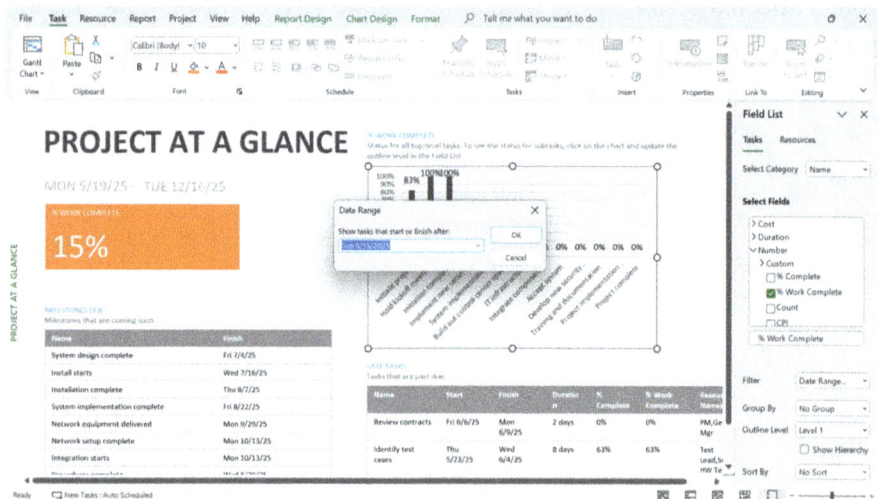

Figure 9-18. Add date June 15, 2025

CHAPTER 9   MICROSOFT PROJECT REPORTS AND ANALYTICS

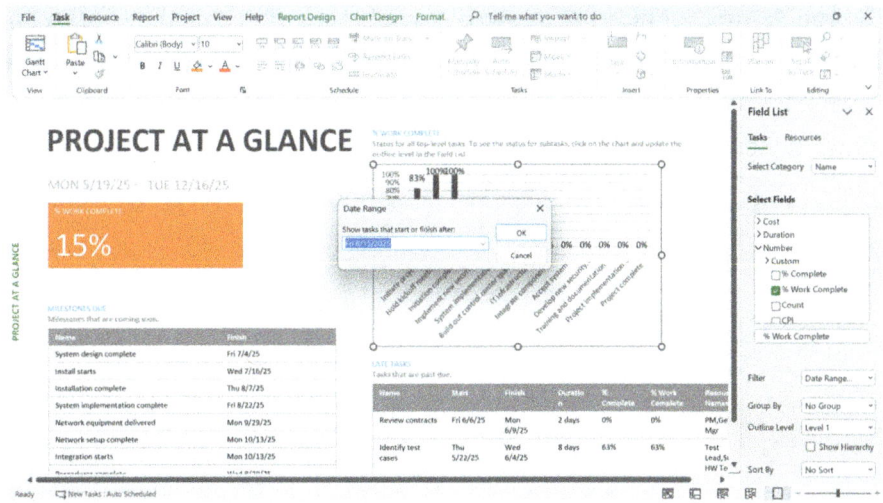

Figure 9-19. *Add date August 15, 2025*

Step 4: When you click OK, the chart displays only tasks within that date range, simplifying focus on the initial project phase as shown in Figure 9-20.

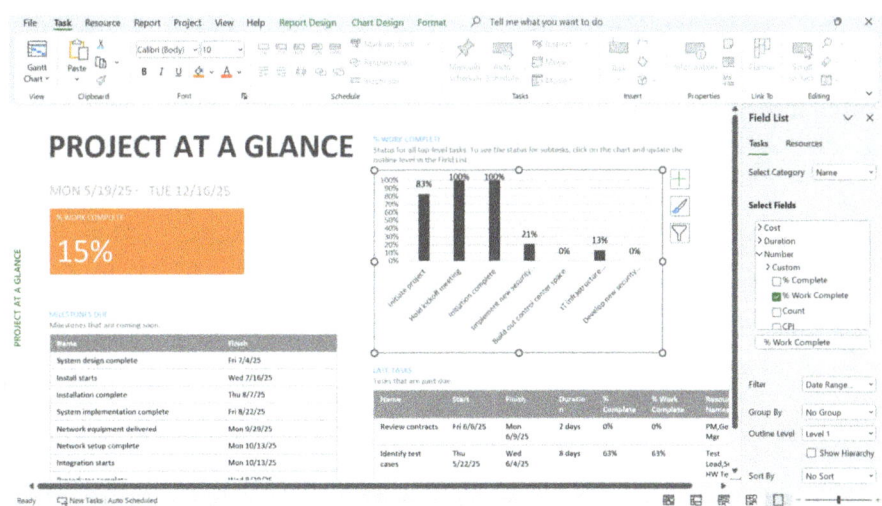

Figure 9-20. *The chart displays in the specific date range of June 15, 2025, and August 15, 2025*

263

CHAPTER 9   MICROSOFT PROJECT REPORTS AND ANALYTICS

Step 5: Another filtering method is available by clicking the Filter icon on the chart's right side. Upon clicking the chart, the Filter icon will appear. Clicking it reveals categories where check boxes can be toggled on or off as shown in Figure 9-21.

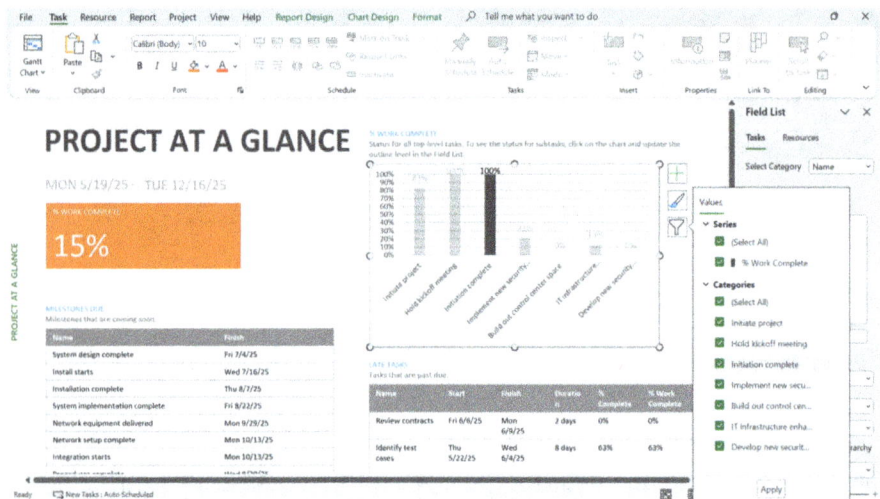

Figure 9-21. *Filter chart based on categories*

Step 6: Turn off Initiation complete, as it is a milestone and provides limited information as shown in Figure 9-22.

CHAPTER 9 MICROSOFT PROJECT REPORTS AND ANALYTICS

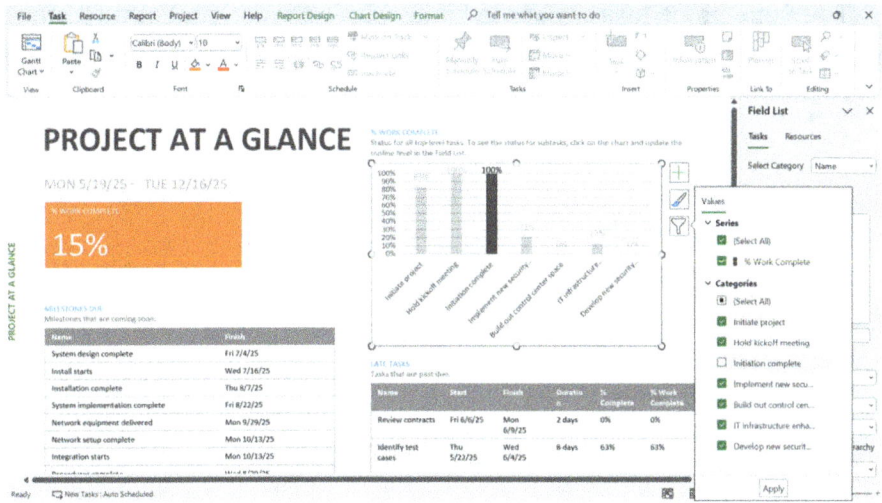

Figure 9-22. *Turn off the category "Initiation complete"*

Step 6: Click Apply to see the results as shown in Figure 9-23.

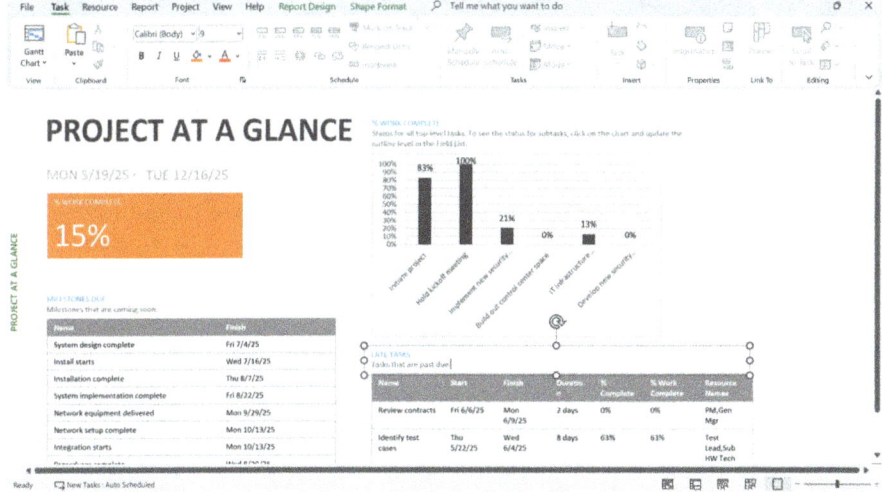

Figure 9-23. *Updated chart after turning off the category "Initiation complete"*

265

CHAPTER 9   MICROSOFT PROJECT REPORTS AND ANALYTICS

The same procedure applies to tables with below steps. For the Late Tasks table, click to open the Field List pane, as shown in Figure 9-24.

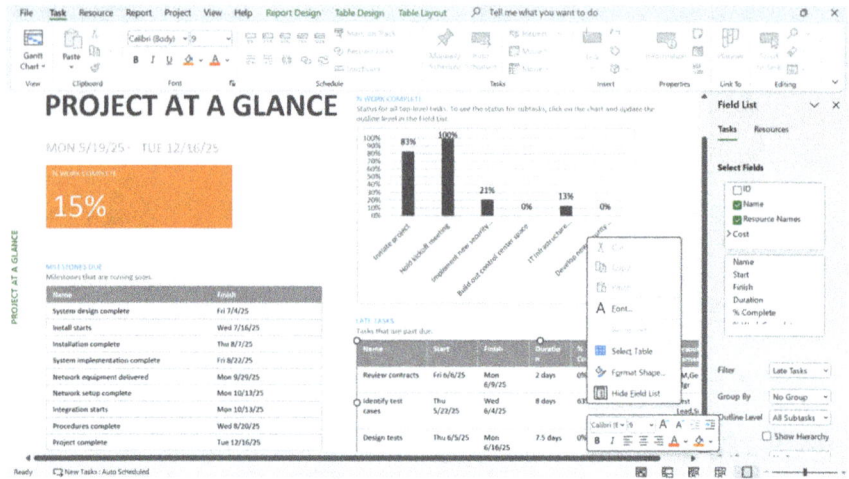

Figure 9-24. Access to Hide Field List

Step 2: Go to the Filter box, and click the down arrow. For this case, switch from Late Tasks to Work Overbudget tasks, indicating more work than scheduled as shown in Figures 9-25 and 9-26, respectively.

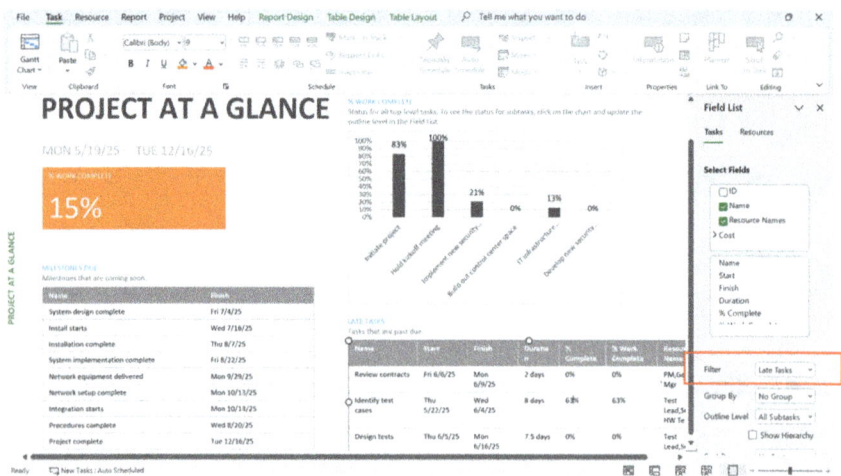

Figure 9-25. Access Filter box

CHAPTER 9   MICROSOFT PROJECT REPORTS AND ANALYTICS

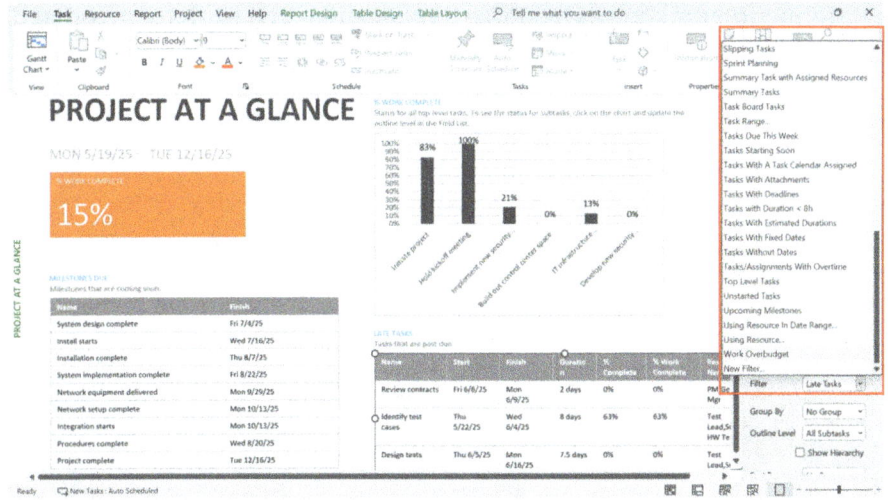

***Figure 9-26.** Select "Work Overbudget" from the filter*

Step 3: Applying this filter updates the table's visible tasks. You may revert to the original filter if desired. Grouping applies solely to charts as shown in Figure 9-27.

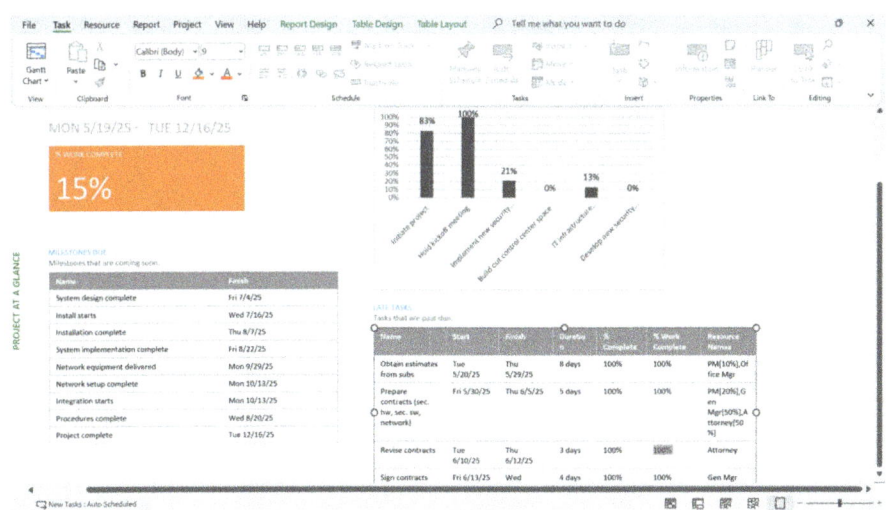

***Figure 9-27.** Chart with Work Overbudget filter*

267

CHAPTER 9 MICROSOFT PROJECT REPORTS AND ANALYTICS

Another report such as resource management can be demonstrated through the following steps:

Step 1: Select Report ➤ Resources ➤ More Reports options as shown in Figure 9-28.

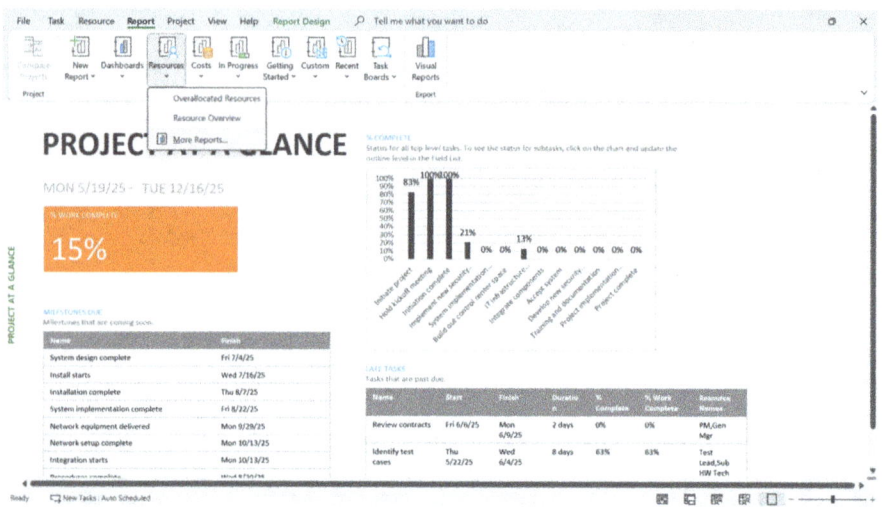

Figure 9-28. *Access Resources reports*

Step 2: In the below dialog box, select "Resources" and "Resource Overview," and click the Select button as shown in Figure 9-29.

CHAPTER 9   MICROSOFT PROJECT REPORTS AND ANALYTICS

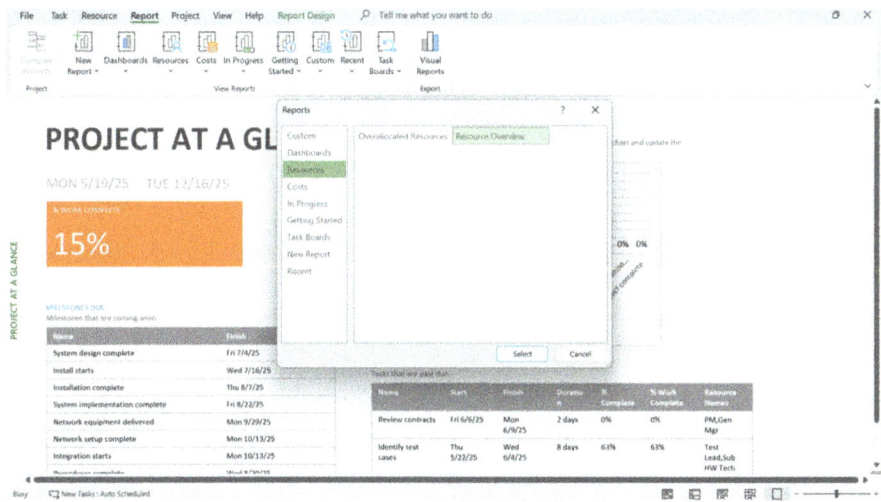

Figure 9-29.   *Choose Resource Overview report*

Step 3: The Resource Overview report is shown in Figure 9-30.

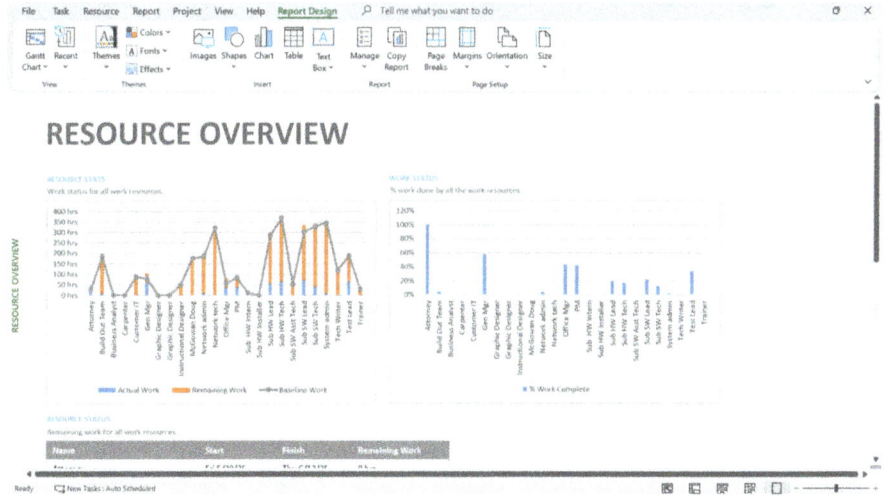

Figure 9-30.   *Resource Overview report*

Step 4: Grouping modifies how values are displayed on the x axis. Select the Resource Stats graph, and the Field List will be displayed on the right-hand side as shown in Figure 9-31.

269

CHAPTER 9 MICROSOFT PROJECT REPORTS AND ANALYTICS

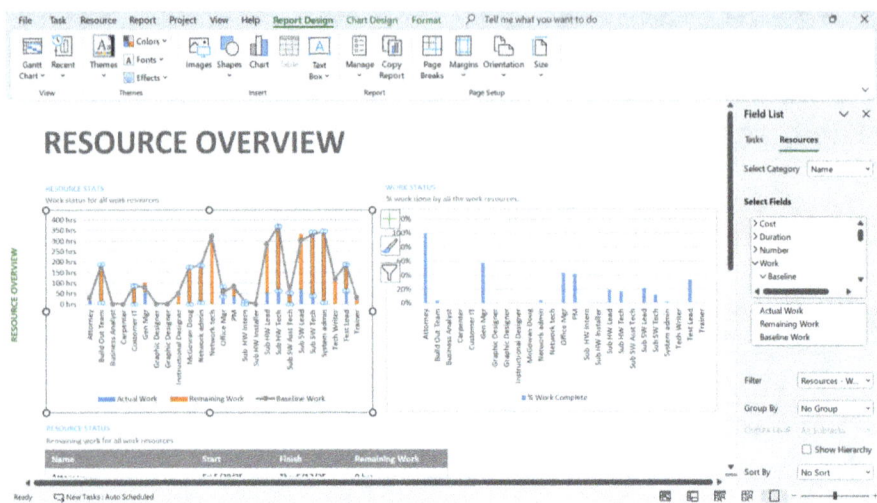

Figure 9-31. Field List for the Resource Stats chart

Step 5: In the Field List pane, go to Group By filter as shown in Figure 9-32.

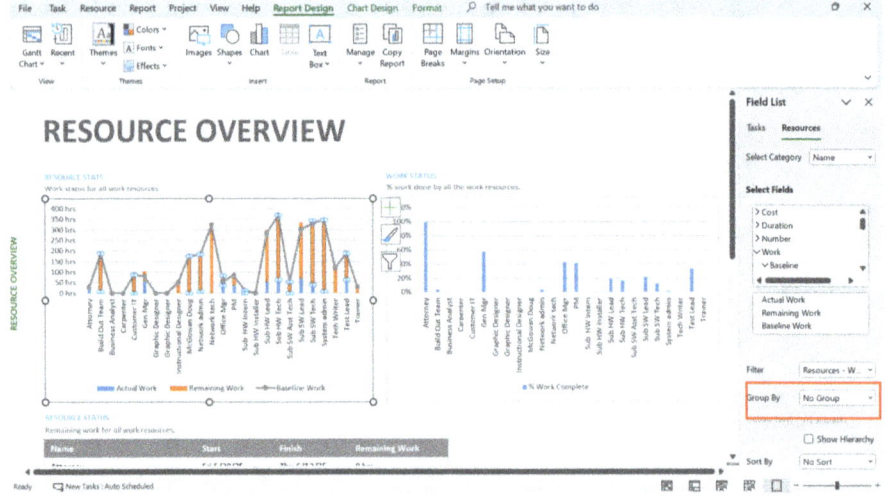

Figure 9-32. Group By filter

CHAPTER 9 MICROSOFT PROJECT REPORTS AND ANALYTICS

Step 6: Click the down arrow, and select Resource Group as shown in Figure 9-33.

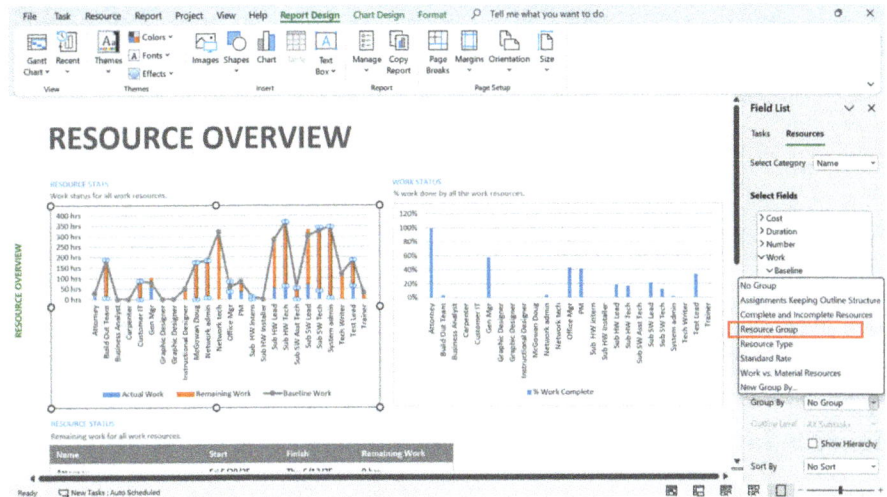

Figure 9-33. *Select Resource Group*

Step 7: The actual remaining and baseline work is now grouped by internal group, subcontractor group, and unassigned resources as shown in Figure 9-34.

CHAPTER 9   MICROSOFT PROJECT REPORTS AND ANALYTICS

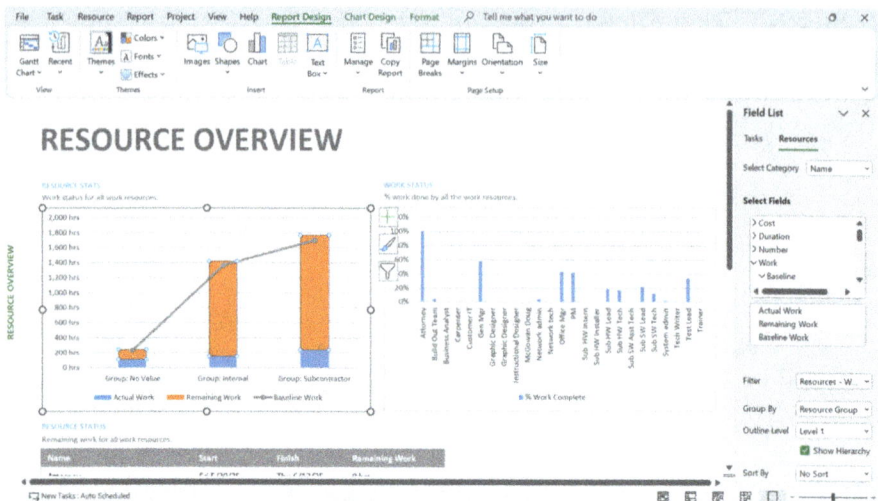

Figure 9-34. *Resource Stats report Group By Resource Group*

Having learned to filter and group results, take some time to experiment with these features in your reports.

With this, we have come to the end of this chapter. In this chapter, we have had a cursory introduction of already explored different types of reports in Microsoft Project in the first chapter of this book under the section "Reporting and Analytics"; then, in detail, we studied how to play with a Microsoft Project report by choosing its different set fields and focusing on the key results in a graphical report. In the next and final chapter, we will be focusing on the advanced features of Microsoft Project and future trends in project management which will cover earned value analysis, risk management and quality control, emerging technologies, future updates in Microsoft project, and preparing for the future and expert tips for efficiency.

CHAPTER 10

Advanced Features of Microsoft Project and Future Trends in Project Management

In the previous chapter, we introduced different types of reports in Microsoft Project. We then detailed how to customize a report using various fields and key results. In this final chapter, we will explore advanced features of Microsoft Project and future trends in project management. Topics include earned value analysis, risk management, quality control, emerging technologies, future updates, and expert tips for efficiency.

Saving time in Project is a compilation of efficient tips and techniques designed to enhance your expertise, introduce innovative methods for utilizing Project, or reminding you of features that may have been overlooked. In this chapter, we will touch base upon some new features of Microsoft Project and also some expert tips for efficient analysis, risk management, and quality control. These are simple, basic and cover

CHAPTER 10 ADVANCED FEATURES OF MICROSOFT PROJECT AND FUTURE TRENDS IN PROJECT MANAGEMENT

copying data into adjacent rows, quickly inserting multiple tasks, entering values quickly with a lookup table, wrapping text in table cells, aligning cell data, copying cell formatting, changing currency formatting, and adjusting column and row size in Project.

Introduction

Microsoft Project 2025 introduces a range of advanced features designed to enhance project management efficiency, collaboration, and overall user experience. From enhanced project planning and improved expense management to advanced collaboration tools and financial management capabilities, the new release offers a comprehensive suite of tools to support project managers in delivering successful projects. The integration of AI-driven features like Copilot, along with seamless integration with Microsoft Teams and Outlook, ensures that project management tasks are streamlined and efficient. With a focus on usability, performance, and reliability, Microsoft Project 2025 is well equipped to meet the needs of modern project management.

In the upcoming sections, let's look at the advanced features of Microsoft Project and some expert tips for efficient analysis, risk management, and quality control.

Advanced Features of Microsoft Project Available

Microsoft Project continues to evolve, offering a range of advanced features designed to enhance project management efficiency, collaboration, and overall user experience. Here's an in-depth look at the features introduced in 2025:

CHAPTER 10   ADVANCED FEATURES OF MICROSOFT PROJECT AND FUTURE TRENDS IN PROJECT MANAGEMENT

- **Work Breakdown Structure (WBS) Templates**: Microsoft Project 2025 introduces support for Work Breakdown Structure (WBS) templates, allowing project managers to create and reuse detailed project plans. This feature simplifies the planning process by providing a structured approach to breaking down projects into manageable tasks.

- **Time Zone-Agnostic Fields**: To accommodate global teams, Microsoft Project now includes time zone-agnostic fields for projects and project tasks. This ensures that deadlines and schedules are consistent regardless of the team members' locations

- **Mobile and Browser Enhancements**: The expense management experience has been significantly improved on both mobile and browser platforms. These enhancements make it easier for team members to submit and track expenses, ensuring that project budgets are managed effectively.

- **Copilot Integration**: One of the most exciting additions is the integration of Copilot capabilities. This AI-driven feature allows for intelligent, natural language interactions, making it easier to manage projects through conversational commands. Copilot can assist with scheduling, task assignments, and more, streamlining project management tasks.

- **Teams and Outlook Integration**: Microsoft Project 2025 offers seamless integration with Microsoft Teams and Outlook. This integration enhances productivity by allowing users to manage project tasks and communications within the tools they use daily.

- **Billing Backlog Review**: Usability improvements have been made to the billing backlog review process, making it more intuitive and efficient. This includes enhancements to the pro forma invoice review, approval, and contract management experiences.

- **Task Details Customization**: Project managers can now customize the task details view to better suit their project management needs. This feature allows for a more personalized and efficient project management experience.

- **Revenue Recognition**: Microsoft Project 2025 introduces flexibility in financial dimensions and revenue recognition based on contract lines. This feature ensures that revenue is accurately tracked and reported, aligning with the financial goals of the organization.

- **Project G/L Journals**: The new release supports the creation of project General Ledger (G/L) journals, providing a more comprehensive financial management tool within the project management framework.

- **Async Dual-Write**: To support larger invoices, Microsoft Project 2025 leverages async dual-write technology. This ensures that data is written asynchronously, improving performance and reliability when handling large volumes of data.

- **Extensibility Patterns**: The new release includes extensibility patterns for additional fields in the invoice summary. This allows organizations to customize their invoicing processes to better meet their specific needs.

CHAPTER 10   ADVANCED FEATURES OF MICROSOFT PROJECT AND FUTURE TRENDS IN PROJECT MANAGEMENT

- **Improved Subcontract Information**: Microsoft Project 2025 provides enhanced support for subcontract information, allowing project managers to manage subcontractor details more effectively. This feature consolidates subcontractor information in one place, improving visibility and management.

- **What-If Analysis on Estimates**: Project managers can now perform what-if analysis on project estimates. This feature allows for better decision-making by analyzing different scenarios and their potential impact on the project.

- **Global Address Book Sync**: The new release supports synchronization with the global address book, ensuring that contact information is up-to-date and consistent across the organization.

- **Integration Troubleshooting**: Microsoft Project 2025 includes tools for troubleshooting integrations with other systems. This feature helps identify and resolve integration issues, ensuring smooth operation of project management processes.

- **New User Experience for Copy Project**: The user experience for copying projects has been improved, making it easier to duplicate and modify existing projects. This feature saves time and ensures consistency across similar projects.

- **Increased WBS Limits**: The limits for the Work Breakdown Structure have been increased, allowing for more detailed and complex project plans. This enhancement supports the management of larger and more intricate projects.

- **Time Zone Independent Milestone Dates**: Milestone dates can now be set to be time zone independent, ensuring that project milestones are consistent regardless of the location of team members.

- **Financial Dimension Defaults**: The new release provides flexibility when determining financial dimension defaults, ensuring that financial data is accurately captured and reported.

Expert Tips for Efficient Analysis, Risk Management, and Quality Control

In this section, we will cover tips such as copying data into adjacent rows, quickly inserting multiple tasks, entering values quickly with a lookup table, wrapping text in table cells, aligning cell data, copying cell formatting, changing currency formatting, and adjusting column and row size in Project.

Copy Data into Adjacent Rows

With a Project keyboard shortcut, you can quickly copy data into adjacent cells in a column. Drag over the cell with the value you want (e.g., "Security Sub) to copy and the cells you want to copy into as shown in Figure 10-1. Then press Ctrl+D; Project copies the value from the first cell into the remaining cells in the selection as shown in Figure 10-2.

CHAPTER 10 ADVANCED FEATURES OF MICROSOFT PROJECT AND FUTURE TRENDS IN PROJECT MANAGEMENT

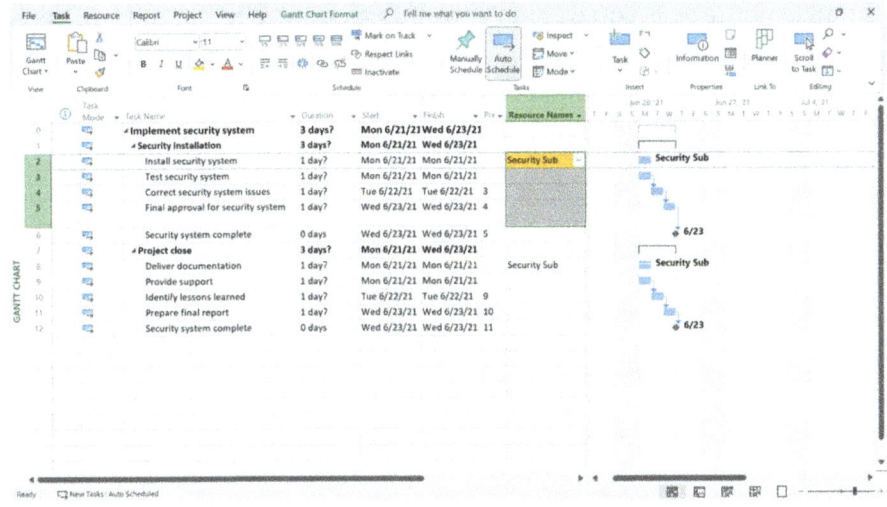

Figure 10-1. Drag over the cell with the value for copy

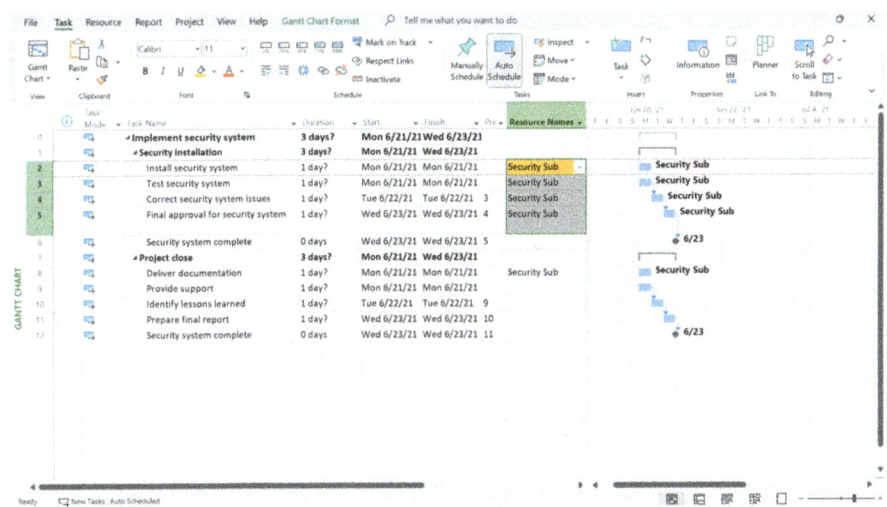

Figure 10-2. Ctrl+D command for copy

You can also use the mouse to copy a value into adjacent cells. Click the cell with the value you want to copy. Hover the pointer over the bottom right corner of the cell. When the pointer changes to a plus sign, drag in the

279

CHAPTER 10 ADVANCED FEATURES OF MICROSOFT PROJECT AND FUTURE TRENDS IN PROJECT MANAGEMENT

column over the cells you want to copy into as shown in Figure 10-3. When you let go of the mouse, Project copies the value from the first cell into the cells you drag over as shown in Figure 10-4.

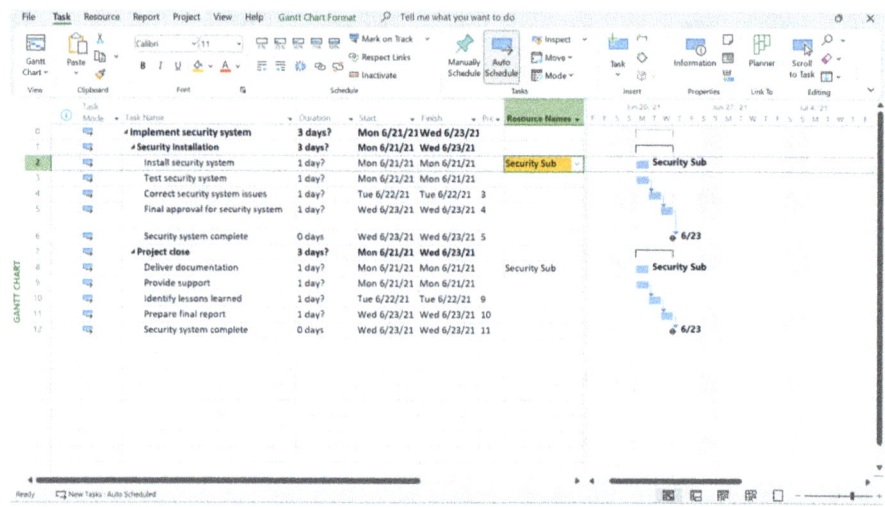

Figure 10-3. Pointer over the bottom right corner of the cell

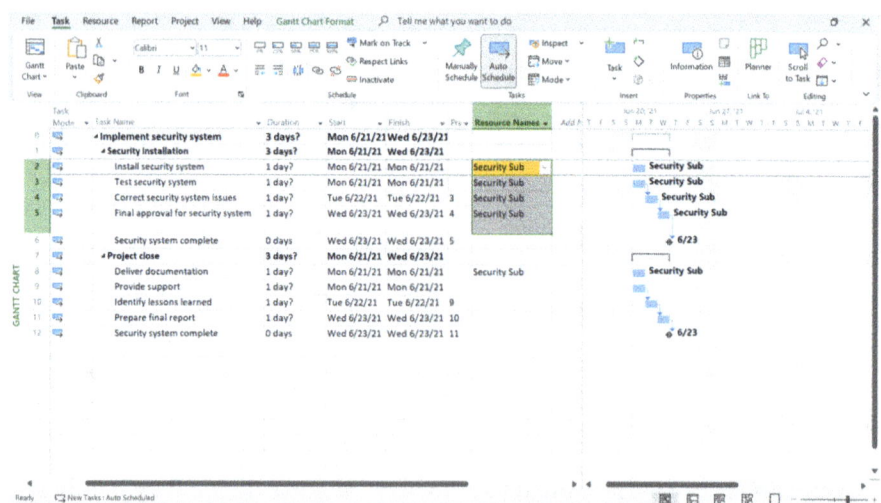

Figure 10-4. Dragging over copies the value from the first cell into the other cells being dragged over

CHAPTER 10   ADVANCED FEATURES OF MICROSOFT PROJECT AND FUTURE TRENDS IN
PROJECT MANAGEMENT

Quickly Insert Multiple Tasks

To insert a single task, right-click a task in the task list, and then choose Insert Task on the shortcut menu as shown in Figure 10-5. The new task appears directly above the selected task as shown in Figure 10-6.

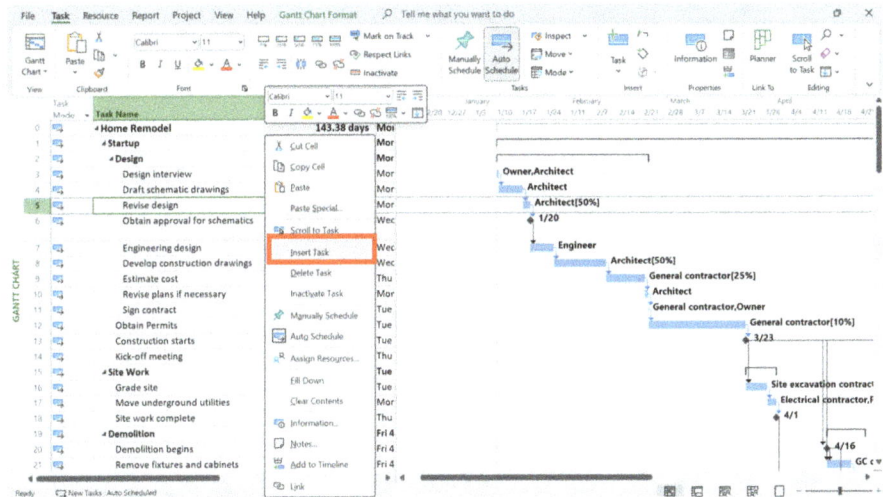

Figure 10-5. Insert new task

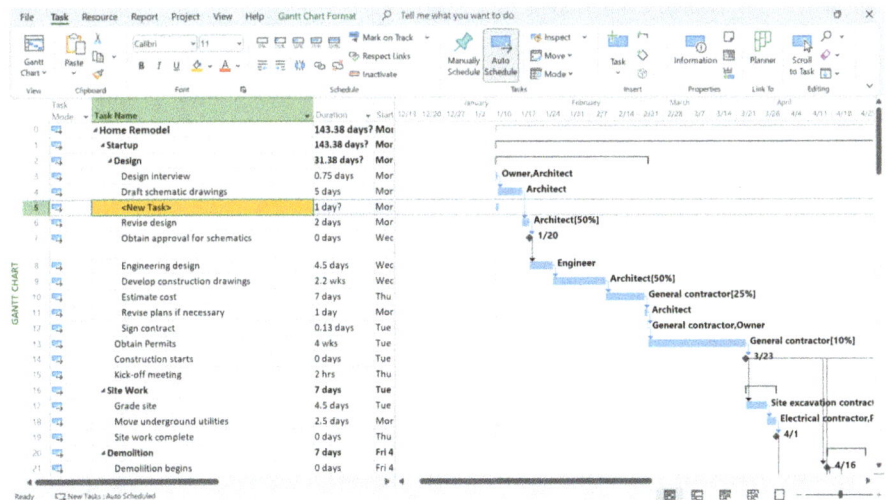

Figure 10-6. New task inserted

281

CHAPTER 10   ADVANCED FEATURES OF MICROSOFT PROJECT AND FUTURE TRENDS IN
             PROJECT MANAGEMENT

To insert multiple tasks, drag over the ID cells for the number of tasks you want to add starting at the desired row. For example, five tasks as shown in Figure 10-7. Right-click within the selection, and choose Insert Task as shown in Figure 10-5. The new tasks appear directly above the first task as shown in Figure 10-8.

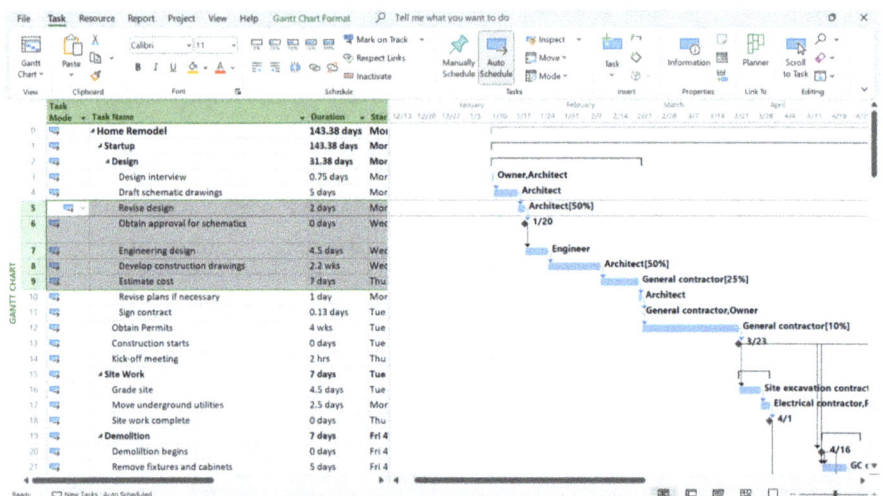

Figure 10-7. Drag over the ID cells for the number of tasks to add

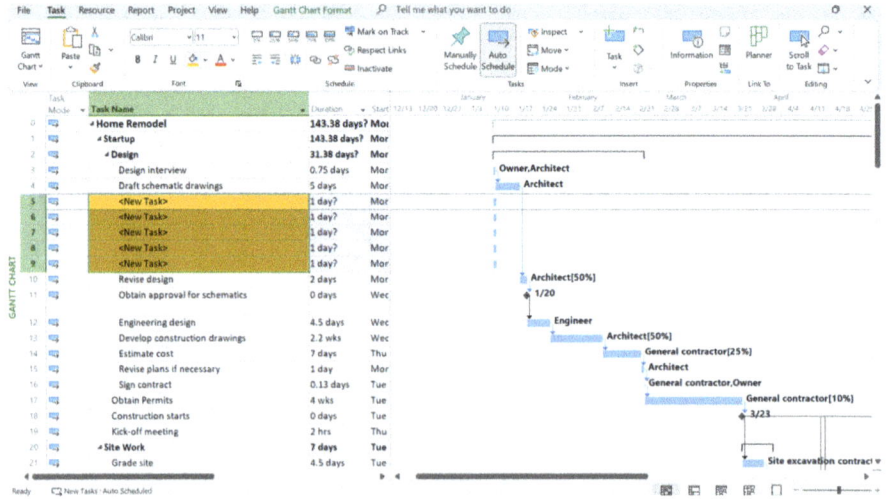

Figure 10-8. Five tasks got added with Insert Task option

282

CHAPTER 10   ADVANCED FEATURES OF MICROSOFT PROJECT AND FUTURE TRENDS IN
PROJECT MANAGEMENT

Enter Values Quickly with a Lookup Table

With a lookup table, you can quickly enter data accurately. To create one, right-click the custom field "Acct Code" heading in a table, and select "custom fields" as shown in Figure 10-9.

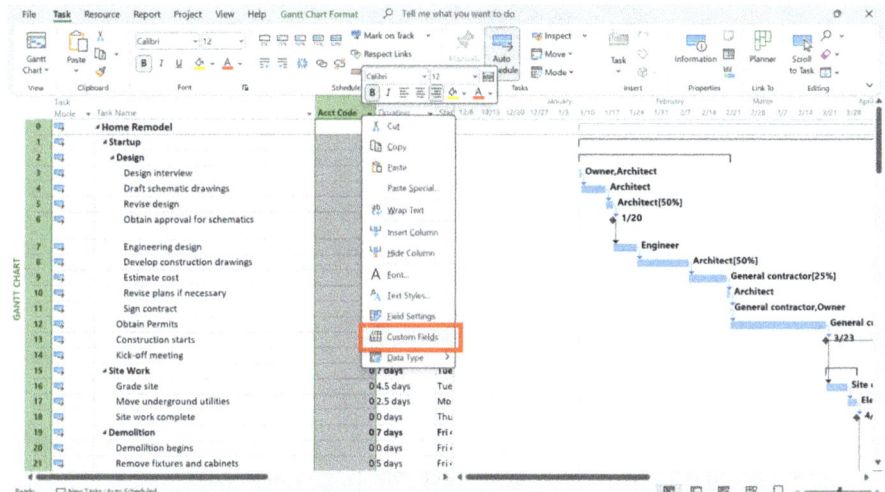

Figure 10-9. Select Custom Fields

In the dialog box, beneath the Field list, click "Lookup" as shown in Figure 10-10.

CHAPTER 10 ADVANCED FEATURES OF MICROSOFT PROJECT AND FUTURE TRENDS IN PROJECT MANAGEMENT

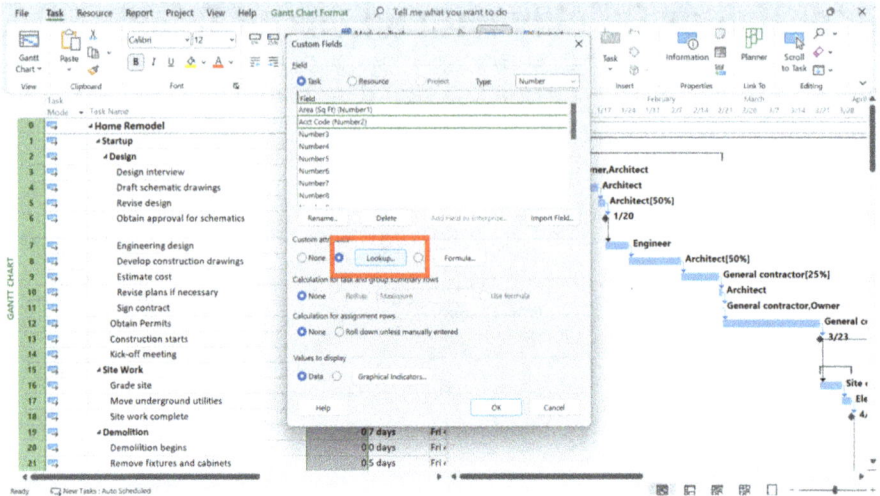

Figure 10-10. Access Lookup option

Enter standard values into the value cells, pressing Enter after each. Optionally, add descriptions for context. Set a default value by checking the box "Use a value from the table as the default entry for the field," selecting a value, and clicking "Set Default," and the default value turns blue as shown in Figure 10-11.

CHAPTER 10   ADVANCED FEATURES OF MICROSOFT PROJECT AND FUTURE TRENDS IN PROJECT MANAGEMENT

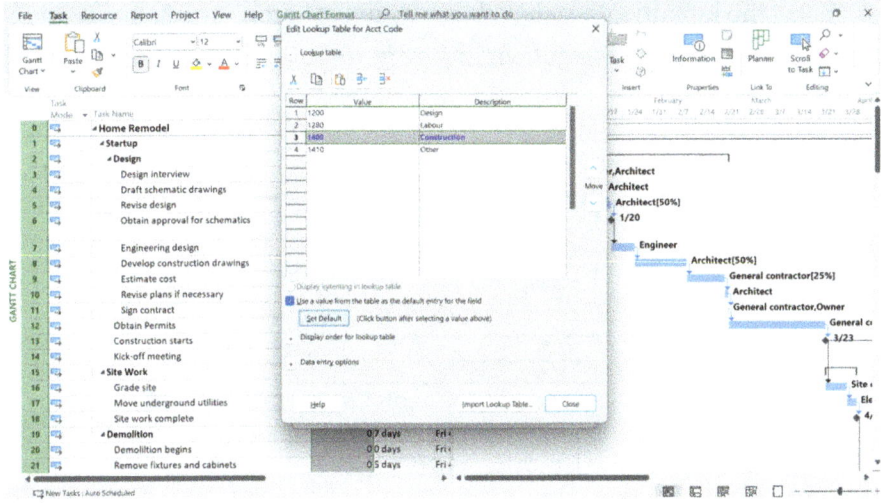

Figure 10-11. Enter Lookup values

Project will automatically use this default when you create a new task. When finished, click "Close" and then "OK" as shown in Figure 10-12.

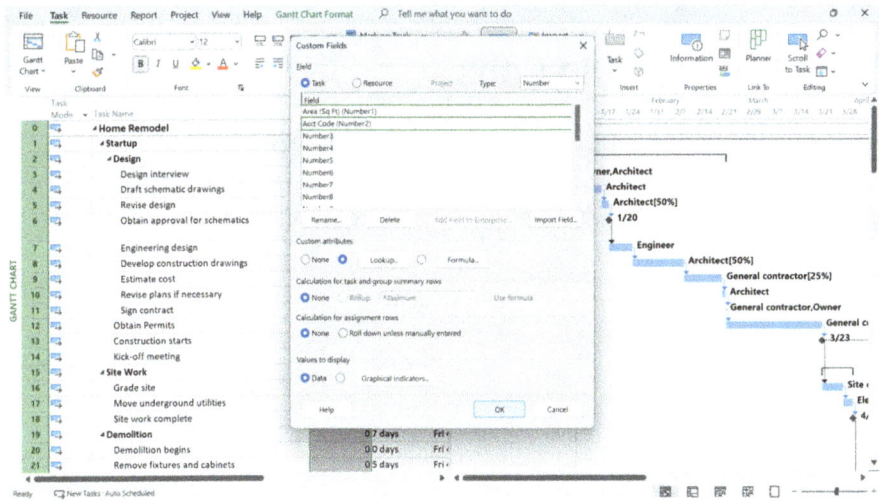

Figure 10-12. Confirm Lookup changes

285

CHAPTER 10   ADVANCED FEATURES OF MICROSOFT PROJECT AND FUTURE TRENDS IN
              PROJECT MANAGEMENT

To use the lookup table, click the cell's down arrow, and select a value from the drop-down list as shown in Figure 10-13.

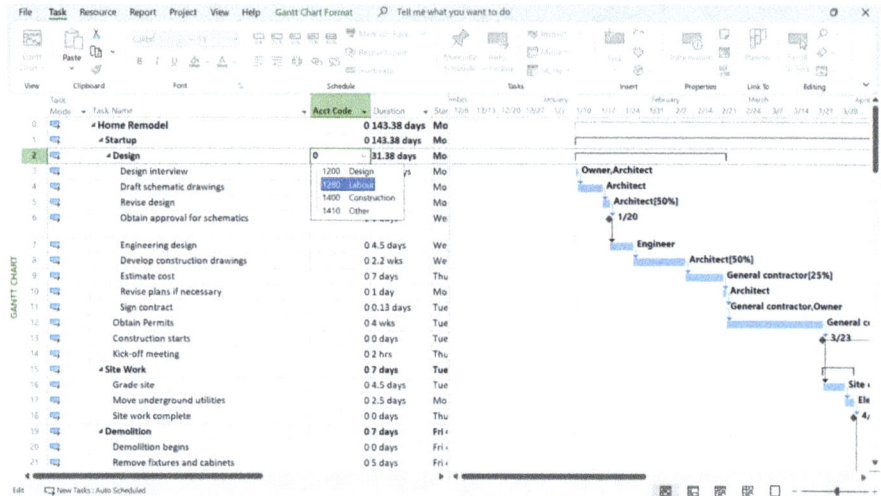

Figure 10-13. Access Lookup values

Wrap Text in Table Cells

You can instruct Project to wrap text over multiple lines when you change a column's width. Let's examine the column "Notes" as shown in Figure 10-14. Project automatically wraps text in the task name column.

CHAPTER 10   ADVANCED FEATURES OF MICROSOFT PROJECT AND FUTURE TRENDS IN PROJECT MANAGEMENT

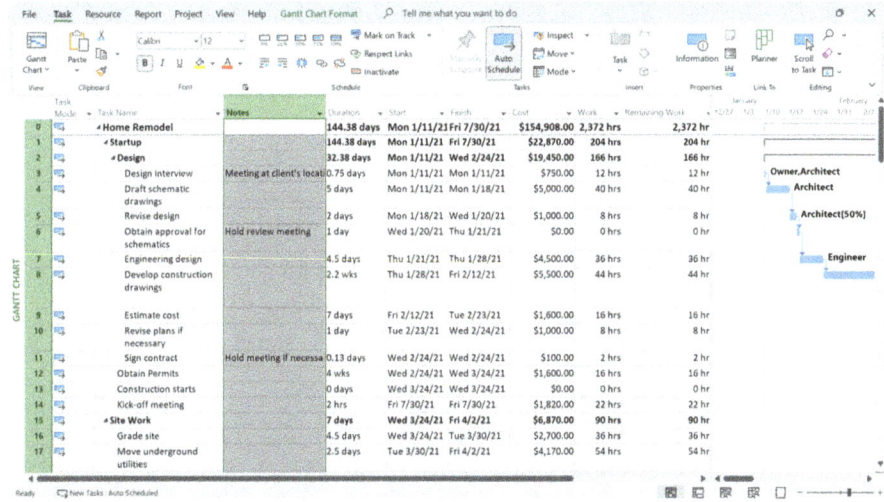

Figure 10-14. Column "Notes" before wrap text

To wrap text in another column, right-click the column heading, and then, choose "Wrap Text" as shown in Figure 10-15. Project will adjust the text to fit the column width as shown in Figure 10-16.

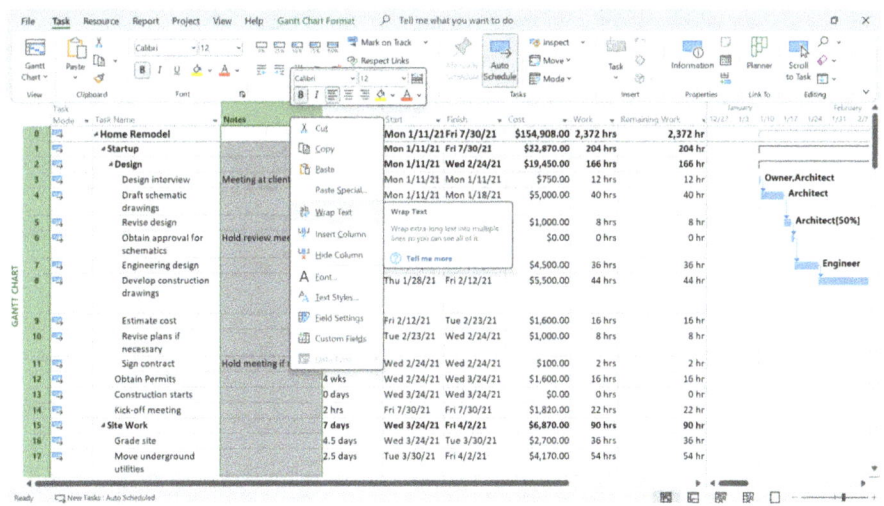

Figure 10-15. Choose Wrap Text option

287

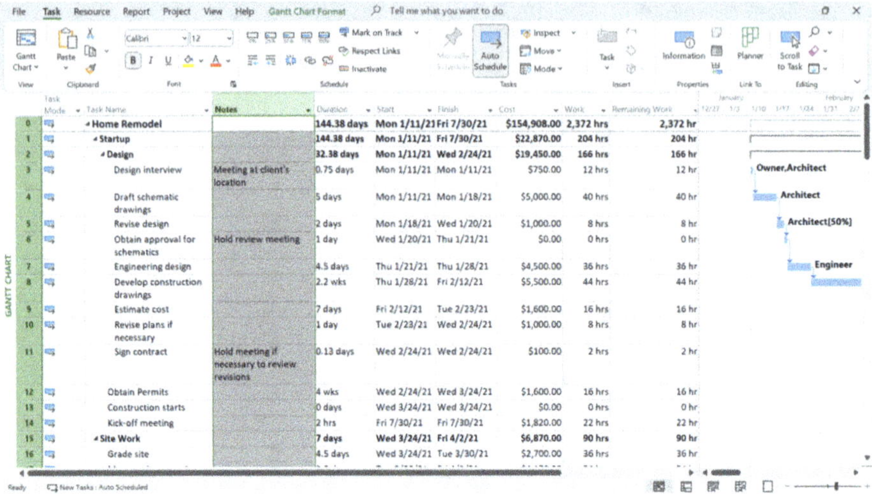

CHAPTER 10   ADVANCED FEATURES OF MICROSOFT PROJECT AND FUTURE TRENDS IN PROJECT MANAGEMENT

Figure 10-16. Column "Notes" after Wrap Text option

When you modify the column width, rows change height accordingly so the text fits. Additionally, you can enable text wrapping in column headings. Right-click the column heading, and select "Field Settings" from the shortcut menu as shown in Figure 10-17.

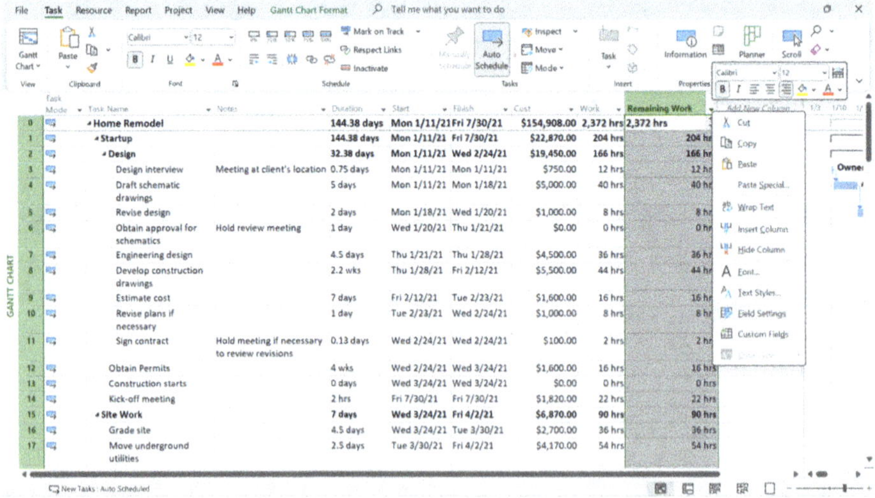

Figure 10-17. Field Settings option

288

CHAPTER 10   ADVANCED FEATURES OF MICROSOFT PROJECT AND FUTURE TRENDS IN PROJECT MANAGEMENT

In the Field Settings dialog box, turn on the Header Text Wrapping check box, and then, click OK as shown in Figure 10-18.

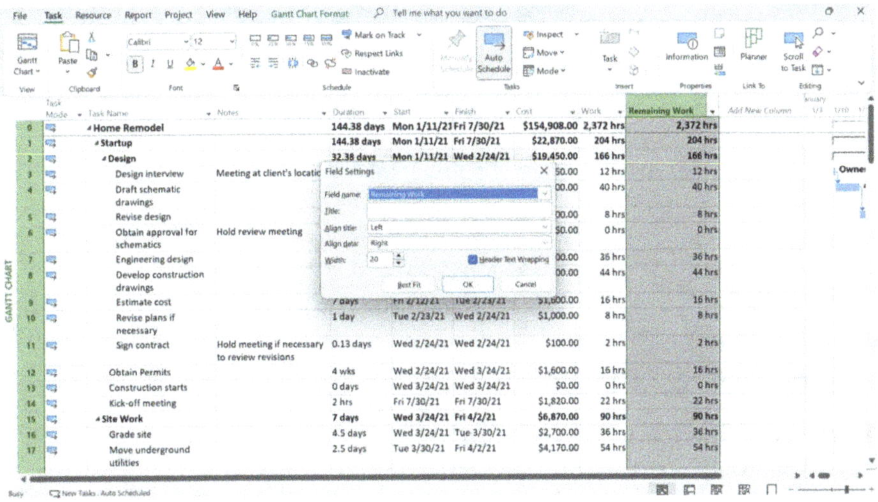

Figure 10-18. Keep "Header Text Wrapping" checked

The header text will wrap to fit the new column width when adjusted as shown in Figure 10-19 for the column "Remaining Work."

289

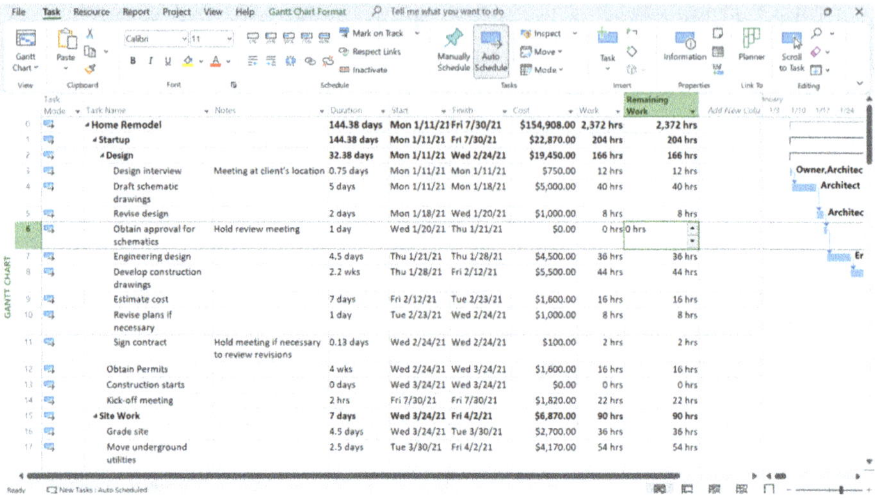

CHAPTER 10   ADVANCED FEATURES OF MICROSOFT PROJECT AND FUTURE TRENDS IN PROJECT MANAGEMENT

Figure 10-19. Text wrap to fit the new column

Align Cell Data

You can adjust the alignment of each column in a project table for better readability. Costs and work fields are typically right aligned to highlight value magnitudes. If adjacent columns' values are difficult to distinguish, alter the alignment. Let's say "% Complete" as shown in Figure 10-20 is chosen under consideration.

CHAPTER 10 ADVANCED FEATURES OF MICROSOFT PROJECT AND FUTURE TRENDS IN PROJECT MANAGEMENT

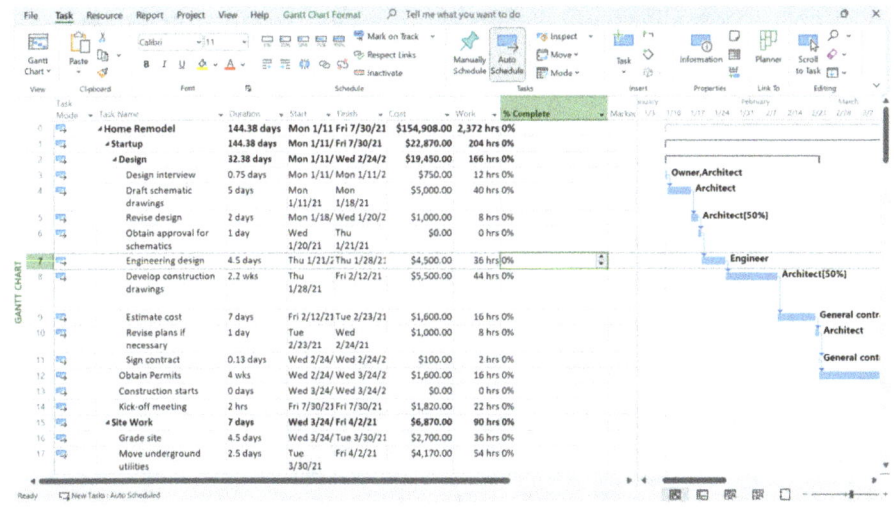

Figure 10-20. Chose "% Completion" column

Right-click the column header, let's say "% Complete" as shown in Figure 10-20. Select Field Settings as shown in Figure 10-21.

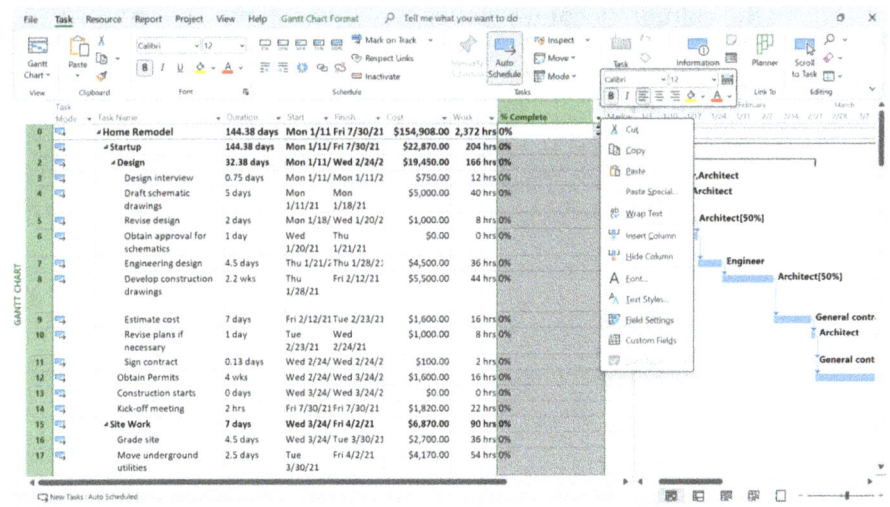

Figure 10-21. Access Field selection column

291

CHAPTER 10 ADVANCED FEATURES OF MICROSOFT PROJECT AND FUTURE TRENDS IN PROJECT MANAGEMENT

Choose a new alignment like Right or Center from the Align data box as shown in Figure 10-22. Click OK to apply.

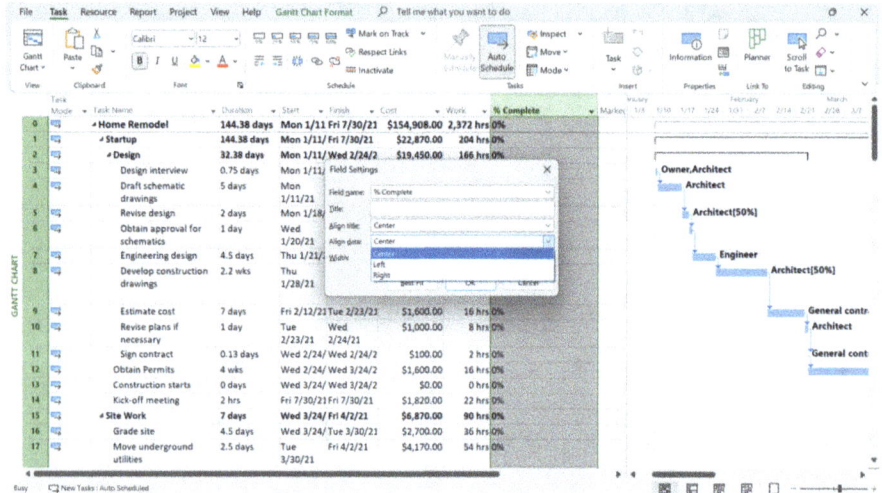

Figure 10-22. *Select data to be center aligned*

Data in the column becomes center aligned as shown in Figure 10-23.

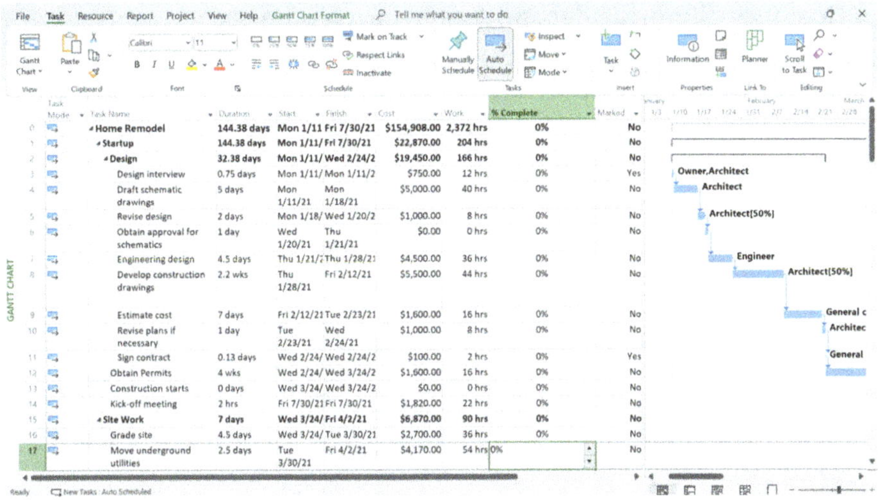

CHAPTER 10   ADVANCED FEATURES OF MICROSOFT PROJECT AND FUTURE TRENDS IN PROJECT MANAGEMENT

Figure 10-23. Data center aligned

To align column headers, right-click the header, choose Field Settings, and select a preferred alignment from the Align title down arrow as shown in Figure 10-24. Click OK to realign.

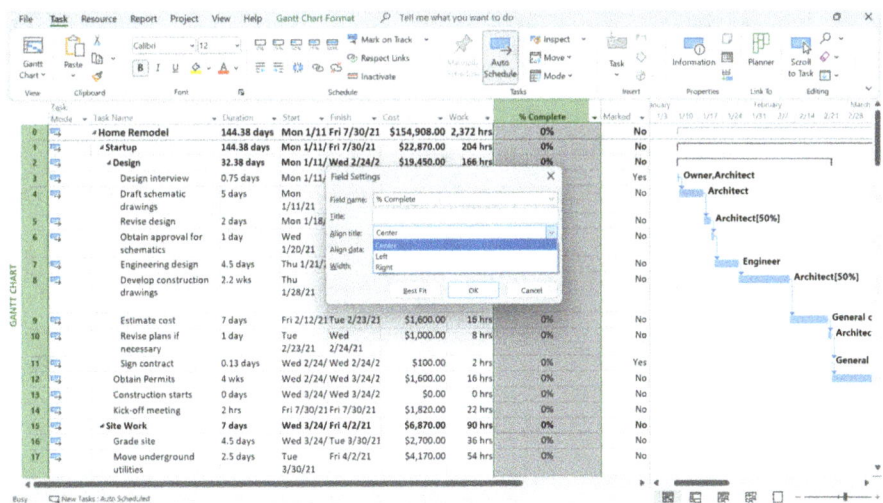

Figure 10-24. Column header to be center aligned

293

CHAPTER 10   ADVANCED FEATURES OF MICROSOFT PROJECT AND FUTURE TRENDS IN PROJECT MANAGEMENT

Both the column header and data in the column become center aligned as shown in Figure 10-25.

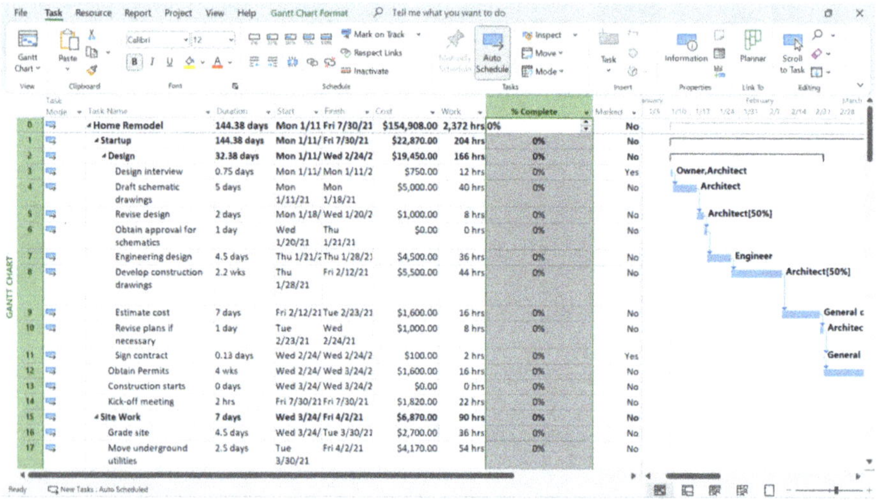

Figure 10-25.   Center aligned "% Completion" column and its data

Copy Cell Formatting

The Format Painter tool allows you to replicate formatting from one cell to another. For instance, in Project, you may wish to apply specific text "Test security system" task 3 formatting to key tasks. Begin by applying the desired formatting to a cell by changing this text to bold and applying a font color as shown in Figure 10-26.

CHAPTER 10 ADVANCED FEATURES OF MICROSOFT PROJECT AND FUTURE TRENDS IN PROJECT MANAGEMENT

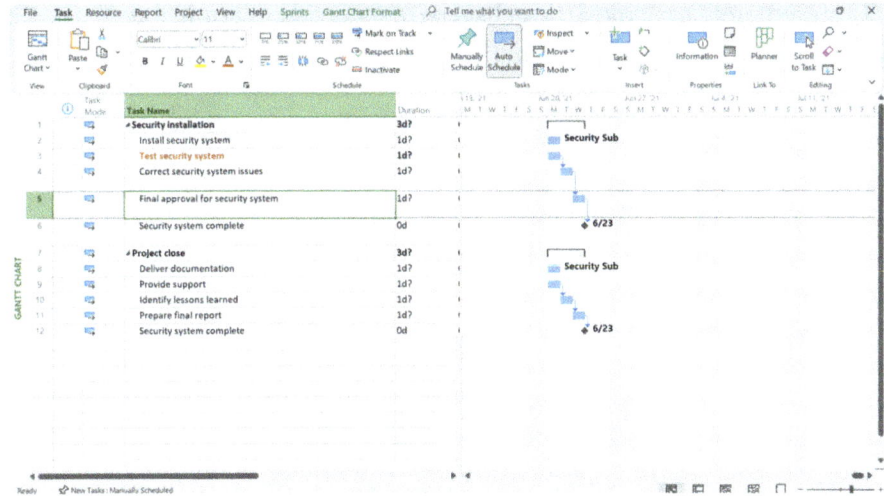

Figure 10-26. Apply formatting

To copy this formatting, navigate to the Task tab within the Clipboard section, and click the Format Painter icon as shown in Figure 10-27.

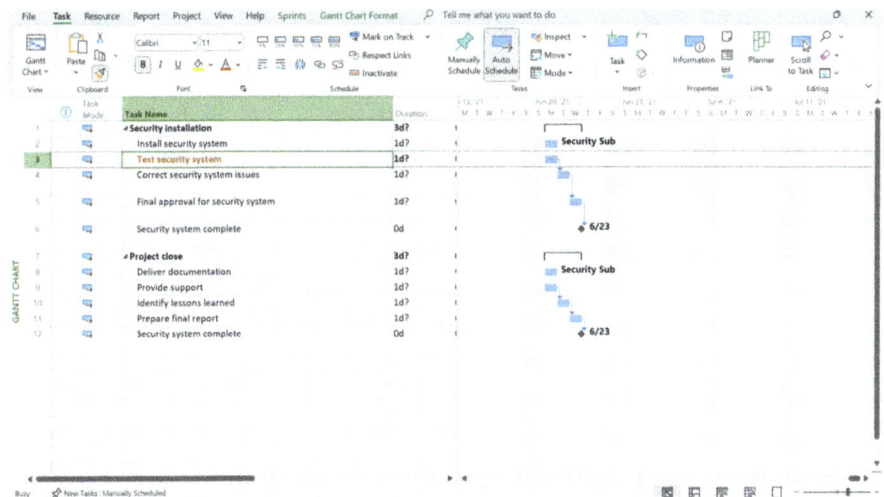

Figure 10-27. Copy formatting with Format Painter

295

CHAPTER 10   ADVANCED FEATURES OF MICROSOFT PROJECT AND FUTURE TRENDS IN
              PROJECT MANAGEMENT

Immediately drag over the cells where you wish to apply the formatting; the changes will take effect instantly as shown in Figure 10-28.

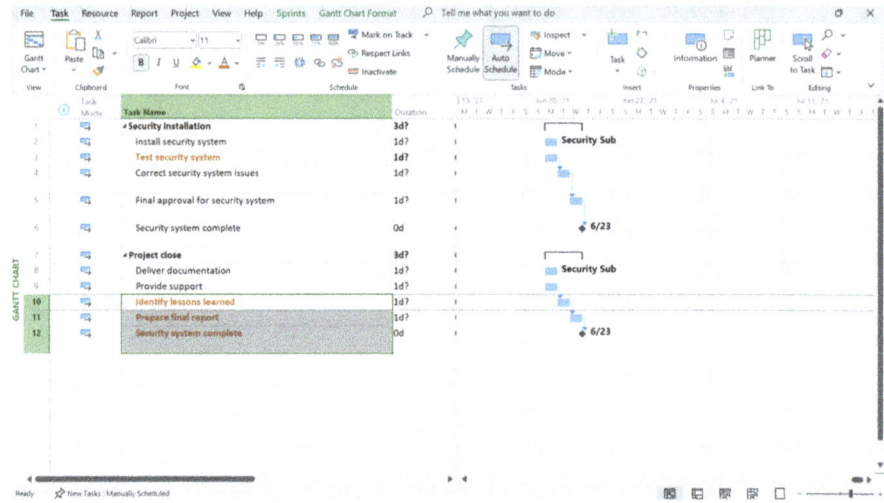

Figure 10-28. Formatting successfully copied

Additionally, you can employ text styles to format text for a category of tasks. Select the Format tab, and then, click Text Styles located on the left side of the ribbon as shown in Figure 10-29. In the Text Styles dialog box, click the "Item to Change" as "Milestone Tasks" drop-down arrow, and select the desired category Font style Bold and color green as shown in Figure 10-29.

296

CHAPTER 10 ADVANCED FEATURES OF MICROSOFT PROJECT AND FUTURE TRENDS IN PROJECT MANAGEMENT

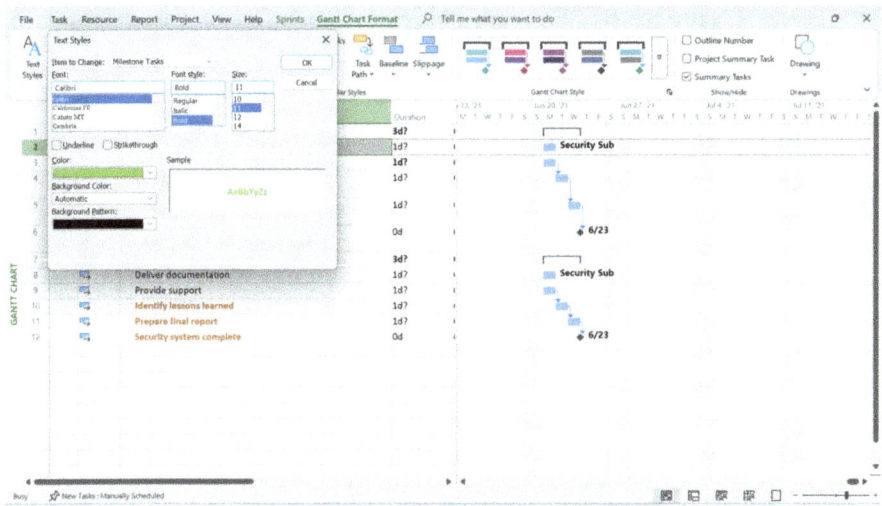

Figure 10-29. Apply Text Style changes

Choose the formatting preferences, such as font, font style, size, and color. Click OK, and the text for all tasks within that category will update accordingly as shown in Figure 10-30.

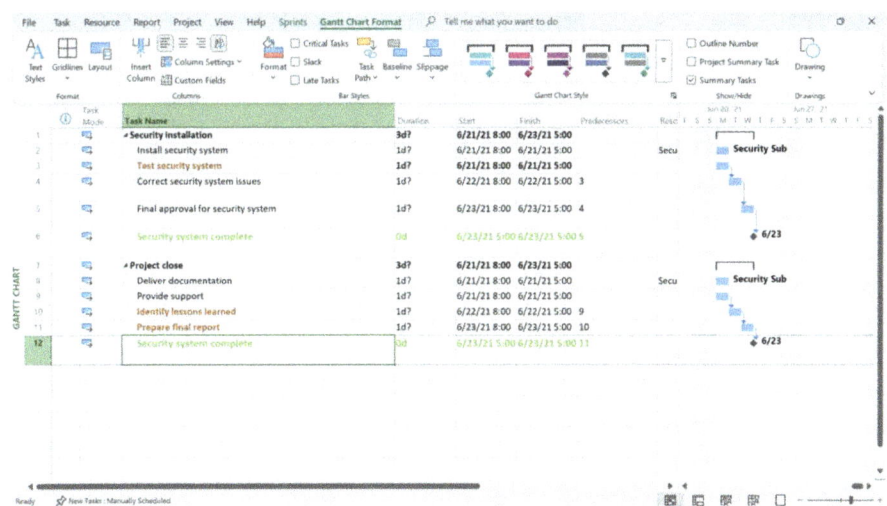

Figure 10-30. Formatting applied to Milestone Tasks

297

CHAPTER 10 ADVANCED FEATURES OF MICROSOFT PROJECT AND FUTURE TRENDS IN
           PROJECT MANAGEMENT

Change Currency Formatting

If you manage a project that uses international currency, for example, $, as shown in Figure 10-31, you can easily change the currency and its formatting in Project. To do this, click the File tab, and then, click Options as shown in Figure 10-32.

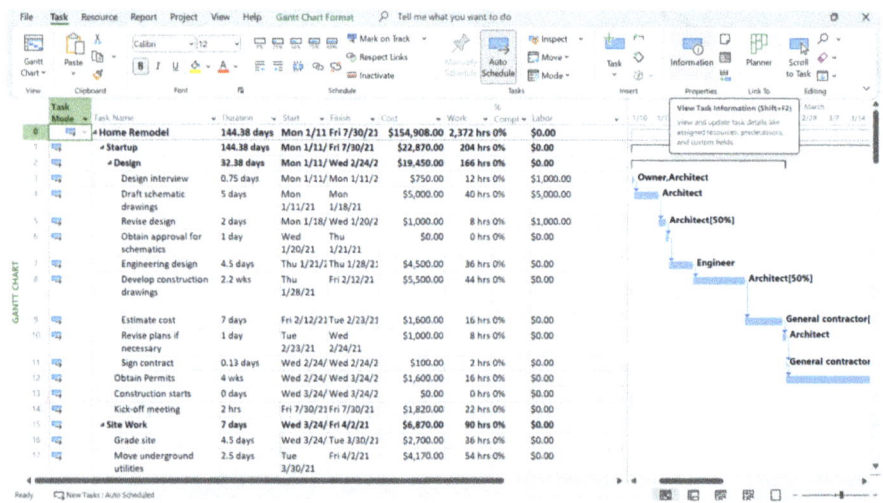

Figure 10-31. Project with $ as currency

CHAPTER 10   ADVANCED FEATURES OF MICROSOFT PROJECT AND FUTURE TRENDS IN PROJECT MANAGEMENT

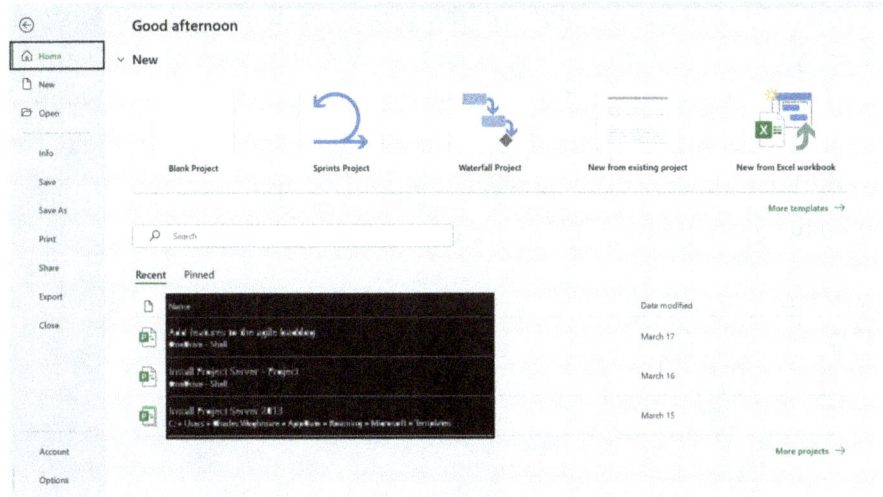

Figure 10-32. Navigation to Options to access change in currency feature

In the Project Options dialog box, select the Display category as shown in Figure 10-33.

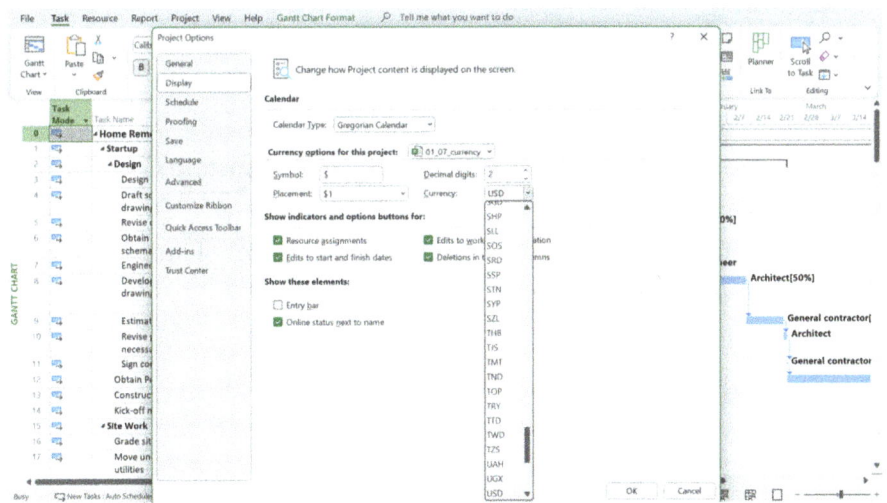

Figure 10-33. Display tab with a list of international currencies

299

CHAPTER 10 ADVANCED FEATURES OF MICROSOFT PROJECT AND FUTURE TRENDS IN PROJECT MANAGEMENT

Under the Currency options for this project section, select the desired currency from the Currency box, adjust the symbol placement, click the placement down arrow and choose whether you want the symbol before or after the value, with or without space, and finally in the Decimal digits box, specify the number of decimal places you wish to appear in Cost fields as shown in Figure 10-34.

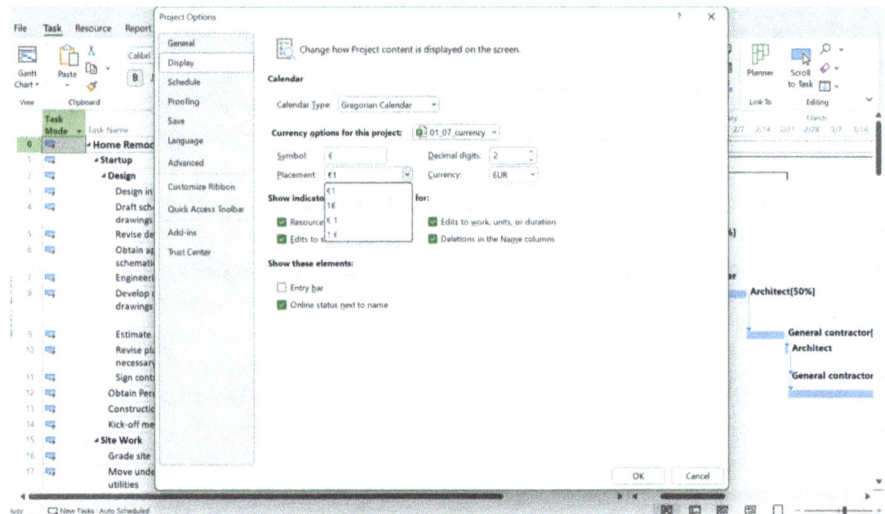

Figure 10-34. *Selection of desired currency*

Click OK, and the values in Project's built-in and custom Cost fields will be updated immediately.

Project will automatically update the currency symbol in the symbol box as shown in Figure 10-35.

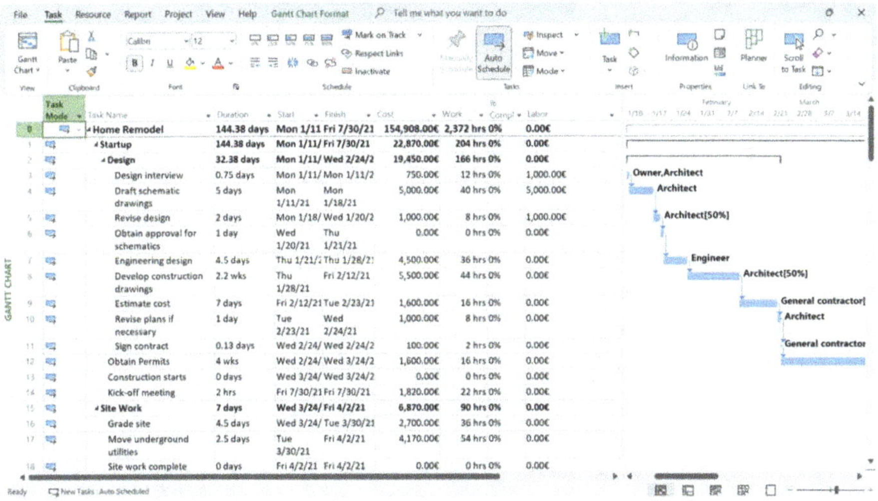

CHAPTER 10   ADVANCED FEATURES OF MICROSOFT PROJECT AND FUTURE TRENDS IN
             PROJECT MANAGEMENT

Figure 10-35. Desired currency got updated

Adjust Column and Row Size in Project

You can easily adjust the width of a column or height of a row. To change the width of a column, let's say "Task Name" column, as shown in Figure 10-36, place your mouse cursor over the right edge of the column header "Task Name," and drag. The final outcome is shown in Figure 10-37.

301

CHAPTER 10 ADVANCED FEATURES OF MICROSOFT PROJECT AND FUTURE TRENDS IN PROJECT MANAGEMENT

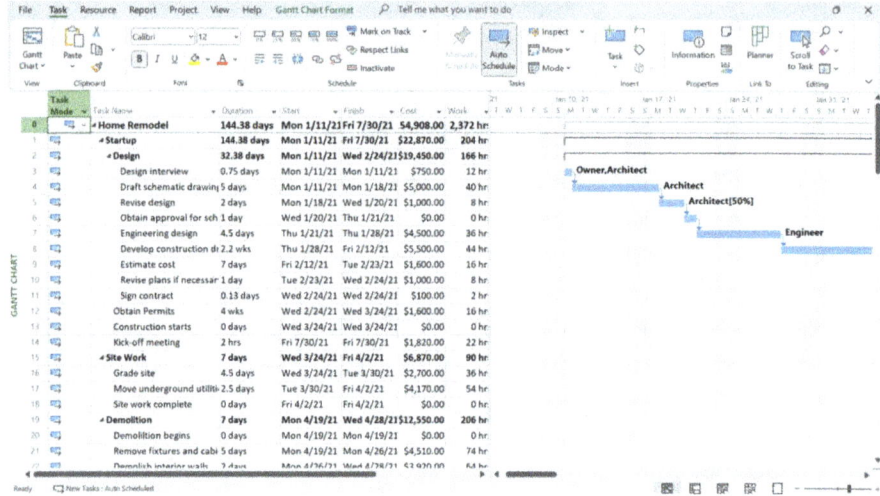

Figure 10-36. Select "Task Name" column

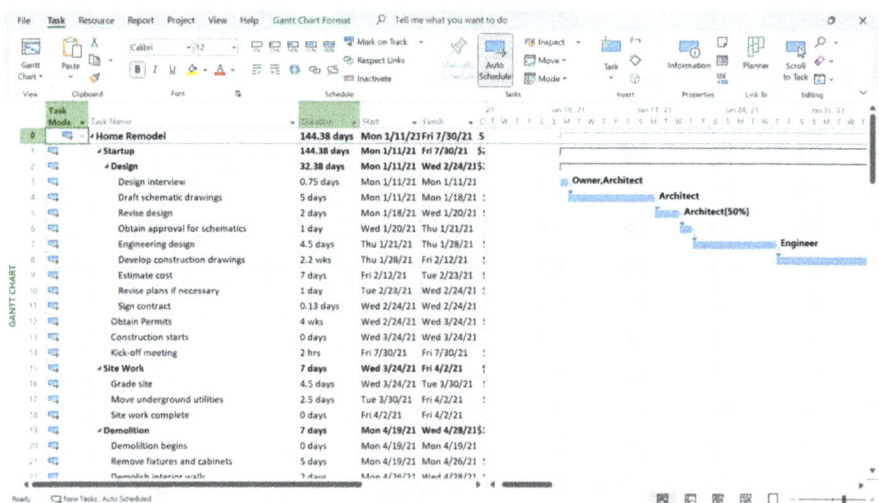

Figure 10-37. Display of "Task Name" column after drag

To set a specific column width, let's say Cost column, right-click the column header, and choose Field Settings as shown in Figure 10-38.

CHAPTER 10 ADVANCED FEATURES OF MICROSOFT PROJECT AND FUTURE TRENDS IN PROJECT MANAGEMENT

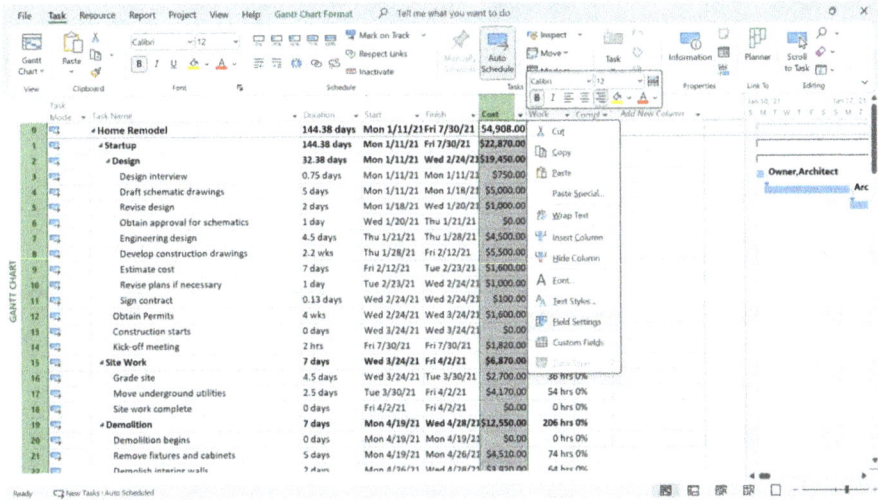

Figure 10-38. Navigating "Field Settings" column

In the Width box, type a numeric value, and click OK as shown in Figure 10-39.

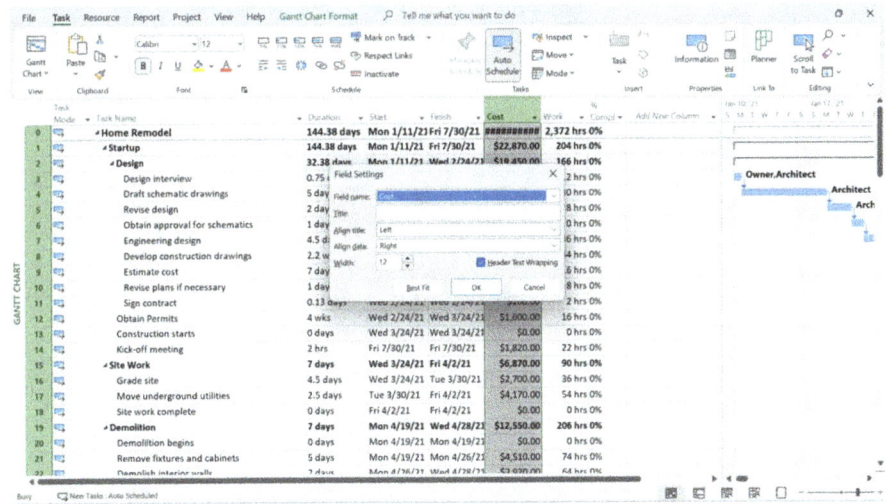

Figure 10-39. Update Width value

303

CHAPTER 10   ADVANCED FEATURES OF MICROSOFT PROJECT AND FUTURE TRENDS IN
             PROJECT MANAGEMENT

Change width value from 12 to 15 as shown in Figure 10-40, and the outcome of updated width is as shown in Figure 10-41.

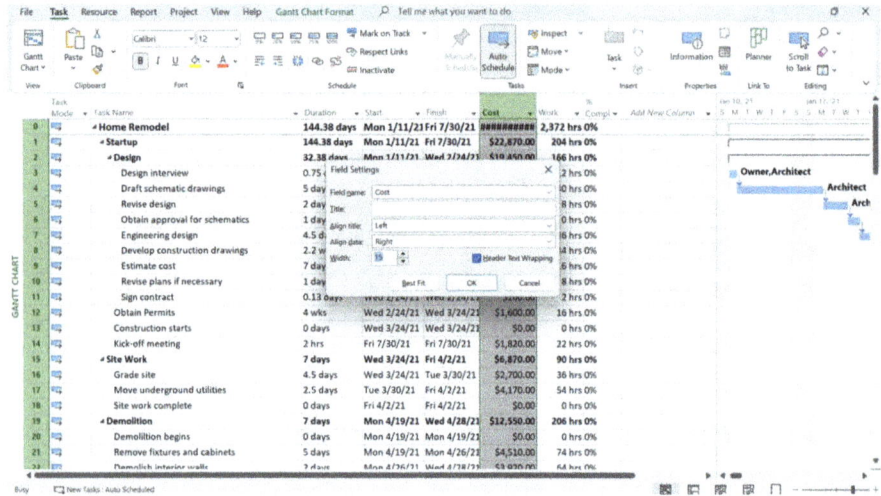

Figure 10-40.   Width value changed to 15

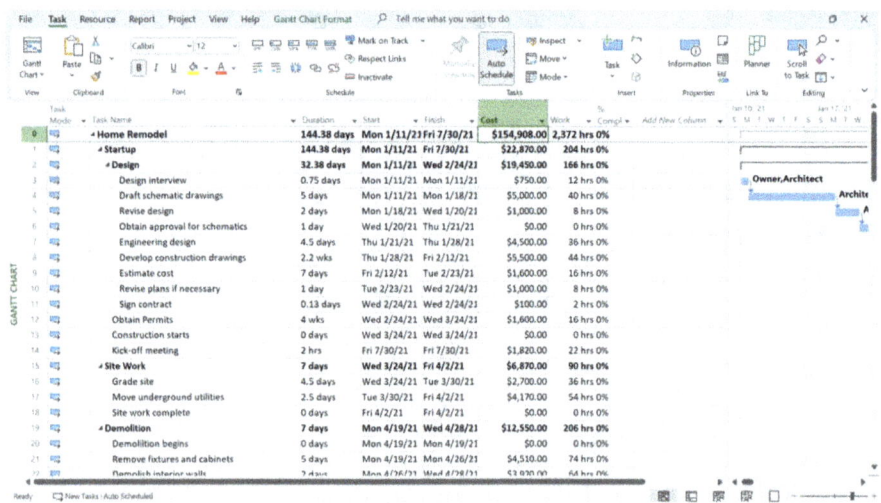

Figure 10-41.   Cost column with width 15

304

CHAPTER 10 ADVANCED FEATURES OF MICROSOFT PROJECT AND FUTURE TRENDS IN PROJECT MANAGEMENT

To resize a column to fit all of its values, let's say for Start column, as shown in Figure 10-42, double-click the right side of the column header. The column width adjusts to fit the longest value in the column as shown in Figure 10-43.

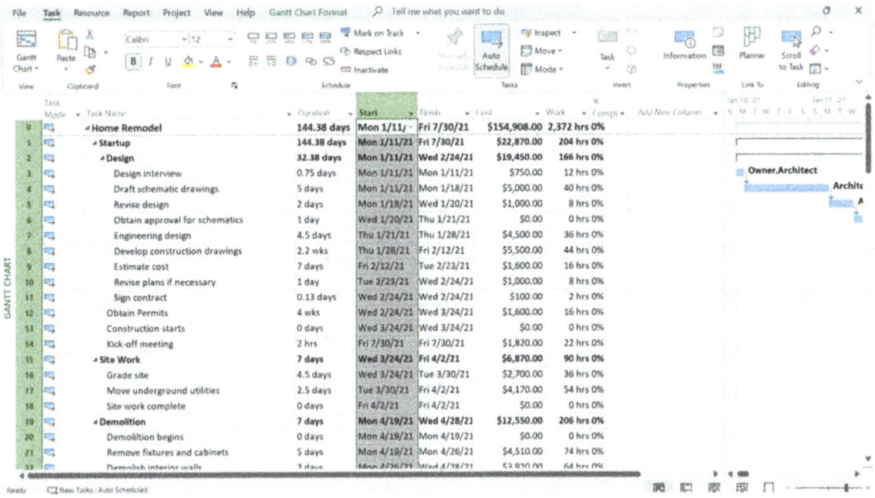

Figure 10-42. Start column under consideration

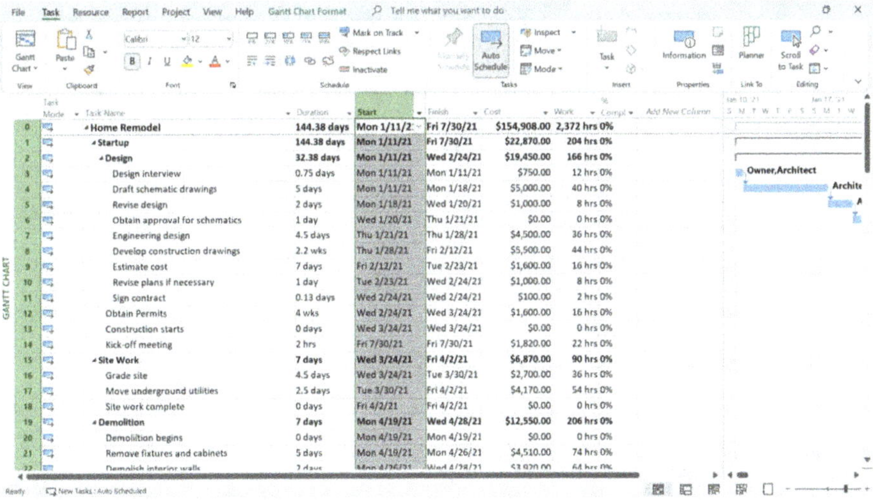

Figure 10-43. Updated width of the column after drag

CHAPTER 10 ADVANCED FEATURES OF MICROSOFT PROJECT AND FUTURE TRENDS IN PROJECT MANAGEMENT

To resize a row, drag the bottom edge of the ID cell, let's say for task 5, as shown in Figures 10-44 and 10-45.

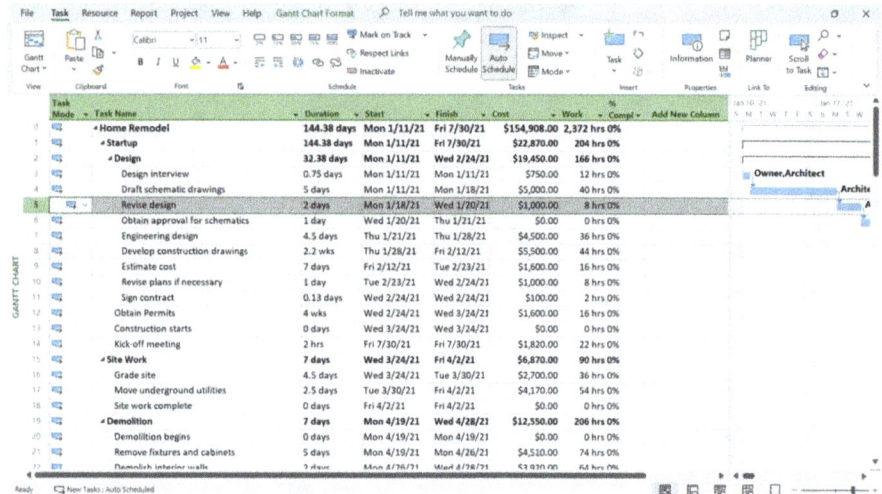

Figure 10-44. Select task 5

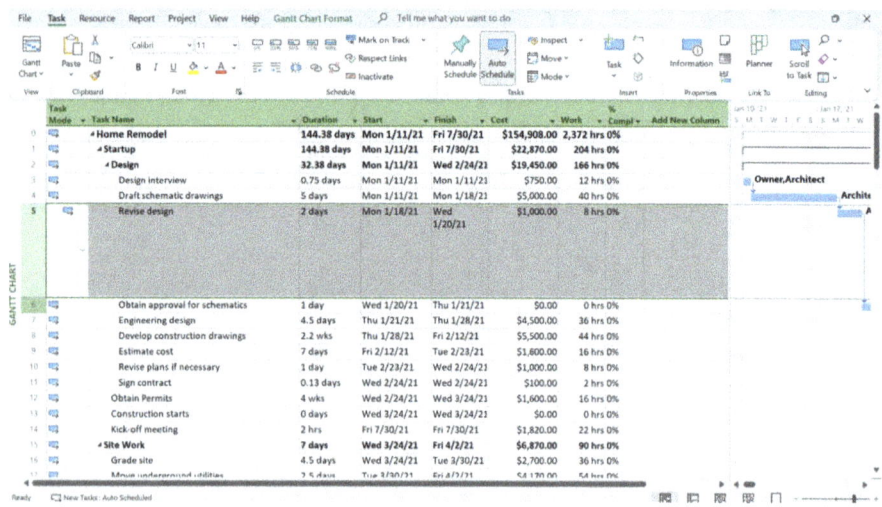

Figure 10-45. Task row resized

CHAPTER 10   ADVANCED FEATURES OF MICROSOFT PROJECT AND FUTURE TRENDS IN PROJECT MANAGEMENT

To change several rows from tasks 5–9 to the same size, select all of them, and then, adjust the size of one of the rows in the range as shown in Figures 10-46 and 10-47.

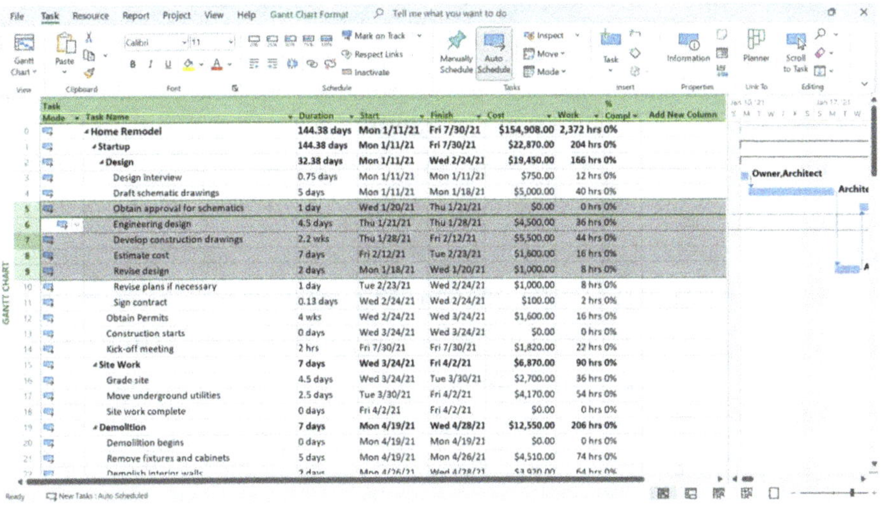

Figure 10-46. Select task 5 resize its row

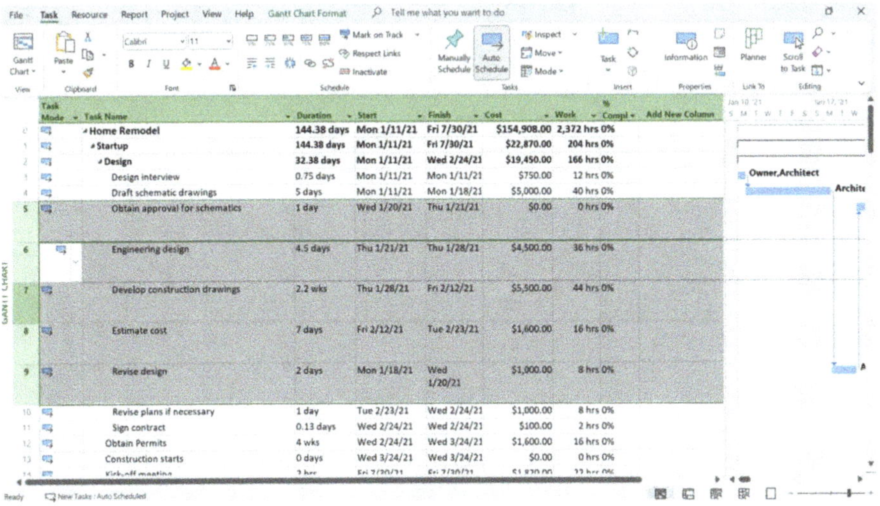

Figure 10-47. Resized task 5 to task 9

307

CHAPTER 10 ADVANCED FEATURES OF MICROSOFT PROJECT AND FUTURE TRENDS IN PROJECT MANAGEMENT

This chapter concludes both the book and our discussion of Microsoft Project's new features. We covered efficiency tips for analysis, risk management, and quality control, including copying data into adjacent rows, quickly inserting multiple tasks, using a lookup table to enter values, wrapping text in table cells, aligning cell data, copying cell formatting, changing currency formatting, and adjusting column and row sizes.

To conclude, Microsoft Project stands as a cornerstone in the realm of project management, offering a comprehensive suite of tools that cater to the diverse needs of modern organizations. Its advanced features, ranging from detailed task management and resource allocation to robust reporting and seamless integration with other Microsoft tools, empower project managers to plan, execute, and monitor projects with unparalleled efficiency. As we navigate the complexities of today's project landscapes, Microsoft Project's continuous evolution ensures that it remains a vital asset, driving successful outcomes and fostering collaboration across teams. Embrace the power of Microsoft Project to transform your project management practices and achieve your organizational goals with confidence and precision. Hope you enjoyed reading the book!

Index

A

Acct Code, 283
Agile project management
    add sprint to existing project, 233, 234
    backlog, 231
    business value over exhaustive documentation, 223
    design documents, 223
    Kanban, 222
    Scrum projects, 222
    user stories, 223
Analytics, 16–23, 104
Async dual-write, 276
Automated scheduling, 23, 24
Auto-scheduled tasks, 70, 72, 73

B

Backlog, 223, 235–243
Baseline, 26
Baseline slippage, 165
Billing backlog review, 276
Budget and cost management, 2, 3, 14, 132
    access cost table, 175
    adjustments, 170
    analyze trends in cost performance, 170
    baseline budget, 169
    cost estimates and resource rates, 168
    cost tab, 172, 173
    cost tracking, 169
    cost view, 176
    estimation, 168
    EVM, 169
    forecasting, 170
    Gantt chart, 174
    monitoring, 170
    network admin and tech rates, 172, 178
    network tech's rate, 171
    proactive, 171
    reporting options, 170
    resource rates, 168
    resource sheet, 172
    scope and objectives, 168
    stakeholders, 170
    templates, 171
    training and support, 171
    WBS, 168
    work and cost resources, 178, 179, 181–183, 185

INDEX

Budget planning, 168
Built-in graphical reports, 251, 253–260

C

Cell data alignment, 290–294
Collaboration, 2, 4, 15, 16, 197
Communication, 2, 15, 16, 41, 197
   and sharing, 15
Conduct full test, 129
Continuous improvement, 9
Copilot integration, 275
Copy cell formatting, 294–297
Copyeditors, 184
Copy formatting with format painter, 295
Cost control, 169, 170
Cost management, 104
Cost reports, 18, 19, 249
Cost resources, 112, 113
Costs and work fields, 290
Cost tracking, 169
Cost variance, 250
Creating resources in Project, 106, 108–110, 112, 113
Critical filter, 140
Critical path, 98
Critical tasks, 98
Currency formatting change, 298–301
Customizable templates, 27
Customization, 25
Custom reports, 249

D

Dashboard Closeout, 242
Dashboards reports, 16–18
Data center alignment, 293
Data-driven decisions, 3, 16
Date range filter, 262
Delegation, 124

E

Earned value management (EVM), 169
Extensibility patterns, 276
External maintenance, 135, 136
External stakeholders, 2, 15

F

Filter chart categories, 264
Filtering and grouping in tables and charts, 260
Fine-tuning project schedule
   arrange external maintenance, 150, 151
   budget management, 132
   concurrent tasks, 147
   critical path, 133–141
   detailed and effective project schedules, 133
   Gantt chart, 133, 150
   leveling Gantt, 149, 150
   manageable tasks, 132
   office manager, 148
   overallocation, 147, 151, 152

progress tracking, 132
reporting features, 133
reports, 132
resource allocation, 132
scheduling problems, 158, 160–166
scope, 132
set dependencies, 132
task management, 131
timeline, 133
timeline visualization, 132
timescale, 161
Float tasks, *see* Slack tasks
Format Painter tool, 294

G

Gantt charts, 1, 11, 58, 67, 113–115, 127, 135, 149, 165, 174, 179, 180
benefits, 100
creation, 98
project schedule, 96
steps, 96, 98
tracking deadlines, 96
types, 98, 99
updation, 100
usage, 100
Global address book, 277
Graphical report
access field list, 261
access filter box, 266
access resources reports, 268
category initiation, 265
date range, 263
filtering and grouping results, 260
Group By filter, 270
hide field list, 266
internal group, 271
resource overview report, 269
resource stats chart, 270
resource stats report, 272
subcontractor group, 271
unassigned resources, 271
work overbudget, 267

H

Header text wrapping, 289
Hiring additional resources, 124

I, J

Inactive tasks in Microsoft, 152–158
Integration, 25
International currencies, 299

K

Kanban approaches, 222–224
Keyboard shortcuts, 215–217, 219

L

Late tasks, 99

311

INDEX

M, N

Manually scheduled tasks, 73
Material resources, 111, 112, 182
Max column, 110
Microsoft 365 subscription, 11
Microsoft Copilot, 91–96
Microsoft Ignite, 11
Microsoft Project
    access start date, 37
    automatic notifications and alerts, 199
    basic operations, 215
    collaboration and communication, 196, 197, 199
    collaboration features, 198
    collaboration tools, 200
    communication plan, 199
    creation, 31, 32
    desktop app icon, 30
    enhancements, 11
    features, 1
        automated scheduling, 23, 24
        baseline and variance analysis, 26
        budget management, 14
        collaboration and communication, 15, 16
        customizable templates, 27
        integration and customization, 25
        portfolio management, 26
        reporting and analytics, 16–23
        resource management, 12
        risk management, 25
        task management, 11, 12
        time tracking, 26
    feedback, 214
    Gantt chart, 96–101
    goals and objectives
        actionable, 40
        benefits, 41
        communication, 41
        document, 40
        key stakeholders, identification, 39
        linking tasks, 41
        project's scope, 39
        review and adjust, 41
        SMART criteria, 40
        steps, 39
        track progress, 41
    importance, 4–10
    improvement areas, 214
    Install Project Server, 33, 34, 37, 38
    instance, 33
    keyboard shortcuts, 215–219
    main window, 217
    managing project scope, 213
    with Microsoft 365 teams, seamless integration
        delete project, 206
        multiple projects or road maps, 205

INDEX

Project app, 202
Project dialog box, 202
project name, 204
Project or Roadmap app, 201
Project tab, 205
remove dialog box, 205
Microsoft 365 tools, 199, 214
monitoring, 200, 214
network diagram, 219
OneDrive/SharePoint, 33, 34
outlining tasks, 218
project management, 196, 211
project objectives, 212
project plan, 42–49
project schedule up-to-date, 213
project templates, 1
regular meetings, 200
reporting and analytics capabilities, 3, 4
reporting tools, 200, 213
resource management, 196, 213
risk management plan, 213
roles and responsibilities, 200
scheduling, 49, 196
(*see also* Project schedule)
select and edit items within dialog boxes, 218
sheet view, 218
sizes and complexities, 3
standardized methods or techniques, 211
status reports, 199
support and resources, 214
task dependencies, 212
templates, 35, 36, 212
timeline view, 217
tracking project, 196
versions, 196
views and windows, 215
Microsoft Project Online Desktop Client, 221
Mitigation strategies, 124
Mobile and browser enhancements, 275

O

Office Art objects, 219
Organizational goals, 6
Outlook, 199
Overallocated tasks, 127
Overallocation threshold, 185
Overtime rate column, 188

P

Planning, 5
Planning complete task, 156
Planning Wizard, 138, 139
Portfolio management, 26
Predecessors, 146
Prioritization, 124
Progress reports, 20, 249
Progress tracking task, 132
Project baseline
choosing baseline view, 47
choosing options, 44, 45

313

INDEX

Project baseline (*cont.*)
    Gantt chart view, 46
    saved date, 45
    setting, 42, 43
    updated fields, 47, 48
    variance, 48, 49
Project Communication Plan, 199
Project for the Web, 196
Project General Ledger (G/L) journals, 276
Project management
    access lookup values, 286
    adaptability and flexibility, 9
    analysis on project estimation, 277
    collaboration and communication, 2, 274
    column and row size adjustment, 301–308
    continuous improvement, 9
    copy data into adjacent cells, 278–280
    efficiency, 274
    enhanced support for subcontract information, 277
    financial dimension defaults, 278
    foundation, 6
    global address book, 277
    importance, 5
    lookup changes, 285
    organizations, 3, 4, 6
    project success, 8
    quality assurance, 8
    resources, 7
    risk management, 8
    set default, 284
    stakeholders, 9
    task list, 281, 282
    team members, 7
    time zone independent, project milestones, 278
    tools, 5
    troubleshooting tools, 277
    user experience, 274, 277
Project managers
    collaboration, 7
    flexibility, 2
    invaluable asset, 3
    methodologies, 8
Project Online, 196
Project Online Desktop Client, 224, 225, 231
Project Overview report, 252
Project planning, 274
Project Professional, 196
Project schedule
    access tracking option, 49, 50
    addition of actual fields, 50
    communication
        choosing tables data, 65
        detail view, purchase MRI equipment, 59
        Gantt view, 67
        inspect equipment, 60

INDEX

    renovation complete, 61
    tables view, 66
    task usage view, 61–63
    timeline view, 59, 60
    tracking Gantt view, 63–65
    work table, 65, 66
  mark on track tasks, 52, 53
  purchase MRI
    equipment, 54–56
  receive equipment, 56, 57
  review lab design, 53, 54
  status date, 51, 52
  update power, 57, 58
  update tasks option, 54, 55
Project success, 8

Q

Quality assurance, 8

R

Real-time collaboration, 15
Regular meetings, 214
Reporting, 104, 132, 170
  access new reports, 20, 21
  costs, 18, 19
  dashboards, 16–18
  MS Project, 16
  progress, 20
  requirements, 16
  resources, 18
  types, 21, 22
  visual, 22, 23

Reporting and analytics, project
    performance
  improvement areas and best
    practices, 247
  key metrics, 248
  types, 248
Resource allocation, 2, 12, 104,
    124, 132
Resource assignments, 113–121
Resource calendars, 104
Resource conflicts, 123
Resource leveling, 104, 124
Resource management, 2, 3, 7, 12
  adding cost column, 120, 121
  allocation, 103
  automation features, 106
  availability and allocation, 105
  availability and skill set, 104
  calendars, 104
  centralized resource pool, 104
  communication, 106
  conflicts, 105
  creation, 106–113
  display, 117
  fixed costs, 104
  planning, 103
  project execution, 105
  reducing waste and increasing
    productivity, 105
  reports and dashboards, 104
  resource information up-to-
    date, 105
  resource utilization, 106
  strategies, 104

INDEX

Resource management (*cont.*)
    Task Form view, 118, 119
    tasks and responsibilities, 105
    task schedules, 104
    tracking resource costs and managing budgets, 105
    training and development, 124
    updating, 117–119
Resource overallocation, 184
    communication among teams, 126
    conflicts over limited resources, 126
    haphazard task assignments, 126
    leveling dialog box, 128
    Level Now feature, 129
    management practices, 125
    organizational dynamics, 125
    overall project cycle, 122–124
    problem, 121, 122
    realistic schedule, 127
    resource task, 128
    unexpected tasks, 126
    unrealistic schedules and budgets, 125
Resource planning, 178, 179, 181, 182
Resource pool, 104
Resource reports, 249
Resource sheet, 12, 13, 107, 172, 179, 181, 191
Resources reports, 18
Revenue recognition, 276
Risk management, 8, 25, 26

S

Schedule training, 129
Scheduling, 5
Scheduling problem, 146
Scrum approach, 222–224, 227
SharePoint site, 207–211
Slack being zero/negative for critical filter, 140
Slack tasks, 99
Slipping tasks, 164, 165
Sprint Planning Board, 226–230
Sprint Planning Sheet, 227–230, 240
Sprint project with Sprint Planning Board view, 232
Sprints, 243–246
Sprints Project, 225, 232
Sprints tab and Task Board, 226
Stakeholder engagement, 197
Stakeholder management, 9
Stakeholders, 123
Streamlining processes, 212
Summary tasks
    creation of subtasks, 78, 79
    indentation, 80
    insert blank subtask, 76, 77
    inserting, 74, 75
    insert new task, 78
    inspect equipment, 76, 77
    procurement, 74, 76
    selecting, 73, 74

T

Task Boards reports, 230, 231
Task dependencies, 113, 212
Task dependency, 85, 89
Task details customization, 276
Task durations, 90, 91
Task Inspector, 141–147
Task links, *see* Task dependency
Task management, 3, 11, 131
    adding milestone
        inserting menu, 81, 82
        prepare room for
          renovation, 80, 81
        procurement
          completed, 81, 83
        ready for final
          approval, 84, 85
        room prep completed,
          83, 84
    configure settings, 70
    creation, 71
    durations, 90
    insertion, 71, 72
    manually scheduled/auto
        scheduled tasks, 72, 73
    planning, 91–96
    sequence, 85–90
    summary tasks, 73–80
Task planning
    access Copilot, 92
    created using Copilot, 95
    creation, 91, 92

    export Excel project, 95, 96
    prompt to generate tasks, 93, 94
Task reports, 248
Task sequence
    chain links, 86, 87
    connections, 88
    dependency, 85
    finish-to-start task links, 89, 90
    list of task selection, 85, 86
    timescale, 87
    update power, 87
Task variance, 250
Team members, 2, 7
Team productivity, 3
Teams and outlook
    integration, 275
Templates, 27, 35
Timeline reports, 250
Timeline visualization, 132
Time tracking, 26
Time zone-agnostic
    fields, 275
Tracking Gantt, 158, 159

U

User feedback, 11

V

Variance analysis, 26
Variance reports, 250
Visual reports, 22, 23, 250

INDEX

W, X, Y, Z

Work breakdown structure (WBS), 168, 275, 277
Working times, 190, 191
Workload reports, 250
Work resources, 108, 110
  maximum capacity, 183–186
  pay rates, 187, 189, 190, 192, 193
Work types, 182
Wrap text over multiple lines in table, 286–290

GPSR Compliance

The European Union's (EU) General Product Safety Regulation (GPSR) is a set of rules that requires consumer products to be safe and our obligations to ensure this.

If you have any concerns about our products, you can contact us on

ProductSafety@springernature.com

In case Publisher is established outside the EU, the EU authorized representative is:

Springer Nature Customer Service Center GmbH
Europaplatz 3
69115 Heidelberg, Germany

www.ingramcontent.com/pod-product-compliance
Lightning Source LLC
LaVergne TN
LVHW010336260326
834688LV00036B/735

9798868815621